PUBLIC

ARCHITECTURE NOW!

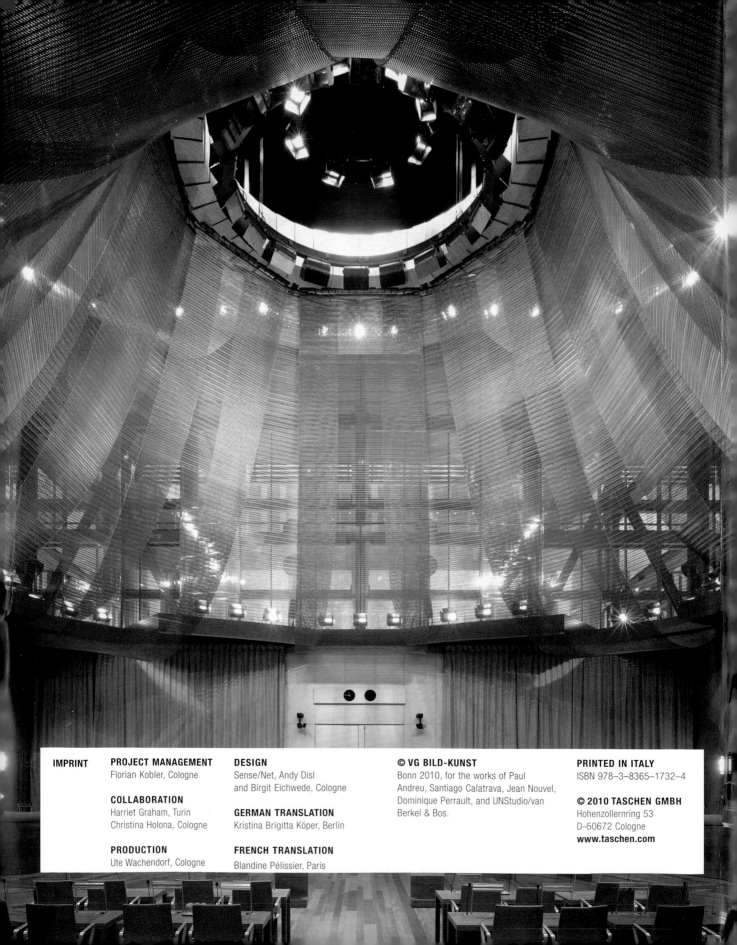

IMPRINT

PROJECT MANAGEMENT
Florian Kobler, Cologne

COLLABORATION
Harriet Graham, Turin
Christina Holona, Cologne

PRODUCTION
Ute Wachendorf, Cologne

DESIGN
Sense/Net, Andy Disl
and Birgit Eichwede, Cologne

GERMAN TRANSLATION
Kristina Brigitta Köper, Berlin

FRENCH TRANSLATION
Blandine Pélissier, Paris

© VG BILD-KUNST
Bonn 2010, for the works of Paul
Andreu, Santiago Calatrava, Jean Nouvel,
Dominique Perrault, and UNStudio/van
Berkel & Bos.

PRINTED IN ITALY
ISBN 978–3–8365–1732–4

© 2010 TASCHEN GMBH
Hohenzollernring 53
D–50672 Cologne
www.taschen.com

PUBLIC

ARCHITECTURE NOW!

ÖFFENTLICHE *Architektur heute!*
L'architecture PUBLIQUE *d'aujourd'hui!*

Philip Jodidio

TASCHEN

CONTENTS

INTRODUCTION

CONTEMPORARY GOES MAINSTREAM

pub·lic (pub'lik)
adjective
1. of, belonging to, or concerning the people as a whole; of or by the community at large, "the public welfare," "a public outcry";
2. for the use or benefit of all; esp., supported by government funds, "a public park";
3. as regards community, rather than private, affairs.
Etymology: ME < L publicus: altered (prob. infl. by pubes, adult) < poplicus, contr. of populicus, public < populus, the people.[1]

Architecture can be classified according to its use, building type, or a host of other criteria. It would seem, though, that buildings can most readily be divided into two basic categories—private structures, such as houses, and public buildings, such as railway stations, stadiums, or museums. Would a courthouse, closed to the general public but open to those concerned by the action of law, be considered a "public" building? Most probably so because it concerns "the people as a whole," even if it is not for the direct use of all. It is also supported by government funds. This apparently simple case does pose questions when the definition of public architecture is at stake. A university building often admits only students and staff, excluding any visit that might perturb the course of learning. Would it still be a public building? If one defines education as being for the common good, and often publically funded, the response should be affirmative. So, too, charging an entrance fee, as most museums or stadiums do, means that a building does not "concern the people as a whole," and yet they are, in the most commonly accepted definition, open to the public.

Prior to the economic difficulties that began in 2008, and for sometime thereafter given the timescale of major building projects, public architecture underwent a tremendous upheaval, an aesthetic awakening of sorts. Where "public" meant solidly classical and staid to earlier generations, awareness that architecture of quality could render public activities more dynamic and efficient took hold. Thus, celebrated architects, from Herzog & de Meuron for the National Stadium (Main Stadium for the 2008 Olympic Games, Beijing, China, 2003–08), or the earlier Allianz Arena (Munich, Germany, 2002–05), to Jean Nouvel for the Quai Branly Museum (Paris, France, 2001–06), emerged as the designers of a new generation of truly public buildings combining access to the many with a quality often previously reserved for the few. Museums, of course, were a major beneficiary of a wave of construction around the world, with architects like Renzo Piano taking a starring role from San Francisco to Bern. Piano is, of course, also the designer of the Kansai International Airport Terminal (Osaka, Japan, 1988–94), another decidedly public manifestation of the rise of architecture that combines functional efficiency with a sense of drama and aesthetic awakening. No one architect can claim responsibility for allowing public authorities to take the risks inherent in betting on creative building design, but, again, Renzo Piano, at the time collaborating with Richard Rogers, imagined the Centre Pompidou in Paris (1971–78), a revolutionary design that also drew 20 000 visitors a day for years and years.

1
Herzog & de Meuron, National Stadium for the 2008 Olympic Games, Beijing, China, 2003–08

THE RAIN IN SPAIN

A number of projects published in this volume are located in Spain. A 2006 exhibition at the Museum of Modern Art (MoMA) in New York highlighted the emergence of Spain as one of the places that count in contemporary architecture. The presentation of the show made things quite clear: "This exhibition documents the most recent architectural developments in a country that has become known in recent years as an international center for design innovation and excellence."[2] And yet Spain has been one of the countries worst hit by the recession, bringing many significant architectural projects, such as Madrid's City of Justice, to a grinding halt. The numerous civic centers, museums, and other public facilities that have sprung up in the past five years, many of them announcing the arrival of talented new architects on the international scene, are very likely to be much less numerous in the immediate future.

This volume may, in a sense, mark the end of a period of architectural innovation and rapid construction because the projects published here were almost all conceived and even built before the property bubble in countries like Spain or the United Kingdom burst. This is not to say that public architecture is by any means a thing of the past—even plans for economic stimulus in many countries clearly take into account the construction of new public buildings and spaces. But there will surely be a slowdown, or a rethinking of many of the large-scale initiatives that have marked the early 21st century. The challenge for architects may well be to design smaller, more economical buildings than they have until now. Green or energy-efficient buildings will come even more to the forefront, especially to the extent that they can justify claims to lower fuel or electricity bills.

Similar conclusions can be drawn about "private" architecture—that which is not meant for use by the general public, or is altogether closed to such use. On the whole, it might well appear that public architecture, since it is meant for the greater number and serves many undeniably useful purposes, is better placed to weather a long economic downturn than the private sector. Public facilities for sports, conventions, or transport generate income, and are indicators of the attractiveness of a given city or region as opposed to competing locations. Though some countries, like the United States, may be harder hit than others during the current economic difficulties, public buildings and spaces are and will remain a constant factor in the development of contemporary architecture. Though designs may be less extravagant, it would seem that the usefulness of calling on talented architects has entered the minds of government officials, promoters, and even the general public in a permanent way. Modestly, this book seeks to show a number of the reasons why such a conclusion is justified.

OLYMPIC AMBITIONS

The upgrading of existing sports facilities, or the creation of new buildings for specific purposes, such as the Olympic Games, constitute a significant part of the work that has taken place in the area of public architecture in recent years. Nor are such initiatives to be found only where they might be expected, such as Beijing in 2008. The celebrated engineering firm Arup recently redeveloped Kensington Oval (2005–07, page 100), a well-known cricket ground in Bridgetown on the easternmost island of the Lesser Antilles, Barbados. With the assis-

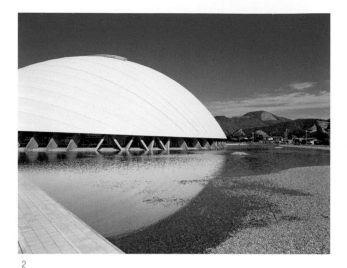

2

tance of the government, which acquired neighboring properties to give the facility more visibility and easier access, Arup upgraded the venue for the final match of the 2007 Cricket World Cup in which Australia beat Sri Lanka on April 28, 2007. The Kensington Oval hosted its first test in 1929–30 and seats 32000 people. The very modern looking curved box imagined by Arup for the main stand clearly updates the appearance of the facility, and the architects took care to use locally available materials and rainwater harvesting to improve the "carbon footprint" of the building.

Another very large firm, Cannon Design, was responsible for the creation of the Richmond Olympic Oval (Richmond, British Columbia, Canada, 2005–08, page 142), the planned venue for the long-track speed-skating events to be held during the 2010 Winter Olympics. At a size of 38000 square meters and a construction cost over $153 million, this is a substantial edifice that includes the anti-doping laboratory for the Winter Games. The covered structure can, of course, also be used in the future for other sports, such as track and field, and basketball. Evidence that the spectacular architecture of past Olympic Games or World Fairs has served no purpose and wound up costing tax payers or investors large sums has finally struck home, convincing organizers and public authorities, such as the City of Richmond in this instance, that the post-event life of such buildings is, if anything, more important than the short initial period that justifies construction.

KAOHSIUNG MEETS JURMALA
On the opposite side of the Pacific, the well-known Japanese architect Toyo Ito was commissioned to build the Main Stadium for the World Games 2009 (Kaohsiung, Taiwan, 2006–09, page 204) by the National Council on Physical Fitness and Sports and the City of Kaohsiung. Seating 40000 people, this is again a large-scale facility. Though there are surely other antecedents for the work of such top architects on a stadium, one of the early, and successful, examples of such an intervention is the Munich Olympic Stadium designed by Günter Behnisch and Frei Otto (Munich, Germany, 1972), with its famous spider-web roof. Kaohsiung is the second-largest city in Taiwan, after Taipei. Toyo Ito, famous for his unusual light metal structures, is here very much at ease working on such a big structure, giving it an unusual dynamism with its 22000-square-meter solar-panel roof and partially open layout that truly invites spectators in. The 8844 solar panels on the stadium's roof allow organizers to bill this as the largest "eco-friendly" sports facility in the world. In optimal conditions, the solar panels can cover about 75 percent of the stadium's energy needs, and, on days when the facility is dormant, the power generated is fed into the local electrical grid, to help the city. Though it is not always the case, Ito's selection for this job was surely facilitated by the fact that he had had previous experience working on sports venues, such as his Odate Jukai Dome Park (Odate, Japan, 1995–97).

Alberto Nicolau's Valdesanchuela Swimming Pool (Valdemoro, Madrid, Spain, 2006–07, page 304) is one of a large number of public facilities in Spain that show the dynamism highlighted in the 2006 show at the MoMA. Born in 1967, Nicolau was formed through work in the offices of Norman Foster and Rafael Moneo, and took on this 5000-square-meter project with a brio and professionalism not always shown by architects in their forties. Imagining the structure like "a series of waves," Nicolau demonstrated that budgetary constraints, as

3

3
Günter Behnisch and Frei Otto,
Olympic Stadium, Munich, Germany,
1972

well as functional ones, are by no means antithetical with architectural inventiveness and intelligence. Though it is certain that public authorities (the client here was Valdemoro Town Hall) have evolved in their approach to contemporary architecture, it must also be apparent that younger architects, coming into their own professionally at this time, have already been made very much aware of practicality and economy as two guiding conditions of their work.

While Canada or Spain have a well-established body of significant contemporary public buildings by talented architects, countries that previously were very much out of the mainstream are now appearing with interesting and even significant work. The Majori Primary School Sports Ground (Jurmala, Latvia, 2007–08, page 372) by Arnis Dimins (born in 1968) and Brigita Barbale (born in 1979) of the firm Substance, both of whom were educated at the Riga Technical University, gives the Baltic Sea resort of Jurmala a glowing sign of faith in contemporary architecture. Usable for track and field, basketball, volleyball, handball, ice hockey, and skating in winter, the facility is topped by a polycarbonate roof with an exterior support system. Inspired by the amber or crystallized resin of pine that sometimes washes up on the seacoast of Jurmala, this design demonstrates that architects trained in a country like Latvia can today be very much at the cutting edge of design, while taking into account the budget and functional capacity desired by the municipality. Young architects have become deadly serious about building, not just daydreaming about the time when their elders will give them a little break. For public architecture the time is now.

FROM THE SOUTHERN CROSS TO OUTER SPACE

After the early days of the glory of rail, public-transportation facilities were all but hidden from public view, sometimes literally buried, like New York's Penn Station. Railway stations or airports are, of course, in good part focused on the obvious technical requirements of a high-speed train or an incoming Airbus. It might be said that two French architects, products of the elite École Polytechnique and Ponts et Chaussées schools did a great deal to change the general attitude about how useful contemporary architecture of the highest quality might be in such circumstances. Paul Andreu was the head architect of the Aéroports de Paris and responsible for the development of the entire Roissy airport terminal complex. Jean-Marie Duthilleul is the chief architect of the SNCF, the French national railways, and responsible for bringing the Gare du Nord, Paris terminal of the Eurostar trains, back to life, but also for building a whole new generation of railway stations for the TGV system—including the recent Aix and Avignon stations. In both cases, the architects convinced their hierarchies that good architecture was worth the investment in terms of public reaction to transport facilities. Where rail transport had been dying in many countries, it took on a new life in France, and subsequently in other countries as well. Nicholas Grimshaw, for example, was the architect of the International Terminal of Waterloo Station (London, 1988–93) at the opposite end of the Eurostar line. More recently, Grimshaw has updated two important rail facilities, with all the talent he showed for the Waterloo Station. One, the Southern Cross Station (Melbourne, Australia, 2002–06, page 194), was billed as an effort to turn an existing facility into a "world-class interchange and new landmark for Melbourne." The "undulating blanket" that forms the roof of the new station areas, like the roof of Waterloo, makes the rail terminal stand out

4
*Nicholas Grimshaw, Amsterdam
Bijlmer ArenA Station, Amsterdam,
The Netherlands, 2002–07*

4

against the background of the city, giving new promise to an old form of transit. The other, the Amsterdam Bijlmer ArenA Station (Amsterdam, The Netherlands, 2002–07, above), concerns a smaller surface, but involves a facility that handles 60 000 travelers per day—a number too significant to allow the station to be closed during construction. Using voids to permit commuters to orient themselves in the station, Grimshaw tackled one of the very obvious flaws of earlier railway stations that must have been designed by engineers who never left their offices. In the new generation of railway station, including those renovated and built by Jean-Marie Duthilleul in France, visibility and light, two elements that had all but disappeared from rail terminals, now have become, on the contrary, the guiding factors of design. This proves that "good" architecture is not only about appearances—it is also about the way it makes people feel. Railway stations like Southern Cross or Bijlmer are seen and used by more people than most other types of building and thus represent an important part of reconciling contemporary architecture and public service.

Another neglected area in transport architecture is the modern highway, usually dotted by disgraceful rest stops or shocking toll structures. The Highway Toll and Control Building (Benavente, Portugal, 2006–07, page 62) by Aires Mateus is the result of careful consideration of the presence of these structures within the landscape. Indeed, the architects consider that the buildings actually become part of the landscape after they are erected, and that their responsibility is not to create ugliness where attention to design and detailing is capable of resetting the motorist's conception of contemporary architecture. It is true that roadside architecture, particularly in places like California, has taken on its own, often quirky existence; highway buildings tend to arise like afterthoughts that blight the landscape. Points of passage and movement, toll booths are, again, highly visible and well placed to break down some of the preconceptions that afflict such "ordinary" architecture.

Though its realization is still some time off, numerous promoters and architects are working on what is likely to be the next generation of travel—into space. Richard Branson of Virgin fame is one of the first to plunge headlong into this adventure, imagining spaceports for his future Virgin Galactic brand. The Space Xperience Center (Hato Airport, Curaçao, Netherlands Antilles, 2011–12, page 324) being designed by the Rotterdam firm ONL is just one of these initiatives, but it demonstrates some of the factors being considered for a type of transport for which position on the globe is more important than positioning in the kind of urban web that feeds into an airport or railway station. On the initiative of Ben Droste and Harry van Hulten, ONL used their trademark parametric modeling to imagine an "iconic" structure on the grounds of the airport in Curaçao. Indeed, it seems difficult to imagine that the first real space tourists would take off from anything other than a futuristic space port—certainly not an ordinary, dull airport. The symbolic function of contemporary architecture, intimately linked in many cases not just to the present, but also to the future, is very much a part of the development of this kind of transport initiative.

5
Jørn Utzon, Opera House, Sydney,
Australia, 1957–73

BIG AND BLUE IN DENMARK

Theaters and concert halls represent an important category in the design of public buildings, but here, too, a bland modernity seems to have swept the globe from one side to the other sometime after World War II. The institutional mindset involved in selecting architects did much to make buildings such as Jørn Utzon's Sydney Opera House (1957-73) an exception to the rule, and few architects have suffered as much as Utzon did to try to complete his masterwork. The 2003 Pritzker Prize citation for Utzon read in part: "There is no doubt that the Sydney Opera House is his masterpiece. It is one of the great iconic buildings of the 20th century, an image of great beauty that has become known throughout the world—a symbol for not only a city, but a whole country and continent." This level of success is attained by few buildings and even fewer architects, but it is clear that recent years have seen a bolder return to "name" architects and audacious projects. Two recent Copenhagen projects, in styles that are somewhat at variance, show how architecture can make even such a historically dense city evolve. The new Royal Playhouse (Copenhagen, Denmark, 2004–07, page 240) by Lundgaard & Tranberg combines wooden decks, dark brick walls, and a dramatic glazed foyer. Theater design has always struggled to some extent with the nature of practical elements, such as the stage tower. The Danish architects who won the international competition for this building covered the stage tower in copper and did not seek to obviate the relation between function and form. Jean Nouvel, on the other hand, with his great blue Concert House for Danish Radio (Copenhagen, Denmark, 2003–09, page 310) willfully sought an air of mystery—a mystery that is "never far from seduction and thus, attraction," according to the architect. Rather than clarity, the Frenchman has sought a labyrinthine complexity, especially within, and a translucid skin on the outside, capable of becoming a kind of billboard for the projection of large-scale images. The interaction between client and architect surely played a role in both instances, but Copenhagen has simultaneously sought architects who, while each remaining in the spirit of the times, interpret the relation between function and form differently. Nouvel has almost always found that buildings should make themselves visible, but not necessarily that they should advertise their function, nor even make such function apparent. Lundgaard & Tranberg can be said to have taken a more traditional approach, and yet their design is by no means outdated. This contrast and comparison says something about the state of public architecture in 2009: nothing is taken for granted but a strong effect is almost universally desired.

RIBBONS AND STONE

Two other theater facilities located at nearly opposite ends of the earth demonstrate the architectural approaches that can be taken to very different situations, which could be assimilated respectively to heaviness and to lightness. Heaviness is, indeed, the feeling that exists in the AllesWirdGut project to redesign a festival site in a Roman quarry in St. Margarethen im Burgenland (Austria, 2006–08, page 72). Rather than trying to oppose the substance of stone with lighter materials, the architects opted to "extend the ambience of the magnificent rock-face scenery to all parts of the theatrical arena so as to make it a more palpable and visually enveloping experience." They used stone from the quarry itself, as well as some oxidized steel plating to bring the facility up to date, giving notes of modernity where ancient stone meets a public of up to 6000 people. Makoto Sei Watanabe has taken a radically different approach for an extension of an

P 12.13

6
Diller Scofidio + Renfro, Institute of Contemporary Art, Boston, Massachusetts, USA, 2004–06

6

existing theater facility located in Taichung City. His RIBBONs Open-Air Theater (Taichung City, Taiwan, 2008–09, page 400) is more a canopy with some backstage facilities than it is an entire theater, but it is clear that Watanabe has sought to weave floating wave-like forms around the stage, and thus to have architecture "play a role in expanding the functions of the theater." Ascribing the word "heaviness" to the work of AllesWirdGut in Austria is by no means intended as a criticism, it is rather quite simply a statement of fact. The location and the options selected by the architects are both firmly anchored in stone, whereas the Japanese architect has chosen to look to lightness and movement as sources of his own inspiration. Again, contemporary architecture readily admits either solution: fundamentally, the preferences of clients and, of course, the architects themselves dictate the direction that might be taken in such circumstances. It seems clear that Watanabe might not have used quarry stone and oxidized steel plates had he been given the Austrian commission.

DOWN IN BEIJING, UP IN NEW YORK

Public architecture can often be exposed to the dissent of users, or local architects, as was the case of Paul Andreu and his National Center for the Performing Arts (Beijing, China, 1999–2007, page 86). Andreu is, of course, the architect of Roissy Airport and 50 other airports across the world, but he has now retired from Aéroports de Paris and struck out on his own, most notably in China. The great shell-like form that he opted for, almost within sight of the Forbidden City, encountered extremely stiff resistance, both within China and, curiously, in his native France as well, where the daily *Le Monde* published an almost vitriolic attack against the design. As Andreu says: "I am not used to projects that receive intense media scrutiny. I must admit that for the Beijing project I have heard quite a few criticisms, some of which are close to being truly insulting. Sometimes the critics make me laugh, for example the fellow who wrote: 'He doesn't have an architect's diploma, he is just an engineer.' Well, I'm sorry if Wright, Le Corbusier, and Ando didn't get their diplomas and I did; well then, I must be the fool. Aside from that they said that I have no culture. I never pretended to be a specialist of Chinese culture … when the press attacks the person as much or more than the project itself, it becomes very tiring. I do my best to avoid getting involved in this kind of debate because I have to reserve my time for the project I have been asked to carry out. Sometimes I make a little smoke though… occasionally even some steam."[3] Although Andreu describes the downward curving roof as the antithesis of the upward curves of the roofs of the Forbidden City, it is more a contemporary building than one influenced by the long history of China. While Andreu's airport buildings have been used by countless millions of air travelers, few are aware that he is the main architect behind these buildings. This takes nothing away from their quality, but it may be that Andreu will be remembered more for his Beijing building than for Roissy Airport, which was a realization of Aéroports de Paris.

In a sense, the architects Diller Scofidio + Renfro were working in an equally complex and architecturally fraught environment when they began extensive renovations of New York's Lincoln Center for the Performing Arts. Their Alice Tully Hall, Lincoln Center (New York, New York, USA, 2006–09, page 168, with FXFowle Architects) is more a case of exhuming a piece of architecture long buried in the volume beneath the Julliard School of Music. They made Alice Tully Hall visible and also worked carefully to shield the concert space from the noise of the nearby 7th Avenue subway line. They also participated in the reconstruction of Lincoln Center's Central Mechanical plant that houses radiant heat and cooling systems for the 11 venues of the complex. Since they clearly accepted to work within the confines of an earlier building designed by Pietro Belluschi, Diller Scofidio + Renfro showed that although they are capable of creating a "signature" building like their recent Institute of Contemporary Art in Boston (2004-06), they are also able to subsume their own egos in the pursuit of a larger goal. It may be asked if the Andreu building in Beijing takes this approach, or rather posits the right of the architect to design a "unique" building that sits on its own, far more closed to the outside world than the Sydney Opera House ever was. This is a matter of taste, and not of absolutes. It does show why public authorities still sometimes hesitate to call on well-known architects.

BATHING CULTURE

Though they are not public buildings in the same sense as a train station or even a theater, bath or spa structures have also benefited from the intervention of celebrated design architects in recent years, as some examples published in this book demonstrate. The Römerbad Thermal Spa Extension (Bad Kleinkirchheim, Carinthia, Austria, 2006–07, page 124) by Behnisch Architekten was a 10 000-square-meter, 15-million-euro project that updated a 1979 facility. They adopted a thematic approach not unrelated to the immediate history of this particular spa. Thus, the "Romanum" is a lower level area that "reflects the bathing culture of Ancient Rome," while the Noricum "reflects the regional level of the spa—the water, forests and cliffs…" This is not to say that architects as qualified as Behnisch have given in to a "Disney" syndrome; rather, they affirm: "As the name itself suggests, the atmosphere and ambience of this 'Roman Bath' is achieved not by merely ornamental means but by conscious abstraction, based on a limited number of essentially sculptural forms and colors."

The Thermal Baths at Panticosa (Huesca, Spain, 2002–08, page 296) by Moneo Brock Studio are in the Pyrenees. The modern-looking design proposed by the architects seeks to address both the natural environment and the urban setting of the existing baths. The combination of glass and stone selected by Moneo Brock succeeds quite admirably in reaching this goal. There is a certain coldness in the exterior materials that is contrasted with the warmer atmosphere of the baths themselves, where water and movement echo the undulating façades. Les Bains des Docks (Le Havre, France, 2006–08, page 318) by Jean Nouvel is inserted into an urban renewal scheme called Port 2000. The mainly dark exterior of the building starkly contrasts with the white, or colored, interior spaces. There is an architectonic composition of geometric solids employed by Nouvel here that is not his most familiar style. The variation between these two projects is surely a matter of location, as well as it is of the architectural feelings and inventiveness of Moneo Brock or Jean Nouvel. Fundamentally, the two serve the same purposes, albeit in differing circumstances. There is an echo of the distant past that can be felt in such projects as the Behnisch baths in Austria, and it is interesting to see how talented architects approach what remains essentially the same set of issues: bringing people together in a bathing experience, where views, to the setting, but also, surely, of other bathers, are part of the equation.

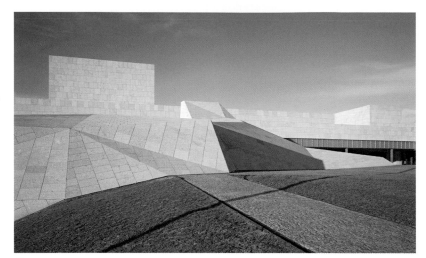

7

7
Francisco Mangado, Ávila Congress
and Municipal Exhibitions Center,
Ávila, Spain, 2004–09

SPANISH CONVENTIONS

Circumstances have indeed encouraged a number of Spanish cities to develop facilities for congresses and professional meetings. Although they may have been known for other reasons already, three Spanish architects—Rafael Beneytez, Nieto Sobejano, and Francisco Mangado—have all completed significant projects in this area in the past months. The first, Rafael Beneytez, is a "graduate" of the office of Rafael Moneo. His Huesca Exhibition and Conference Center (Huesca, Spain, 2005–08, page 44) is a 12 000-square-meter facility that has an apparently orthogonal—even geometrically strict—appearance, but through the architect's careful and inventive manipulation of materials, surfaces, and lighting, the volumes come alive and change between night and day. He even stated that he had designed "two buildings in one; one for the day and the other for the night." This type of architectural design, at the base practical and modular, is made all the more interesting and "current" by the architect's use of the full gamut of possibilities at his disposition within the defined rectilinear range.

The zigzagging forms of Nieto Sobejano's Auditorium and Convention Center of Aragon (Expo 2008, Zaragoza, Spain, 2006–08, page 45) appear to draw out into three dimensions the result of an elevation sketch. The intelligent use of glazing and metal lattices gives the structure a surface variety that is also translated into the interior, manipulating light and developing the volumes in unexpected ways that nonetheless meet programmatic requirements without waste. The architects evoke "landscape of solid light emerging from the ground." Though this notion may somewhat exaggerate the propagation and diffusion of their forms throughout the structure (i.e. light is not geometric), there is something to be said for the excitement and unexpected forms that they do create.

Francisco "Paxti" Mangado is the author of the Ávila Congress and Municipal Exhibitions Center (Ávila, Castilla y León, Spain, 2004–09, page 258), which is in the range of size and cost of the other two projects. When the architect speaks of the "topographical, mineral compactness" of Ávila, he does a great deal to explain the geological appearance of his building, emerging from the earth in planes of stone that are, indeed, related to the earth. This is by no means a green site and the mineral presence of the building confirms and reinforces its own origin. Nearby city walls are evoked as well, which confirms the "rootedness" of the building in its context, again within the confines of the usual requirements of flexibility and efficiency. Mangado, like his colleagues, shows that the constraints imposed by public projects do not exclude truly unexpected and innovative architecture. Mangado gives this city an identity, while also staying within orthogonal limits that obviously facilitate not only the use of the building, but also its construction and maintenance. This is no Guggenheim Bilbao with its unusable corners and surfaces. Beneytez, Nieto Sobejano, and Mangado mean business and they know how to create architecture while they are at it. It can only be hoped that the relative collapse of the Spanish property market and a good part of the economy with it will not prevent these architects from showing their talents in other ways.

8
Frank O. Gehry, Guggenheim Bilbao,
Bilbao, Spain, 1991–97

8

LATIN PRIDE

Libraries, too, like New York's Public Library on Fifth Avenue between 41st Street and 42nd Street (Carrère & Hastings, 1911), have reflected, until very recently, the heaviness and solemnity that was deemed appropriate for public architecture. Libraries, faced with the challenge of the Internet, but also the realization that interesting contemporary architecture can serve the purpose of keeping contact with the present, have evolved dramatically, as a few examples chosen here show. The American architects Line & Space, based in Arizona, recently completed the Cesar Chavez Branch Library (Phoenix, Arizona, USA, 2002–07, page 228). Designed for up to 40 000 visitors per month, the facility measures a relatively modest 2323 square meters. Its dramatic lines and profile certainly speak of a different type of library than the one that Carrère & Hastings erected on Fifth Avenue. This is a library for the present, which of course takes into account the constraints implied by ecological consciousness.

A very different case is that of the Santo Domingo Library Park (Medellín, Colombia, 2006–07, page 264) by Giancarlo Mazzanti. Born in 1963 in Barranquilla, Colombia, Mazzanti is based in Bogotá. This structure, "folded and cut like the mountains that surround it," is located in an area devastated by 1980s drug violence. The triple structure set on a common base includes a library, classrooms, an auditorium, and offices. Rightfully intended as a symbol of this city known more as a drug capital than as one of learning, the library attempts also to "decontextualize the individual from the poverty that surrounds him." Likewise, the University of Deusto Library (Bilbao, Spain, 2001–08, page 292) is interesting in its own right as a piece of architecture, but it is also an effort to stand apart in an environment dominated by Frank O. Gehry's Guggenheim Bilbao. Rafael Moneo is certainly not one for the twisting, metallic forms that Gehry has mastered, in this instance, for the obvious betterment of Bilbao. Instead, he is content to step back and to show that more traditional forms, albeit set in a luminous, sophisticated volume, represent an adequate answer to, or perhaps even an efficient critique of, the American's exuberance.

BIG ARCHITECTS, SMALL CHAPELS

Religion, after having been a primary source of architectural innovation in the relatively distant past, has again become an area where architects can express themselves in creative ways. With architects from Mario Botta (Évry Cathedral, Évry, France, 1988–95; Tamaro Chapel, Monte Tamaro, Switzerland, 1992–96; another chapel in Mogno, Switzerland, 1986–98) to Richard Meier (Jubilee Church, Rome, Italy, 2003) or Tadao Ando (Church of the Light, Ibaraki, Osaka, Japan, 1988–89) creating memorable ecclesiastical architecture, it is no surprise that other architects continue in this vein. The New York-based architect Stan Allen created the small CCV Chapel (Tagaytay, Cavite, Philippines, 2007–08, page 66) at the entrance to the campus of the Chosen Children's Village Foundation, a non-profit organization "dedicated to the creation of a home environment for physically and mentally challenged children." With an area of 240 square meters, the concrete structure nonetheless rises to a height of seven meters, its white, articulated forms creating a space of worship that belies the very low budget. Built to withstand the conditions of a tropical climate and seismic risks, this structure relies on natural ventilation, surely a better way to deal with energy saving than the most sophisticated computer-driven systems employed in more sophisticated buildings.

9
Tadao Ando, Punta della Dogana Renovation, Venice, Italy, 2007–09

Another innovative chapel was designed by the Swiss group Localarchitecture. Their Temporary Chapel of St. Loup (Pompaples, Switzerland, 2008, page 234) is a 130-square-meter structure erected to serve as a place of worship during work on the home of the Deaconesses of St. Loup in the Canton of Vaud. They used CAD-CNC methods, which is to say computer-assisted design leading to numerically controlled cutting of the wood, plastic, and fabric building. The temporary nature of the structure permitted it to be erected without foundations, but it is interesting to note that this Protestant group was open to the idea of contemporary forms for their place of prayer, and indeed to call on architects who are under 40 years of age.

The Santa Monica Parish Church (Rivas Vaciamadrid, Madrid, Spain, 2004–09, page 394) by Vicens + Ramos Architects was built for the Bishop of Alcalá. Where more traditional church and parish designs very often separate functions in terms of the architecture, Vicens + Ramos opted instead for a "continuum" linking the building housing the priests, the parish center, and the church. They also agreed with the client to call on a number of contemporary artists, and indeed to use Cor-ten steel as the most visible exterior cladding element. Corten is, of course, the material most often used by sculptors, such as Richard Serra, thus in a sense the entire project evokes a work of art. However, the interior design does not in any sense give an impression of an art gallery, nor does the architecture appear to be an expression of the ego of the architects; it is rather a place of contemplation and worship, where art and architecture have not only been admitted, but provide an uplifting element that makes a very contemporary statement. The harmonious use of art in a religious and architectural context is, of course, deeply rooted in the traditions of the church, but the 20th century did not always follow this inspiration as much as earlier times. The Santa Monica Parish Church would appear rather to revive this tradition with a very contemporary aesthetic response to the needs of the church and the parish.

BRIDGES FROM PAST TO PRESENT

Museums are one of the most obvious expressions of the recent development of public architecture. A companion volume to this book, *Architecture Now! Museums*, explores this area more fully than is possible here, but there are nonetheless several examples in this volume as well. The Pritzker Prize-winning Japanese architect Tadao Ando, for example, inaugurated the Punta della Dogana (Venice, Italy, 2007-09, page 78) for the François Pinault Foundation on June 4, 2009. Every tourist who has set foot in Venice is familiar with the image of the Basilica of Santa Maria della Salute. Located near the point of Dorsoduro, designed by the architect Baldassare Longhena (1598–1682), and dedicated to the Virgin Mary, protector of the Republic, the church was commissioned by the Venetian Senate in 1630, marking the devastation brought to the city by the plague, and was completed in 1681. The very tip of Dorsoduro, long the site of salt warehouses, had been occupied by a customshouse for seaborne goods since 1525. As the new Basilica rose, it was decided for aesthetic reasons to rebuild the neighboring Dogana da Mar. It was Giuseppe Benoni (1618–84) who built a low, rusticated structure ending in a tower at the point of land opposite Saint Mark's, built between 1676 and 1682. It is here, working with Tadao Ando, that François Pinault decided to create a second Venetian site for his Foundation dedicated to contemporary art. As might have been expected, Tadao Ando has cho-

10
*Santiago Calatrava, Quarto Ponte
sul Canal Grande, Venice, Italy,
1999–2006*

10

sen to see the existing building in terms of its basic, geometric form. He says: "The Punta della Dogana building is characterized by a simple, rational structure. The volume creates a triangle, a direct reference to the shape of the tip of the island of Dorsoduro, while the interiors are divided into long rectangles, with a series of parallel walls." Though a great deal of attention was paid to the renovation of the existing structure, Tadao Ando did make a powerful geometric gesture in the middle of the triangular plan of the building: a concrete cube that rises to the full height of the structure and becomes the axis of all paths leading through the renewed space.

It might be noted in passing that another Venetian structure by a leading contemporary architect is also featured in this book. Santiago Calatrava's Quarto Ponte sul Canal Grande (Venice, Italy, 1999–2006, page 136) is only the fourth bridge to arch over the Grand Canal. Ninety-four meters long, it is situated very close to the main railway station of the city. The elegance and modernity of this bridge is undeniable, and yet some controversy did greet its design and construction. This is all the more bewildering since bridges such as that of the Accademia have long been allowed to stand despite their rather obvious lack of aesthetic or architectural significance. Calatrava's bridge, on the other hand, is neither too bold, nor too timid a gesture: it is an ideal sign that Venice continues to live, despite being so firmly locked in other areas into its decaying past. With architects like Ando and Calatrava adding to its more ancient forms in such intelligent ways, it may be that Venice can continue to live on as a real city and not just a postcard stop for tour boats. In any case, few structures could more appropriately be deemed good public architecture than the Quarto Ponte.

Kuehn Malvezzi's renovation of an early 20th-century factory building for the Julia Stoschek Collection (Dusseldorf, Germany, 2005–07, page 222) clearly posed different problems from Ando's remake of the Punta della Dogana. Working with a listed building, the architects maintained the original façade while gutting the interiors and building a new perimeter within the older walls of the former factory. Public authorities did give the architects permission to replace the old factory sign with a new glass box. Since the structure also contains the apartment of the donor, Julia Stoschek, this is something of a hybrid design, but the architects did use a continuous palette of colors and materials in both public and private areas. This project, of course, fits in with the trend of reusing of old buildings for cultural purposes. Whether because they are in some way protected, as was the case in Dusseldorf, or because their volumes and materials are of interest aesthetically or structurally, older buildings provide elements to architects that break with a purely modern approach. In this instance, a factory building that could not have really been considered "public" architecture becomes one that is open to those who have the curiosity to step through its doors.

SUNDAY IN THE PARK WITH FRANK
Pavilion structures have become another popular point of encounter between architects of the highest level and the general public. Often temporary, like the summer Serpentine pavilions in London, these buildings sometimes go on to be used in other circumstances, as was the case of Frank O. Gehry's own Serpentine Pavilion (Kensington Gardens, London, UK, 2008, page 180). Measuring 418 square

11

11
Frank O. Gehry, Jay Pritzker Pavilion
Millennium Park, Chicago, Ilinois,
USA, 1999–2004

meters, this structure with an exoskeleton made of timber, in good part covered by multiple glazed roof surfaces, evoking the "juxtaposition of random elements," was intended to be used for events or concerts receiving up to 275 spectators. In this context, Gehry was able to look back to the real source of his architectural innovation, the houses he built early in his career in Santa Monica or Venice, California, where "found" materials like chain-link fence or asphalt used in unexpected ways made for a new approach to architecture in general, somehow closer to the freedom of contemporary art. Fittingly, the Gehry Serpentine Pavilion was purchased by the Irish owner of the Château La Coste vineyards located near Aix-en-Provence in the south of France. This domain will open to the public in 2010 with works by various other celebrated artists and architects surrounding the actual wine-growing and producing facilities.

A real point of encounter between contemporary art, architecture, and the general public is the Millennium Park in Chicago. Artists such as Jaume Plensa and Anish Kapoor created works for the Park, as did the ubiquitous Frank O. Gehry. His Jay Pritzker Pavilion (Millennium Park, Chicago, IL, USA, 1999–2004) is a 36-meter-high billowing structure made of stainless-steel ribbons and an accompanying trellis of steel pipes. With 4000 fixed seats and accommodation for 7000 more, the outdoor concert venue quickly became a new symbol of Chicago. As Gehry states his goal: "How do you make everyone—not just the people in the seats, but the people sitting 400 feet (121 meters) away on the lawn—feel good about coming to this place to listen to music? And the answer is, you bring them into it. You make the proscenium larger; you build a trellis with a distributed sound system. You make people feel part of the experience." Work on the Park did not cease with its inauguration, and new pavilions have recently been installed by Zaha Hadid and the Dutch architects UNStudio (both Chicago, IL, USA, 2009). The UNStudio project—the Burnham Pavilion (page 390)—is a 300-square-meter, steel-and-wood structure that evokes a "floating and multidirectional space" that is intended as an homage to Daniel Burnham's 1909 orthogonal plan of Chicago. In this instance, new architecture provides a critique at the same time as it evokes past building in this still-dynamic city.

CONTEMPORARY GOES MAINSTREAM

In a way, the Burnham Pavilion by UNStudio is symbolic of the evolution of contemporary public architecture. Here, new forms, conceived and executed with computer-driven methods, emerge in a highly visible location, where the general public is free to admire (or detest) work that is at the cutting edge of contemporary design. Though economic difficulties will surely curtail some projects for public buildings that would have been architecturally interesting, it would seem that the earlier time of prosperity did a great deal to open spirits and allow contemporary creativity to truly enter the mainstream of architecture. This volume is in a sense a celebration of what might be termed a historic shift in perception, which has allowed inventive architects from Spain to Taiwan to create new forms for the general public, or at any rate for a use that goes far beyond the elite that may have appreciated the avant-garde of the past. It cannot be said that any particular style emerges from this diverse group of realizations, but the imprint of the computer is visible in most instances, at least for those who know how to see its impact. In reality the flexibility introduced by computer-driven design and manufacturing has now reached the mainstream of architecture, allowing a variety of forms that previously could not have existed without exorbitant cost overruns. It does seem

12
Zaha Hadid, Burnham Pavilion,
Millennium Park, Chicago, Ilinois,
USA, 2009

12

apparent from the selection in this book that architects had already learned the lessons of economic and functional efficiency that clients demanded of them even before the recession clouded the horizon. The public buildings published here are for the most part not only innovative aesthetically, but also highly usable, and, what is more, usually conceived with a respect for the environment that was surely not a concern in earlier (modern) times. These signs—the ability of quality architects to engage in large projects conscious of cost, functional efficiency, and environmental responsibility—bode well for the future, even with fewer projects to build and less money to spend. With these buildings and others from recent years across the world, high-quality contemporary architecture has become publically acceptable, and is no longer confined to an insignificant number of usually isolated locations. Contemporary architecture that is more than an ugly box has gone mainstream.

Philip Jodidio, Grimentz, July 6, 2009

1   See http://www.yourdictionary.com/public accessed on July 4, 2009.
2   "On-Site: New Architecture in Spain," February 12, 2006–May 1, 2006. See http://www.moma.org/visit/calendar/exhibitions/86 accessed on July 5, 2009.
3   Excerpts from an interview with Paul Andreu published in *Upstreet* magazine, February 2001.

EINLEITUNG

ANGEKOMMEN IM MAINSTREAM

öffentlich <Adj.>
[mhd. offenlich, ahd. offanlih]
1. für jeden hörbar und sichtbar; nicht geheim
2. für die Allgemeinheit zugänglich, benutzbar
3. die Gesellschaft allgemein, die Allgemeinheit betreffend, von ihr ausgehend, auf sie bezogen[1]

Will man Architektur klassifizieren, so kann man dies entsprechend ihrer Nutzung tun, nach Gebäudetyp oder nach einer ganzen Flut weiterer Kriterien. Dennoch scheint es, dass sich Bauten am ehesten in zwei Grundkategorien einordnen lassen – in private Bauten, wie etwa Wohnbauten, oder öffentliche Bauten, darunter Bahnhöfe, Stadien oder Museen. Doch wie sieht es bei einem Gerichtsgebäude aus, das der breiten Öffentlichkeit verschlossen, dabei aber allen zugänglich ist, die vom Rechtsvollzug betroffen sind – kann man dieses ebenfalls als „öffentlich" bezeichnen? Aller Wahrscheinlichkeit nach schon, betrifft dieses Gebäude doch „die Allgemeinheit", selbst wenn es nicht von allen unmittelbar genutzt wird. Hinzu kommt, dass es aus öffentlichen Geldern finanziert wird. Schon dieser scheinbar eindeutige Fall wirft also Fragen auf, wie sich öffentliche Architektur definieren lässt. Ein Universitätsgebäude etwa gewährt oft nur Studierenden und Mitarbeitern Zutritt und schließt Besucher aus, die den Lehralltag stören könnten. Handelt es sich hierbei dennoch um ein öffentliches Gebäude? Definiert man Bildung als etwas zum Wohl der Allgemeinheit, das noch dazu meistens öffentlich finanziert wird, dürfte die Antwort „ja" lauten. Selbst das Erheben eines Eintrittsgelds wie bei den meisten Museen oder Sportstadien – was diese Einrichtungen eben *nicht* frei „für die Allgemeinheit zugänglich" macht – scheint kein Hinderungsgrund zu sein, auch diese Art von Bauten als öffentlich zu bezeichnen.

Noch bevor die gegenwärtige Wirtschaftskrise 2008 begann und einige Zeit danach (begründet durch die Dauer großer Bauprojekte), war in der öffentlichen Architektur ein gewaltiger Umbruch zu spüren, eine Art ästhetisches Erwachen. Während „öffentlich" für frühere Generationen gleichbedeutend mit „klassisch-konservativ" und „seriös" war, setzt sich inzwischen zunehmend ein neues Bewusstsein durch: Qualitätvolle Architektur darf öffentliche Einrichtungen und Veranstaltungsorte nun dynamischer und effizienter gestalten. Im Zuge dieser Entwicklung etablierten sich renommierte Architekten als Gestalter einer neuen Generation öffentlicher Bauten, die der breiten Öffentlichkeit zugänglich sind und zwar auf einem Qualitätsniveau, das bis dato oft nur wenigen Privilegierten vorbehalten war. Beispiele hierfür reichen von Herzog & de Meuron mit ihrem Nationalstadion in Peking (Hauptaustragungsort der Olympischen Spiele 2008, 2003–08) und ihrer etwas älteren Allianz Arena (München, 2002–05) bis hin zu Jean Nouvel mit seinem Musée du Quai Branly (Paris, 2001–06). Zweifellos profitierten auch Museen maßgeblich von dieser internationalen Bauwelle, wobei besonders Architekten wie Renzo Piano mit Projekten von San Francisco bis Bern eine Rolle spielten. Piano entwarf auch das Terminalgebäude am Kansai International Airport (Osaka, Japan, 1988–94), ein weiteres höchst öffentliches Beispiel für eine Architektur, in der sich funktionale Effizienz mit Dramatik und ästhetischem Neuaufbruch verbinden.

13
Herzog & de Meuron, Allianz Arena,
Munich, Germany, 2002–05

Sicherlich ist es nicht das Verdienst eines einzelnen Architekten, die öffentlichen Träger davon überzeugt zu haben, dass sich das Einlassen auf kreative Entwürfe lohnt. Dennoch war es ebenfalls Renzo Piano, diesmal in Zusammenarbeit mit Richard Rogers, der das Centre Pompidou erdacht hatte (1971–78), einen revolutionären Entwurf, der jahrelang 20 000 Besucher täglich anzog.

ES GRÜNT SO GRÜN, WENN SPANIENS BLÜTEN BLÜH'N

Etliche in diesem Band vorgestellte Projekte sind in Spanien zu finden. Schon 2006 hob eine Ausstellung im Museum of Modern Art in New York die wachsende Bedeutung Spaniens als einen der entscheidenden Schauplätze der zeitgenössischen Architektur hervor, woran die Ankündigung keinen Zweifel ließ: „Diese Ausstellung dokumentiert die jüngsten architektonischen Entwicklungen in einem Land, das in den letzten Jahren als internationales Zentrum für innovatives und exzellentes Design bekannt geworden ist."[2] Da Spanien eines jener Länder ist, die am schwersten von der Rezession getroffen wurden, sind viele bedeutende Bauprojekte, darunter das Justizviertel in Madrid, inzwischen zum Erliegen gekommen. Die Zahl der Gemeindezentren, Museen und anderen öffentlichen Einrichtungen, die in den vergangenen fünf Jahren noch aus dem Boden geschossen sind – viele von ihnen ein erster Hinweis auf neue Talente in der internationalen Architekturszene – wird in nächster Zukunft höchstwahrscheinlich weitaus geringer sein.

Der vorliegende Band markiert möglicherweise das Ende einer Ära architektonischer Innovation und rascher Baufortschritte, denn fast alle der hier präsentierten Projekte wurden entworfen und gebaut, bevor die Immobilienblase in Ländern wie Spanien oder Großbritannien zerplatzte. Das muss jedoch nicht heißen, dass öffentliche Architektur ab jetzt Vergangenheit ist – viele Länder berücksichtigen bei ihren Investitionsanreizen sogar explizit die Errichtung neuer öffentlicher Bauten. Trotzdem wird es zweifellos zu einer Verlangsamung oder zumindest einem Umdenken bei vielen Großprojekten kommen, wie sie den Beginn des 21. Jahrhunderts geprägt haben. Die Herausforderung für Architekten wird darin bestehen, kleinere und ökonomischere Bauten zu entwerfen als bisher. Grüne oder energieeffiziente Bauten werden immer wichtiger werden – schließlich unterstreichen sie wirkungsvoll die Appelle, die Energiekosten zu senken.

Ähnliche Schlüsse ließen sich im Hinblick auf „private" Bauten ziehen, die nicht für eine Nutzung durch die breite Öffentlichkeit vorgesehen sind oder eine solche Nutzung sogar ausschließen. Insgesamt scheint es, als sei die öffentliche Architektur, weil sie breiter genutzt wird und zahlreichen, zweifellos sinnvollen Zwecken dient, besser in der Lage als der private Sektor, einer langfristigen ökonomischen Krise standzuhalten. Öffentliche Bauten für Sport, Messen oder Verkehr generieren Umsatz und steigern die Attraktivität der jeweiligen Stadt oder Region im Vergleich zur Konkurrenz. Auch wenn manche Länder, wie etwa die USA, stärker von der Wirtschaftskrise betroffen sind als andere, werden öffentliche Einrichtungen weiterhin eine Konstante in der Entwicklung der zeitgenössischen Architektur sein. Die Entwürfe mögen weniger extravagant ausfallen, dennoch scheint es in den Köpfen von Regierungsbeamten, Lobbyisten und sogar der breiten Öffentlichkeit dauerhaft angekommen zu sein, dass es sinnvoll ist, talentierte Architekten mit Projekten zu betrauen. Dieses Buch will nicht mehr, als eine Reihe von Gründen aufzeigen, warum ein solcher Schluss gerechtfertigt sein dürfte.

14
Renzo Piano, Kansai International
Airport Terminal, Osaka, Japan,
1988–94

14

OLYMPISCHE AMBITIONEN

Die Modernisierung bestehender Sporteinrichtungen ebenso wie das Realisieren von Neubauten für spezielle Anlässe, etwa die Olympischen Spiele, haben in den vergangenen Jahren einen erheblichen Anteil der Bautätigkeit im öffentlichen Sektor ausgemacht. Solche Vohaben sind jedoch nicht nur dort zu finden, wo man sie erwartet, wie 2008 in Peking. Das gefeierte Ingenieurbüro Arup Associates modernisierte unlängst das Kensington Oval (2005–07, Seite 100), ein bekanntes Kricketstadion in Bridgetown auf der östlichsten Insel von Barbados. Mit Unterstützung der Regierung, die die angrenzenden Grundstücke erwarb, um höhere Sichtbarkeit und leichteren Zugang zum Stadion zu gewährleisten, modernisierte Arup Associates das Stadion für das Endspiel des Cricket World Cup am 28. April 2007, in dem Australien über Sri Lanka siegte. Im Kensington Oval mit Platz für 32 000 Zuschauer wurden bereits 1929 bis 1930 die ersten Testspiele ausgetragen. Die von Arup Associates entworfene, höchst modern wirkende, geschwungene „Box" der Haupttribüne trägt zweifellos dazu bei, das Erscheinungsbild der Einrichtung zu aktualisieren. Dabei achteten die Architekten darauf, lokale Materialien und Regenwasser zu nutzen, um die CO_2-Bilanz des Gebäudes zu verbessern.

Ein weiteres großes Büro, Cannon Design, zeichnete für das Richmond Olympic Oval (Richmond, British Columbia, Kanada, 2005–08, Seite 142) verantwortlich, den geplanten Austragungsort für die Eisschnelllaufwettkämpfe der Olympischen Winterspiele 2010. Mit einer Fläche von 38 000 m² und Baukosten von 153 Millionen Dollar ist es ein beachtliches Bauwerk, in dem auch die Anti-Dopinglabors für die Winterspiele untergebracht sind. Der überdachte Komplex wird sich in Zukunft auch für andere Sportarten wie für Leichtathletik oder Basketball nutzen lassen. Die Erkenntnis, dass die spektakulären Bauten vergangener Olympischer Spiele oder Weltausstellungen keinen sinnvollen Zweck mehr erfüllen, die Steuerzahler oder Investoren jedoch Unsummen gekostet haben, scheint langsam bei Organisatoren und öffentlichen Behörden angekommen zu sein. So auch in Richmond, wo man sich bewusst ist, dass die Lebensspanne des Bauwerks *nach* solchen Großveranstaltungen wichtiger ist als die kurze Anfangsphase, die ihren Bau rechtfertigt.

ZWISCHEN KAOHSIUNG UND JURMALA

Unterdessen erhielt der renommierte japanische Architekt Toyo Ito auf der anderen Seite des Pazifiks den Auftrag, eine große Sportarena für die World Games 2009 zu realisieren (Kaohsiung, Taiwan, 2006–09, Seite 204). Mit Platz für 40 000 Besucher ist auch dies ein Großprojekt. Auftraggeber waren der taiwanische Nationalrat für körperliche Gesundheit und Sport sowie die Stadt Kaohsiung. Auch wenn es zahlreiche Vorläufer für Stadionbauten von Toparchitekten gibt, so ist doch eines der frühesten und gelungensten Beispiele das von Günter Behnisch und Frei Otto entworfene Münchner Olympiastadion (München, 1972) mit seiner berühmten spinnennetzartigen Dachkonstruktion. Doch zurück nach Kaohsiung, der nach Taipeh zweitgrößten Stadt Taiwans. Toyo Ito, berühmt geworden durch seine ungewöhnlichen Leichtbaukonstruktionen aus Metall, ist bei diesem großen Bauprojekt offensichtlich ganz in seinem Element. Er verleiht dem Stadion mit seinem 22 000 m² großen Solardach und teilweise offenen Grundriss, der die Zuschauer buchstäblich in den Komplex hineinzieht, ungewöhnliche Dynamik. Dank der 8844 Solarpaneele auf dem Dach des Stadions konnten die Organisatoren den Bau zur größten „umweltfreundlichen"

15
Toyo Ito, Main Stadium for the World
Games 2009, Kaohsiung, Taiwan,
2006–09

15

Sporteinrichtung der Welt erklären. Unter optimalen Bedingungen decken die Solarpaneele rund 75 Prozent des Energiebedarfs des gesamten Stadions. Wird die Arena nicht genutzt, kann die erzeugte Energie in das lokale Stromnetz eingespeist werden, wovon die Stadt profitiert. Auch wenn dies sicherlich nicht die Regel ist – in diesem Fall dürfte die Wahl auch deshalb auf Ito als Architekten gefallen sein, weil er bereits über Erfahrungen mit dem Bau von Sportarenen verfügte, so etwa mit seinem Odate Jukai Dome Park (Odate, Japan, 1995–97).

Alberto Nicolaus Schwimmbad Valdesanchuela (Valdemoro, Region Madrid, 2006–07, Seite 304) zählt zu jenen dynamischen öffentlichen Bauprojekten in Spanien, die 2006 in der MoMA-Ausstellung besonders hervorgehoben wurden. Der 1967 geborene Nicolau, geprägt durch seine Erfahrungen bei Norman Foster und Rafael Moneo, meisterte das mehr als 5000 m² große Projekt mit einem Elan und einer Professionalität, die bei Architekten in den 40ern nicht immer zu finden sind. Mit seinem wie „eine Wellenserie" konzipierten Bau stellte Nicolau unter Beweis, dass Einschränkungen im Hinblick auf Budget und Funktion keineswegs architektonischen Erfindungsreichtum und Intelligenz ausschließen müssen. Nicht nur die Einstellung öffentlicher Behörden zur zeitgenössischen Architektur hat sich zweifellos gewandelt (Auftraggeber war hier das Rathaus von Valdemoro), sondern jüngeren Architekten, die sich in diesem Zeitraum beruflich etabliert haben, ist auch längst deutlich bewusst, dass praktische Gesichtspunkte und Wirtschaftlichkeit zwei Leitgedanken ihrer Tätigkeit sein müssen.

Während Kanada oder Spanien bereits auf eine beachtliche Anzahl zeitgenössischer öffentlicher Bauten von talentierten Architekten zurückblicken können, präsentieren sich jetzt auch Länder, die bisher außerhalb des Mainstreams lagen, mit interessanten und bedeutenden Projekten. Die Sportanlagen der Majori-Grundschule (Jurmala, Lettland, 2007–08, Seite 372) von Arnis Dimins (geboren 1968) und Brigita Barbale (geboren 1979) vom Büro Substance setzen im Ostseebad Jurmala ein leuchtendes Zeichen für den Glauben an die zeitgenössische Architektur. Sowohl Dimins als auch Barbale studierten an der Technischen Universität Riga. Die Sportanlage für Leichtathletik, Basketball, Volleyball, Handball sowie Eishockey und Eislauf im Winter wird von einem Polycarbonatdach überspannt, das von einem außen liegenden Tragwerk abgehängt ist. Inspiriert wurde der Entwurf vom Bernstein, der an den Stränden von Jurmala mitunter angespült wird. Dieses Projekt zeigt, wie Architekten, die in Ländern wie Lettland ausgebildet wurden, hochaktuelles Design gestalten und dabei zugleich den von der Stadtverwaltung gewünschten Anforderungen im Hinblick auf Funktion und Budget gerecht werden. Junge Architekten nehmen das Bauen heute so ernst wie nie zuvor und begnügen sich nicht mehr mit Tagträumen von einer Zukunft, in der ihnen die Älteren womöglich eine Chance geben. Für öffentliche Architektur heißt es: jetzt oder nie.

VOM KREUZ DES SÜDENS BIS IN DEN WELTRAUM

Nach der frühen Glanzzeit der Eisenbahn verschwanden Einrichtungen des öffentlichen Verkehrs fast gänzlich aus dem Blickfeld der Öffentlichkeit oder wurden sogar buchstäblich unter die Erde versenkt, wie die New Yorker Penn Station. Natürlich sind Bahnhöfe oder Flughäfen zum großen Teil auf die technischen Anforderungen zugeschnitten, die ein Hochgeschwindigkeitszug oder ein landender Airbus ihnen abverlangen. Man könnte sagen, dass zwei französische Architekten – Absolventen der Elitehochschulen École Polytechnique sowie der Ponts

16

et Chaussées – maßgeblich dazu beigetragen haben, die allgemeinen Vorstellungen davon zu verändern, wie anspruchsvolle, aber auch zweckorientierte zeitgenössische Architektur unter solchen Umständen auszusehen hat. Paul Andreu war Chefarchitekt der Aéroports de Paris und verantwortlich für die Entwicklung des Flughafenkomplexes in Roissy. Jean-Marie Duthilleul ist leitender Architekt der SNCF, der französischen Bahnbetriebe. Er war nicht nur für die Erneuerung des Gare du Nord, des Pariser Endbahnhofs der Eurostar-Züge, verantwortlich, sondern ebenso für den Bau einer ganzen Generation neuer TGV-Bahnhöfe – darunter auch die jüngst errichteten Bahnhöfe von Aix und Avignon. In beiden Fällen gelang es den Architekten, ihre Verwaltung davon zu überzeugen, dass gute Architektur eine lohnenswerte Investition ist, gerade im Hinblick auf das öffentliche Echo, das Verkehrseinrichtungen finden. Während der Bahnverkehr in vielen Ländern am Aussterben war, lebte er in Frankreich, und schließlich auch in anderen Ländern wieder auf.

Nicholas Grimshaw z. B. ist der Architekt des Internationalen Terminals der Waterloo Station (London, 1988–93), des englischen Endbahnhofs des Eurostar. In letzter Zeit konnte Grimshaw zwei weitere bedeutende Bahnhöfe modernisieren und zeigte dabei mindestens so viel Talent wie bei der Waterloo Station. Einer dieser Bahnhöfe, die Southern Cross Station (Melbourne, Australien, 2002–06, Seite 194), wurde mit dem Ziel geplant, einen bestehenden Bahnhof „zum Umsteigebahnhof von Weltformat und zum neuen Wahrzeichen für Melbourne" zu machen. Die Dachkonstruktion über den neuen Bahnhofsabschnitten wurde wie eine „Daunendecke" gestaltet und sorgt dafür, dass sich der Bahnhof, wie schon das Dach der Waterloo Station, als Kontrast vor der Kulisse der Stadt abzeichnet. Zugleich entstehen hier ermutigende Perspektiven für die Zukunft eines traditionellen Verkehrsmittels. Der zweite Bahnhof, Bijlmer ArenA in Amsterdam (2002–07, Seite 10), wird trotz seiner kleineren Grundfläche täglich von 60 000 Reisenden frequentiert – eine zu hohe Fahrgastzahl, als dass man den Bahnhof während der Umbauarbeiten hätte schließen können. Grimshaw nutzte „voids" (Leerräume), um den Pendlern die Orientierung im Bahnhof zu erleichtern. Zugleich setzte er sich so mit bekannten Schwachpunkten älterer Bahnhofsbauten auseinander, die offenbar von Ingenieuren geplant wurden, die nie ihr Büro verlassen haben. Bei dieser neuen Generation von Bahnhöfen, einschließlich der von Jean-Marie Duthilleul in Frankreich gebauten und sanierten Bahnhöfe, sind auffällige gute Orientierung und Licht – zwei Elemente, die aus Bahnhofsbauten so gut wie verschwunden waren – inzwischen zu entscheidenden Faktoren der Entwürfe geworden. Dies belegt, dass es bei „guter" Architektur nicht nur um das Erscheinungsbild geht, sondern auch darum, welches Gefühl sie den Menschen vermittelt. Bahnhöfe wie Southern Cross oder Bijlmer werden von mehr Menschen gesehen und genutzt als viele andere Gebäudetypen. Damit leisten sie einen entscheidenden Beitrag dafür, zeitgenössische Architektur und öffentliche Dienstleistung miteinander zu versöhnen.

Ein weiterer Bereich öffentlicher Architektur, der meist vernachlässigt wird, ist die moderne Schnellstraße, die oft von tristen Raststätten oder Mautstationen gesäumt wird. Dem Bau der Mautstelle und Autobahnwacht von Aires Mateus (Benavente, Portugal, 2006–07, Seite 62) gingen sorgfältige Überlegungen voraus, welche Wirkung solche Bauten auf die Landschaft haben. Dabei gingen die Architekten sogar so weit, die Bauten so zu konzipieren, dass sie nach ihrer Fertigstellung zu einem Teil der Landschaft werden konnten. Sie verstehen es als Aufgabe, keine unansehnlichen Konstrukte zu realisieren, sondern wollen vielmehr die Chance nutzen, das Bild, das Autofahrer von zeitgenössi-

17
Jean Nouvel, Concert House for
Danish Radio, Copenhagen, Denmark,
2003–09

17

scher Architektur haben, positiv zu verändern. Dies erreichen sie durch besondere Aufmerksamkeit beim Entwurf und den baulichen Details. Natürlich ist es so, dass sich Architektur am Straßenrand, gerade in Gegenden wie Kalifornien, zu einer ganz eigenen, nicht selten skurrilen Spezies entwickelt hat; an den Highways springen Bauten wie nachträgliche Einfälle aus dem Boden und verschandeln die Landschaft. Trotzdem sind auch Mautstellen – Orte des Transits und der Bewegung – von größter Sichtbarkeit und ideal, um so manche Vorurteile über „profane" Architektur zu widerlegen.

Obwohl deren Realisierung noch einige Zeit auf sich warten lassen dürfte, arbeiten bereits zahlreiche Organisatoren und Architekten an der wahrscheinlich nächsten Generation des Reisens – der Reise in den Weltraum. Richard Branson, bekannt geworden durch seine Firma Virgin, ist einer der Ersten, die sich mit Entwürfen von Weltraumbahnhöfen für seine zukünftige Marke Virgin Galactic kopfüber in dieses Abenteuer gestürzt hat. Das Space Xperience Center (Hato Airport, Curaçao, Niederländische Antillen, 2011–12, Seite 324) des Rotterdamer Büros ONL ist nur eine dieser Initiativen. Dennoch illustriert dieses Projekt einige der Faktoren, die bei einer Verkehrsart zur berücksichtigen sind, bei der der Standort auf dem Globus wichtiger ist als die Einbindung in ein urbanes Netzwerk, das einen Flughafen oder Bahnhof versorgt. Auf Anregung von Ben Droste und Harry van Hulten arbeitete ONL mit der für das Büro typischen parametrischen Konstruktionsweise, um ein unverwechselbares Bauwerk auf dem Gelände des Flughafens von Curaçao zu entwerfen. Ohnehin ist es kaum vorstellbar, dass die ersten Weltraumtouristen von etwas anderem als einer futuristischen Basis aus starten könnten – mit Sicherheit nicht von einem gewöhnlichen, langweiligen Flughafen. Auch deshalb kommt der zeitgenössischen Architektur, die in vielen Fällen nicht nur mit der Gegenwart, sondern eng mit der Zukunft verwoben ist, eine hohe Symbolwirkung bei der Entwicklung solcher Verkehrswege zu.

GROSS UND BLAU IN DÄNEMARK

Theater und Konzertsäle sind eine wichtige Kategorie öffentlicher Bauten, besonders in gestalterischer Hinsicht. Dennoch scheint nach dem Zweiten Weltkrieg auch in diesem Bereich eine Welle fader Modernität über den Globus gefegt zu sein. Die Mentalität öffentlicher Amtsträger, deren Aufgabe es war, Architekten zu beauftragen, war maßgeblich dafür verantwortlich, dass Bauten wie Jørn Utzons Opernhaus in Sydney die Ausnahme blieben. Nur wenige Architekten mussten ähnlich viel durchmachen wie Utzon, um sein Meisterwerk zu realisieren. Bei der Verleihung des Pritzker-Preises an Utzon 2003 hieß es: „Zweifellos ist das Opernhaus von Sydney sein Meisterwerk. Es ist eines der großen zeichenhaften Bauten des 20. Jahrhunderts, ein Bild großer Schönheit, das weltweit bekannt wurde – ein Symbol nicht nur für eine Stadt, sondern für ein ganzes Land und einen ganzen Kontinent." Ein solcher Erfolg ist nur wenigen Bauten und noch wenigeren Architekten vergönnt.

Klar ist jedoch, dass es in den vergangenen Jahren eine Rückkehr zu „namhaften" Architekten und mutigeren Projekten gegeben hat. Zwei jüngere Projekte in Kopenhagen, stilistisch durchaus unterschiedlich, stellen unter Beweis, wie sehr Architektur zur Weiterentwicklung

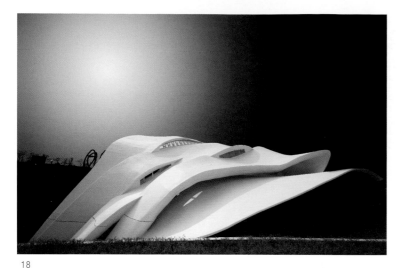

18
Makoto Sei Watanabe, RIBBONs Open-
Air Theater, Taichung City, Taiwan,
2008–09

einer historisch so dichten Stadt beitragen kann. Im neuen Königlichen Schauspielhaus (Kopenhagen, 2004–07, Seite 240) kombinieren Lundgaard & Tranberg Holzterrassen mit dunklen Backsteinwänden und einem dramatischen Glasfoyer. Entwürfe für Theater haben bis zu einem gewissen Grad stets mit praktischen Aspekten zu kämpfen, etwa mit dem Bühnenturm. Die dänischen Architekten, die den internationalen Wettbewerb für dieses Gebäude gewannen, verblendeten den Bühnenturm mit Kupfer und versuchten erst gar nicht, das Verhältnis von Form und Funktion zu kaschieren.

Ganz anders Jean Nouvel, der seinem beeindruckenden blauen Konzerthaus für den dänischen Rundfunk (Kopenhagen, 2003–09, Seite 310) bewusst eine geheimnisvolle Aura verleihen wollte – ein Geheimnis, das dem Architekten zufolge „nie weit davon entfernt ist, zu verführen und deshalb fasziniert". Statt für Klarheit entschied sich der Franzose für labyrinthische Komplexität, besonders im Innern des Baus, und eine transparente Außenhaut, die zugleich als Anzeigetafel für großformatige Bildprojektionen genutzt werden kann. Sicherlich spielte das Gespräch zwischen Auftraggeber und Architekten in beiden Fällen eine Rolle. Doch Kopenhagen hat zeitgleich zwei Büros ausgewählt, die jeweils dem Geist ihrer Zeit verpflichtet sind, aber die Beziehung von Funktion und Form auf unterschiedliche Weise interpretieren. Nouvel vertrat fast immer die Ansicht, dass Bauten sehr sichtbar sein sollten, dabei aber nicht unbedingt ihre Funktion herausstreichen oder zumindest nach außen vermitteln müssen. Lundgaard & Tranberg hingegen wählten sicherlich einen traditionelleren Ansatz, trotzdem ist ihr Entwurf alles andere als unzeitgemäß. Dieser Vergleich und Kontrast gibt Aufschluss über den Stand der öffentlichen Architektur im Jahr 2009: Nichts wird als selbstverständlich vorausgesetzt, doch eine ausdrucksstarke Wirkung ist fast immer erwünscht.

BÄNDER UND STEIN

Zwei weitere Theaterprojekte in fast entgegengesetzten Ecken der Erde illustrieren Ansätze, die in sehr unterschiedlichen Situationen zum Einsatz kommen und die mit den Prinzipien Schwere und Leichtigkeit gleichgesetzt werden können. Tatsächlich ist Schwere ein Eindruck, der bei AllesWirdGut zu spüren ist, einem Team, das einen ehemaligen römischen Steinbruch in St. Margarethen im Burgenland (Österreich, 2006–08, Seite 72) neu zu gestalten hatte. Statt der Stofflichkeit des Steins leichtere Materialien entgegenzusetzen, entschieden sich die Architekten dafür, „sämtliche Teile des Theaters an der gewaltigen Felskulisse teilhaben zu lassen. Es gilt, das räumliche Schauspiel sichtbar und erlebbar zu machen." Dabei nutzten sie das Material aus dem Steinbruch sowie oxidierte Stahlplatten, um den Veranstaltungsort zu erneuern und Zeichen von Modernität zu setzen, wo der uralte Stein ein Publikum von bis zu 6000 Personen empfängt.

Im Gegensatz hierzu entschied sich Makoto Sei Watanabe für einen radikal anderen Ansatz, als er den Erweiterungsbau für ein Theater in Taichung realisierte. Sein Freilufttheater RIBBONs (Taichung, Taiwan, 2008–09, Seite 400) ist eher eine Dachkonstruktion mit Bühnenanbau als ein vollständiger Theaterbau. Klar ist jedoch, dass Watanabe bemüht war, schwebende, wellenförmige Elemente um die Bühne herum in seinen Entwurf einzufügen, wodurch die Architektur aktiv „die Rolle übernimmt, die Wirkung des Theaters zu erweitern". Den Entwurf von AllesWirdGut in Österreich mit dem Begriff „Schwere" zu assoziieren, ist keineswegs als Kritik zu verstehen, sondern vielmehr eine schlichte

19
*Paul Andreu, National Center for
the Performing Arts, Bejing, China,
1999–2007*

19

Feststellung. Sowohl der Standort als auch die Optionen, für die sich die Architekten entschieden, sind engstens mit dem Material Stein verbunden, während der japanische Architekt beschloss, Leichtigkeit und Bewegung als Inspirationsquelle zu wählen. Wieder einmal zeigt sich, dass die zeitgenössische Architektur beide Lösungen ermöglicht: Letztlich bestimmen die Präferenzen der Auftraggeber und natürlich der Architekten selbst, welchen Weg sie unter den gegebenen Umständen einschlagen. Watanabe hätte sich wohl nicht für Stein aus dem Steinbruch und oxidierte Stahlplatten entschieden, wenn er den Auftrag in Österreich erhalten hätte.

BUHRUFE IN PEKING, JUBEL IN NEW YORK

Öffentliche Bauten sind oftmals der Kritik durch ihre Nutzer oder ortsansässige Architekten ausgesetzt, was auf das Nationale Zentrum für darstellende Künste von Paul Andreu (Peking, 1999–2007, Seite 86) zutrifft. Andreu ist Architekt des Flughafens Roissy und 50 weiterer Flughäfen weltweit, hat sich inzwischen jedoch von seiner Tätigkeit für die Aéroports de Paris zurückgezogen und arbeitet selbstständig, insbesondere in China. Die monumentale, muschelförmige Konstruktion, für die er sich entschied, liegt fast in Sichtweite der Verbotenen Stadt. Das Projekt erfuhr erbitterten Widerstand, sowohl in China als auch erstaunlicherweise in seinem Heimatland Frankreich, wo *Le Monde* einen geradezu giftigen Angriff auf seinen Entwurf publizierte. Andreu erinnert sich: „Ich bin nicht gewohnt, dass Projekte so starke Aufmerksamkeit in der Presse erregen. Ich gebe gern zu, dass ich im Hinblick auf mein Projekt in Peking eine Menge Kritik einstecken musste, die geradezu beleidigend war. Manchmal muss ich über die Kritiker lachen, z. B. über den Kerl, der schrieb: ‚Er hat keinen Architekturabschluss, er ist nichts weiter als ein Bauingenieur.' Nun ja, es tut mir leid, aber wenn Wright, Le Corbusier und Ando kein Diplom in Architektur gemacht haben, ich aber eins hätte, dann wäre ich doch ein Idiot. Abgesehen davon hat man mir vorgeworfen, ich hätte keine Kultur. Ich habe nie vorgegeben, ein Fachmann für chinesische Kultur zu sein. […] Wenn die Presse die Person ebenso sehr, wenn nicht gar stärker angreift als das eigentliche Projekt, wird das ziemlich ermüdend. Ich gebe mir alle Mühe, mich nicht in solche Debatten verwickeln zu lassen, weil ich meine Zeit für das Projekt brauche, mit dem man mich beauftragt hat. Manchmal allerdings lasse ich es ein bisschen rauchen … hier und da lasse ich sogar richtig Dampf ab."[3] Obwohl Andreu den Abwärtsschwung seiner Dachkonstruktion in Peking als Antithese zu den aufwärts geschwungenen Dächern der Verbotenen Stadt bezeichnet, ist sein Bau doch eher zeitgenössisch als durch die lange Geschichte Chinas inspiriert. Andreus Flughäfen werden von Millionen Fluggästen genutzt, doch nur wenige wissen, dass er als Architekt hinter diesen Bauten steht. Diese Tatsache schmälert ihre Qualität zwar in keiner Weise, doch es könnte durchaus sein, dass man Andreu eher wegen seines Baus in Peking in Erinnerung behalten wird als wegen Roissy, einem Projekt für die Aéroports de Paris.

In gewisser Weise fanden die Architekten Diller Scofidio + Renfro ein ähnlich komplexes und architektonisch vorbelastetes Umfeld vor, als sie mit ihren umfangreichen Umbaumaßnahmen am New Yorker Lincoln Center begannen. Die von ihnen gestaltete Alice Tully Hall am Lincoln Center (New York, 2006–09, Seite 168, mit FXFowle Architects) ist beinahe so etwas wie die Exhumierung einer Architektur, die lange Zeit unter der Juilliard School of Music begraben war. Dem Team gelang es, die Alice Tully Hall wieder ins Blickfeld zu rücken und den Kon-

20
Line & Space, Cesar Chavez Branch
Library, Phoenix, Arizona, USA,
2002–07

20

zertsaal zugleich vom Lärm der unweit verlaufenden U-Bahnlinie der 7th Avenue abzuschirmen. Außerdem waren die Architekten an der Sanierung der zentralen Haustechnikeinrichtung des Lincoln Center beteiligt, in der die Heiz- und Kühlanlagen für die elf Veranstaltungsorte des Kulturkomplexes untergebracht sind. Mit ihrer Bereitschaft, in den gesteckten Grenzen des bereits bestehenden Gebäudes von Pietro Belluschi zu arbeiten, zeigten Diller Scofidio + Renfro, dass sie nicht nur zeichenhafte Gebäude wie das Institute of Contemporary Art in Boston (2004–06) entwerfen können, sondern auch fähig sind, ihr persönliches Ego einem größeren Ziel unterzuordnen. Man könnte fragen, ob Andreu mit seinem Bauwerk in Peking diesen zurückhaltenden Ansatz verfolgt oder vielmehr für das Recht des Architekten eintritt, ein „einzigartiges" Gebäude zu gestalten, das für sich selbst steht und sich weitaus stärker von der Außenwelt abschließt, als es die Oper in Sydney je tat. Doch natürlich ist dies eine Frage des Geschmacks und keine Frage absoluter Standpunkte. Es erklärt jedoch, warum die öffentliche Hand nach wie vor oft zögert, bekannte Architekten zu beauftragen.

BADEKULTUR

Obwohl Bäder und Spas nicht im gleichen Maß als öffentliche Bauten zu bezeichnen sind wie Bahnhöfe oder gar Theater, konnten sie in den letzten Jahren von den Entwürfen renommierter, designbewusster Architekten profitieren, wie etliche Beispiele in diesem Band belegen. Die Erweiterung des Römerbads (Bad Kleinkirchheim, Kärnten, Österreich, 2006–07, Seite 124) durch Behnisch Architekten ist ein 10 000 m² großes, 15 Millionen Euro teures Projekt zur Modernisierung der 1979 entstandenen Einrichtung. Die Architekten entschieden sich für einen thematischen Ansatz, der die Geschichte des Wellnessbads aufgriff. Entsprechend spiegelt die untere Ebene, das Romanum, „die Badekultur des alten Rom", während das Noricum „den regionalen Kontext des Spas reflektiert – Wasser, Wälder und Felsen ...". Dies bedeutet jedoch keineswegs, so anspruchsvolle Architekten wie Behnisch seien dem „Disney"-Syndrom aufgesessen, vielmehr bekräftigt das Team: „Wie schon der Name sagt, werden Atmosphäre und Flair des ‚Römerbads' nicht allein durch dekorative Elemente geschaffen, sondern durch bewusste Abstraktion, auf Grundlage einer begrenzten Anzahl im Grunde skulpturaler Formen und Farben."

Die von Moneo Brock Studio realisierten Thermalbäder in Panticosa (Huesca, Spanien, 2002–08, Seite 296) liegen in den Pyrenäen. Der modern anmutende Entwurf der Architekten sucht sowohl die Auseinandersetzung mit der landschaftlichen Umgebung als auch mit dem urbanen Kontext der bestehenden Bäderarchitektur. Mit der gewählten Kombination aus Glas und Stein gelingt es dem Team eindrucksvoll, dieses Ziel zu erreichen. Die Materialien des Außenbaus sind von einer gewissen Kühle und kontrastieren mit der wärmeren Atmosphäre der Bäder, wo Wasser und Bewegung die Themen für die geschwungenen Fassaden liefern. Les Bains des Docks (Le Havre, Frankreich, 2006–08, Seite 318), ein Projekt von Jean Nouvel, ist eingebettet in das Stadterneuerungsprogramm „Port 2000". Der überwiegend dunkle Außenbau bildet einen auffälligen Kontrast zu den weißen bzw. farbigen Innenräumen. Die hier von Nouvel zum Einsatz gebrachte architektonische Komposition aus geometrischen Körpern findet sich bei ihm sonst eher selten. Zweifellos erklären sich die Unterschiede zwischen beiden Projekten aus ihrem Standort, ebenso jedoch aus dem architektonischen Gespür und Erfindungsreichtum von Moneo Brock und Jean Nouvel. Letztlich verfolgen beide dasselbe Ziel, wenn auch unter verschiedenen Vorzeichen. In Projekten wie dem von Behnisch gestalteten Bad in

21
*Giancarlo Mazzanti, Santo Domingo
Library Park, Medellin, Colombia,
2006–07*

Österreich klingt eine ferne Vergangenheit nach. Es ist durchaus interessant zu sehen, wie talentierte Architekten an Problemstellungen herangehen, die im Kern dieselben sind: Wie lassen sich Menschen im Kontext eines Badeerlebnisses zusammenbringen, wenn es zugleich gilt, Aussicht, Umgebung und nicht zuletzt die anderen Badegäste zu berücksichtigen?

SO TAGT MAN IN SPANIEN

Aus gegebenem Anlass entschloss sich eine ganze Reihe spanischer Städte unlängst zum Bau von Tagungs- und Kongresseinrichtungen. Drei spanische Architekten, bereits bekannt aus anderen Zusammenhängen, – Rafael Beneytez, Nieto Sobejano und Francisco Mangado – konnten in den vergangenen Monaten bedeutende Projekte auf diesem Gebiet abschließen. Zunächst ist da Rafael Beneytez, ehemaliger „Absolvent" des Büros von Rafael Moneo. Sein Messe- und Konferenzzentrum in Huesca (Spanien, 2005–08, Seite 44), ein Komplex mit 12 000 m², wirkt ausgesprochen geradlinig – fast schon geometrisch streng. Dennoch werden die einzelnen Baukörper dank der sorgfältigen und einfallsreichen Behandlung der Materialien, Oberflächen und der Beleuchtung lebendig und erscheinen bei Tag und bei Nacht höchst unterschiedlich. Beneytez ging sogar so weit zu erklären, er habe „zwei Bauten in einem" entworfen, „einen für den Tag und einen für die Nacht". Diese Art von architektonischer Gestaltung, im Prinzip pragmatisch und modular, wird umso interessanter und aktueller, je stärker der Architekt das gesamte Spektrum an Möglichkeiten ausschöpft, das ihm im Rahmen der rechtwinkligen Formensprache zur Verfügung steht.

Nieto Sobejanos Entwurf hingegen, die zickzackähnlichen Formen seines Auditoriums und Messezentrums in Aragon (Expo 2008, Saragossa, Spanien, 2006–08, Seite 45), wirkt, als hätte man eine Aufrisszeichnung unmittelbar ins Dreidimensionale übersetzt. Der geschickte Einsatz von Verglasung und Metallrosten verleiht der Oberfläche des Baus Abwechslung, die sich auch im Innern fortsetzt. Dort werden Licht und Volumen auf ungewöhnliche Weise manipuliert und gestaltet, ohne dabei Verluste in der Umsetzung des Programms in Kauf zu nehmen. Die Architekten entwarfen eine „Landschaft aus massivem Licht, das aus dem Boden aufzusteigen scheint". Auch wenn dieser Anspruch leicht überzeichnet scheinen mag, was die Umsetzung und Präsenz der Formensprache im gesamten Komplex angeht (schließlich ist Licht eben kein massiver Körper), so sprechen der Reiz und die überraschenden Ideen des Architekten doch für sich.

Francisco „Paxti" Mangado schließlich entwarf das Städtische Kongress- und Messezentrum in Ávila (Castilla y León, Spanien, 2004–09, Seite 258), das den anderen beiden Projekten in Dimension und Budget durchaus ebenbürtig ist. Der Architekt verweist auf die „topografische, mineralische Dichte" der Umgebung und verrät damit zugleich viel über das fast geologisch anmutende Bauwerk, das wie Gesteinsschichten aus dem Boden aufzuwachsen scheint und erdverbunden ist. Der Standort des Komplexes ist alles andere als grün, und so bekräftigt und unterstreicht die steinerne Präsenz des Gebäudes seine Herkunft. Aufgegriffen werden auch die Stadtmauern in der Nähe, wodurch die „Verwurzelung" des Bauwerks in seinem Kontext einmal mehr hervorgestrichen wird. Dies alles geschieht wie immer unter Berücksichtigung der üblichen Auflagen von Flexibilität und Effizienz. Wie seine Kollegen, so beweist auch Mangado, dass Beschränkungen,

22
Mario Botta, Tamaro Chapel, Monte
Tamaro, Switzerland, 1990–96

22

denen öffentliche Bauvorhaben unterworfen sind, keineswegs überraschende und innovative Architektur ausschließen müssen. Und so gelingt es Mangado, der Stadt ein Gesicht zu geben, obwohl er sich auf ein orthogonales Raster beschränkt. Dies erleichtert natürlich nicht nur die Nutzung des Gebäudes, sondern ebenso Bau und Instandhaltung. Dieser Komplex ist kein Guggenheim Bilbao mit schlicht nicht nutzbaren Nischen und Wandflächen. Beneytez, Nieto Sobejano und auch Mangado ist es ernst mit ihrem Metier, sie wissen, wie man Architektur gestaltet. Es bleibt zu hoffen, dass der fast vollständige Zusammenbruch des spanischen Immobilienmarkts und weiter Teile der spanischen Wirtschaft diese Architekten nicht daran hindert, ihr Talent auch auf anderem Gebiet zu zeigen.

GELEHRTER STOLZ

Bibliotheken – etwa die New Yorker Public Library auf der Fifth Avenue zwischen 41st Street und 42nd Street (Carrère und Hastings, 1911) – haben bis vor kurzem eine Schwere und Feierlichkeit vermittelt, die öffentlicher Architektur angemessen schien. Die unumgängliche Auseinandersetzung mit dem Internet jedoch, ebenso wie die Erkenntnis, dass ansprechende zeitgenössische Architektur dazu beitragen kann, Anschluss an die Gegenwart zu finden, haben Bibliotheksbauten zu einem dramatischen Entwicklungsschub verholfen, wie einige hier vorgestellte Beispiele illustrieren. Das in Arizona ansässige Büro Line and Space konnte kürzlich die Zweigbibliothek Cesar Chavez fertigstellen (Phoenix, Arizona, 2002–07). Die für monatlich bis zu 40 000 Besucher ausgelegte Einrichtung verfügt über relativ bescheidene 2323 m² Fläche. Schon die dramatische Linienführung und Profilgebung des Baus zeugen davon, dass wir es mit einem anderen Typ von Bibliothek zu tun haben, als dem von Carrère und Hastings an der Fifth Avenue realisierten Bauwerk. Die Bibliothek in Arizona richtet ihren Blick fest auf die Gegenwart, was natürlich ebenso bedeutet, Einschränkungen zu bejahen, die ein ökologisches Bewusstsein diktiert.

Ein vollkommen anderer Fall ist die Bibliothek Santo Domingo in Medellín (Kolumbien, 2006–07, Seite 264) von Giancarlo Mazzanti. Mazzanti wurde 1963 im kolumbianischen Barranquilla geboren und hat sein Büro in Bogotá. Der Bau, „gefaltet und zerklüftet, wie die Berge, die ihn umgeben", liegt inmitten eines Viertels, das von der Drogengewalt der 1980er-Jahre gezeichnet ist. Der dreiteilige Bau sitzt auf einem gemeinsamen Sockel und umfasst eine Bibliothek, Schulräume, einen Hörsaal sowie Büros. Bewusst als Wahrzeichen einer Stadt geplant, die man eher als Drogenhauptstadt und weniger als akademische Metropole kennt, geht es hier darum, „den Einzelnen aus dem Kontext der ihn umgebenden Armut" herauszulösen. Auf ähnliche Weise ist auch die Bibliothek der Universität Deusto in Bilbao (Spanien, 2001–08, Seite 290) von Rafael Moneo ein architektonischer Entwurf, der für sich selbst steht und zugleich der Versuch, sich in einem Umfeld zu behaupten, das von Frank Gehrys Guggenheim Bilbao dominiert wird. Moneo ist sicherlich niemand, der metallische Volumina verdreht – eine Disziplin, die Gehry hingegen meisterhaft beherrscht, in diesem Fall zweifellos zugunsten der Stadt. Vielmehr reicht es Moneo, sich zurückzunehmen und traditionellere Formen zu präsentieren. Trotzdem verpackt er diese in einen strahlenden, komplexen Baukörper und gestaltet so ein würdiges Pendant, wenn nicht gar eine pointierte Kritik zum überschwänglichen Stil des Amerikaners.

23
Richard Meier, Jubilee Church, Rome,
Italy, 2003

23

GROSSE ARCHITEKTEN, KLEINE KIRCHEN

Nachdem Religion bereits in früheren Zeiten eine der Hauptquellen architektonischer Innovation war, wird sie nun wieder zu einem Bereich, in dem sich Architekten kreativ verwirklichen können. Es überrascht nicht, dass heutige Architekten eine Tradition fortführen, in der schon Mario Botta (Kathedrale von Évry, Frankreich, 1988–95, Kirche in Tamaro, Monte Tamaro, Schweiz, 1992–96 und Kirche in Mogno, Schweiz, 1986–98), Richard Meier (Jubiläumskirche, Rom, 2003) oder Tadao Ando (Kirche des Lichts, Ibaraki, Osaka, Japan, 1988–89) mit ihren unverwechselbaren Sakralbauten stehen. Der New Yorker Architekt Stan Allen entwarf die kleine CCV-Kapelle (Tagaytay, Cavite, Philippinen, 2007–08, Seite 66) am Eingang des Campusgeländes der Chosen Children's Village Foundation. Anliegen der gemeinnützigen Organisation ist die „Schaffung eines Heims für körperlich und geistig behinderte Kinder". Der Betonbau mit einer Grundfläche von 240 m^2 erhebt sich bis zu 7 m hoch. Seine weißen, markanten Formen umreißen ein Gotteshaus, das sein höchst bescheidenes Budget nicht ahnen lässt. Geplant mit Blick auf das tropische Klima und die Erdbebengefahr, ist der Bau auf natürliche Belüftung angewiesen. Dies ist zweifellos ein sinnvollerer Weg, Energie zu sparen als der Einsatz technisch aufwendigerer, computergesteuerter Systeme in komplexeren Bauten.

Ein weiterer innovativer Kirchenentwurf stammt vom Schweizer Team Localarchitecture. Ihre temporäre Kapelle in St. Loup (Pompaples, Schweiz, 2008, Seite 234) ist eine 130 m^2 große Konstruktion, die als provisorisches Gotteshaus errichtet wurde, während das Mutterhaus der Diakonissengemeinschaft von St. Loup im Kanton Waadt saniert wird. Die Architekten arbeiteten mit CAD-CNC-Tools, sprich mit computergestützten Entwurfswerkzeugen, um den numerisch gesteuerten Zuschnitt der Formteile für ihre Konstruktion aus Holz, Kunststoff und textilem Material zu berechnen. Wegen der temporären Nutzung konnte die Konstruktion ohne Fundament errichtet werden. Interessant ist jedoch, dass die protestantische Glaubensgemeinschaft offen für ein zeitgenössisch gestaltetes Gebetshaus war sowie dafür, Architekten zu verpflichten, die jünger als 40 Jahre sind.

Die Pfarrkirche Santa Monica (Rivas Vaciamadrid, Madrid, 2004–09, Seite 394) wurde von Vicens + Ramos für den Bischof von Alcalá erbaut. Während traditionellere Kirchen- und Gemeindebauten ihre Funktionen architektonisch sehr oft trennen, entschieden sich Vicens + Ramos dafür, ein „Kontinuum" zu gestalten und Wohnungen für die Priester, Gemeindezentrum und Kirche miteinander zu verbinden. Darüber hinaus vereinbarten sie mit dem Bauherrn, eine Reihe zeitgenössischer Künstler mit einzubeziehen und wählten Cor-Ten-Stahl als markante Verkleidung für die Fassade. Da Cor-Ten-Stahl auch ein Material ist, das sehr häufig von Bildhauern wie etwa Richard Serra genutzt wird, wirkt das gesamte Projekt wie eine Skulptur. Trotzdem lässt die Gestaltung des Innenraums keineswegs an eine Galerie denken, und ebenso wenig wirkt die Architektur wie ein Akt der Selbstverwirklichung des Architekten. Vielmehr ist sie ein Ort der Kontemplation und des Gebets, in dem Kunst und Architektur nicht nur geduldet werden, sondern zum inspirierenden Beitrag werden, der dezidiert zeitgenössisch ist. Obwohl die harmonische Einbindung von Kunst in religiöse und architektonische Kontexte tief in der Tradition der Kirche verwurzelt ist, folgte das 20. Jahrhundert diesem historischen Vorbild nicht immer so ausgeprägt wie in früheren Zeiten. Die Pfarrkirche Santa Monica scheint diese Tradition wieder zu beleben – mit einer zweifellos zeitgenössischen Ästhetik, die auf die Bedürfnisse der Kirche und Gemeinde reagiert.

BRÜCKENSCHLAG ZWISCHEN VERGANGENHEIT UND GEGENWART

Museen sind der wohl auffälligste Ausdruck der jüngsten Entwicklung in der öffentlichen Architektur. Eine Partnerpublikation zu diesem Band, *Architecture Now! Museums*, beschäftigt sich mit diesem Bereich weitaus ausführlicher, als es in diesem Rahmen möglich ist. Dennoch sind auch hier einige Beispiele vertreten. So konnte der mit dem Pritzker-Preis ausgezeichnete japanische Architekt Tadao Ando am 4. Juni 2009 die Punta della Dogana (Seite 78) für François Pinaults Kunststiftung in Venedig einweihen. Jedem Touristen, der schon einmal in Venedig gewesen ist, ist das Bild der Basilika Santa Maria della Salute vertraut. Die Kirche, unweit der Spitze des Bezirks Dorsoduro gelegen, ist ein Entwurf des Architekten Baldassare Longhena (1598–1682) und der Jungfrau Maria geweiht, der Schutzpatronin der Republik. Der 1681 vollendete Bau wurde 1630 vom venezianischen Senat in Auftrag gegeben und ist dem Gedenken an die verheerende Pest gewidmet, die die Stadt heimgesucht hatte. An der eigentlichen Spitze von Dorsoduro befanden sich lange Zeit Salzlagerhallen, seit 1525 steht hier ein Zollhaus für Seegüter, die Dogana da Mar. Mit dem Bau der neuen Basilika entschied man sich aus ästhetischen Gründen, die angrenzende Dogana umzubauen. Es war Giuseppe Benoni (1618–84), der zwischen 1676 und 1682 einen niedrigen Bau mit Bossenwerk realisierte, der an seiner Spitze mit einem Turm gegenüber dem Markusplatz bekrönt wurde. An diesem Standort wollte François Pinault in Zusammenarbeit mit Tadao Ando eine zweite venezianische Galerie für seine Stiftung für zeitgenössische Kunst eröffnen. Wie zu erwarten, interpretierte Ando den Altbau ausgehend von seiner geometrischen Grundform: „Die Punta della Dogana zeichnet sich durch eine einfache, rationale Struktur aus. Der Baukörper bildet ein Dreieck und nimmt damit unmittelbar Bezug auf die Landspitze der Dorsoduro-Insel. Die Innenräume indessen sind durch eine Reihe paralleler Wände in längliche Rechtecke gegliedert." Das bestehende Gebäude wurde mit größter Sorgfalt renoviert, und Ando entschied sich darüber hinaus, eine ausdrucksstarke geometrische Geste in das Herz des dreieckigen Grundrisses zu setzen und realisierte einen Betonkubus, der die gesamte Höhe des Baus einnimmt und zur zentralen Achse sämtlicher Wege durch den neu gestalteten Raum wird.

Vielleicht sollte erwähnt werden, dass in diesem Band ein weiteres Bauwerk in Venedig vorgestellt wird, das von einem führenden zeitgenössischen Architekten stammt. Santiago Calatravas Quarto Ponte sul Canal Grande (1999–2006, Seite 136) ist tatsächlich erst die vierte Brücke, die den Canal Grande überspannt. Die 94 m lange Konstruktion liegt unweit des Hauptbahnhofs der Stadt. Zwar stehen die Eleganz und Modernität des Bauwerks außer Frage, dennoch wurden Entwurf und Bau von Kontroversen begleitet. Dies ist umso erstaunlicher, als Brücken wie die an der Accademia seit Langem geduldet werden, trotz ihres offensichtlichen Mangels an Ästhetik oder architektonischer Bedeutung. Calatravas Brücke hingegen ist weder eine zu gewagte, noch eine zu verhaltene Geste: Sie ist das ideale Signal, dass Venedig noch immer lebendig ist, obwohl die Stadt in anderen Bereichen allzu sehr in ihrer langsam verfallenden Vergangenheit gefangen ist. Dank Architekten wie Ando und Calatrava, die die altehrwürdigen Formen der Stadt so intelligent bereichern, könnte Venedig als reale Stadt weiterleben

24
*Frank O. Gehry, Serpentine Pavilion,
Kensington Gardens, London, United
Kingdom, 2008*

24

und nicht nur als Postkartenmotiv für Touristen. Jedenfalls lassen sich nur wenige Bauten ebenso rechtmäßig als gelungene öffentliche Architektur bezeichnen wie die Quarto Ponte.

Kuehn Malvezzis Umbau eines Industriegebäudes aus dem frühen 20. Jahrhundert für die Sammlerin Julia Stoschek (Düsseldorf, 2005–07, Seite 222) warf ganz andere Fragen auf als Andos Umgestaltung der Punta della Dogana. Hier arbeiteten die Architekten mit einem denkmalgeschützten Gebäude und behielten die ursprüngliche Fassade bei, entkernten jedoch das Innere und zogen neue Wände innerhalb der alten Fabrikmauern ein. Die zuständigen Ämter genehmigten, das alte Fabrikschild durch eine Glasbox zu ersetzen. Da im Gebäude auch die Wohnung der Sammlerin untergebracht ist, ist das Projekt im Grunde ein Hybrid. Dennoch entschieden sich die Architekten für eine durchgängige Farb- und Materialpalette in den öffentlichen und privaten Bereichen. Zweifellos ist dieses Projekt dem vorherrschenden Trend zuzuordnen, alte Industriebauten für kulturelle Zwecke umzunutzen. Sei es nun, weil solche Altbauten denkmalgeschützt sind, wie hier in Düsseldorf, oder weil ihre Bauteile und -materialien ästhetisch oder konstruktiv von Interesse sind – so oder so bieten sie Architekten die Gelegenheit, sich von einem rein modernistischen Ansatz zu lösen. Und so wird ein kaum „öffentlich" zu nennendes Fabrikgebäude zu einem Ort, der jedem offen steht, der neugierig genug ist, ihn zu betreten.

SONNTAG IM PARK MIT FRANK

Auch Pavillonbauten sind zu einem beliebten Ort der Begegnung zwischen renommierten Architekten und der breiten Öffentlichkeit geworden. Die oft temporären Konstruktionen, wie etwa die Sommerpavillons der Serpentine Gallery in London, werden z. T. an anderer Stelle weitergenutzt. Dies gilt auch für Frank O. Gehrys Serpentine Pavilion (Kensington Gardens, London, 2008, Seite 180). Die freiliegende Holzskelettkonstruktion mit einer Fläche von 418 m^2 war überwiegend mit einer Vielzahl von Glassegmenten bedeckt – einer „kontrastreichen Kombination zufällig wirkender Elemente" – und bot bei Konzerten und Veranstaltungen bis zu 275 Besuchern Platz. Hier konnte Gehry auf die ursprüngliche Inspirationsquelle seiner innovativen Entwürfe zurückgreifen: jene Häuser im kalifornischen Santa Monica oder Venice, die er zu Beginn seiner Laufbahn aus „gefundenen" Materialien wie Maschendraht oder Asphalt errichtet hatte. Die Baustoffe hatte er auf überraschende Weise verarbeitet und so einen neuartigen architektonischen Ansatz definiert, der Ähnlichkeit mit der Freiheit zeitgenössischer Kunst hatte. Treffenderweise wurde Gehrys Serpentine Pavilion vom irischen Besitzer des Weinguts Château La Coste unweit von Aix-en-Provence in Südfrankreich erworben. Geplant ist, das Gut 2010 für die Öffentlichkeit zugänglich zu machen, mit Werken zahlreicher weiterer berühmter Künstler und Architekten, die neben dem eigentlichen Weinberg und den Produktionsstätten zu sehen sein werden.

Ein wahrer Ort der Begegnung für zeitgenössische Kunst, Architektur und Öffentlichkeit ist der Millennium Park in Chicago. Künstler wie Jaume Plensa und Anish Kapoor haben Projekte für den Park realisiert, ebenso wie der allgegenwärtige Frank Gehry. Sein Jay-Pritzker-Pavillon (Millennium Park, Chicago, Illinois, 1999–2004) ist eine 36 m hohe, wogende Konstruktion aus Edelstahlbändern mit einem spalierartigen Gerüst aus Stahlrohren. Die Freiluftbühne mit ihren 4000 festen Sitzen und Platz für 7000 weitere Besucher wurde innerhalb kürzester Zeit zu

25
*UNStudio, Burnham Pavilion, Chicago,
IL, 2009*

einem neuen Wahrzeichen Chicagos. Gehry führt aus: „Wie schafft man es, dass sich alle Besucher – nicht nur die Gäste auf den festen Plätzen, sondern auch diejenigen, die 120 m weiter auf dem Rasen sitzen – wohlfühlen, wenn sie hierher kommen, um Musik zu hören? Die Antwort ist: Man muss sie hineinnehmen. Man konzipiert eine größere Vorderbühne, man baut ein spalierartiges Gerüst mit einer Soundanlage.
Man vermittelt den Besuchern das Gefühl, Teil des Geschehens zu sein." Selbst nach Einweihung des Parks wurde hier weiter gebaut –
unlängst konnten neue Pavillonbauten von Zaha Hadid und dem niederländischen Architekturbüro UNStudio installiert werden. Das Projekt von
UNStudio – der Burnham-Pavillon (Chicago, Illinois, 2009, Seite 390) – ist eine 300 m² große Konstruktion aus Holz und Stahl, die als „fließender, multidirektionaler Raum" und als Hommage an den orthogonalen Stadtgrundriss von Chicago konzipiert wurde, den Daniel Burnham
1909 entwarf. Hier bezieht die aktuelle Architektur kritisch Position und knüpft zugleich an die gebaute Vergangenheit in einer nach wie vor
dynamischen Stadt an.

ANGEKOMMEN IM MAINSTREAM

In gewisser Weise ist der Burnham-Pavillon von UNStudio ein Symbol für die Entwicklung zeigenössischer öffentlicher Architektur. Hier
treten neuartige Formen, mithilfe computergestützter Methoden entworfen und realisiert, an prominenten Standorten in Erscheinung. Die breite Öffentlichkeit kann nun Projekte bewundern (oder ablehnen), die zur Avantgarde zeitgenössischer Architektur zählen. Ohne Frage werden
wirtschaftliche Engpässe in Zukunft dafür sorgen, dass so manche öffentliche Bauvorhaben, die architektonisch interessant wären, nicht realisiert werden können. Dennoch scheint es, als habe die frühere finanzielle Freiheit mehr Offenheit geschaffen und dafür gesorgt, dass zeitgenössische Kreativität nachhaltig in den Mainstream der Architektur Einzug gehalten hat. So gesehen ist dieser Band auch die Würdigung eines
schon fast historisch zu nennenden Sinneswandels. Ihm ist zu verdanken, dass innovative Architekten von Spanien bis Taiwan der breiten
Öffentlichkeit eine neue Formensprache präsentieren konnten oder zumindest einem Publikum, das weit über jene Elite hinausgeht, die diese
Avantgarde bisher zu schätzen wusste. Zwar zeichnet sich bei diesen höchst unterschiedlichen Projekten kein einheitlicher Stil ab, doch der
zunehmende Einfluss des Computers ist in den meisten Fällen sichtbar, zumindest für den, der einen Blick dafür hat. Die Flexibilität, die com-
putergestützte Entwurfs- und Fertigungstechniken mit sich gebracht haben, ist inzwischen längst im Mainstream der Architektur angekommen. Unterschiedlichste Formen, die früher nicht ohne exorbitante Budgetüberschreitungen möglich gewesen wären, können nun realisiert
werden.

Die Projektauswahl für diesen Band legt nahe, dass Architekten schon lange bevor die dunklen Wolken der Rezession am Himmel auf-
zogen, die Lektionen „Sparsamkeit" und „funktionale Effizienz" gelernt hatten. Die hier präsentierten Bauten sind in den meisten Fällen nicht
nur ästhetisch innovativ, sondern auch ausgesprochen nutzerfreundlich und darüber hinaus mit einer Rücksicht auf die Umwelt geplant, die in
früheren (modernen) Zeiten kein Thema war. Diese Zeichen – die Fähigkeit anspruchsvoller Architekten, sich für Großprojekte zu engagieren
und dabei Kosten, funktionale Effizienz sowie die Umwelt zu berücksichtigen – lassen Gutes für die Zukunft hoffen, auch wenn zunächst weniger Projekte realisiert werden und weniger Finanzmittel zur Verfügung stehen sollten. Dank dieser Bauten und anderer Projekte, die in den

letzten Jahren weltweit realisiert wurden, hat qualitativ anspruchsvolle Architektur mehr und mehr an öffentlicher Akzeptanz gewonnen und beschränkt sich nicht länger auf eine kleine Zahl eher isoliert liegender Standorte. Zeitgenössische Architektur, die mehr ist als nur eine unansehnliche Box, ist längst im Mainstream angekommen.

Philip Jodidio, Grimentz, 6. Juli 2009

[1] Siehe *Großes Wörterbuch der deutschen Sprache*, Mannheim: F.A. Brockhaus, 1995, S. 2428.
[2] „On-Site: New Architecture in Spain", 12. Februar 2006 – 1. Mai 2006. Siehe http://www.moma.org/visit/calendar/exhibitions/86, aufgerufen am 5. Juli 2009.
[3] Auszüge aus einem Interview mit Paul Andreu, erschienen in der Zeitschrift *Upstreet*, Februar 2001.

INTRODUCTION

LE CONTEMPORAIN SE GÉNÉRALISE

public, -ique
adjectif

1. D'État, qui est sous contrôle de l'État, qui appartient à l'État, qui dépend de l'État, géré par l'État.
Établissement public ; économie, prospérité publique ; recettes, subventions, publiques.
2. Qui concerne tout un peuple, l'ensemble de la population. Bonheur, ordre public ; morale publique ; mœurs publiques ;
contributions publiques ; hygiène publique ; travaux d'utilité publique.
3. Qui est général, commun à tous.
Étymologie : empr. au lat. publicus *« qui concerne le peuple ou l'État ; d'un usage public ; commun à tous », adj. corr. au subst.* populus.[1]

On peut classer l'architecture par types d'usage ou de constructions, ou recourir à une foule d'autres critères. Mais les bâtiments semblent pouvoir très facilement être classés suivant deux catégories essentielles: les bâtiments privés, comme les maisons d'habitation, et les bâtiments publics, comme les gares, les stades ou les musées. Un palais de justice, fermé au grand public mais ouvert à tous ceux qui ont affaire à la justice, peut-il être considéré comme un bâtiment « public » ? C'est très probable, puisqu'il concerne « la population dans son ensemble », même si tout le monde n'en a pas un usage direct. Il est également soutenu par des fonds publics. Ce cas, apparemment simple, pose la question de la définition de l'architecture publique. Un bâtiment universitaire n'est souvent ouvert qu'aux étudiants et au personnel, excluant toute visite qui pourrait perturber les cours. Est-ce néanmoins un bâtiment public ? Si l'on définit l'éducation comme étant pour le bien de tous, et souvent financée par des fonds publics, la réponse devrait être affirmative. Ainsi, faire payer un droit d'entrée, comme le font la plupart des musées ou des stades, signifie que le bâtiment ne « concerne pas la population dans son ensemble », et pourtant ils sont, dans leur définition la plus généralement acceptée, ouverts au public.

Avant la crise économique qui a débuté en 2008, et jusqu'à une date indéterminée étant donnés les calendriers d'exécution des grands projets, l'architecture publique a connu un formidable bouleversement, un véritable réveil esthétique. Là où « publique » signifiait résolument classique et guindée pour les générations antérieures, la conscience qu'une architecture de qualité pouvait redynamiser et rendre plus efficaces les activités publiques a fait son chemin. Ainsi, des architectes renommés, comme Herzog et de Meuron pour le Stade national (principale installation olympique des Jeux olympiques de 2008 à Pékin, Chine, 2003–08), ou le stade plus ancien Allianz Arena (Munich, Allemagne, 2002–05), ou Jean Nouvel pour le musée du quai Branly (Paris, France, 2001–06), sont apparus comme les concepteurs d'une nouvelle génération de bâtiments vraiment publics, conciliant l'accès au plus grand nombre et une esthétique autrefois réservée à une minorité. Les musées, bien sûr, ont été des bénéficiaires importants de cette vague de construction mondiale, avec des architectes comme Renzo Piano qui a brillé de San Francisco à Berne. Piano est également le dessinateur de l'aéroport international du Kansai (Osaka, Japon,

26
Renzo Piano and Richard Rogers,
Centre Pompidou, Paris, France,
1971–78

1988–94), une autre manifestation résolument publique de la montée d'une architecture qui allie à la fonctionnalité le sens d'un éveil théâtral et esthétique. Aucun architecte ne peut revendiquer la responsabilité de permettre aux pouvoirs publics une prise de risque inhérente au pari sur des architectures innovantes, mais c'était déjà Renzo Piano, à l'époque en collaboration avec Richard Rogers, qui avait imaginé le Centre Pompidou à Paris (1971–78), un design révolutionnaire qui a attiré plus de 20 000 visiteurs par jour pendant des années.

MAUVAIS TEMPS SUR L'ESPAGNE

Plusieurs projets présentés dans ce volume sont situés en Espagne. Une exposition de 2006 au Musée d'art moderne de New York (MoMA) mettait l'accent sur l'émergence de l'Espagne dans l'architecture contemporaine. La présentation précisait : « Cette exposition détaille les développements architecturaux les plus récents dans un pays qui est devenu, ces dernières années, un centre international d'innovation et d'excellence dans le design. »[2] Et pourtant, l'Espagne a été l'un des pays les plus touchés par une récession qui a arrêté net de nombreux projets architecturaux comme le Palais de justice de Madrid. Les nombreux centres administratifs, musées et autres équipements publics, qui ont poussé comme des champignons au cours des cinq dernières années, et dont plusieurs annonçaient l'arrivée de nouveaux talents sur la scène internationale, seront probablement beaucoup moins nombreux dans l'avenir immédiat.

Cet ouvrage marquera peut-être la fin d'une période d'innovation architecturale et de construction rapide, car les projets présentés ici ont presque tous été conçus et même construits avant l'éclatement de la bulle immobilière qui a touché des pays comme l'Espagne ou l'Angleterre. Il n'est pas dit pour autant que l'architecture publique soit une chose du passé – des projets de stimulation économique dans de nombreux pays prennent même nettement en compte la construction de nouveaux bâtiments et espaces publics. Mais nombre des initiatives à grande échelle qui ont marqué le début du XXIe siècle seront sans doute ralenties ou repensées. Les architectes auront peut-être pour défi de dessiner des bâtiments plus petits et plus économiques qu'ils ne l'ont fait jusqu'à présent. Des bâtiments verts ou à énergie positive viendront d'autant plus au premier plan qu'ils pourront justifier de factures effectivement moins importantes de combustible ou d'électricité.

De semblables conclusions peuvent être tirées en ce qui concerne l'architecture « privée » – non destinée au grand public, ou complètement fermée à cet usage. Dans l'ensemble, on peut supposer que l'architecture publique, puisqu'elle est destinée au plus grand nombre et sert des desseins indéniablement utiles, est mieux placée pour survivre à un long ralentissement de l'économie que le secteur privé. Les équipements publics pour le sport, les salons, ou les transports génèrent des revenus et sont des indicateurs de l'attrait de telle ville ou telle région par opposition à une concurrence entre emplacements. Même si certains pays, comme les États-Unis, sont peut-être plus durement touchés que d'autres par les difficultés économiques actuelles, les bâtiments et les espaces publics sont et resteront un facteur constant du développement de l'architecture contemporaine. Même si les conceptions en sont moins extravagantes, l'utilité de faire appel à des architectes de talent semble être entrée de façon durable dans l'esprit des fonctionnaires du gouvernement, des promoteurs et même du grand public. Cet ouvrage cherche modestement à présenter certaines des raisons pour lesquelles cette conclusion est justifiée.

DES AMBITIONS OLYMPIQUES

L'amélioration des équipements sportifs existants ou la création de nouveaux bâtiments pour des besoins spécifiques, comme les Jeux olympiques par exemple, constituent une partie significative des travaux réalisés dans le domaine de l'architecture publique ces dernières années. De telles initiatives ne se trouvent pas seulement là où on peut s'y attendre, comme à Pékin en 2008. Le célèbre bureau d'études Arup a récemment réaménagé Kensington Oval (2005–07, page 100), le stade de cricket bien connu de Bridgetown, sur l'île de la Barbade. Avec l'aide du gouvernement qui a acheté des propriétés avoisinantes pour donner au stade plus de visibilité et un accès plus facile, Arup a modernisé les lieux pour la finale de la Coupe du monde de cricket de 2007, au cours de laquelle l'Australie a battu le Sri Lanka, le 28 avril 2007. Le stade Kensington Oval a accueilli son premier test match en 1929–30 et peut recevoir 32 000 spectateurs. La très moderne boîte arrondie imaginée par Arup pour la tribune principale actualise franchement l'apparence des équipements, et les architectes ont pris soin d'utiliser des matériaux locaux ou de récupérer les eaux pluviales pour minimiser l'« empreinte carbone » du bâtiment.

Un autre très grand cabinet, Cannon Design, a été chargé de la création de l'Anneau olympique de Richmond (Richmond, Colombie-Britannique, Canada, 2005–08, page 142), prévu pour accueillir les compétitions de patinage de vitesse longue piste lors des Jeux olympiques d'hiver de 2010. D'une superficie de 38 000 mètres carrés et d'un coût de plus de 153 millions de dollars, c'est un grand édifice qui héberge également le laboratoire de contrôle antidopage des Jeux d'hiver. La structure couverte pourra, bien sûr, être utilisée à l'avenir pour d'autres sports, comme l'athlétisme et le basket. Après s'être finalement rendus à l'évidence que l'architecture spectaculaire des Jeux olympiques ou des Expositions universelles du passé ne servait à rien d'autre et finissait par coûter une fortune aux contribuables et aux investisseurs, les organisateurs et les pouvoirs publics, comme ceux de la ville de Richmond par exemple, ont été convaincus que la vie post-événementielle de tels bâtiments est sans doute un enjeu plus important que la courte période justifiant leur construction.

KAOHSIUNG RENCONTRE JURMALA

De l'autre côté du Pacifique, le Conseil national de la forme physique et du sport (National Council on Physical Fitness and Sports) et la ville de Kaohsiung ont demandé au célèbre architecte Toyo Ito de construire le stade principal pour les Jeux mondiaux de 2009 (Kaohsiung, Taiwan, République de Chine, 2006–09, page 204). Ce stade pouvant recevoir 40 000 spectateurs est encore un équipement de grandes dimensions. Même s'il y a probablement eu de grands architectes bâtisseurs de stades par le passé, l'un des premiers exemples fameux de ce genre d'intervention est le stade olympique de Munich, conçu par Gunter Behnisch et Frei Otto (Munich, Allemagne, 1972), avec son célèbre toit en toile d'araignée. Kaohsiung est la deuxième plus grande ville de Taiwan après Taipei. Toyo Ito, célèbre pour ses singulières armatures métalliques légères, est ici très à l'aise sur une structure aussi grande, lui offrant un dynamisme inhabituel avec son toit de 22 000 mètres carrés de panneaux solaires et son agencement, en partie ouvert, qui invite les spectateurs à entrer. Les 8 844 panneaux solaires revêtant le toit du stade permettent aux organisateurs de le vanter comme le plus grand équipement sportif « respectueux de l'environnement » du monde. Dans des conditions optimales, les panneaux solaires couvrent environ 75 % des besoins énergétiques du stade, et, quand

27 + 28
Jean Nouvel, Quai Branly Museum,
Paris, France, 2001–06

27   28

le stade n'est pas en activité, l'énergie générée alimente le réseau électrique local pour aider la ville. Bien que ce ne soit pas toujours le cas, le choix d'Ito a été probablement influencé par le fait qu'il avait déjà travaillé sur des équipements sportifs, comme le Odate Jukai Dome Park (Odate, Japon, 1995–97).

La piscine Valdesanchuela d'Alberto Nicolau (Valdemoro, Madrid, Espagne, 2006–07, page 304) fait partie des nombreux équipements publics espagnols faisant foi du dynamisme souligné par l'exposition du MoMA en 2006. Né en 1967 et formé dans les cabinets de Norman Foster et Rafael Moneo, Nicolau a pris en charge ce projet de 5000 mètres carrés avec un brio et un professionnalisme que l'on ne retrouve pas toujours chez les architectes quadragénaires. Imaginant la structure comme « une série de vagues », Nicolau a démontré que les contraintes budgétaires et fonctionnelles ne sont pas antithétiques d'une inventivité et d'une intelligence architecturale. Même s'il est certain que les pouvoirs publics (le client étant ici la mairie de Valdemoro) ont évolué dans leur approche de l'architecture contemporaine, il est également clair qu'on a déjà fait prendre conscience aux architectes plus jeunes qui s'installent dans la profession, qu'aspect pratique et économie sont les deux conditions de base de leur travail.

Alors que le Canada ou l'Espagne ont un ensemble établi de longue date de bâtiments publics contemporains d'architectes de talent, d'autres pays, jusque-là très en dehors du courant dominant, révèlent maintenant un travail intéressant et même significatif. Le terrain sportif de l'école primaire Majori (Jurmala, Lettonie, 2007–08, page 372) réalisé par Arnis Dimins (né en 1968) et Brigita Barbale (née en 1979) du cabinet Substance, sortis tous deux de l'Université technique de Riga, donne à Jurmala, station balnéaire de la mer Baltique, un éclatant signe de foi en l'architecture contemporaine. Ces équipements, utilisables en terrains ou pistes pour le basket, le volley, le handball, et, en hiver, le hockey sur glace et le patinage, sont recouverts d'un toit en polycarbonate supporté par une structure extérieure. Inspiré de l'ambre ou de la résine de pin cristallisée parfois rejetés sur les côtes de Jurmala, ce design prouve que des architectes ayant fait leurs études dans un pays comme la Lettonie peuvent être aujourd'hui à la pointe de la modernité, tout en tenant compte du budget et des fonctionnalités réclamés par la municipalité. Les jeunes architectes considèrent le fait de construire comme une affaire très sérieuse, et ils ne se contentent plus de rêver du jour où leurs aînés leur laisseront leur chance. Pour l'architecture publique, c'est le moment.

DE LA CROIX DU SUD À L'ESPACE

Après les premiers jours glorieux du rail, les équipements de transports publics ont été cachés à la vue, quelquefois littéralement enterrés, comme par exemple la gare Penn Station, à New York. Les gares et les aéroports sont en grande partie centrés sur les exigences techniques évidentes d'un train à grande vitesse ou d'un Airbus. Deux architectes français, issus de l'École polytechnique et de celle des Ponts et Chaussées, ont beaucoup fait pour modifier l'attitude générale concernant l'utilité de l'architecture contemporaine de haute qualité sous de telles modalités. Paul Andreu était l'architecte en chef des Aéroports de Paris et responsable du développement de tout le complexe de l'aéroport de Roissy. On doit à Jean-Marie Duthilleul, architecte en chef de la SNCF, non seulement la renaissance de la gare du Nord, terminal

29
Jean-Marie Duthilleul/SNCF, Avignon Station, Avignon, France, 2001

29

parisien des trains Eurostar, mais aussi toute une nouvelle génération de gares TGV – dont celles, récentes, d'Aix et d'Avignon. Dans les deux cas, les architectes ont convaincu leur hiérarchie qu'une bonne architecture était un investissement rentable en terme de réaction du public vis-à-vis des équipements de transports. Alors que le transport par rail se meurt dans de nombreux pays, il a pris un nouvel essor en France et, par la suite, dans d'autres pays. Nicholas Grimshaw, par exemple, a été l'architecte du terminal international de la gare de Waterloo (Londres, 1988–93), à l'autre extrémité de la ligne Eurostar. Plus récemment, Grimshaw a rénové deux infrastructures ferroviaires importantes avec le même talent dont il avait fait preuve pour la gare de Waterloo. L'une, la gare Southern Cross (Melbourne, Australie, 2002–06, page 194), a été présentée comme un effort pour transformer des équipements existants en « échangeur de niveau mondial et nouveau symbole pour Melbourne ». La « couverture ondoyante » qui forme le toit des nouvelles gares, comme celle de Waterloo, fait ressortir les bâtiments sur le fond urbain, offrant de nouvelles promesses à un moyen de transport ancien. L'autre, la gare Bijlmer ArenA d'Amsterdam (Amsterdam, Pays-Bas, 2002–07, page 10), bien que d'une surface plus petite, concerne 60 000 voyageurs par jour – un nombre trop important pour envisager la fermeture de la gare durant les travaux de construction. Se servant de vides pour permettre aux voyageurs de s'orienter dans la gare, Grimshaw s'est attaqué à l'un des défauts les plus évidents des anciennes gares, qui avaient dû être conçues par des ingénieurs n'étant jamais sortis de leur bureau. Dans la nouvelle génération de gares, dont celles rénovées et construites par Jean-Marie Duthilleul en France, la visibilité et la lumière, deux éléments qui avaient disparu des terminaux ferroviaires, deviennent au contraire les éléments moteurs de la conception. Cela prouve que la question de la « bonne » architecture ne concerne pas uniquement son apparence, mais aussi le sentiment qu'elle provoque chez le public. Des gares comme Southern Cross ou Bijlmer sont vues et utilisées par un public beaucoup plus nombreux que d'autres genres de bâtiments et font ainsi beaucoup pour réconcilier architecture contemporaine et service public.

Un autre secteur négligé de l'architecture des transports est celui des autoroutes modernes, souvent parsemées d'aires de repos honteuses ou de péages disgracieux. Le péage d'autoroute Brisa toll plaza (Benavente, Portugal, 2006–07, page 62) de Aires Mateus tient soigneusement compte du paysage pour y inclure ces structures. Les architectes considèrent que les bâtiments deviennent vraiment partie du paysage une fois construits, et que leur responsabilité n'est pas de créer de la laideur là où une attention portée au design et aux détails est capable d'actualiser l'opinion de l'automobiliste sur l'architecture contemporaine. Il est vrai que l'architecture des bords de route, en particulier dans des endroits comme la Californie, a pris sa propre existence souvent décalée ; les bâtiments d'autoroute ont tendance à surgir comme des ajouts défigurant le paysage. Points de passage et d'allées et venues, les cabines de péage sont, ici aussi, très visibles et bien placées pour briser certains préjugés qui affectent ces architectures « banales ».

Bien que sa réalisation soit encore à venir, de nombreux promoteurs et architectes travaillent déjà sur ce qui sera probablement la prochaine génération du voyage – dans l'espace. Richard Branson de Virgin Fame est l'un des premiers à se lancer tête baissée dans cette aventure, imaginant des bases de lancement pour sa future marque Virgin Galactic. Une de ces initiatives, le Space Xperience Center (Hato Airport, Curaçao, Antilles néerlandaises, 2011–12, page 324) en cours de conception par le cabinet de Rotterdam ONL, fait la démonstration de certains des facteurs à prendre en compte pour un type de transport où la position sur le globe est plus importante que le positionnement d'un aéroport ou d'une gare par rapport au réseau urbain qui les alimente. À l'initiative de Ben Droste et Harry van Hulten, ONL a utilisé sa modélisation paramétrable caractéristique pour imaginer une structure « iconique » sur le terrain de l'aéroport de Curaçao. On s'imagine difficilement les premiers vrais touristes de l'espace en train de décoller d'un quelconque aéroport ordinaire, et non d'un spatioport futuriste. La fonction symbolique de l'architecture contemporaine, souvent intimement liée au temps présent comme au futur, est une composante intrinsèque du développement de ce genre d'initiatives de transport.

LA GRANDE BLEUE AU DANEMARK

Les théâtres et les salles de concert représentent une catégorie importante des bâtiments publics, mais, ici aussi, une fade modernité semble avoir balayé le globe d'un bout à l'autre après la Seconde Guerre mondiale. La mentalité institutionnelle participant du choix des architectes a fait beaucoup pour que des bâtiments comme celui de l'Opéra de Sydney de Jørn Utzon restent l'exception, et peu d'architectes ont autant souffert qu'Utzon pour mener son chef-d'œuvre à terme. Dans la citation du prix Pritzker 2003 pour Utzon, on pouvait lire ceci : « L'Opéra de Sidney est sans nul doute son chef-d'œuvre. C'est l'un des grands bâtiments emblématiques du XXe siècle, une image d'une grande beauté qui est devenue connue du monde entier – un symbole non seulement de la ville, mais aussi de tout le pays et continent. » Bien peu de bâtiments et encore moins d'architectes connaissent un tel succès, mais ces dernières années ont vu un retour résolu des architectes de renom et des projets audacieux. Deux projets récents à Copenhague, dans des styles un peu divergents, montrent comment l'architecture peut faire évoluer une ville aussi dense en bâtiments historiques. Le nouveau Théâtre royal (Copenhague, Danemark, 2004–07, page 240) de Lundgaard & Tranberg conjugue ponts de bois, murs de briques sombres et un foyer vitré spectaculaire. L'architecture des théâtres a toujours dû tenir plus ou moins compte d'éléments concrets comme la tour de scène. Les architectes danois qui ont gagné le concours international pour ce bâtiment ont recouvert la tour de scène de cuivre, sans chercher à dissimuler la relation entre la fonction et la forme. Jean Nouvel, d'un autre côté, avec sa grande salle de concert bleue pour la radio danoise (Copenhague, Danemark, 2003–09, page 310), a cherché délibérément un air de mystère – un mystère qui n'est « jamais loin de la séduction, et donc de l'attractivité », selon l'architecte. Plutôt que la clarté, le Français a recherché, surtout à l'intérieur, une complexité labyrinthique, et, à l'extérieur, un revêtement translucide capable de se transformer en une sorte de grand panneau pour la projection d'images à grande échelle. L'interaction entre client et architecte a probablement joué un rôle dans les deux cas, mais Copenhague a cherché des architectes qui, tout en restant tous deux dans l'esprit du temps, interprètent de façon différente la relation entre la fonction et la forme. Pour Nouvel, les bâtiments doivent toujours se faire remarquer, sans nécessairement afficher leur fonction, ni même rendre cette fonction visible. Mais si Lundgaard & Tranberg ont choisi une approche plus traditionnelle, leur design n'est en rien démodé. Cette comparaison et ce contraste racontent quelque chose de l'état de l'architecture publique en 2009 : rien n'est pris pour acquis, mais un effet puissant est presque universellement désiré.

30
AllesWirdGut, Redesign of festival site in a Roman quarry, St. Margarethen im Burgenland, Austria, 2006–08

30

RUBANS ET PIERRE

Deux autres théâtres, situés en deux endroits presque opposés de la terre, illustrent des approches architecturales, dans des situations très différentes, qui pourraient être assimilées respectivement à la pesanteur et à la légèreté. La pesanteur est ce qui ressort du projet Alles-WirdGut pour redessiner le site d'un festival dans une carrière romaine à St. Margarethen im Burgenland (Autriche, 2006–08, page 72). Plutôt que d'opposer la matière de la pierre à des matériaux plus légers, les architectes ont opté pour « l'élargissement de l'ambiance du magnifique décor de pierres à toutes les parties de l'arène théâtrale, pour en faire une expérience enveloppante plus manifeste et visuelle ». Ils ont utilisé la pierre de la carrière elle-même, ainsi qu'un placage en acier oxydé, pour mettre le lieu au goût du jour, mettant des notes de modernité là où la pierre ancienne rencontre un public de 6 000 personnes. Makoto Sei Watanabe a choisi une approche radicalement différente quand il s'est agi d'agrandir un théâtre de Taichung. Son RIBBONs Open-Air Theater (Taichung, Taiwan, République de Chine, 2008–09, page 400) est plus un auvent avec des installations d'arrière-scène qu'un théâtre entier, et Watanabe a cherché à entrelacer des formes flottantes à l'aspect de vagues autour de la scène, de sorte que l'architecture « joue un rôle en élargissant les fonctions du théâtre ». Attribuer le mot « pesanteur » au travail de AllesWirdGut en Autriche n'est en aucun cas péjoratif, il s'agit simplement d'un état de fait. Le lieu et les choix faits par les architectes sont fermement ancrés dans la pierre, alors que l'architecte japonais a choisi la légèreté et le mouvement comme source d'inspiration. Encore une fois, l'architecture contemporaine admet volontiers les deux solutions : fondamentalement, les préférences des clients et, bien sûr, les architectes eux-mêmes dictent la direction qui pourra être prise en de telles circonstances. Le choix de Watanabe ne se serait probablement pas porté sur la pierre de carrière et un revêtement d'acier oxydé s'il avait obtenu la commande autrichienne.

EN BAISSE À PÉKIN, EN HAUSSE À NEW YORK

L'architecture publique se retrouve souvent exposée aux divergences d'opinion des utilisateurs, ou des architectes locaux, comme ce fut le cas pour Paul Andreu et son Opéra de Pékin (Pékin, Chine, 1999–2007, page 86). Andreu, l'architecte de l'aéroport de Roissy et de cinquante autres aéroports à travers le monde, a quitté les Aéroports de Paris et travaille maintenant à son compte, notamment en Chine. La grande forme en coque qu'il a choisie, presqu'en vue de la Cité interdite, a rencontré une résistance extrêmement sévère, aussi bien en Chine qu'en France, curieusement, où *Le Monde* a publié un article au vitriol contre l'esthétique de son projet. Comme le dit Andreu : « Je n'ai pas l'habitude que mes projets soient examinés de près par les médias. Je dois admettre que, pour le projet de l'Opéra de Pékin, j'ai entendu pas mal de critiques, dont certaines presque injurieuses. Quelquefois, les critiques me font rire, par exemple le type qui a écrit : " Il n'a pas de diplôme d'architecte, c'est juste un ingénieur. " Eh bien, je suis désolé que Wright, Le Corbusier et Ando n'aient pas eu leur diplôme, alors que moi j'ai eu le mien ; donc c'est moi qui doit être le charlot. Ils ont dit aussi que je n'avais aucune culture. Je n'ai jamais prétendu être un spécialiste de la culture chinoise [...] quand la presse s'attaque à la personne autant ou plus qu'au projet, ça devient très fatigant. Je fais de mon mieux pour éviter d'être mêlé à ce genre de débat car je dois réserver mon temps pour le projet qu'on m'a demandé de mener à bien. Mais quelquefois, je fais un peu de fumée... et même à l'occasion de la vapeur. »[3] Bien qu'Andreu voie dans la courbure descendante de son toit l'antithèse des courbes ascendantes des toits de la Cité interdite, c'est plus un bâtiment contemporain qu'un bâtiment influencé par la longue

31
Jean Nouvel, Les Bains des Docks,
Le Havre, France, 2006–08

31

histoire de la Chine. Parmi les millions de voyageurs aériens qui sont passés par les aéroports construits par Andreu, peu d'entre eux savent qu'il en est l'architecte principal. Si cela n'enlève rien à leur qualité, il est possible qu'on se souvienne plus d'Andreu pour son Opéra de Pékin que pour l'aéroport de Roissy qui était une réalisation des Aéroports de Paris.

En un sens, les architectes Diller Scofidio + Renfro travaillaient dans un environnement aussi complexe et dangereux du point de vue architectural quand ils ont commencé la rénovation extensive du Lincoln Center for the Performing Arts de New York. En ce qui concerne la salle Alice Tully Hall, Lincoln Center (New York, 2006–09, page 168, avec FXFowle Architects), il s'agissait plutôt d'exhumer une pièce d'architecture depuis longtemps enfouie sous l'École de musique Juilliard. Ils ont rendu le Alice Tully Hall visible, et ont travaillé également à protéger soigneusement la salle de concert des bruits de la ligne de métro de la 7ᵉ Avenue. Ils ont également participé à la reconstruction de la centrale mécanique du Lincoln Center qui abrite les systèmes de chauffage et de refroidissement pour les onze lieux du complexe. En ayant accepté de travailler dans les limites d'une première structure conçue par Pietro Belluschi, Diller Scofidio + Renfro ont montré que, tout en étant capables de créer un bâtiment « signature », comme leur récent Institut d'art contemporain à Boston (Institute of Contemporary Art, 2006), ils peuvent contenir leur ego au service d'un but plus grand. On peut se demander si le bâtiment d'Andreu à Pékin suit cette approche ou, au contraire, pose comme postulat le droit de l'architecte à concevoir un édifice « unique » qui vaille pour lui-même, bien plus fermé au monde extérieur que ne le fut jamais l'Opéra de Sidney. Ceci est affaire de goût, et non d'absolu. Voilà pourquoi les pouvoirs publics hésitent encore parfois à faire appel à des architectes reconnus.

CULTURE THERMALE

Bien qu'il ne s'agisse pas de bâtiments publics au sens d'une gare ou même d'un théâtre, les établissements de bains ou thermaux ont également bénéficié de l'intervention d'architectes célèbres ces dernières années, comme le montrent certains exemples de cet ouvrage. L'agrandissement de l'établissement thermal Römerbad (Bad Kleinkirchheim, Kärnten, Autriche, 2006–07, page 124) par Behnisch Architekten était un projet de 10 000 mètres carrés et de 15 millions d'euros pour rénover des équipements datant de 1979. Ils ont adopté une approche thématique non sans lien avec l'histoire immédiate de ces bains thermaux particuliers. Ainsi, le « Romanum », situé au niveau inférieur, « évoque la culture des bains de la Rome Antique », alors que le « Noricum » « évoque l'aspect régional des thermes – l'eau, les forêts et les à-pics… » Cela ne signifie pas que des architectes aussi qualifiés que Behnisch ont cédé au syndrome « Disney ». Ils affirment plutôt : « Comme le suggère leur nom, l'atmosphère et l'ambiance de ces "Bains romains" ne sont pas simplement créés par le décor, mais par une abstraction consciente fondée sur un nombre restreint de formes sculpturales et de couleurs. »

Les thermes de Panticosa (Huesca, Espagne, 2002–08, page 296), de Moneo Brock Studio, sont situés dans les Pyrénées. L'esthétique moderne proposée par les architectes cherche à traiter à la fois l'environnement naturel et le cadre urbain des bains existants. L'association du verre et de la pierre choisie par Moneo Brock réussit admirablement à atteindre ce but. Une certaine froideur des matériaux extérieurs

32

32
Rafael Beneytez, Huesca Exhibition
and Conference Center, Huesca,
Spain, 2005–08

contraste avec l'atmosphère plus chaude des bains eux-mêmes, où l'eau et le mouvement font écho aux façades ondoyantes. Les Bains des Docks (Le Havre, France, 2006–08, page 318), de Jean Nouvel, s'insèrent dans un schéma de rénovation urbaine appelé Port 2000. L'extérieur essentiellement noir de l'édifice contraste vivement avec des espaces intérieurs blancs ou colorés. La composition architectonique des solides géométriques employés ici par Nouvel diffère de son style habituel. Les différences entre ces deux projets sont probablement imputables aux lieux autant qu'aux sensibilités architecturales et à l'inventivité de Moneo Brock et Jean Nouvel. Les deux servent au fond les mêmes objectifs, bien que dans des circonstances différentes. On sent l'écho du passé dans des projets tels que celui des Bains Behnisch en Autriche, et il est intéressant de voir comment des architectes de talent abordent ce qui reste finalement la même série de questions : rassembler des baigneurs autour de la même expérience, où la vue du cadre, mais aussi des autres baigneurs, fait partie de l'équation.

CONVENTIONS ESPAGNOLES

Certaines villes espagnoles ont été encouragées par les circonstances à développer des équipements pour les congrès et les rencontres professionnelles. Déjà connus pour d'autres raisons, trois architectes espagnols, Rafael Beneytez, Nieto Sobejano et Francisco Mangado, ont achevé, ces derniers mois, des projets importants dans ce domaine. Le premier, Rafael Beneytez, est « diplômé » du cabinet de Rafael Moneo. Son Palais de congrès et des expositions (Palacio de Congresos y Exposiciones de Huesca, Espagne, 2005–08, ci-dessus) est un édifice de 12 000 mètres carrés à l'apparence orthogonale, voire strictement géométrique, mais, grâce à une utilisation inventive et soignée des matériaux, des surfaces et de l'éclairage, les volumes s'animent et diffèrent de jour et de nuit. L'architecte a même déclaré avoir conçu « deux édifices en un ; un pour le jour et l'autre pour la nuit ». Ce type d'architecture, à la base pratique et modulaire, est rendu a fortiori plus intéressant et « actuel » par l'utilisation que fait l'architecte de toute la gamme de possibilités à sa disposition à l'intérieur du registre rectilinéaire défini.

Les formes en zigzag de l'auditorium et du Palais des congrès d'Aragón (Palacio de Congresos de Aragón) de Nieto Sobejano (Expo 2008, Zaragoza, Espagne, 2006–08, ci-dessus) semblent étirer en trois dimensions le résultat d'une épure d'élévation. L'utilisation adroite d'un treillis de verre et de métal donne à la structure une diversité de surfaces se traduisant également à l'intérieur par un traitement de la lumière et un déploiement des volumes inattendu, le tout sans gaspillage et en respectant les exigences programmatiques. Les architectes évoquent un « paysage de lumière solide émergeant du sol ». Bien qu'il soit un peu excessif d'appliquer cette notion à la propagation et la diffusion de leurs formes à travers la structure (c'est-à-dire la lumière n'est pas géométrique), l'émotion et les formes inattendues qu'ils produisent sont indéniables.

Francisco « Patxi » Mangado est l'auteur de l'auditorium et du Centre municipal des congrès et des expositions d'Ávila (Ávila, Castilla-León, Espagne, 2004–09, page 258), qui appartient à la même gamme de projets en termes de dimension et de budget. Quand l'architecte parle de la « compacité topographique, minérale » d'Ávila, il explique en grande partie l'apparence géologique de son édifice qui sort de terre

33
Nieto Sobejano, Auditorium and Con-
vention Center of Aragon, Expo 2008,
Zaragoza, Spain, 2006–08

33

en plans de pierre ayant un lien évident avec la terre. Le site n'est en rien verdoyant et la présence minérale du bâtiment confirme et renforce sa propre origine. Les murs proches de la ville sont également évoqués, confirmant l'« enracinement » de l'édifice dans son contexte, toujours dans le cadre des exigences habituelles d'efficacité et de souplesse d'emploi. Mangado, tout comme ses confrères, prouve que les contraintes imposées par des projets publics n'excluent pas une architecture innovante et vraiment surprenante. Mangado donne à cette ville une identité, tout en restant dans les limites orthogonales qui facilitent non seulement l'utilisation du bâtiment mais aussi sa construction et son entretien. Rien à voir avec le Guggenheim de Bilbao, avec ses coins et ses surfaces inutilisables. Beneytez, Nieto Sobejano et Mangado ne plaisantent pas et savent créer de l'architecture. On ne peut qu'espérer que l'effondrement relatif du marché immobilier en Espagne et, avec lui, d'une bonne partie de l'économie, n'empêchera pas ces architectes de faire montre de leurs talents d'autres façons.

ORGUEIL LATIN

Les bibliothèques, comme la Bibliothèque publique de New York (New York Public Library) sur la 5e Avenue entre la 41e et la 42e Rue (Carrère et Hastings, 1911), reflétaient aussi jusqu'à très récemment la pesanteur et la solennité censées convenir à l'architecture publique. Les bibliothèques, confrontées au défi de l'Internet, mais aussi à la prise de conscience qu'une architecture contemporaine intéressante peut aider à garder le contact avec le présent, ont évolué de façon spectaculaire, comme le montrent quelques exemples choisis ici. Les archi-tectes américains Line and Space, installés en Arizona, ont achevé récemment la bibliothèque Cesar Chavez Branch Library (Phoenix, Arizona, États-Unis, 2002–07, page 228). Conçu pour accueillir jusqu'à 40 000 visiteurs par mois, l'édifice mesure un relativement modeste 2323 mètres carrés. Ses lignes et son profil spectaculaires parlent assurément d'un tout autre type de bibliothèque que celle érigée par Carrère et Hastings sur la 5e Avenue. C'est une bibliothèque pour le présent qui prend en compte les contraintes imposées par une conscience écolo-gique.

Le cas de la Bibliothèque publique du parc Santo Domingo (Parque Biblioteca Pública Santo Domingo, Medellín, Colombie, 2006–07, page 264) de Giancarlo Mazzanti est très différent. Né en 1963 à Barranquilla, Colombie, Mazzanti vit à Bogota. Cet édifice, « plissé et décou-pé comme les montagnes environnantes », est situé dans une zone dévastée par la violence liée à la drogue des années 80. La triple structu-re assise sur une base commune comprend une bibliothèque, des salles de cours, un auditorium et des bureaux. Légitimement voulue comme un symbole de cette ville plus connue comme capitale de la drogue que comme celle des études, la bibliothèque tente aussi d'« extraire l'indi-vidu de la pauvreté qui l'entoure ». De même, la bibliothèque de l'université de Deusto à Bilbao, intéressante en tant que réalisation architec-turale, représente aussi un effort pour se démarquer dans un environnement dominé par le Guggenheim Bilbao de Frank Gehry. Les formes sinueuses de métal que Ghery a maîtrisées, en l'occurrence, pour l'amélioration évidente de Bilbao, ne sont certainement pas le fort de Rafael Moneo. Il se contente, lui, de montrer que des formes plus traditionnelles, bien que sises dans un volume lumineux et sophistiqué, représen-tent une réponse adaptée, voire même une critique efficace, à l'exubérance de l'Américain.

34

34
Mario Botta, Évry Cathedral, Évry,
France, 1988–95

GRANDS ARCHITECTES, PETITES CHAPELLES

La religion, après avoir été une des sources principales d'innovation en matière d'architecture dans un passé relativement lointain, est redevenue un domaine où les architectes peuvent s'exprimer de façon créative. Avec des architectes comme Mario Botta (cathédrale d'Évry, Évry, France, 1988–95 ; la chapelle de Tamaro, Monte Tamaro, Suisse, 1992–96 ; une autre chapelle à Mogno, Suisse, 1986–98), Richard Meier (l'église du Jubilée, Rome, Italie, 2003) ou encore Tadao Ando (l'église de la Lumière, Ibaraki, Osaka, Japon, 1988–89) qui ont créé une architecture religieuse mémorable, il n'est guère surprenant que d'autres architectes continuent dans cette même veine. L'architecte new-yorkais Stan Allen a imaginé la petite chapelle CCV (Tagaytay, Cavite, Philippines, 2007–08, page 66) à l'entrée du campus de la fondation Chosen Children's Village, une organisation à but non lucratif « consacrée à la création d'un lieu d'accueil pour des enfants handicapés physiques ou mentaux ». D'une superficie de 240 mètres carrés, la structure de béton s'élève néanmoins à sept mètres de hauteur, ses formes blanches articulées créant un lieu de culte qui dément la grande modestie du budget. Construite pour résister au climat tropical et aux risques de séisme, cette structure s'appuie sur une ventilation naturelle, un meilleur moyen de faire des économies d'énergie que les systèmes beaucoup plus élaborés, gérés par ordinateur, employés dans des bâtiments plus sophistiqués.

Le groupe suisse Localarchitecture a imaginé une autre chapelle d'un type novateur. Leur chapelle temporaire de Saint-Loup (Pompaples, Suisse, 2008, page 234) est une structure de 130 mètres carrés bâtie pour servir de lieu de culte pendant les travaux de la maison des diaconesses de Saint-Loup, dans le canton de Vaud. Les architectes ont utilisé le système CAD-CNC, c'est-à-dire le dessin assisté par ordinateur et la découpe à commande numérique du bois, du plastique et du matériau textile. La nature temporaire de la structure lui a permis d'être érigée sans fondations, mais il est intéressant de noter que cette communauté protestante était ouverte à l'idée de formes contemporaines pour son lieu de culte et a fait appel à des architectes de moins de quarante ans.

L'église de Santa Mónica (Rivas Vaciamadrid, Madrid, Espagne, 2004–09, page 394) des architectes Vicens + Ramos a été construite pour l'évêque d'Alcalá. Alors que les projets d'églises ou de locaux paroissiaux plus traditionnels traduisent souvent la séparation des fonctions dans l'architecture, Vicens + Ramos ont opté pour un *continuum* reliant le bâtiment logeant les prêtres, le centre paroissial et l'église. Ils se sont également mis d'accord avec le client pour faire appel à des artistes contemporains, et pour utiliser eux-mêmes l'acier Corten comme élément du revêtement extérieur le plus visible. L'acier Corten étant le matériau le plus utilisé par des sculpteurs comme Richard Serra, le projet entier évoque inévitablement une œuvre d'art. Toutefois, le design intérieur ne suggère en aucune façon une galerie d'art, et l'architecture n'apparaît pas comme une expression de l'ego des architectes ; c'est plutôt un lieu de contemplation et de culte, où l'art et l'architecture, non contents d'y être admis, fournissent un élément inspirant qui en fait une formulation très contemporaine. L'utilisation harmonieuse de l'art dans un contexte religieux et architectural est profondément enracinée dans les traditions de l'église, mais le XXe siècle a souvent moins suivi cette inspiration que dans des temps plus reculés. Avec une réponse esthétique très contemporaine aux besoins de l'église et de la paroisse, l'église de Santa Mónica semble raviver cette tradition.

35
Tadao Ando, Church of the Light,
Ibaraki, Osaka, Japan, 1988–89

DES PONTS DU PASSÉ AU PRÉSENT

Les musées sont l'une des expressions les plus évidentes des récentes avancées de l'architecture publique. Un volume pendant à cet ouvrage, *L'architecture d'aujourd'hui! Musées,* explore ce champ plus en profondeur qu'il n'est possible ici, ou l'on retrouvera néanmoins plusieurs exemples. Par exemple, l'architecte japonais lauréat du prix Pritzker, Tadao Ando, a inauguré la Punta della Dogana (page 78) à Venise, en Italie, pour la fondation François Pinault, le 4 juin 2009. Tous les touristes qui ont visité Venise connaissent l'image familière de la basilique Santa-Maria della Salute. Située près du Dorsoduro, dessinée par l'architecte Baldassare Longhena (1598–1682), et dédiée à la Vierge Marie, protectrice de la République, l'église fut commandée par le Sénat de Venise en 1630, après les ravages causés par la peste, et achevée en 1681. La pointe extrême du Dorsoduro, le long des entrepôts à sel, avait été occupée par un poste de douane pour les marchandises maritimes depuis 1525. Pendant les travaux de la nouvelle basilique, il fut décidé pour des raisons esthétiques de reconstruire la Dogana da Mar (douane de mer) voisine. C'est Giuseppe Benoni (1618–84) qui construisit, entre 1676 et 1682, une structure basse et rustique terminée par une tour, à la pointe de terre en face de la place Saint-Marc. C'est ici, travaillant de concert avec Tadao Ando, que François Pinault a décidé de créer un deuxième site vénitien pour sa fondation consacrée à l'art contemporain. Comme on aurait pu s'y attendre, Tadao Ando a retenu la forme géométrique élémentaire du bâtiment existant. Il explique : « Le bâtiment de la Punta della Dogana se caractérise par une structure simple et rationnelle. Le volume crée un triangle, une référence directe à la forme de la pointe de l'île du Dorsoduro, alors que les intérieurs sont divisés en longs rectangles, avec une série de murs parallèles. » Tout en portant une très grande attention à la rénovation du bâtiment existant, Tadao Ando s'est autorisé un geste géométrique puissant au beau milieu du plan triangulaire de l'édifice : un cube de béton qui s'élève sur toute la hauteur de la structure et devient l'axe de toutes les allées qui traversent l'espace rénové.

On notera au passage une autre structure à Venise d'un grand architecte contemporain présente dans cet ouvrage. Il s'agit du Quarto Ponte sul Canal Grande (Venise, Italie, 1999–2006, page 136) de Santiago Calatrava, le quatrième pont à enjamber le Grand Canal. Long de 94 mètres, il est situé à proximité de la principale gare de la ville. L'élégance et la modernité de ce pont sont indéniables, et pourtant sa conception et sa construction ont suscité une certaine controverse. Ceci est d'autant plus surprenant que des ponts comme celui de l'Accademia sont restés en place depuis longtemps malgré leur manque évident d'importance esthétique ou architecturale. Le pont de Calatrava, au contraire, est un geste ni trop audacieux ni trop timide : il est un signe idéal prouvant que Venise, bien que fortement immobilisée dans d'autres secteurs dans un passé qui se dégrade, continue à vivre. Avec des architectes comme Ando et Calatrava complétant ses formes plus anciennes de façon aussi intelligente, Venise pourrait continuer à vivre comme une vraie ville et non juste comme un arrêt carte postale pour touristes en croisière. En tout cas, en dehors du Quarto Ponte, il existe peu d'ouvrages d'architecture publique dignes de l'épithète honorable.

La rénovation, par Kuehn Malvezzi, d'une ancienne usine du début du XXe siècle pour la collection Julia Stoschek (Düsseldorf, Allemagne, 2005–07, page 222) a clairement posé des problèmes différents de la réfection de la Punta della Dogana d'Ando. Travaillant sur un monument classé, les architectes n'ont conservé que la façade originale et ont construit un nouveau périmètre à l'intérieur des murs de l'an-

36

cienne usine. Les pouvoirs publics ont donné aux architectes l'autorisation de remplacer la vieille enseigne de l'usine par un cube de verre. Comme la structure renferme également l'appartement de la donatrice, Julia Stoschek, il s'agit un peu d'une conception hybride, mais les architectes ont utilisé la même palette de couleurs et de matériaux dans les parties publiques et privées. Ce projet s'inscrit dans la tendance à la réutilisation des vieux bâtiments dans un but culturel. Qu'ils soient protégés, comme c'était le cas à Düsseldorf, ou que leurs volumes ou leurs matériaux présentent un intérêt esthétique ou architectural, les bâtiments plus anciens offrent aux architectes des éléments en rupture avec une approche purement moderne. Dans ce cas, un bâtiment d'usine qui n'aurait pas vraiment pu être considéré comme de l'architecture « publique » s'ouvre à ceux qui ont la curiosité de franchir ses portes.

DIMANCHE AU PARC AVEC FRANK

La construction de pavillons est devenue un autre point de rencontre populaire entre les architectes de haute volée et le grand public. Souvent temporaires, comme les pavillons d'été de la Serpentine Gallery à Londres, ces édifices en viennent à être utilisés dans d'autres circonstances, comme ce fut le cas du pavillon Serpentine de Frank O. Gehry (Kensington Gardens, Londres, 2008, page 180). D'une superficie de 418 mètres carrés, cette structure dotée d'un exosquelette de bois, en grande partie recouverte de multiples surfaces de toiture vitrée, évoquant la « juxtaposition aléatoire d'éléments », était destinée à accueillir des événements ou des concerts pour un nombre de spectateurs pouvant aller jusqu'à 275. Dans ce contexte, Gehry fut capable de revenir sur la vraie source de son innovation architecturale, les maisons qu'il avait construites dans les premiers temps de sa carrière à Santa Monica ou à Venice, en Californie, où des matériaux « récupérés » comme du grillage ou de l'asphalte utilisés de manière inattendue avaient contribué à une nouvelle approche de l'architecture en général, plus proche de la liberté de l'art contemporain. Le pavillon Serpentine de Gehry a été acheté par le propriétaire irlandais des vignobles de Château La Coste, près d'Aix-en-Provence, dans le Sud de la France. Ce domaine ouvrira ses portes au public en 2010, avec des œuvres d'autres artistes et architectes célèbres entourant les vraies installations viticoles.

Le Millennium Park de Chicago est un vrai point de rencontre entre art contemporain, architecture et grand public. Des artistes comme Jaume Plensa ou Anish Kapoor ont réalisé des œuvres pour ce parc, tout comme l'incontournable Frank Gehry. Son pavillon Jay Pritzker (Millennium Park, Chicago, Illinois, États-Unis, 1999–2004) est une structure en volutes de 36 mètres de haut faite de rubans en acier inoxydable accompagnés d'un treillage de tubes d'acier. Avec 4000 sièges fixes et de la place pour 7000 personnes de plus, ce lieu de concert en plein air est devenu très vite un nouveau symbole de Chicago. Gehry définit ainsi son but : « Comment fait-on pour que tout le monde – et pas seulement le public assis sur les sièges – ait envie de venir ici écouter de la musique ? La réponse est : on les y amène. On fait un proscenium plus grand ; on construit un treillage avec une sono bien répartie. On fait en sorte que le public ait le sentiment de partager l'aventure. » Les travaux sur le parc n'ont pas cessé avec son inauguration, et de nouveaux pavillons ont été installés récemment par Zaha Hadid et les architectes hollandais UNStudio. Le projet d'UNStudio, le pavillon Burnham (Chicago, Illinois, États-Unis, 2009, page 390), une structure d'une superficie de 300 mètres carrés en bois et acier qui évoque un « espace flottant et multidirectionnel », est conçu comme un hommage au tra-

37
Vicens + Ramos, Santa Monica Parish
Church, Rivas Vaciamadrid, Madrid,
Spain, 2004–09

37

cé orthogonal de Chicago de 1909 de Daniel Burnham. Dans ce cas précis, une nouvelle architecture apporte une critique, tout en évoquant les édifices du passé dans cette ville toujours dynamique.

LE CONTEMPORAIN SE GÉNÉRALISE

Le Burnham Pavilion de UNStudio est, d'une certaine façon, symbolique de l'évolution de l'architecture publique contemporaine. Ici, de nouvelles formes, conçues et réalisées avec des méthodes assistées par ordinateur, surgissent dans un lieu très visible, où le grand public est libre d'aimer (ou de détester) une œuvre à la pointe du design contemporain. Bien que la crise économique risque de réduire certains projets de bâtiments publics qui auraient été architecturalement intéressants, les temps anciens de la prospérité ont fait beaucoup pour ouvrir les esprits et permettre à la créativité contemporaine de vraiment pénétrer l'architecture traditionnelle. Ce volume est une célébration de ce qu'on pourrait appeler un tournant historique dans la perception, qui a permis à des architectes inventifs, de l'Espagne à Taïwan, de créer de nouvelles formes pour le grand public, ou du moins pour un usage qui va bien au-delà de l'élite qui aurait pu apprécier l'avant-garde par le passé. Sans pouvoir dire qu'un style particulier ait émergé de ces différentes réalisations, on retrouve l'empreinte de l'ordinateur dans la plupart des cas, du moins pour ceux qui sont capables de voir son impact. En réalité, la souplesse introduite par le dessin et la fabrication assistés par ordinateur a aujourd'hui atteint l'architecture conventionnelle, permettant une variété de formes qui n'aurait pu se faire auparavant sans dépassements de coûts exorbitants. La sélection de cet ouvrage montre à l'évidence que les architectes avaient déjà retenu les leçons d'efficacité économique et fonctionnelle que les clients exigeaient d'eux avant même que la récession n'assombrisse l'horizon. Les édifices publics présentés ici sont pour la plupart non seulement d'une esthétique très novatrice, mais aussi très fonctionnels, et, qui plus est, souvent conçus dans un respect de l'environnement qui n'était sûrement pas une préoccupation dans des temps (modernes) plus anciens. Ces signes – l'aptitude d'architectes de qualité à s'engager dans de gros projets en étant conscients des coûts, de la fonctionnalité et de la responsabilité environnementale – augurent bien de l'avenir, même avec moins de projets à construire et moins d'argent à dépenser. Ces dernières années, grâce à ces bâtiments et à d'autres, dans le monde entier, une architecture contemporaine de haute qualité – qui ne se limite plus à un nombre insignifiant de lieux habituellement isolés – s'est fait accepter du grand public. Une architecture contemporaine ne se réduisant pas à de vilaines boîtes s'est généralisée.

Philip Jodidio, Grimentz, 6 juillet 2009

1   Voir http://www.cnrtl.fr/lexicographie/public (visité le 4 juillet 2009).
2   « On-Site : New Architecture in Spain » 12 février 2006–1er mai 2006.
Voir http://www.moma.org/visit/calendar/exhibitions/86 (visité le 5 juillet 2009).
3   Extraits d'une interview de Paul Andreu parue dans la revue *Upstreet*, février 2001.

3XN

3XN A/S
Strandgade 73
1401 Copenhagen
Denmark

Tel: +45 70 26 26 48
Fax: +45 70 26 26 49
E-mail: 3xn@3xn.dk
Web: www.3xn.com

Kim Herforth Nielsen was born in Sønderborg, Denmark, in 1954 and graduated from the Aahus School of Architecture in 1981. He is the founder, principal partner, and artistic director of **3XN**. Michael Kruse was born in 1970 and also graduated from the Aarhus School of Architecture (1998). Prior to joining 3XN, he worked with Schmidt Hammer Lassen (Aarhus, 1998–2001) and with David Chipperfield in London (2001–02). He is a partner and head of competition design at 3XN. He was also the Competition Design Manager for the Ørestad College (Copenhagen, 2005–07, published here). The three other partners of the firm are Jan Ammundsen, Bo Boje Larsen, and Tommy Bruun. Other recent and current work (with expected completion dates) includes the Saxo Bank (Copenhagen, 2008); Horten Headquarters (Copenhagen, 2009); Middelfart Savings Bank (Middelfart, 2010); Museum of Liverpool (Liverpool, UK, 2010); Bella Hotel (Copenhagen, 2011); Theatre and Jazzhouse (Molde, Norway, 2011); Buen Cultural Center (Mandal, Norway, 2011); and Blue Planet Aquarium (Copenhagen, 2012), all in Denmark unless stated otherwise.

Kim Herforth Nielsen wurde 1954 in Sønderborg, Dänemark, geboren und schloss sein Studium 1981 an der Hochschule für Architektur in Århus ab. Er ist Gründer, Seniorpartner und Artdirector bei **3XN**. Michael Kruse wurde 1970 geboren und machte seinen Abschluss ebenfalls an der Hochschule für Architektur in Århus (1998). Vor seiner Zeit bei 3XN arbeitete er für Schmidt Hammer Lassen (Århus, 1998–2001) und David Chipperfield in London (2001–02). Er ist ebenfalls Partner bei 3XN und zuständig für Wettbewerbsentwürfe. Auch beim Wettbewerb für das Ørestad College (Kopenhagen, 2005–07, hier vorgestellt) betreute er den Entwurf. Drei weitere Partner des Büros sind Jan Ammundsen, Bo Boje Larsen und Tommy Bruun. Aktuelle Projekte sind u. a. (mit voraussichtlichen Fertigstellungsdaten) die Saxo Bank (Kopenhagen, 2008), die Firmenzentrale von Horten (Kopenhagen, 2009), die Sparkasse Middelfart (Middelfart, 2010), das National Museum of Liverpool (Liverpool, 2010), das Hotel Bella (Kopenhagen, 2011), ein Theater und Jazzklub (Molde, Norwegen, 2011) das Buen-Kulturzentrum (Mandal, Norwegen, 2011) sowie das Blue-Planet-Aquarium (Kopenhagen, 2012).

Kim Herforth Nielsen est né en 1954 à Sønderborg, au Danemark. Il obtient son diplôme de l'École d'architecture d'Aahus en 1981. Il est le fondateur, principal associé et directeur artistique de **3XN**. Michael Kruse, né en 1970, obtient également son diplôme de l'École d'architecture d'Aahus en 1998. Avant de rejoindre 3XN, il travaille avec Schmidt Hammer Lassen (Aarhus, 1998–2001) et David Chipperfield, à Londres (2001–02). Il est associé de 3XN et dirige les concours de design. Il dirige également les concours à l'Ørestad College (Copenhague, 2005–07, publié ici). Les trois autres associés de l'agence sont Jan Ammundsen, Bo Boje Larsen, et Tommy Bruun. Leurs projets récents ou en cours (avec dates prévues d'achèvement) sont le siège de la banque Saxo (Copenhague, 2008); le siège de Horten (Copenhague, 2009); le siège de la banque Middelfart Sparekasse (Middelfart, 2010); le musée de Liverpool (Liverpool, Royaume-Uni, 2010); l'hôtel Bella (Copenhague, 2011); le théâtre et la Maison du jazz de Molde (Molde, Norvège, 2011); le Centre culturel de Mandal (Mandal, Norvège 2011); et l'aquarium Blue Planet de Copenhague (Copenhague, 2012), tous situés au Danemark, sauf mention contraire.

ØRESTAD COLLEGE
Copenhagen, Denmark, 2005–07

Address: Ørestads Boulevard 75, 2300 Copenhagen, Denmark, +45 82 30 22 22, www.oerestadgym.dk
Area: 12 000 m². Client: Municipality of Copenhagen, Danish University, and Property Agency
Cost: € 27 million

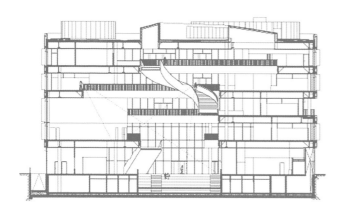

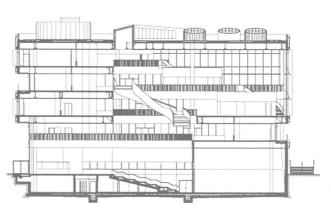

The architects declare that "Ørestad Gymnasium (**ØRESTAD COLLEGE**) is the first college in Denmark based on the new visions of content, subject matter, organization and learning systems in the reform of the educational system of the Danish 'high-school' (gymnasium) for students of the age of 16 to 19." Placing an emphasis on IT, the new system is intended to be more dynamic and flexible, encouraging teamwork. Four boomerang shapes were used by the architects to create interconnected spaces. The rotation of these forms allows for the creation of a central atrium for community contact—but the main emphasis is on concentrating teaching and learning spaces on each floor to encourage overlapping and interaction between student groups.

Nach Angaben der Architekten ist das „**GYMNASIUM ØRESTAD** die erste Sekundarschule Dänemarks, die auf Basis der neuen inhaltlichen, organisatorischen und didaktischen Visionen konzipiert wurde, die im Zug der Bildungsreform entwickelt wurden. Diese betreffen dänische Gymnasien für Schüler im Alter von 16 bis 19 Jahren." Das neue System legt besonderen Wert auf Computertechnik, ist dynamischer und flexibler und fördert Teamarbeit. Die Architekten entwarfen vier bumerangartige Formen und verschränkten sie ineinander. Durch die Drehung der Elemente entsteht ein zentrales Atrium, in dem sich die Schüler begegnen und austauschen können. Hauptanliegen ist jedoch, die Lehr- und Lernräume auf jeder Ebene zu bündeln, sodass es zu Überschneidungen und Interaktionen zwischen den einzelnen Schülergruppen kommen kann.

Selon ses architectes, « l'Ørestad Gymnasium (**LYCÉE ØRESTAD**) est le premier lycée danois fondé sur la nouvelle politique de contenus, d'organisation et de système d'enseignement mise en place par la réforme du système éducatif des lycées danois pour les étudiants de 16 à 19 ans ». Le nouveau système, qui met l'accent sur l'informatique pour un dynamisme et une flexibilité accrus, favorise le travail en équipe. Les architectes ont utilisé quatre éléments en forme de boomerang pour créer des espaces interconnectés. La rotation de ces formes crée un atrium central, point de rencontre pour la communauté, mais l'accent est porté sur la concentration des espaces d'enseignement sur chaque étage, favorisant la rencontre et l'interaction des groupes d'étudiants.

Sections show the large spiraling staircase that links the upper levels. Right, the blocky façade is rendered cheerful by colored fins of varying height.

Schnittzeichnungen zeigen die geschwungene Treppe, die die oberen Geschosse miteinander verbindet. Rechts die blockhafte Fassade, aufgelockert durch farbige Lamellen unterschiedlicher Länge.

Les coupes montrent le large escalier en spirale reliant les étages supérieurs. Page de droite, les façades compactes sont égayées par des ailerons colorés de différentes hauteurs.

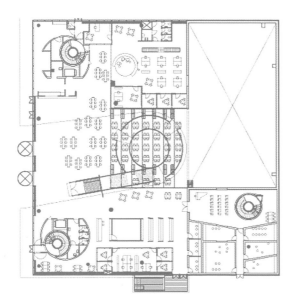

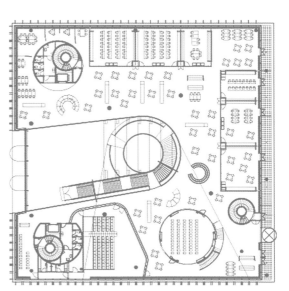

Plans and photos (left and below) show the curving staircase and open spaces inside the building. Texts silkscreened on the windows are outlined on the floor in the image to the right.

Grundrisse und Aufnahmen (linke Seite und unten) zeigen die geschwungene Treppe und die offene Raumsituation. Rechts Schattenspiele der Fenster-Siebdrucktexte auf dem Boden.

Les plans et les photos (ci-dessous et à gauche) montrent l'escalier incurvé et les espaces ouverts à l'intérieur du bâtiment. Sur la photo de droite, les textes sérigraphiés sur les fenêtres se découpent sur le sol.

ADJAYE/ASSOCIATES

Adjaye/Associates
23–28 Penn Street
London N1 5DL
UK

Tel: +44 20 77 39 49 69
Fax: +44 20 77 39 34 84
E-mail: info@adjaye.com
Web: www.adjaye.com

DAVID ADJAYE was born in 1966 in Dar es Salaam, Tanzania. He studied at the Royal College of Art in London (M.Arch, 1993), and worked in the offices of David Chipperfield and Eduardo Souto de Moura, before creating his own firm in London in 2000. He has been widely recognized as one of the leading architects of his generation in the United Kingdom, in part because of the talks he has given in various locations such as the Architectural Association, the Royal College of Art, and Cambridge University, as well as Harvard, Cornell, and the Universidad de Luisdad in Lisbon. His office employs a staff of 35, and some of his key works are: a house extension (Saint John's Wood, 1998); studio/home for Chris Ofili (1999); the SHADA Pavilion (2000, with artist Henna Nadeem); Siefert Penthouse (2001); Elektra House (2001); and a studio/gallery/home for Tim Noble and Sue Webster (2002), all in London. Recent work includes the Nobel Peace Center (Oslo, Norway, 2002–05); Bernie Grant Performing Arts Center (London, 2001–06); Stephen Lawrence Center (London, 2004–06); a visual arts building for the London-based organizations inIVA/Autograph at Rivington Place (London, 2003–07); the Museum of Contemporary Art/Denver (Denver, Colorado, USA, 2004–07); and the Sclera Pavilion (Size + Matter, London Design Festival, London, 2008, published here), all in the UK unless stated otherwise. Current work includes the African Contemporary Arts Center (Lisbon, Portugal, 2012); and the National Museum of African American History and Culture (Smithsonian Institution, Washington D.C., USA, 2015).

DAVID ADJAYE wurde 1966 in Daressalam, Tansania, geboren. Er studierte am Royal College of Art in London (M. Arch., 1993) und arbeitete für David Chipperfield und Eduardo Souto de Moura, bevor er 2000 in London sein eigenes Büro gründete. Er gilt weithin als einer der führenden Architekten seiner Generation in Großbritannien, u. a. wegen seiner Vorträge an so verschiedenen Institutionen wie der Architectural Association, dem Royal College of Art, der Universität Cambridge, den Universitäten von Harvard und Cornell sowie der Universidad de Luisdad in Lissabon. Sein Büro beschäftigt 35 Mitarbeiter. Zu seinen wichtigsten Projekten zählen eine Hauserweiterung (Saint John's Wood, 1998), ein Atelier und Haus für Chris Ofili (1999), der SHADA Pavilion (2000, mit der Künstlerin Henna Nadeem), das Siefert Penthouse (2001), das Elektra House (2001) sowie eine Kombination aus Atelier, Galerie und Wohnhaus für Tim Noble und Sue Webster (2002), alle in London. Zu seinen jüngeren Arbeiten gehören das Nobel-Friedenszentrum (Oslo, 2002–05), das Bernie Grant Performing Arts Center (London, 2001–06), das Stephen Lawrence Center (London, 2004–06), ein Haus für visuelle Künste für die Londoner Organisation inIVA/Autograph am Rivington Place (London, 2003–07) und der Sclera Pavilion (Size + Matter, London Design Festival, London, 2008, hier vorgestellt). Aktuelle Projekte sind u. a. das Zentrum für zeitgenössische afrikanische Kunst (Lissabon, 2012) sowie das National Museum of African American History and Culture (Smithsonian Institution, Washington D. C., 2015).

DAVID ADJAYE est né en 1966 à Dar es Salaam, en Tanzanie. Il étudie au Royal College of Art, à Londres (master d'architecture, 1993), et travaille dans les agences de David Chipperfield et d'Eduardo Souto de Moura, avant de créer sa propre agence à Londres, en 2000. Il est considéré comme l'un des architectes les plus importants de sa génération au Royaume-Uni, en partie grâce aux conférences qu'il donne en divers lieux, comme l'Architectural Association, le Royal College of Art, et l'université de Cambridge, ainsi qu'à Harvard, à Cornell, et à l'université de Luisdad à Lisbonne. Son agence emploie 35 personnes, et parmi ses réalisations importantes, on peut citer une extension d'habitation (Saint John's Wood, 1998) ; un atelier-logement pour Chris Ofili (1999) ; le pavillon SHADA (2000, avec l'artiste Henna Nadeem) ; l'appartement de grand standing Siefert (2001) ; la maison Elektra (2001) et un atelier-galerie-logement pour Tim Noble et Sue Webster (2002) ; tous situés à Londres. Ses projets récemment réalisés sont le Centre Nobel de la Paix (Oslo, Norvège, 2002–05) ; le Centre Bernie Grant Performing Arts (Londres, 2001–06) ; le Centre Stephen Lawrence (Londres, 2004–06) ; un immeuble dédié aux arts visuels pour l'organisation inIVA/Autograph, à Rivington Place (Londres, 2003–07) ; le Musée d'art contemporain de Denver (Denver, Colorado, États-Unis, 2004–07) ; et le pavillon Sclera (Size + Matter, London Design Festival, Londres, 2008, publié ici), tous situés au Royaume-Uni, sauf mention contraire. Ses projets en cours comprennent le Centre culturel d'art contemporain africain (Lisbonne, Portugal, 2012) ; et le Musée national d'histoire et de culture afro-américaine (Smithsonian Institution, Washington D.C., États-Unis, 2015).

SCLERA, SIZE + MATTER

London Design Festival, London, UK, June–September 2008

Area: 40 m². Client: London Design Festival. Cost: not disclosed
Collaboration: American Hardwood Export Council (Sponsorship: tulipwood), Hess Wohnwerk (Fabricator),
Jochen A. Stahl, TU-Darmstadt FB Architektur (Structural Engineer)

This ephemeral pavilion was intended both to explore the ways in which the eye perceives light and to find new uses for tulipwood (Yellow Poplar). The elliptical structure measures 12 meters by 8 meters and was put in place on the South Bank Centre Square near the Thames. Adjaye explains that the name "sclera" means the "domain of parentheses, or the outer enclosure of the eyeball." The undulating pattern of wood appears random, but is in fact based on a loose system of varying timber lengths, with an open roof and gaps on the sides. Adjaye's work has often explored new uses for relatively common materials such as the wood employed here—and he has also played on the rules of perception in an innovative way, making apparently simple structures much more intriguing and challenging than they might at first appear. The very visible location selected for this installation also sought to bring intelligent design closer to the general public.

Bei dem temporären Pavillon setzte sich Adjaye sowohl mit der Lichtwahrnehmung des Auges als auch mit neuen Nutzungsmöglichkeiten für Rosenholz auseinander. Die elliptische, 8 x 12 m große Konstruktion wurde unweit des South Bank Centre Square nahe der Themse realisiert. Adjaye erläutert, dass „Sclera" das „Umschlossene oder die äußere Hülle des Augapfels" bezeichnet. Die wellenförmige Anordnung der Holzelemente wirkt wie zufällig, beruht jedoch auf einem lockeren System verschiedener Lattenlängen. Neben einem offenen Dach hat die Konstruktion auch seitlich Öffnungen. Adjaye befasst sich, wie so oft in seinem Werk, mit neuartigen Einsatzmöglichkeiten für eher gewöhnliche Baumaterialien wie das hier verwendete Holz. Zugleich spielt er auf innovative Weise mit den Gesetzmäßigkeiten der Wahrnehmung, wodurch scheinbar einfache Konstruktionen wesentlich faszinierender und anspruchsvoller wirken, als auf den ersten Blick zu vermuten wäre. Der prominente Standort der Installation wurde auch deshalb gewählt, um der Öffentlichkeit intelligentes Design näher zu bringen.

Ce pavillon éphémère avait pour objectifs d'explorer les manières dont l'œil perçoit la lumière et de trouver de nouveaux usages pour le bois de tulipier (Yellow Poplar). La structure elliptique de 12 mètres par 8 était installée sur le South Bank Centre Square, près de la Tamise. Adjaye explique que le nom « sclera » signifie « domaine de parenthèses, ou paroi externe du globe oculaire ». Le motif de bois ondulant semble aléatoire, mais est en fait basé sur un système relâché de poutres de longueurs variées, avec un toit ouvert et des vides sur les côtés. Dans ses projets, Adjaye explore souvent des usages nouveaux de matériaux relativement banals, comme le bois utilisé ici, et joue souvent de manière innovante avec les lois de la perception, pour rendre des structures apparemment simples beaucoup plus intrigantes et stimulantes qu'elles ne le semblent à première vue. L'emplacement très visible de cette installation visait aussi à mettre le grand public en contact avec un design éclairé.

The simple elliptical plan of the structure is rendered complex by the orchestration of the wooden slats that form the structure.

Der schlichte ellipsenförmige Grundriss des Pavillons gewinnt an Komplexität durch die ausgeklügelte Anordnung der Holzlatten, aus denen die Konstruktion besteht.

L'orchestration des lattes de bois de la structure enrichit le plan en simple ellipse du bâtiment.

Calling on imagery that might vary between a forest and a cave with its stalactites, there is also a musical presence in the dense arrangement of the wooden slats.

Der Raum erinnert an einen Wald oder an Stalaktiten in einer Höhle. Zugleich hat die dichte Anordnung der Holzlatten etwas Musikalisches.

La structure évoque des images de forêt ou de grotte à stalactites. L'arrangement dense des lattes de bois lui donne également une présence musicale.

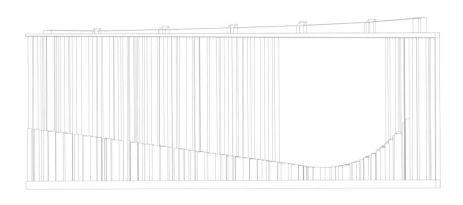

AIRES MATEUS

Francisco Aires Mateus Arquitectos
Rua de Campolide, 62
1070-037 Lisbon
Portugal

Tel: +351 21 382 75 00
Fax: +351 21 382 75 09
E-mail: f@airesmateus.com
Web: www.airesmateus.com

MANUEL ROCHA DE AIRES MATEUS was born in Lisbon in 1963. He graduated as an architect from the Faculty of Architecture at the Universidade Técnica de Lisboa (FA-UTL; Lisbon, 1986). He worked with Gonçalo Byrne beginning in 1983 and with his brother Francisco Aires Mateus beginning in 1988. He has taught at the Harvard GSD (2002, 2005), and the Accademia di Architectura (Mendrisio, Switzerland, since 2001). **FRANCISCO XAVIER DE AIRES MATEUS** was born in Lisbon in 1964. He also graduated from the FA-UTL (Lisbon, 1987). He began working with Gonçalo Byrne beginning in 1983, before his collaboration with his brother. He has likewise taught at Harvard and in Mendrisio. Their work includes Fontana Park Hotel (Lisbon, 2002–07); Santa Marta Light House Museum (Cascais, 2003–07); the Highway Toll and Control Building (Benavente, 2006–07, published here); school complex (Vila Nova da Barquinha, 2006–08); 14 private houses, Vila Utopia-Wise (Lisbon, 2005–09); social housing (Madrid, Spain, 2007–09); EDP headquarters, Portuguese Electric Company (Lisbon, 2008–09); Portugal Telecom Call Center (Santo Tirso, 2008–09); Parque de los Cuentos Museum (Málaga, Spain, 2008–09); and an urban plan for the Parque Mayer and Botanical Gardens (Lisbon, 2008–09), all in Portugal unless otherwise indicated.

MANUEL ROCHA DE AIRES MATEUS wurde 1963 in Lissabon geboren. Sein Studium beendete er an der Architekturfakultät der Universidade Técnica de Lisboa (FA-UTL, Lissabon, 1986). Ab 1983 arbeitete er mit Gonçalo Byrne zusammen, seit 1988 dann mit seinem Bruder **FRANCISCO XAVIER DE AIRES MATEUS**. Nach Lehraufträgen an der Harvard Graduate School of Design (2002, 2005) lehrt er inzwischen an der Accademia di Architectura (Mendrisio, Schweiz, seit 2001). Francisco Xavier de Aires Mateus wurde 1964 in Lissabon geboren. Auch er absolvierte sein Architekturstudium an der FA-UTL (Lissabon, 1987) und arbeitete ab 1983 bei Gonçalo Byrne, bevor er die Kooperation mit seinem Bruder begann. Er lehrte ebenfalls in Harvard und Mendrisio. Zu den Projekten der Brüder zählen das Hotel Fontana Park (Lissabon, 2002–07), das Leuchtturmmuseum Santa Marta (Cascais, 2003–07), eine Mautstelle und Autobahnwacht (Benavente, 2006–07, hier vorgestellt), ein Schulkomplex (Vila Nova da Barquinha, 2006–08), Vila Utopia-Wise, 14 private Wohnbauten (Lissabon, 2005–09), ein soziales Wohnbauprojekt in Madrid (Spanien, 2007–09), die Firmenzentrale der portugiesischen Elektrizitätswerke EDP (Lissabon, 2008–09), ein Callcenter für Portugal Telecom (Santo Tirso, 2008–09), das Museum im Parque de los Cuentos (Málaga, Spanien, 2008–09) sowie die Stadtplanung für den Parque Mayer und den Botanischen Garten in Lissabon (2008–09), alle in Portugal soweit nicht anders angegeben.

MANUEL ROCHA DE AIRES MATEUS est né à Lisbonne en 1963. Il est diplômé de la Faculté d'architecture de l'Université technique de Lisbonne (FA-UTL, Lisbonne, 1986). Il commence à travailler avec Gonçalo Byrne en 1983, puis avec son frère, **FRANCISCO XAVIER DE AIRES MATEUS**, en 1988. Il a enseigné à la Harvard GSD (2002, 2005) et, depuis 2001, à l'Accademia di Architectura (Mendrisio, Suisse). Francisco Xavier de Aires Mateus est né à Lisbonne en 1964. Il est également diplômé de la FA-UTL (Lisbonne, 1987). Il commence également à travailler avec Gonçalo Byrne en 1983, avant de s'associer à son frère. Il a également enseigné à Harvard et à Mendrisio. Leurs projets réalisés comprennent l'hôtel Fontana Park (Lisbonne, 2002–07), le musée du Phare de Santa Marta (Cascais, 2003–07) ; le péage de Benavente (Benavente, 2006–07, publié ici) ; un complexe scolaire (Vila Nova da Barquinha, 2006–08) ; quatorze maisons privées, Vila Utopia-Wise (Lisbonne, 2005–09) ; des logements sociaux (Madrid, Espagne, 2007–09) ; le siège EDP, la compagnie portugaise d'électricité (Lisbonne, 2008–09) ; le Centre d'appel de Portugal Telecom (Santo Tirso, 2008–09) ; le musée du Parc de los Cuentos (Malaga, Espagne, 2008–09) ; et un plan d'urbanisme pour le parc Mayer et le Jardin botanique (Lisbonne, 2008–09) ; tous situés au Portugal sauf mention contraire.

HIGHWAY TOLL AND CONTROL BUILDING

Benavente, Portugal, 2006–07

Area: 1115 m². Client: Brisa. Cost: not disclosed
Collaboration: Giacomo Brenna, Felipe Boim

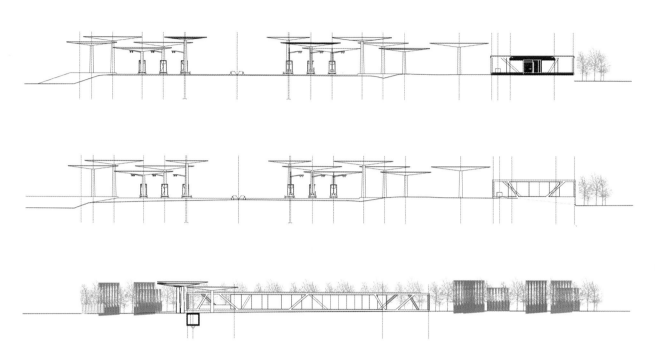

The architects conceived this project in terms of time and speed—and also in terms of the mark it leaves on the land. "A mandatory stop in a continuous flow," it is also an "artificial gateway erected in a territory." Rather than ignoring the natural setting as many designers of highway structures do, Aires Mateus has chosen to provoke an interaction between the site and its function. The connection between the architecture and time is revealed in what they call a "tense" design—perhaps "taut" might be a more appropriate word. They conclude: "The building of a highway is of enormous initial impact on a virgin landscape. At the same time, it is guaranteed that both time and the complex tissue of history and culture will transform it into simply a mark—similar to all the marks that the territory is made of (and without which it is not)." This sensitivity not only to the process of transportation by motor vehicle, but also the healing virtues of time, gives a special presence to what might have been a banal intervention.

Die Architekten entwarfen ihr Projekt mit den Leitmotiven Zeit und Geschwindigkeit – sowie mit Blick auf die Spuren, die Architektur in der Landschaft hinterlässt. Der Komplex ist „ein zwingender Haltepunkt in einem unaufhörlichen Fluss" und zugleich „ein künstliches Tor mitten in der Landschaft". Statt die Landschaft zu ignorieren, wie das zahlreiche Autobahnbauten tun, sorgten Aires Mateus für ein Zusammenspiel zwischen Umfeld und Funktion. Das Verhältnis von Architektur und Zeit spiegelt sich den Architekten zufolge im „zügigen" Entwurf – wobei „straff" es vielleicht besser treffen würde. Zusammenfassend führen sie aus: „Der Bau einer Schnellstraße hat anfänglich enorme Auswirkungen auf die unberührte Landschaft. Zugleich jedoch steht fest, dass sie im Lauf der Zeit durch die komplexe Verflechtung von Geschichte und Kultur zu einer bloßen Spur werden wird – wie all jene Markierungen, die ein Territorium ausmachen (und ohne die es nicht existiert)." Dieses Gespür für das Prozesshafte des Motorverkehrs, ebenso wie für die heilenden Kräfte der Zeit, trägt dazu bei, dass dieses Projekt keine banale Intervention ist, sondern eine ganz eigene Präsenz besitzt.

Les architectes ont conçu ce projet en partant des notions de temps et de vitesse, mais aussi d'empreinte laissée dans le paysage. « Arrêt obligé dans un flux continu », c'est aussi une « porte artificielle érigée sur un territoire ». Plutôt que d'ignorer le site naturel comme beaucoup de structures autoroutières, ils ont choisi de provoquer une interaction entre le site et sa fonction. La relation entre l'architecture et le temps est mise en évidence dans ce qu'ils appellent un dessin « tendu » – « rigoureux » serait peut-être un terme plus approprié. Ils concluent : « Un bâtiment d'autoroute a un énorme impact initial sur un paysage vierge. Mais on sait que le temps et le tissu complexe de l'histoire et de la culture le transformeront en une simple marque – similaire à toutes les marques qui constituent le territoire (lequel n'existe pas sans elles). » Cette sensibilité, non seulement au mode de transport, mais aussi aux vertus curatives du temps, confère une présence singulière à ce qui aurait pu n'être qu'une intervention banale.

As the drawings above imply, the architects have sought to integrate the Highway Toll and Control structures into the site as subtly as possible.

Wie die Zeichnungen oben illustrieren, ging es den Architekten darum, die Mautstation und Autobahnwacht so stark wie möglich in ihr Umfeld zu integrieren.

Comme le suggèrent les dessins ci-dessus, les architectes ont cherché autant que possible à intégrer les installations du péage d'autoroute dans le site.

Clean, simple lines and a distinct modernity are the hallmarks of this design, with its sharply inclined support columns.

Klare, schlichte Linien und eine deutlich moderne Formensprache kennzeichnen den Entwurf mit seinen dramatisch geneigten Stützen.

Avec ses piliers de soutien très obliques, ce projet se caractérise par de simples lignes épurées et une indéniable modernité.

STAN ALLEN ARCHITECT

SAA/Stan Allen Architect
68 Jay Street no. 426
Brooklyn, NY 11201
USA

Tel: +1 718 624 7827
E-mail: studio@stanallenarchitect.com
Web: www.stanallenarchitect.com

STAN ALLEN received his B.A. from Brown University (1978), a B.Arch degree from the Cooper Union (1981), and an M.Arch degree from Princeton (1988). He started his career in the office of Richard Meier (1981–83) and then worked for Rafael Moneo in Madrid and Cambridge, Massachusetts (1984–87). He created his own firm, SAA/ Stan Allen Architect, in 1991 and also became a Principal and Director of the collaborative, interdisciplinary firm Field Operations (1999–2003). He was an Assistant Professor of Architecture (1990–97) and then Associate Professor of Architecture (1998–2002) at the Columbia University GSAP. He has been Dean and George Dutton Class of '27 Professor at the School of Architecture, Princeton University, since 2002. Recent projects include the Taichung Gateway Park (Taichung, Taiwan, 2007); CCV Chapel (Tagaytay, Philippines, 2007–08, published here); Bada Publishing Company (Paju Book City, Seoul, South Korea, 2008); Gwanggyo Lakeside Park (Suwon, South Korea, 2008); and the Yan-Ping Waterfront in Taipei (Taiwan, 2009).

STAN ALLEN machte seinen B. A. zunächst an der Brown University (1978), anschließend einen B. Arch. an der Cooper Union (1981) und schließlich einen M. Arch. an der Universität Princeton (1988). Seine Laufbahn begann im Büro von Richard Meier (1981–83), anschließend war er für Rafael Moneo in Madrid und Cambridge, Massachusetts, tätig (1984–87). Sein eigenes Büro SAA/Stan Allen Architect gründete er 1991. Darüber hinaus war er Seniorpartner und Direktor des interdisziplinären Büros Field Operations (1999–2003). Allen war Lehrbeauftragter (1990–97) und außerordentlicher Professor für Architektur (1998–2002) an der Graduate School of Architecture der Columbia University. Seit 2002 ist er Dekan an der Fakultät für Architektur in Princeton und hat die Professur „George Dutton Class of '27" inne. Zu seinen jüngsten Projekten zählen der Taichung Gateway Park (Taichung, Taiwan, 2007), die CCV-Kapelle (Tagaytay, Philippinen, 2007–08, hier vorgestellt), der Bada-Verlag (Paju Book City, Seoul, Südkorea, 2008), der Gwanggyo Lakeside Park (Suwon, Südkorea, 2008) sowie die Yan-Ping-Promenade in Taipeh (Taiwan, 2009).

STAN ALLEN a obtenu sa licence en arts à la Brown University (1978), sa licence en architecture à la Cooper Union (B. Arch., 1981) et son master en architecture à Princeton (M. Arch., 1988). Il débute sa carrière dans l'agence de Richard Meier (1981–83), puis travaille pour Rafael Moneo à Madrid et Cambridge, dans le Massachusetts (1984–87). Il fonde sa propre agence, SAA/ Stan Allen Architect, en 1991 et devient également directeur de l'agence multidisciplinaire Field Operations (1999–2003). Il est maître-assistant en architecture (1990–97), puis professeur associé en architecture (1998–2002) à la GSAP de l'université Columbia. Il est doyen et professeur « George Dutton Class of '27 » de l'École d'architecture de Princeton depuis 2002. Ses projets récents comprennent le parc Taichung Gateway (Taichung, Taiwan, 2007); la chapelle CCV (Tagaytay, Philippines, 2007–08, publié ici); le siège de la maison d'édition Bada (Paju Book City, Séoul, Corée du Sud, 2008); Gwanggyo Lakeside Park (Suwon, Corée du Sud, 2008); et le front de mer de Yan-Ping à Taipei (Taiwan, 2009).

CCV CHAPEL

Tagaytay, Cavite, Philippines, 2007–08

Address: Km. 48, Lalaan II, Silang, Cavite, Philippines, +63 46 414 2667
Area: 240 m². Client: Ricardo Delgado and CCV Foundation
Cost: $250 000. Collaboration: Carlos Arnaiz (Project Architect), David Orkand, Marc McQuade

This very small chapel marks the entrance to the campus of the Chosen Children's Village Foundation, a non-profit organization "dedicated to the creation of a home environment for physically and mentally challenged children." Designed and built by professionals who donated their services, the structure had a small budget and was erected in a tropical area with a high earthquake risk. "Our response," says the architect, "is a simple pavilion created out of a single line that folds back on itself. The walls are canted in plan for structural stiffness; the resulting figure embraces the congregation and frames the altar. In elevation, the walls are treated like screens to allow for natural air circulation and to filter the strong sunlight." Built largely with cast-in-place concrete, the seven-meter-high space creates a considerable effect.

Die ausgesprochen kleine Kapelle bestimmt den Eingang zum Campus der Chosen Children's Village Foundation, einer gemeinnützigen Organisation, die sich die „Schaffung eines Heims für körperlich und geistig behinderte Kinder" zur Aufgabe gemacht hat. Der Bau, geplant und realisiert von Fachleuten, die ihre Arbeit kostenlos zur Verfügung stellten, musste mit einem kleinen Budget auskommen und wurde in einer tropischen Gegend errichtet, die stark erdbebengefährdet ist. „Unsere Reaktion darauf", so der Architekt, „war ein schlichter Pavillon, der von einer einzigen, in sich gefalteten Linie umrissen wird. Die Kanten der Wände schieben sich in den Grundriss hinein, was dem Bau zusätzliche Steifigkeit verleiht; die so entstandene Form umfängt die Gemeinde und rahmt den Altar. Im Aufriss wirken die Mauern wie Wandschirme. Sie lassen natürliche Belüftung zu und filtern das starke Sonnenlicht." Die überwiegend aus Ortbeton erbaute Kapelle wirkt mit ihrer Höhe von 7 m durchaus beeindruckend.

Cette très petite chapelle marque l'entrée du campus de la fondation Chosen Children's Village, une organisation caritative « dédiée à la création d'un lieu d'accueil pour des enfants handicapés physiques ou mentaux ». Conçu et construit par des professionnels bénévoles, ce bâtiment était doté d'un budget modeste et situé dans une zone tropicale à haut risque sismique. « Notre réponse », dit l'architecte, « est un simple pavillon créé à partir d'une ligne unique se repliant sur elle-même. Les murs sont obliques pour solidifier la structure ; la forme obtenue enlace l'assemblée et encadre l'autel. En élévation, les murs sont traités comme des écrans qui permettent une circulation naturelle de l'air et filtrent la forte lumière. » L'espace de sept mètres de haut, largement construit en béton coulé sur place, produit un bel effet.

The unusual, columnar design of the chapel gives it a musical appearance, with varying roof heights and openings beneath the roof plane. Right, the chapel seen from another angle, with a site plan and axonometric drawing.

Die ungewöhnliche Stützenoptik der Kapelle mit ihren unterschiedlichen Dachniveaus und Fensteröffnungen unterhalb der Dachlinie weckt musikalische Assoziationen. Rechts die Kapelle aus einem anderen Blickwinkel, ein Lageplan und eine Axonometrie.

Avec ses ouvertures de hauteur variable sous un toit, lui aussi de hauteur variable, le dessin inhabituel de la chapelle évoque des orgues basaltiques. À droite, la chapelle vue d'un autre angle, un plan de situation et une axonométrie.

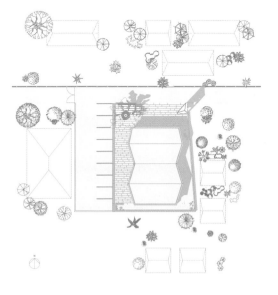

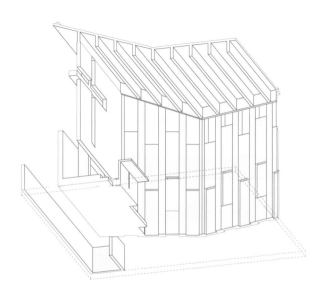

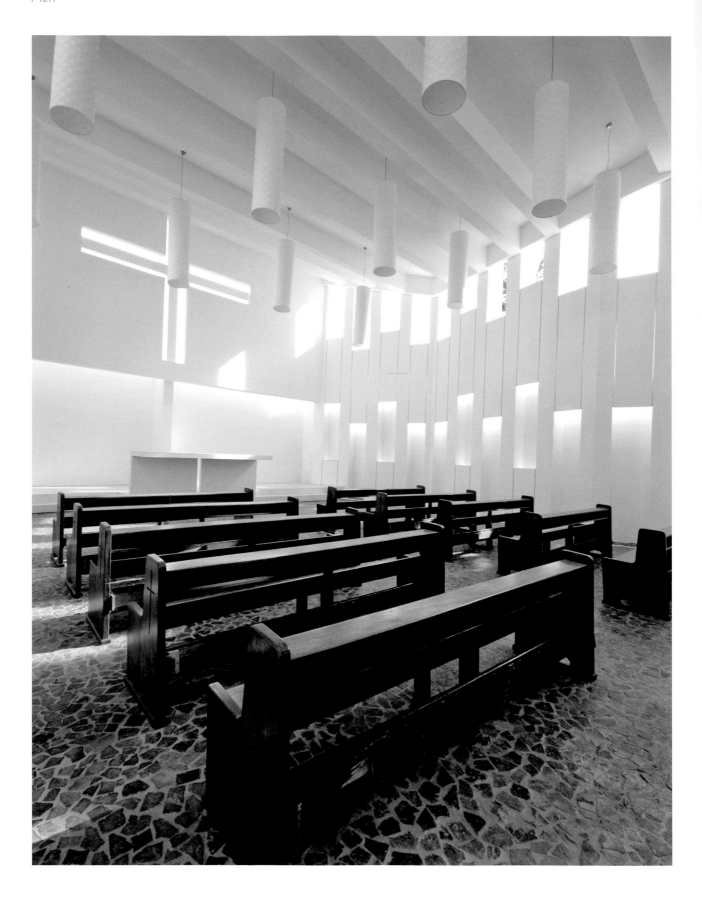

The white orchestration of forms and
light is contrasted with the darker
wooden entry and pews, and the
irregular stone paving.

Das Zusammenspiel von Licht und
weißen Elementen kontrastiert mit
dem dunklen Holz der Eingangstür
und der Kirchenbänke sowie der
unregelmäßigen Bodenpflasterung.

L'orchestration blanche des formes et
de la lumière contraste avec le bois
sombre de l'entrée et des bancs et le
pavement en pierres irrégulières.

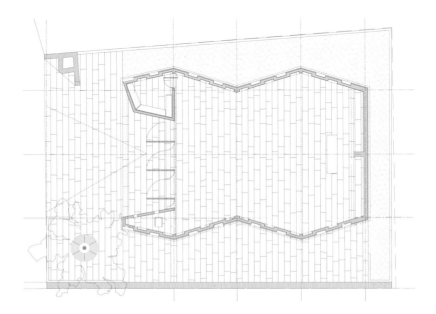

ALLESWIRDGUT

AllesWirdGut
Josefstädter Str. 74B
1080 Vienna
Austria

Tel: +43 1 96 10 43 70
Fax: +43 1 96 10 437 11
E-mail: awg@alleswirdgut.cc
Web: www.alleswirdgut.cc

ALLESWIRDGUT, or AWG, was created in 1999 by Andreas Marth (born in 1969 in Zams, Austria), Friedrich Passler (born in 1969 in Bruneck, Italy), Herwig Spiegl (born in 1973 in Innsbruck, Austria), and Christian Waldner (born in 1971 in Tscherms, Italy). They met at the Technical University in Vienna, from which they all received their diplomas. Their recent work includes the entry, concert, and event area, Château Lackenbach (Burgenland, 2007); Housing Rauchfangkehrergasse (Vienna, 2005–08); ROM, the redesign of a Roman quarry for Opera festivals, Römersteinbruch (St. Margarethen im Burgenland, 2006–08, published here); Alma Boutique Hotel (Vienna, 2006–08); the reorganization of Maria Theresien Strasse (Innsbruck, 2008–09); and Housing Erzherzog-Karl-Strasse (Vienna, 2009–10), all in Austria.

ALLESWIRDGUT (AWG) wurde 1999 von den Partnern Andreas Marth (geboren 1969 in Zams, Österreich), Friedrich Passler (geboren 1969 in Bruneck, Italien), Herwig Spiegl (geboren 1973 in Innsbruck, Österreich) und Christian Waldner (geboren 1971 in Tscherms, Italien) gegründet. Sie begegneten sich an der Technischen Universität Wien, wo alle ihr Diplom machten. Zu den jüngeren Projekten des Teams zählen der Eingangspavillon, Konzertsaal und Veranstaltungsbereich für Schloss Lackenbach (Burgenland, 2007), das Wohnbauprojekt Rauchfangkehrergasse (Wien, 2005–08), ROM, die Umgestaltung eines römischen Steinbruchs zur Festspielstätte Römersteinbruch (St. Margarethen im Burgenland, 2006–08, hier vorgestellt), das Hotel Alma Boutique (Wien, 2006–08), die Umgestaltung der Maria-Theresien-Straße (Innsbruck, 2008–09) sowie das Wohnbauprojekt Erzherzog-Karl-Straße (Wien, 2009–10), alle in Österreich.

ALLESWIRDGUT, ou AWG, a été créée en 1999 par Andreas Marth (né en 1969 à Zams, en Autriche), Friedrich Passler (né en 1969 à Bruneck, en Italie), Herwig Spiegl (né en 1973 à Innsbruck, en Autriche) et Christian Waldner (né en 1971 à Tscherms, en Italie). Ils sont tous diplômés de l'Université technique de Vienne, où ils se sont rencontrés. Leurs projets récents incluent l'accueil et les espaces de concert et d'événements du château de Lackenbach (Burgenland, 2007); l'ensemble d'habitations Rauchfangkehrergasse (Vienne, 2005–08); ROM, le réaménagement d'une carrière romaine pour le festival d'opéra de Römersteinbruch (St. Margarethen im Burgenland, 2006–08, publié ici); l'Alma Boutique Hotel (Vienne, 2006–08); la réorganisation de la Maria Theresien Strasse (Innsbruck, 2008–09); et l'ensemble d'habitations Erzherzog-Karl-Strasse (Vienne, 2009–10), tous situés en Autriche.

ROM – REDESIGN OF FESTIVAL SITE IN A ROMAN QUARRY

St. Margarethen im Burgenland, Austria, 2006–08

Address: 7062 St. Margarethen, Austria, +43 26 80 42 042, www.ofs.at
Area: 4430 m². Client: Fürst Esterházy Familienprivatstiftung. Cost: not disclosed

The architects explain that their work in a Roman quarry, a unique festival venue in Austria, was intended to "extend the ambience of the magnificent rock-face scenery to all parts of the theatrical arena so as to make it a more palpable and visually enveloping experience." The architects were the winners of a 2005 competition and began construction in December 2006 on the site that includes 4430 square meters of outdoor space. Seating up to 6000 people, the theater is reached through a handicapped-accessible ramp leading 400 meters along the rock faces to the actual site, situated 19 meters below. The main construction material is the stone of the quarry itself, with some Cor-ten steel plates added where required.

Den Architekten zufolge war es Ziel des Projekts in einem römischen Steinbruch – einem einzigartigen Festspielort in Österreich – „sämtliche Teile des Theaters an der gewaltigen Felskulisse teilhaben zu lassen. Es gilt, das räumliche Schauspiel sichtbar und erlebbar zu machen." 2005 hatte das Büro den Wettbewerb gewonnen und konnte 2006 mit den Bauarbeiten beginnen. Zum Grundstück gehört auch ein 4430 m² großes Freiluftgelände. Die Arena mit Sitzplätzen für bis zu 6000 Besucher ist barrierefrei über eine 400 m lange Rampe zu erreichen, die entlang der Felswand hinunter bis zur 19 m tiefer gelegenen Bühne führt. Hauptbaumaterial war der vor Ort gebrochene Stein, hinzu kamen an gegebener Stelle Platten aus Cor-Ten-Stahl.

Les architectes expliquent que leur projet pour le site exceptionnel d'une carrière romaine accueillant un festival autrichien visait à « étendre l'ambiance du magnifique décor de parois rocheuses à toutes les parties du lieu théâtral pour créer une sensation plus visuelle et plus enveloppante ». Les architectes ont remporté le concours en 2005 et la construction a démarré en décembre 2006 sur le site de 4430 mètres carrés en plein air. On arrive sur le site, d'une capacité de 6000 spectateurs, par une rampe de 400 mètres de long, également accessible aux handicapés, le long des parois rocheuses du site, jusqu'au théâtre situé à 19 mètres en contrebas. Le matériau de construction utilisé est principalement la pierre provenant de la carrière elle-même, et des plaques d'acier Corten, quand nécessaire.

A general view suggests how the architects have inserted the walkways and new forms into the existing volumes of the former quarry.

Eine Gesamtaufnahme des Areals zeigt die Rampen sowie die neuen Elemente, die von den Architekten in die bestehende Anlage des ehemaligen Steinbruchs integriert wurden.

Une vue générale montrant la façon dont les architectes ont inséré les allées et de nouvelles formes dans les volumes existants de l'ancienne carrière.

With its low-lying angular forms, the
new structure stands out from the
quarry walls without impeding views.

Der niedrige, rechtwinklige Neubau
hebt sich von den Felswänden des
Steinbruchs ab, ohne dabei die Sicht
zu verstellen.

Avec ses formes basses et anguleuses, la nouvelle structure se
détache sur les parois de la carrière
sans bloquer la vue.

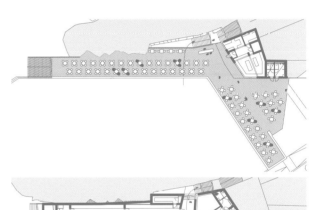

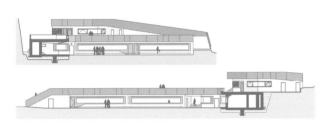

TADAO ANDO

Tadao Ando Architect & Associates
5–23 Toyosaki 2-Chome
Kita-ku
Osaka 531
Japan

Tel: +81 6 6375 1148
Fax: +81 6 6374 6240

Born in Osaka in 1941, **TADAO ANDO** was self-educated as an architect, largely through his travels in the United States, Europe, and Africa (1962–69). He founded Tadao Ando Architect & Associates in Osaka in 1969. He has received the Alvar Aalto Medal, Finnish Association of Architects (1985); the Medaille d'or, French Academy of Architecture (1989); the 1992 Carlsberg Prize; and the 1995 Pritzker Prize. Notable buildings include Church on the Water (Hokkaido, 1988); Japan Pavilion Expo '92 (Seville, Spain, 1992); Forest of Tombs Museum (Kumamoto, 1992); Rokko Housing (Kobe, 1983–93); the Suntory Museum (Osaka, 1994); and Awaji Yumebutai (Awajishima, Hyogo, 1997–2000), all in Japan unless stated otherwise. His work outside Japan includes the Pulitzer Foundation for the Arts (Saint Louis, Missouri, USA, 1997–2000); the Modern Art Museum of Fort Worth (Fort Worth, Texas, USA, 1999–2002); an expansion of the Clark Art Institute (Williamstown, Massachusetts, USA, 2006–08); and the renovation of the Punta della Dogana (Venice, Italy, 2007–09, published here). He completed the Chichu Art Museum on the Island of Naoshima in the Inland Sea in 2004, part of the continuing project that led him to create the Benesse House Museum and Hotel there beginning in the early 1990s. Other recent work in Japan includes the Omote Sando Hills complex (Tokyo, 2006); 21_21 Design Sight (Tokyo, 2004–07); and Tokyu Toyoko Line Shibuya Station (Shibuya-ku, Tokyo, 2006–08). He is working on the Abu Dhabi Maritime Museum (Abu Dhabi, UAE, 2006–); and a house for the designer Tom Ford near Santa Fe, New Mexico.

TADAO ANDO wurde 1941 in Osaka geboren. Als Architekt ist er Autodidakt und bildete sich in erster Linie durch seine Reisen in den USA, Europa und Afrika zwischen 1962 und 1969. 1969 gründete er Tadao Ando Architect & Associates in Osaka. 1985 erhielt er die Alvar-Aalto-Medaille des finnischen Architektenverbands, 1989 die Medaille d'Or der französischen Académie d'Architecture, 1992 den Carlsberg-Preis sowie 1995 den Pritzker-Preis. Zu seinen beachtenswerten Bauten zählen die Kirche auf dem Wasser (Hokkaido, 1988), der japanische Pavillon auf der Expo '92 (Sevilla, Spanien, 1992), das Museum im Gräberwald (Kumamoto, 1992), die Wohnanlage Rokko (Kobe, 1983–93) sowie das Suntory Museum (Osaka, 1994) und das Awaji Yumebutai (Awajishima, Hyogo, 1997–2000), alle in Japan, sofern nicht anders vermerkt. Zu seinen Projekten außerhalb Japans zählen die Pulitzer Foundation for the Arts (St. Louis, Missouri, 1997–2000), das Modern Art Museum in Fort Worth (Fort Worth, Texas, 1999–2002), eine Erweiterung des Clark Art Institute (Williamstown, Massachusetts, 2006–08) und der Umbau der Punta della Dogana (Venedig, 2007–09, hier vorgestellt). 2004 konnte das Chichu Art Museum auf der Insel Naoshima in der Seto-Inlandsee fertiggestellt werden, Teil eines fortlaufenden Projekts, für das Ando Anfang der 1990er Jahre bereits das Benesse House (Museum und Hotel) realisiert hatte. Weitere jüngere Projekte in Japan sind u. a. der Omotesando-Hills-Komplex (Tokio, 2006), das 21_21 Design Sight (Tokio, 2004–07) sowie der U-Bahnhof Shibuya der Tokyu-Toyoko-Linie (Shibuya-ku, Tokio, 2006–08). Tadao Ando arbeitet derzeit am Meeresmuseum von Abu Dhabi (Abu Dhabi, VAE, seit 2006) sowie an einem Haus für den Modedesigner Tom Ford unweit von Santa Fe, New Mexico.

Né à Osaka en 1941, **TADAO ANDO** s'est formé à l'architecture en autodidacte, principalement à travers ses voyages aux États-Unis, en Europe et en Afrique (1962–69). Il fonde Tadao Ando Architect & Associates à Osaka en 1969. Il reçoit la médaille Alvar Aalto, de l'Association finlandaise des architectes (1985), la médaille d'or de l'Académie française d'architecture (1989), le prix Carlsberg 1992, et le prix Pritzker 1995. Ses projets réalisés les plus remarquables incluent l'Église sur l'eau (Hokkaido, 1988); le Pavillon japonais de l'Exposition universelle de 1992 (Séville, Espagne, 1992); le musée de la Forêt des tombes (Kumamoto, 1992); la maison Rokko (Kobe, 1983–93); le musée Suntory (Osaka, 1994); et le complexe Awaji Yumebutai (Awajishima, Hyogo, 1997–2000), tous situés au Japon, sauf mention contraire. Son œuvre hors du Japon inclut la fondation Pulitzer pour les arts (Saint-Louis, Missouri, États-Unis, 1997–2000); le Musée d'art moderne de Fort Worth (Fort Worth, Texas, États-Unis, 1999–2002); une extension du Clark Art Institute (Williamstown, Massachusetts, États-Unis, 2006–08); et la rénovation de la Punta della Dogana (Venise, Italie, 2007–09, publié ici). En 2004, il termine le Chichu Art Museum, sur l'île Naoshima dans la Mer Intérieure, dans la continuité d'un projet global commencé au début des années 1990 avec la construction du musée et de l'hôtel Benesse House. D'autres projets récents incluent, au Japon, le complexe Omote Sando Hills (Tokyo, 2006); le Centre « 21_21 Design Sight », un établissement dédié au design (Tokyo, 2004–07); et la station de métro Shibuya sur la ligne Tokyu Toyoko (Shibuya-ku, Tokyo, 2006–08); et hors du Japon; le Musée maritime d'Abou Dhabi (Abou Dhabi, EAU, 2006–); et une maison pour le designer Tom Ford près de Santa Fe, au Nouveau-Mexique.

PUNTA DELLA DOGANA RENOVATION

Venice, Italy, 2007–09

Address: Dorsoduro 2, 30173 Venice, Italy, +39 41 523 1680,
www.palazzograssi.it/en/punta-della-dogana/museo/punta-della-dogana-venice.html
Area: 3800 m². Client: François Pinault Foundation. Cost: not disclosed

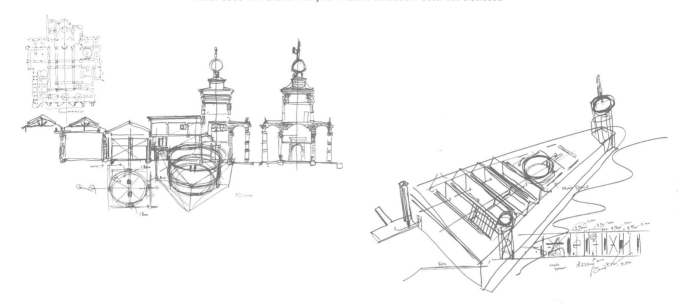

The Dogana di Mare (sea customshouse) is a 15th-century structure renovated in the second half of the 17th century that forms the point opposite Saint Mark's Square at the entrance to the Grand Canal in the Dorsoduro district of Venice. The city of Venice considered competing proposals put forth by Zaha Hadid Architects with the Guggenheim Foundation and Tadao Ando with the Pinault Foundation. François Pinault, who had already had the Palazzo Grassi redesigned by Tadao Ando, won this competition with the Japanese architect. The building is essentially triangular, corresponding to the shoreline site. "Just as with the Palazzo Grassi," says Tadao Ando, "for the exterior as well as the interior, alterations other than a return to the original appearance are severely restricted under the laws concerning the preservation of historical structures. Within these constraints, we were again faced with the theme of how to produce a space possessing modernity while drawing out the latent power of the original building. By exposing the bricks of hidden walls and the wooden roof trusses that had been concealed during the frequent renovations, I wanted to further emphasize the charm of the spaces by adding just a few new architectural elements, while manifesting the individuality of the building." Though a great deal of attention was paid to the renovation of the existing structure, Tadao Ando did allow himself a powerful geometric gesture in the middle of the triangular plan of the building— a concrete cube that rises to the full height of the structure and becomes the axis of all paths leading through the renewed space.

Die Dogana di Mare (das Seezollamt) ist ein Gebäudekomplex aus dem 15. Jahrhundert, der in der zweiten Hälfte des 17. Jahrhunderts umgebaut wurde. Das Gebäude liegt im Stadtviertel Dorsoduro auf der Landspitze gegenüber dem Markusplatz, an der Mündung des Canal Grande. Venedig musste sich zwischen zwei rivalisierenden Entwürfen entscheiden – einem Entwurf Zaha Hadids im Auftrag der Guggenheim Foundation sowie einem Entwurf Tadao Andos für die Fondation Pinault. François Pinault, der bereits den Palazzo Grassi nach Entwürfen des japanischen Architekten hatte umbauen lassen, gewann schließlich den Wettbewerb. Formal bildet das Gebäude ein Dreieck und folgt damit den Konturen des Ufergrundstücks. „Wie schon beim Palazzo Grassi", berichtet Ando, „unterlagen sämtliche Eingriffe sowohl außen als auch innen, die vom ursprünglichen Erscheinungsbild abwichen, strengsten Denkmalschutzauflagen. Aufgrund dieser Rahmenbedingungen waren wir erneut vor die Herausforderung gestellt, einen Raum zu gestalten, der modern ist, jedoch die Ausdruckskraft des historischen Baus hervorhebt. Durch das Freilegen der Ziegelmauern und der Holzbinder der Dachkonstruktion, die bei zahlreichen früheren Sanierungen verborgen geblieben waren, wollte ich die Ausstrahlung der Räume besonders unterstreichen. Ich fügte nur wenige neue architektonische Elemente hinzu und arbeitete die Individualität des Gebäudes heraus." Neben der äußerst sorgsamen Sanierung des alten Gebäudes realisierte Ando eine ausdrucksstarke geometrische Geste im Herzen des dreieckigen Grundrisses – einen Betonkubus, der die gesamte Höhe des Baus einnimmt und sich in der zentralen Achse sämtlicher Wege durch den neu gestalteten Raum befindet.

La Dogana di Mare (douane de mer) est un bâtiment du XVe siècle, rénové dans la deuxième moitié du XVIIe siècle, qui forme la pointe faisant face à la place Saint-Marc, à l'entrée du Grand Canal, dans le quartier du Dorsoduro, à Venise. La ville de Venise a examiné les propositions élaborées par Zaha Hadid, pour la fondation Guggenheim, et Tadao Ando pour la fondation Pinault. François Pinault, qui avait déjà fait appel à Tadao Ando pour le réaménagement du Palazzo Grassi, remporte le concours avec l'architecte japonais. Le bâtiment, essentiellement triangulaire, coïncide avec les rives du site. « Comme pour le Palazzo Grassi », dit Tadao Ando, « pour l'extérieur comme pour l'intérieur, les transformations autres que la restitution de l'aspect original sont sévèrement soumises aux restrictions réglementant la conservation des monuments historiques. Dans ce cadre restreint, nous étions confrontés à la même problématique, à savoir, comment produire un espace empreint de modernité tout en faisant ressortir la puissance sous-jacente du bâtiment original. En révélant les briques de murs cachés et les fermes en bois qui avaient été dissimulées au cours de fréquentes restaurations, j'ai voulu amplifier le charme des espaces en ajoutant juste quelques éléments architecturaux, et révéler l'originalité du bâtiment. » Tout en portant une très grande attention à la rénovation du bâtiment existant, Tadao Ando s'est autorisé un geste géométrique puissant au beau milieu du plan triangulaire de l'édifice : un cube de béton qui s'élève sur toute la hauteur de la structure et devient l'axe de toutes les allées qui traversent l'espace rénové.

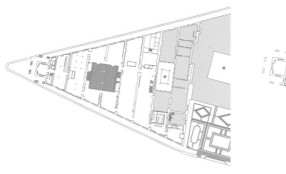

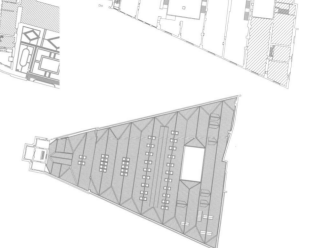

Sketches by Ando (left), floor and roof plans and a view of one of the exhibition galleries show how the architect has retained most of the existing structure while rendering the volumes modern.

Skizzen von Ando (linke Seite), Grundrisse und die Dachaufsicht sowie der Blick in einen Ausstellungsraum zeigen, dass der Architekt zwar einen Großteil des Altbaus erhalten, den Volumina aber trotzdem zu moderner Raumwirkung verholfen hat.

Les croquis d'Ando (page de gauche), les plans du sol et du toit, et la vue de l'une des salles d'exposition montrent comment l'architecte a conservé la plupart du bâtiment existant, tout en donnant un aspect moderne aux volumes.

Works by Maurizio Cattelan and other well-known figures of contemporary art are juxtaposed within the brick and wood structure where Ando has added a number of his signature concrete walls.

Arbeiten von Maurizio Cattelan und anderen bekannten zeitgenössischen Künstlern kontrastieren mit der Ziegel- und Holzkonstruktion des Baus, den Ando um einige seiner typischen Betonmauern ergänzte.

Des œuvres de Maurizio Cattelan et d'autres artistes contemporains de renom se partagent l'espace de la structure de briques et de bois où Ando a ajouté plusieurs de ses murs caractéristiques en béton.

A work by Rudolph Stingel (Untitled, Alpino, 1976) hangs on a concrete wall in the central cubic volume that was added by the architect to the original building.

Ein Werk von Rudolph Stingel (Untitled, Alpino, 1976) an einer Betonwand im zentralen Betonwürfel, den der Architekt in den Altbau integrierte.

Une œuvre de Rudolph Stingel (Sans titre, Alpino, 1976) est accrochée sur un mur de béton dans le cube central ajouté par l'architecte au bâtiment d'origine.

PAUL ANDREU

Paul Andreu Architecte Paris
15 rue du Parc Montsouris
75014 Paris
France

Tel: +33 1 58 10 05 15
Fax: +33 1 53 62 02 20
E-mail: carole.rami@paul-andreu.com
Web: www.paul-andreu.com

PAUL ANDREU was born in 1938 in Caudéran in the Gironde region of France. He obtained diplomas from the École Polytechnique (1961), the École Nationale des Ponts et Chaussées (1963, as an engineer), and as an architect from the École des Beaux-Arts in Paris (1968). As Chief Architect of the Aéroports de Paris, he was responsible not only for the architecture of Charles de Gaulle (Roissy) Airport (Paris, 1967–97), but also for the development of approximately 50 airports around the world, such as those of Jakarta (1986); Teheran (1996); Harare, Zimbabwe (1996); and Shanghai-Pudong (1999). Andreu has also worked on other large-scale projects, such as the French terminal for the Eurotunnel project (1987) and the National Center for the Performing Arts (Beijing, China, 1999–2007, published here). Other recent work includes the Museum of Maritime History in Osaka (Japan, 2000); a sports complex in Guangzhou (China, 2001); and the Center for Oriental Arts (Shanghai, China, 2004).

PAUL ANDREU wurde 1938 in Caudéran im französischen Département Gironde geboren. Diplomabschlüsse absolvierte er an der École Polytechnique (1961), der École Nationale des Ponts et Chaussées (1963, als Bauingenieur) sowie als Architekt an der École des Beaux-Arts in Paris (1968). Als Chefarchitekt der Aéroports de Paris zeichnete er nicht nur für die Architektur des Flughafens Charles de Gaulle (Roissy) verantwortlich (Paris, 1967–97), sondern auch für die Entwicklung von rund 50 Flughäfen in aller Welt, darunter in Jakarta (1986), Teheran (1996), Harare, Simbabwe (1996), und Shanghai-Pudong (1999). Andreu arbeitete zudem an anderen Groß-projekten, wie dem französischen Endbahnhof des Eurotunnels (1987) oder dem Nationalen Zentrum für darstellende Künste (Peking, 2007, hier vorgestellt). Aktuellere Projekte sind das Museum für Meeresgeschichte in Osaka (Japan, 2000), eine Sportanlage in Guangzhou (China, 2001) sowie das Zentrum für orientalische Kunst (Shanghai, China, 2004).

PAUL ANDREU est né en 1938 à Caudéran, dans la Gironde, en France. Il est ingénieur diplômé de l'École polytechnique (1961), et de l'École nationale des ponts et chaussées (1963) et architecte diplômé de l'École nationale supérieure des beaux-arts (1968). Comme architecte en chef des Aéroports de Paris, il était non seulement responsable de l'architecture de l'aéroport Charles-de-Gaulle de Roissy (Paris, 1967–97), mais aussi du développement de près de cinquante aéroports dans le monde, comme Jakarta (1986), Téhéran (1996), Harare, au Zimbabwe (1996) et Shanghai-Pudong (1999). Andreu a également travaillé sur des projets de grande ampleur comme le terminal français d'Eurotunnel (1987) et le Centre national des arts du spectacle, plus connu sous le nom d'Opéra de Pékin (Pékin, Chine, 2007, publié ici). D'autres créations récentes incluent le Musée maritime d'Osaka (Japon, 2000) ; un complexe sportif à Guangzhou (Chine, 2001) ; et le Centre des arts orientaux (Shanghai, Chine, 2004).

NATIONAL CENTER
FOR THE PERFORMING ARTS

Bejing, China, 1999–2007

Address: No.2 West Chang'an Avenue, Xicheng District, Beijing, China, +86 10 6655 0989, www.chncpa.org
Area: 150 000 m². Client: Grand National Theater Committee. Cost: €300 million
Collaboration: François Tamisier, Olivia Faury, Mario Flory, Serge Carillion

The spectacular shell of the Opera sits on an artificial basin, with visitors entering through a tunnel.

Die spektakuläre Gebäudehülle des Opernhauses ragt inmitten eines Wasserbeckens auf; die Besucher betreten den Bau durch einen Tunnel.

La coque impressionnante de l'Opéra est posée sur un bassin artificiel, tandis que l'accès des visiteurs se fait par un tunnel.

Awarded to Paul Andreu in August 1999 as a result of an international competition that he won in the last phase against Carlos Ott, author of the Paris Bastille Opera, and the English architect Terry Farrell, as well as a Chinese group from Xinghua University, this large structure was erected just behind the Great Hall of the People, near Tien An Men Square, and thus very close to the entrance to the Forbidden City. Its 212-meter-long ellipsoidal titanium shell houses three halls of 2416 seats (opera), 2017 seats (concerts), and 1040 seats (theater). The shorter axis of the structure is 143 meters and the height of the shell is 46 meters. In order to leave the external shell intact, the architect decided to provide public access through a 60-meter-long tunnel passing beneath the basin that surrounds the building. Andreu emphasizes that the tunnel is an essential design element since it represents a transition space between the busy outside world and the world of culture within. Andreu faced stiff resistance to his project, both within China, and, curiously, in France as well.

Im August 1999 konnte sich Paul Andreu in der letzten Phase eines internationalen Wettbewerbs gegen Carlos Ott durchsetzen, den Architekten der Pariser Bastille-Oper, sowie gegen den englischen Architekten Terry Farrell und eine chinesische Bewerbergruppe von der Universität Xinghua. Erbaut wurde das Großprojekt hinter der Großen Halle des Volkes, unweit des Tian'anmen-Platzes, also ganz nah am Eingang zur Verbotenen Stadt. In der 212 m langen ovalen Titanhülle sind drei Säle mit 2416 Plätzen (Opernbühne), 2017 Plätzen (Konzertsaal) und 1040 Plätzen (Theaterbühne) untergebracht. Die kürzere Achse des Baus misst 143 m, die Gebäudehülle ist 46 m hoch. Um die Außenhülle des Baus nicht aufbrechen zu müssen, entschied sich der Architekt für einen 60 m langen Tunnel als Zugang zum Gebäude, der unterhalb des Wasserbeckens verläuft, das den Komplex umgibt. Andreu betont die Bedeutung des Tunnels als Schlüsselelement seines Entwurfs, weil dieser den Übergang aus der geschäftigen Außenwelt hinein in das kulturelle Leben im Herzen des Baus markiere. Andreu sah sich bei diesem Projekt mit massivem Widerstand konfrontiert, sowohl in China als auch – erstaunlicherweise – in Frankreich.

Attribué à Paul Andreu en août 1999, à l'issue d'un concours international qui l'opposait dans la phase finale à Carlos Ott, architecte de l'Opéra Bastille de Paris, et à l'architecte anglais Terry Farrell, ainsi qu'à un groupe chinois de l'université de Xinghua, ce grand édifice a été construit juste derrière le Palais de l'Assemblée du peuple, près de la place Tien-an-Men, et donc très près de l'entrée de la Cité interdite. Sa coque ellipsoïde en titane, d'une longueur de 212 mètres, abrite trois salles de capacités respectives de 2416 places (opéra), 2017 places (concerts) et 1040 places (théâtre). Son petit axe mesure 143 mètres et sa hauteur 46 mètres. Pour laisser la coque externe intacte, l'architecte a opté pour un accès du public par un tunnel de 60 mètres de long passant sous les bassins entourant le bâtiment. Andeu souligne que le tunnel est un élément essentiel du projet, car il représente un espace de transition entre l'agitation du monde extérieur et le monde intérieur de la culture. Le projet d'Andreu a rencontré une vive résistance, non seulement en Chine, mais aussi curieusement en France.

The sweeping curves of the building and its large scale can be judged by the size of the figures seen in the image above, right.

Die ausgreifenden Kurven des Gebäudes und seine Dimensionen lassen sich anhand der Figuren im Bild oben rechts ahnen.

Une idée de l'ample courbe et de la taille imposante du bâtiment est fournie par la taille des personnages visibles dans la photo, ci-dessus à droite.

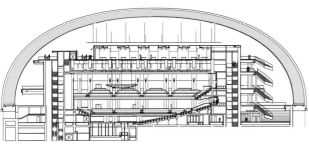

The actual performance spaces are
arranged in a box-like form beneath
the great, curving shell, as can be
seen in the section drawing and plan,
and the image above.

Die eigentlichen Bühnenräume liegen
in einer Box unterhalb der großen
Gebäudekuppel, wie Schnitte, Grundriss und Abbildung oben zeigen.

La salle de spectacle proprement dite
est emboîtée dans un volume situé
sous la grande coque curviligne,
comme le montrent la coupe, le plan
et la photo ci-dessus.

ARM

ARM
Level 11, 522 Flinders Lane
Melbourne, Victoria 3000
Australia

Tel: +61 3 8613 1888
Fax: +61 3 8613 1889
E-mail: arm.melb@a-r-m.com.au
Web: www.a-r-m.com.au

ARM is named after its three founding directors, Stephen Ashton, Howard Raggatt, and Ian McDougall. They have since been joined by a fourth director, Tony Allen. Neil Masterton was appointed design director in 2007. Stephen Ashton has been a director of ARM since the creation of the firm in 1988. He has degrees in Architecture (B.Arch) and in Business Administration. Howard Raggatt received his M.Arch degree from RMIT University in Melbourne. He was appointed the first Adjunct Professor of Architecture at RMIT in 1993, where he and Ian McDougall developed the new Master's course in Urban Design. All three founding directors are Life Fellows of the Australian Institute of Architects. Ian McDougall also received his architectural training at RMIT (B.Arch, M.Arch). He is a Professor of Architecture and Urban Design at the University of Adelaide. Tony Allen received his B.Arch degree from the University of New South Wales, and began his career at Ancher Mortlock Woolley (Sydney). Their work includes Storey Hall, RMIT (Melbourne, 1996); the National Museum of Australia (Canberra, 2001); master planning for the Melbourne Docklands (1996–2004); the remodeling of the Melbourne Central Shopping Center (2005); Albury Library Museum (Albury, New South Wales, 2006–07); the Melbourne Recital Centre and MTC Theatre (2006–08, published here); Perth Arena (Western Australia, under construction); and the Southbank Cultural Precinct Redevelopment (Melbourne, appointed April 2009), all in Australia.

Das Kürzel **ARM** steht für die drei Partner des Büros – Stephen Ashton, Howard Raggatt und Ian McDougall – wobei sich das Team mit Tony Allen inzwischen um einen vierten Partner erweitert hat. Seit 2007 leitet Neil Masterton das Entwurfsteam. Stephen Ashton ist bereits seit Gründung des Büros 1988 Partner. Er absolvierte Abschlüsse in Architektur (B. Arch.) sowie in Betriebswirtschaft. Howard Raggatt machte seinen M. Arch. an der RMIT University in Melbourne. 1993 wurde er zum ersten außerordentlichen Professor für Architektur an der RMIT berufen, wo er gemeinsam mit Ian McDougall den neuen Masterstudiengang Städtebau einführte. Alle drei Gründungspartner von ARM sind Mitglieder auf Lebenszeit des Australian Institute of Architects. Auch Ian McDougall studierte Architektur an der RMIT (B. Arch., M. Arch.). Er ist Professor für Architektur und Städtebau an der Universität Adelaide. Tony Allen absolvierte seinen B. Arch. an der Universität New South Wales und begann seine Laufbahn bei Ancher Mortlock Woolley (Sydney). Zu den Projekten des Büros zählen die Storey Hall, RMIT (Melbourne, 1996), das Nationalmuseum von Australien (Canberra, 2001), der Masterplan für das Hafenviertel in Melbourne (1996–2004), die Neuplanung der Einkaufszone im Zentrum von Melbourne (2005), das Museum der Bibliothek Albury (Albury, New South Wales, 2006–07), das Melbourne Recital Centre und das MTC Theatre (Konzerthaus und Theater, 2006–08, hier vorgestellt), die Perth Arena (Westaustralien, im Bau) sowie die Neuplanung des Kulturquartiers an der Southbank (Melbourne, Auftragserteilung April 2009), alle in Australien.

ARM doit son nom à ses trois directeurs fondateurs, Stephen Ashton, Howard Raggatt et Ian McDougall. Ils ont été rejoints depuis par un quatrième directeur, Tony Allen. Neil Masterton a été nommé directeur du design en 2007. Stephen Ashton est directeur d'ARM depuis sa création en 1988. Il est diplômé en architecture (B. Arch.) et en administration des affaires. Howard Raggatt obtient son master en architecture à l'université RMIT de Melbourne. Il est nommé professeur d'architecture associé au RMIT en 1993, où il développe avec Ian McDougall le nouveau Master de design urbain. Les trois directeurs fondateurs sont membres à vie de l'Institut australien des architectes. Ian McDougall a également un master en architecture du RMIT (B. Arch. et M. Arch.). Il est professeur d'architecture et de design urbain à l'université d'Adelaide. Tony Allen obtient sa licence en architecture (B. Arch.) à l'université de Nouvelle-Galles du Sud, et débute sa carrière chez Ancher Mortlock Woolley (Sydney). Leurs réalisations incluent le réaménagement du Storey Hall, RMIT (Melbourne, 1996) ; le Musée national d'Australie (Canberra, 2001) ; le plan directeur des Docklands, le quartier des docks de Melbourne (Melbourne, 1996–2004) ; la restructuration du Centre commercial Melbourne Central (2005) ; l'Albury Library Museum (Albury, Nouvelle-Galles du Sud, 2006–07) ; le complexe du Centre de récital de Melbourne et du théâtre MTC (2006–08, publié ici) ; le stade Perth Arena (Australie-Occidentale, en construction) ; et la restructuration du quartier culturel de Southbank (Melbourne, projet retenu en avril 2009), toutes situés en Australie.

MELBOURNE RECITAL CENTRE AND MELBOURNE THEATRE COMPANY THEATRE

Melbourne, Australia, 2006–08

Address Recital Centre: Cnr Southbank Boulevard & Sturt Street Southbank, VIC 3006, Australia, +61 3 9699 3333, www.melbournerecital.com.au
Area: 4700 m². Clients: Arts Victoria / Melbourne Recital Centre. Cost: not disclosed

Address MTC Theatre: 140 Southbank Blvd, Southbank, VIC 3006, Australia, +61 3 8688 0800, www.mtc.com.au
Area: 5500 m². Clients: The University of Melbourne / Melbourne Theatre Company. Cost: not disclosed

These two buildings were designed by ARM at the same time, share the same site, and were built at the same time by the same contractor—but they are distinct buildings intended for different public groups. The **MELBOURNE RECITAL CENTRE** includes the 1000-seat Dame Elisabeth Murdoch Hall and a 150-seat Salon. The architects explain: "The design is fundamentally ordered around a procession from the street to the foyer to the main spaces." Though influenced by European concert halls, both the appearance and the design of this Recital Centre are very contemporary. The **MELBOURNE THEATRE COMPANY** is housed in a structure with a 500-seat theater making use of the latest available technology and backstage facilities. The larger, Sumner Theatre has no balcony and provides ideal sight lines to the stage. The smaller Lawler Studio can be used for rehearsals or small performances, seating 150 people. A café, patrons' lounges, and bars are located in the front of the structure. Glowing tubes surrounding a black-box design mark the appearance of the theater.

Die beiden hier vorgestellten Bauten wurden zeitgleich von ARM entworfen, teilen sich einen Standort und wurden parallel von demselben Bauunternehmer realisiert – trotzdem sind es zwei klar unterscheidbare Gebäude, die sich an verschiedene Zielgruppen wenden. Zum **MELBOURNE RECITAL CENTRE** gehören u. a. die Dame Elisabeth Murdoch Hall mit 1000 Sitzplätzen sowie ein Salon mit 150 Plätzen. Die Architekten führen aus: „Der Entwurf ist im Prinzip um eine festliche Passage von der Straße bis ins Foyer und die Haupträume hinein angeordnet." Obwohl das Recital Centre formal von europäischen Konzerthäusern beeinflusst ist, sind Erscheinungsbild und Gestaltung dennoch klar zeitgenössisch. Die **MELBOURNE THEATRE COMPANY** ist in einem Theaterbau mit 500 Sitzplätzen untergebracht, der über neueste Technologien und Bühnentechnik verfügt. Der größere Saal, das Sumner Theatre, verzichtet auf obere Ränge und bietet optimale Sicht auf die Bühne. Das kleinere Lawler Studio mit 150 Sitzplätzen kann für Proben und kleinere Aufführungen genutzt werden. Ein Café, Lounges und Bars sind im vorderen Teil des Baus untergebracht. Leuchtende Röhren, die sich über den gesamten schwarzen Kubus ziehen, prägen das Äußere des Theaters.

Ces deux bâtiments, qui ont été conçus en même temps par ARM, partagent le même site et ont été construits par le même maître d'ouvrage – mais les deux bâtiments qui diffèrent ne sont pas destinés aux mêmes publics. Le **CENTRE DE RÉCITAL DE MELBOURNE** abrite une salle de 1000 places, la salle Dame Elisabeth Murdoch, et un salon de 150 places. Les architectes expliquent que « la conception est fondamentalement commandée par un parcours depuis la rue vers le foyer et les espaces principaux ». Bien qu'inspirées des salles de concert européennes, l'apparence et la conception de ce Centre de récital sont très contemporaines. La **COMPAGNIE DE THÉÂTRE DE MELBOURNE** est hébergée dans un bâtiment disposant d'une salle de 500 places, utilisant les technologies et les équipements scéniques les plus récents. La plus grande salle, le Théâtre Sumner, n'a pas de balcons et offre un angle de vision idéal de la scène. La plus petite, le Lawler Studio, destinée aux répétitions ou à des petits spectacles, a une jauge de 150 places. Un café, des salons et des bars réservés au public sont disposés en façade du bâtiment. Des tubes étincelants enveloppant la boîte noire du théâtre marquent sa présence.

The Melbourne Theatre Company
building is seen to the left, while the
photo above and the plan to the right
show both structures, with the Recital
Centre in the foreground (above).

Links im Bild das Gebäude der
Melbourne Theatre Company. Oben
und auf dem Grundriss rechts beide
Bauten, im Vordergrund das Recital
Centre (oben).

La photo de gauche montre le
bâtiment de la Compagnie de théâtre
de Melbourne, tandis que la photo
ci-dessus et le plan à droite montrent
les deux bâtiments, dont le Centre de
récital au premier plan (ci-dessus).

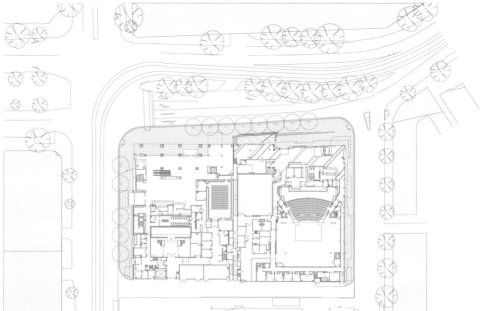

Interior views of the Melbourne Theatre Company and its 500-seat Sumner Theatre, and, below, the smaller Lawler Studio for rehearsals or smaller performances.

Innenansichten der Melbourne Theatre Company mit dem Sumner Theatre (500 Plätze) sowie dem kleineren Lawler Studio (unten), das als Probenbühne und für kleinere Produktionen genutzt wird.

Vues intérieures de la Compagnie de théâtre de Melbourne avec, ci-dessus, la salle de 500 places du Théatre Sumner et, ci-dessous, la salle plus petite du Studio Lawler, dédiée aux répétitions ou à de petits spectacles.

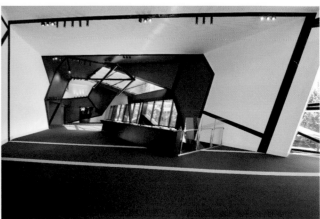

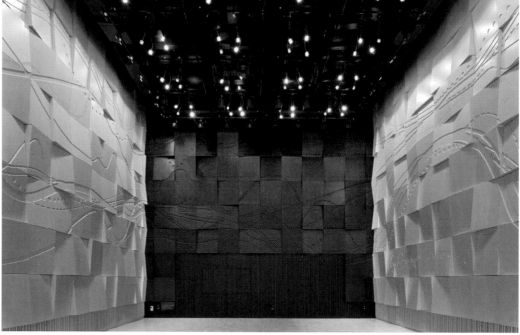

Above, interior views of the Melbourne Recital Centre with its 1000-seat Dame Elisabeth Murdoch Hall and, below, the 150-seat Salon.

Innenansichten des Melbourne Recital Centre mit der Dame Elisabeth Murdoch Hall (oben, 1000 Plätze) und dem darunter gelegenen Salon mit 150 Plätzen.

Ci-dessus, vues intérieures du Centre de récital de Melbourne, avec la salle Dame Elisabeth Murdoch et, dessous, le Salon de 150 places.

ARUP ASSOCIATES

Arup Associates
38 Fitzroy Square
London W1T 6EY
UK

Tel. +44 20 7755 2525
E-mail: pressoffice@arup.com
Web: www.arupassociates.com

ARUP ASSOCIATES is the integrated design studio of the multinational consulting engineering group Arup. Started by Sir Ove Arup more than four decades ago, the studio practices multidisciplinary design where engineers and architects work side-by-side in embedded teams in a single practice. Dipesh Patel is an architect and urban designer who joined Arup Associates in 1992. He was the lead architect for the City of Manchester Stadium (Manchester, UK), venue for the 2002 Commonwealth Games, now converted into the home of Manchester City Football Club, and he was responsible for the design of the redevelopment of Kensington Oval (Bridgetown, Barbados, 2005–07, published here) for the 2007 Cricket World Cup. Other recent work by the firm includes the Druk White Lotus School (Ladakh, northern India, 2007); Arup Campus (Solihull, West Midlands, UK, 2007); Citi Data Center (Frankfurt am Main, Germany, 2008); Coventry University, Engineering and Computing Building (Coventry, West Midlands, UK, 2001), where the future Faculty Building is under construction (2011); and Harlequin 1, BSkyB Transmission and Recording Facility (West London, due for completion 2010).

ARUP ASSOCIATES ist das Entwurfsteam der multinationalen Ingenieurgruppe Arup. Das von Sir Ove Arup vor über vier Jahrzehnten gegründete Studio entwirft fachübergreifend, indem Ingenieure und Architekten Seite an Seite in vernetzten Teams in einem Büro zusammenarbeiten. Der Architekt und Stadtplaner Dipesh Patel ist seit 1992 für Arup Associates tätig. Als leitender Architekt betreute er das City of Manchester Stadium (Manchester, Großbritannien), Austragungsort der Commonwealth Games 2002 und inzwischen das Stadion des Manchester City Football Club, und zeichnete verantwortlich für die Umgestaltung des Kensington Oval (Bridgetown, Barbados, 2005–07, hier vorgestellt) für die Kricketweltmeisterschaften 2007. Jüngere Projekte des Büros sind u. a. die Druk White Lotus School (Ladakh, Nordindien, 2007), der Arup-Campus (Solihull, West Midlands, Großbritannien, 2007), das Citi Data Center (Frankfurt am Main, 2008), die Fakultät für Ingenieurwissenschaften und Informatik der Universität Coventry (Coventry, West Midlands, Großbritannien, 2001), wo ein weiteres Fakultätsgebäude in Bau ist (2011), sowie die Sende- und Aufnahmestudios Harlequin 1 für BSkyB (Westlondon, geplante Fertigstellung 2010).

ARUP ASSOCIATES est l'atelier de design du groupe international de consultants en ingénierie ARUP. Fondé par Sir Ove Arup, il y a plus de quarante ans, l'atelier conçoit des projets multidisciplinaires pour lesquels les ingénieurs et architectes travaillent en accord, dans des équipes intégrées au sein d'une seule agence. Dipesh Patel, architecte et urbaniste, rejoint Arup Associates en 1992. Il est l'architecte principal du stade de Manchester (Manchester, Royaume-Uni), site des Jeux du Commonwealth 2002 et à présent résidence du Manchester City Football Club, et le responsable du projet de restructuration du stade Kensington Oval (Bridgetown, Barbade, 2005–07, publié ici) pour la Coupe du monde de cricket de 2007. D'autres chantiers récents du groupe incluent la Druk White Lotus School (Ladakh, Inde du nord, 2007) ; le campus Arup (Solihull, Midlands de l'Ouest, Royaume-Uni, 2007) ; le Centre de traitements des données du groupe Citi (Francfort, Allemagne, 2008) ; l'Engineering et Computing Building de l'université de Coventry (Coventry, Midlands de l'Ouest, Royaume-Uni, 2001), où le nouveau bâtiment de la faculté est en cours de construction (2011) ; et le Centre de transmission et d'enregistrement de BSkyB, Harlequin 1 (Londres, fin prévue pour 2010).

KENSINGTON OVAL

Bridgetown, Barbados, 2005–07

Address: Fontabelle, St. Michael, Bridgetown, Barbados, +1 246 436 1397
Area: not available. Client: World Cup Barbados. Cost: £35 million

The original brief was an assessment of the feasibility of redeveloping **KENSINGTON OVAL CRICKET GROUND** into a modern test venue, in particular for the final match of the 2007 Cricket World Cup. Arup Associates decided to maintain a collection of stands as opposed to a stadium-type design. These were designed according to three fundamental principles: the stands provide shaded seating, some light transmission through the roof to reduce differential in light levels, and maximized airflow to aid cooling. The government acquired properties near the "land-locked" site of the existing facility, allowing for greater visibility and openness for the ground. Rainwater harvesting and brackish water-resistant grass are used to reduce water consumption for the facility. Locally available materials were used wherever possible in the design, which had to take into account hurricane and seismic risks. A curved box form with a simplified cladding system was used for the main stands, and the player's pavilion was carefully thought out to make the use of Kensington Oval agreeable not only for spectators, but also for the athletes.

Ursprünglich ging es zunächst darum, ein Gutachten zu erstellen, ob sich das **KRICKETSTADION DES KENSINGTON OVAL** überhaupt zu einer modernen Einrichtung umbauen ließe, insbesondere für das Endspiel der Kricketweltmeisterschaften 2007. Arup Associates plädierte dafür, die Konfiguration mit mehreren Tribünen beizubehalten, statt ein konventionelles Stadion zu konzipieren. Der Entwurf fußt auf drei Grundprinzipien: Erstens bieten die Tribünen Sitzplätze im Schatten, zweitens reduziert eine gewisse Lichtdurchlässigkeit der Überdachung allzu große Unterschiede in den Lichtverhältnissen, während drittens eine Maximierung der Luftzirkulation zur Kühlung beiträgt. Die Regierung erwarb Grundstücke auf der Landseite des bestehenden Gebäudes, um dem Stadion größere Sichtbarkeit und Offenheit zu verschaffen. Regenwassernutzung sowie die Pflanzung einer brackwasserverträglichen Rasenart tragen dazu bei, den Wasserverbrauch des Komplexes zu minimieren. Für den Entwurf wurden soweit wie möglich Materialien aus der Region verwendet, wobei Erdbeben- und Wirbelsturmrisiken berücksichtigt werden mussten. Bei der Haupttribüne entschied man sich für einen geschwungenen Kasten mit schlichtem Verblendsystem. Große Aufmerksamkeit wurde auf den Spielerpavillon verwendet, sodass der Aufenthalt im Kensington Oval nicht nur für Besucher, sondern auch für die Sportler so angenehm wie möglich ist.

Le programme original était une étude de faisabilité pour la rénovation du **KENSINGTON OVAL CRICKET GROUND** en un terrain de cricket moderne, notamment pour accueillir la finale de la Coupe du monde de cricket de 2007. Arup Associates ont préféré maintenir un ensemble de tribunes séparées plutôt que d'opter pour un stade classique. La conception des tribunes répond à trois principes de base : offrir de l'ombre aux places assises, laisser passer une certaine quantité de lumière à travers le toit pour réduire les écarts de luminosité et contribuer au rafraîchissement de l'air en maximisant son écoulement. L'État a acquis les propriétés proches du site « enclavé » de l'installation existante, pour donner au stade plus de visibilité et un accès plus facile. La récupération des eaux de pluie et une pelouse résistante aux eaux saumâtres permettent de réduire sa consommation d'eau. Des matériaux produits localement ont été utilisés partout où le permettait le projet qui devait également prendre en compte les risques sismique et cyclonique. Une forme de boîte arrondie avec un système de revêtement simplifié a été utilisée pour les tribunes principales, et le pavillon des joueurs a été soigneusement conçu de manière à rendre l'usage du Kensington Oval agréable aux spectateurs comme aux athlètes.

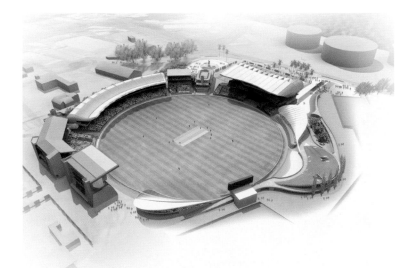

Drawings show the overall layout of the complex (left) as well as document factors such as airflow. To the right, at night, the Oval has a futuristic appearance, highlighted by its curving, segmented canopy.

Zeichnungen verdeutlichen die Gesamtanlage des Komplexes (links) und dokumentieren die Luftströme. Rechts Ansichten des Oval-Stadions, das nachts geradezu futuristisch wirkt, besonders wegen seines geschwungenen, mehrteiligen Tribünendachs.

Les dessins montrent l'ensemble du complexe (à gauche) et fournissent des informations sur des facteurs comme l'écoulement de l'air. Page de droite, la nuit, l'aspect futuriste de l'Oval est souligné par son toit incurvé et segmenté.

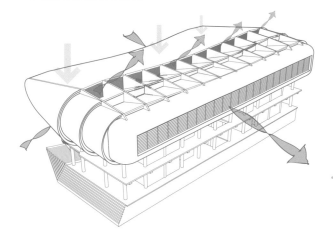

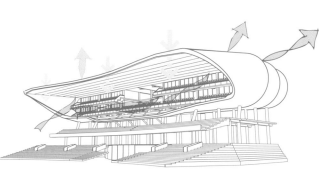

ASSADI + PULIDO

Felipe Assadi + Francisca Pulido Architects
Carmencita 262, oficina 202
Las Condes, Santiago
Chile

Tel: +56 234 5558
E-mail: info@assadi.cl
Web: www.felipeassadi.com

Felipe Assadi was born in 1971. He received his degree in Architecture from the Finis Terrae University (Santiago, 1996) and his M.Arch degree from the Pontificia Universidad Católica de Chile in Santiago in 2006. He teaches at the Andrés Bello University in Santiago. Francisca Pulido also received her degree in Architecture from the Finis Terrae University in 1996 and teaches at Andrés Bello University. They created **ASSADI + PULIDO** in 1999 on an informal basis, incorporating the firm in 2006. Their work, concentrated on private residences for the moment, includes the Schmitz House (Calera de Tango, Santiago, 2001); Bar El Tubo (Lima, Peru, 2003); Park Theater (Santiago, 2004); 20x20 House (Santiago, 2005); Gatica House (Rancagua, 2006); Russo Club (Talca, 2006); Serrano House (Santiago, 2006); Deck House (Santiago, 2006); Guthrie House (Santiago, 2007); as well as the Chilean Architecture Biennale 2008 (Santiago, 2008, published here), all in Chile unless stated otherwise.

Felipe Assadi wurde 1971 geboren. Er machte seinen Abschluss in Architektur an der Universidad Finis Terrae (Santiago, 1996) und 2006 seinen M. Arch. an der Pontificia Universidad Católica de Chile in Santiago. Er unterrichtet an der Universidad Andrés Bello in Santiago. Auch Francisca Pulido schloss ihr Architekturstudium 1996 an der Universidad Finis Terrae ab und lehrt an der Universidad Andrés Bello. 1999 gründeten sie **ASSADI + PULIDO** zunächst auf informeller Basis, die offizielle Firmengründung folgte 2006. Ihr Werk, das sich bislang auf private Wohnbauten konzentriert, umfasst u. a. die Casa Schmitz (Calera de Tango, Santiago, 2001), die Bar El Tubo (Lima, Peru, 2003–04), das Teatro del Parque (Santiago, 2004), das Haus 20 x 20 (Santiago, 2005), die Casa Gatica (Rancagua, 2006), den Klub Russo (Talca, 2006), die Casa Serrano (Santiago, 2006), die Casa Deck (Alto Rungue, Santiago, 2006), die Casa Guthrie (Santiago, 2007) sowie Bauten für die chilenische Architekturbiennale 2008 (Santiago, 2008, hier vorgestellt), alle in Chile, sofern nicht anders vermerkt.

Felipe Assadi est né en 1971. Il obtient sa licence en architecture à l'université Finis Terrae (Santiago, 1996) et son master (M. Arch.) à l'Université pontificale catholique du Chili, à Santiago en 2006. Il enseigne à l'université Andrés Bello, à Santiago. Francisca Pulido obtient également son diplôme d'architecte à l'université Finis Terrae en 1996, et enseigne également à l'université Andrés Bello. Ils débutent leur agence **ASSADI + PULIDO** en 1999 sur une base informelle, avant de la constituer en société en 2006. Leurs réalisations, qui concernent pour l'instant surtout des résidences privées, incluent la maison Schmitz (Calera de Tango, Santiago, 2001) ; le bar El Tubo (Lima, Pérou, 2003) ; le Théâtre Park (Santiago, 2004) ; la maison 20x20 (Santiago, 2005) ; la maison Gatica (Rancagua, 2006) ; le club Russo (Talca, 2006) ; la maison Serrano (Santiago, 2006) ; la maison Deck (Santiago, 2006) ; et la maison Guthrie (Santiago, 2007) ; ainsi qu'un pavillon temporaire pour la Biennale chilienne d'architecture 2008 (Santiago, 2008, publié ici), tous situés au Chili sauf mention contraire.

CHILEAN ARCHITECTURE BIENNALE 2008

Santiago, Chile, 2008

Area: 1500 m² (temporary pavilion 400 m²). Client: Colegio de Arquitectos
Cost: not disclosed

The 16th Architecture Biennale was to be held in Santiago's Museum of Contemporary Art (MAC). Though not large enough to house the event, the museum presented advantages in terms of its location and accessibility. A 400-square-meter temporary pavilion was added, with proportions roughly similar to those of the central space of the MAC. Aluzinc strip was used for the exterior of the pavilion, as well as InterfaceFLOR carpets made up with 80 percent recycled fiber, permitting the reuse of almost all the materials employed in the Biennale pavilion. Corrugated cardboard blocks 160 centimeters high and 40 centimeters thick were used to display the works to be exhibited in the MAC. Relying on their physical mass to hold them in place, these blocks can easily be reconfigured for other uses, or other planned locations, in the provinces for example. An international conference held in the central courtyard of the MAC was made possible through the use of compressed blocks of wood agglomerate provided by the Chilean forest-products company Masisa, again confirming the principle of 100 percent reuse of the materials employed.

Ursprünglich sollte die 16. Architekturbiennale im Museum für zeitgenössische Kunst (MAC) stattfinden. Trotz Platzmangel bot der Standort Vorteile aufgrund seiner Lage und Erreichbarkeit. Ein 400 m² großer temporärer Pavillon wurde gebaut, dessen Proportionen in etwa denen des MAC-Hauptgebäudes entsprechen. Das Äußere des Pavillons wurde mit Streifen aus Aluzink verblendet. Auch InterfaceFLOR-Auslegeware mit bis zu 80 Prozent Recyclingfaser kam zum Einsatz, sodass fast sämtliche Baumaterialien des Biennalepavillons wiederverwertbar sind. Blöcke aus Wellpappe, 160 cm hoch und 40 cm tief, dienten zur Präsentation der ausgestellten Arbeiten. Die durch ihre Masse stabilen Blöcke lassen sich problemlos für andere Zwecke oder an anderen Ausstellungsorten in der Provinz verwenden. Außerdem wurden komprimierte Blöcke aus Pressholz eingesetzt, sodass eine internationale Konferenz im zentralen Innenhof des MAC veranstaltet werden konnte. Die Blöcke wurden von der chilenischen Holzbaufirma Masisa zur Verfügung gestellt, das verwendete Material war zu 100 Prozent wiederverwertbar.

La XVIᵉ Biennale d'architecture devait se tenir au Musée d'art contemporain (MAC). En dépit de sa taille insuffisante pour un tel événement, le musée offrait les avantages de sa situation et sa facilité d'accès. Un pavillon temporaire de dimensions assez semblables à celles de l'espace central du MAC lui fut ajouté. L'utilisation d'Aluzinc en bande pour l'extérieur et de moquettes InterfaceFLOR constituées à 80 % de fibres recyclées, a permis la réutilisation de la quasi totalité des matériaux employés pour le pavillon de la Biennale. Des blocs en carton ondulé de 160 centimètres de hauteur et de 40 centimètres d'épaisseur furent utilisés pour l'exposition des œuvres à l'intérieur du MAC. Ces blocs, qui se maintiennent en place sous l'effet de leur propre masse, sont facilement réutilisables pour d'autres applications, ou sur d'autres sites prévus en province, par exemple. Un colloque international a pu se tenir dans la cour centrale du MAC grâce à l'utilisation de blocs de bois aggloméré comprimés produits par la compagnie chilienne de produits forestiers Masisa, confirmant le principe d'un emploi de matériaux recyclables à 100 %.

Seen in the image to the left and the elevation drawing below, the Biennale pavilion contrasts markedly with its Neo-classical neighbor. Sitting lightly on the ground, it declares its difference openly.

Wie links im Bild und im Aufriss unten zu sehen, kontrastiert der Biennale-Pavillon auffällig mit seinem klassizistischen Nachbargebäude. Der scheinbar leicht über dem Baugrund schwebende Pavillon zeigt seine Verschiedenartigkeit ganz offen.

Sur la photo à gauche et l'élévation ci-dessous, le pavillon de la Biennale contraste avec son voisin néo-classique. Délicatement posé sur le sol, il affirme sa différence.

Using a tubular metal structure the architects make inventive use of the light and space of the pavilion.

Mithilfe einer Metallgerüstkonstruktion gelingt es den Architekten, auf ungewöhnliche Weise mit Licht und Raum zu arbeiten.

Grâce à une structure métallique tubulaire, les architectes font une utilisation inventive de la lumière et de l'espace du pavillon.

Corrugated cardboard blocks seen in the drawing and photo below are deployed to allow the exhibition of the works. Above, an entrance bridge and a view into the building at night.

Blöcke aus Wellpappe, unten im Bild und in der Zeichnung zu sehen, dienen der Präsentation der ausgestellten Arbeiten. Oben eine Zugangsbrücke und ein nächtlicher Blick in den Pavillon.

Des blocs en carton ondulé, visibles sur les dessins et les photos ci-dessous sont déployés pour l'accrochage des œuvres exposées. Ci-dessus, une passerelle d'accès et une vue nocturne de l'intérieur du bâtiment.

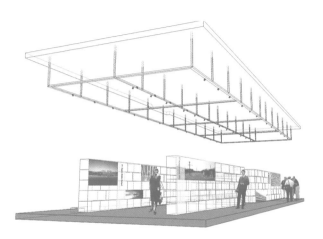

The Lantern ▶

ATELIER OSLO + AWP

Atelier Oslo / A. Mogata 6C / 0464 Oslo / Norway / Tel: +47 21 66 34 22
E-mail: jonas@www.atelieroslo.no / Web: www.atelieroslo.no
AWP / 25 rue Henry Monnier / 75009 Paris / France / Tel: +33 1 46 54 10 03
E-mail: awp@awp.fr / Web: www.awp.fr

ATELIER OSLO was created in 2006 by Nils Ole Bae Brandtzæg (born in 1975), Thomas Liu (born in 1978), Marius Mowe (born in 1973), and Jonas Norsted (born in 1973). The partners all graduated from the Oslo School of Architecture, and worked in the offices of Sverre Fehn, Knut Hjeltnes, Jensen & Skodvin, and Lund Hagem. They were awarded First Prize in a competition for a residential high rise (Lervig, with Lund Hagem, 2008). They completed the Leilighetshotell Medical Spa (Verdens Ende, Tjøme, in collaboration with Lund Hagem, 2007); the Skihotel (Geilo, in collaboration with Lund Hagem); and The Lantern (Sandnes, with AWP, 2008–09, published here), all in Norway. Atelier Oslo was nominated for The Lantern, with AWP, for the 2009 Mies van der Rohe Award. **AWP** was created in 2003. The three current partners are Matthias Armengaud, an architect and urban planner (ENSA Versailles), Marc Armengaud, a philosopher (Paris I, Sorbonne), and Alessandra Cianchetta, an architect and landscape architect ("La Sapienza," Rome; ETSA Barcelona; ETSA Madrid). Their focus is on a renewed relationship between master planning, landscape architecture, and architecture. Alessandra Cianchetta explains that AWP was the team leader in the competition phase for The Lantern, and that Atelier Oslo was the team leader for the development and construction phase of the project. The project is the result of a "co-conception." The work of AWP includes the French Pavilion for the Architecture Biennale in São Paulo (Brazil, 2007); the landscape design for the Museum of Modern Art of Villeneuve D'Ascq (France, 2010); and enlargement of a water purification plant (Évry, France, 2003–12).

ATELIER OSLO wurde 2006 von Nils Ole Bae Brandtzæg (geboren 1975), Thomas Liu (geboren 1978), Marius Mowe (geboren 1973) und Jonas Norsted (geboren 1973) gegründet. Alle Partner schlossen ihr Studium an der Oslo School of Architecture ab und waren für die Büros von Sverre Fehn, Knut Hjeltnes, Jensen & Skodvin und Lund Hagem tätig. Das Team gewann den ersten Preis in einem Wettbewerb für ein Wohnhochhaus (Lervig, mit Lund Hagem, 2008). Darüber hinaus realisierten die Architekten das Leilighetshotell Medical Spa (Verdens Ende, Tjøme, in Zusammenarbeit mit Lund Hagem, 2007), das Skihotel (Geilo, ebenfalls mit Lund Hagem) sowie das Projekt Lantern (Sandnes, mit AWP, 2008–09, hier vorgestellt), alle in Norwegen. Für Lantern wurden Atelier Oslo + AWP 2009 für den Mies-van-der-Rohe-Preis nominiert. **AWP** wurde 2003 gegründet. Aktuell hat das Büro mit dem Architekten und Stadtplaner Matthias Armengaud (ENSA Versailles), dem Philosophen Marc Armengaud (Paris I, Sorbonne) und der Architektin und Landschaftsarchitektin Alessandra Cianchetta („La Sapienza", Rom, ETSA Barcelona, ETSA Madrid) drei Partner. Ihr Hauptanliegen ist es, ein neues Verhältnis zwischen Masterplanung, Landschaftsarchitektur und Architektur zu gestalten. Alessandra Cianchetta zufolge übernahm AWP die Teamleitung für das Lantern-Projekt während des Wettbewerbs, während Atelier Oslo die Entwicklungs- und Bauphase leitete. Somit ist das Projekt Ergebnis einer „Co-Entwicklung". Zu den Arbeiten von AWP zählen der französische Pavillon für die Architekturbiennale in São Paulo (Brasilien, 2007), die Landschaftsgestaltung für das Museum für moderne Kunst in Villeneuve d'Ascq (Frankreich, 2010) sowie die Erweiterung einer Wasseraufbereitungsanlage (Evry, Frankreich, 2003–12).

ATELIER OSLO a été créé en 2006 par Nils Ole Bae Brandtzæg (né en 1975), Thomas Liu (né en 1978), Marius Mowe (né en 1973) et Jonas Norsted (né en 1973). Les associés sont tous diplômés de l'École d'architecture d'Oslo et ont travaillé dans les agences de Sverre Fehn, Knut Hjeltnes, Jensen & Skodvin, et Lund Hagem. Ils ont remporté le premier prix d'un concours pour une tour d'habitations (Lervig, avec Lund Hagem, 2008), ont réalisé l'hôtel thermal Leilighetshotell (Verdens Ende, Tjøme, en collaboration avec Lund Hagem, 2007) ; l'hôtel Skihotel (Geilo, en collaboration avec Lund Hagem) ; et la Lanterne (Sandnes, avec AWP, 2008–09, projet publié ici), tous situés en Norvège. Atelier Oslo, a été sélectionné, avec AWP, pour la Lanterne, pour le prix Mies van der Rohe 2009. **AWP** a été créé en 2003. Les trois collaborateurs actuels sont Matthias Armengaud, architecte et urbaniste (ENSA Versailles), Marc Armengaud, philosophe (Paris I, Sorbonne) et Alessandra Cianchetta, architecte et architecte paysagiste (« La Sapienza », Rome, ETSA Barcelone, ETSA Madrid). Ils mettent l'accent sur un nouveau type de relations entre plan directeur, architecture du paysage et architecture. Alessandra Cianchetta explique qu'AWP a joué un rôle moteur dans la phase de compétition pour le projet de la Lanterne, et Atelier Oslo dans sa phase de développement et de construction. Ce projet est le fruit d'une « co-conception ». Les projets d'AWP incluent le pavillon de la France de la Biennale d'architecture de São Paulo (Brésil, 2007) ; le traitement paysager du Musée d'art moderne de Villeneuve d'Ascq (France, 2010) ; et l'agrandissement de la station d'épuration d'Évry (Évry, France, 2003–12).

THE LANTERN

Sandnes, Norway, 2008–09

Area: 140 m². Client: Sandnes Municipality. Cost: €1.1 million
Team: Atelier Oslo—Thomas Liu (Project leader), Nils Ole Bae Brandtzæg, Marius Mowe, Jonas Norsted, Bosheng Gan
AWP—Matthias Armengaud, Marc Armengaud, Alessandra Cianchetta, Arnaud Hirschauer

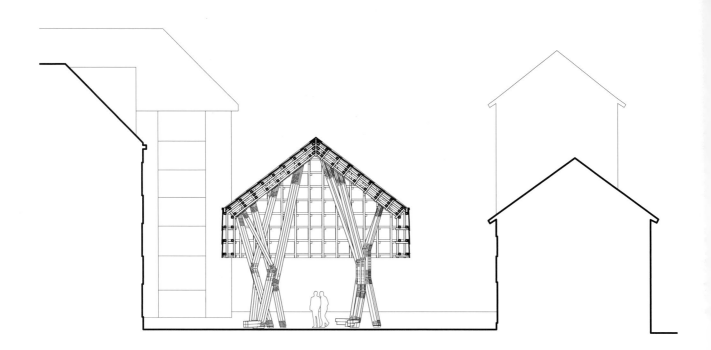

Subsequent to the selection of Sandnes and Stavanger as the European cultural capitals for 2008, a series of competitions called Norwegian Wood was initiated, to promote "contemporary, sustainable timber architecture." The city of Sandnes sought, in this context, to create a canopy over a small pedestrian square. The aim was to revitalize the square and to provide a location for a market, informal concerts, or simple meetings. The competition for a structure intended to be visible from a certain distance was won by Atelier Oslo and the French firm AWP. The design, completed in November 2008, is meant to echo a traditional wooden house, whose transparency allows it to glow from within at night, hence the name—**THE LANTERN**. 90x90-millimeter laminated pine elements are used for most of the structure with steel reinforcement for the joints. Glass panels mounted directly on the wood in an overlapping pattern replace the traditional slate roof. Individual "sculptural" oak columns, which turn into benches at the juncture with the ground, hold up the structure.

Nach der gemeinsamen Ernennung der norwegischen Städte Sandnes und Stavanger zur Europäischen Kulturhauptstadt 2008 wurde eine Reihe von Wettbewerben unter dem Arbeitstitel „Norwegian Wood" zur Förderung „zeitgenössischer, nachhaltiger Holzarchitektur" initiiert. In diesem Zusammenhang beschloss die Stadt Sandnes, eine Pavillonkonstruktion auf einem kleinen Platz der örtlichen Fußgängerzone zu realisieren. Ziel war es, den Platz neu zu beleben und einen Standort für Märkte, spontane Konzerte oder kleinere Versammlungen zu schaffen. Den Wettbewerb für die Konstruktion, die auch aus einiger Entfernung sichtbar sein sollte, konnten Atelier Oslo und das französische Büro AWP gemeinsam für sich entscheiden. Der im November 2008 fertiggestellte Bau erinnert an ein traditionelles Holzhaus, das dank der transparenten Konstruktion nachts von innen leuchtet – daher der Name „**LATERNE**". Konstruktives Hauptelement sind 90 x 90 mm starke Kiefernschichtholzstreben mit stahlverstärkten Verbindungsstücken. Statt eines traditionellen Schieferdachs wurden einander überlappende Glasplatten direkt auf das Holz montiert. „Skulpturale" Eichenholzpfeiler, die sich am Boden zu Bänken verbreitern, stützen den Bau.

Le choix de Sandnes et Stavanger comme capitales culturelles européennes 2008 a donné lieu au lancement d'un ensemble de concours baptisé Norwegian Wood, destiné à promouvoir une « architecture en bois contemporaine et durable ». Dans ce contexte, la ville de Sandnes souhaitait couvrir une petite place piétonne. Le but était de revitaliser la place en offrant un lieu pour un marché, des concerts informels ou de simples rencontres. Ce sont Atelier Oslo et l'agence française AWP qui ont remporté le concours pour une structure qui devait être visible de loin. Le projet, achevé en novembre 2008, évoque une maison en bois traditionnelle. Sa transparence lui permet d'irradier de l'intérieur dans la nuit, d'où son nom, **LANTERNEN (LA LANTERNE)**. Des éléments en pin lamellé de 90 x 90 millimètres sont utilisés pour la majorité du bâtiment, avec des renforts en acier pour les joints. Des panneaux vitrés, montés directement sur le bois et se chevauchant, remplacent le traditionnel toit d'ardoise. La structure est supportée par des colonnes « sculpturales » individuelles en chêne, formant des banquettes au niveau du sol.

A drawing (left) and two photos show the full structure in its setting, echoing the sloped roofs of neighboring structures.

Eine Zeichnung (linke Seite) und zwei Fotos zeigen den Bau, der die Satteldächer der Nachbarbauten aufgreift, in seinem baulichen Umfeld.

Un dessin (page de gauche) et deux photos montrent l'implantation de l'ensemble du bâtiment répondant aux toits en pente des édifices voisins.

AUER+WEBER+ASSOZIIERTE

Auer+Weber+Assoziierte
Haussmannstr. 103a
70188 Stuttgart
Germany

Tel: +49 711 268 40 40
Fax: +49 711 26 84 04 88
E-mail: stuttgart@auer-weber.de
Web: www.auer-weber.de

FRITZ AUER, born in Tübingen, Germany, in 1933, became a Partner in the firm of Behnisch & Partner in 1966 and created the office Auer+Weber in 1980. **CARLO WEBER** was born in Saarbrücken, Germany, in 1934 and also attended the Technical University of Stuttgart before going to the Beaux-Arts in Paris. Like Auer, he became a Partner at Behnisch & Partner in 1966. They have worked extensively on urban renewal in Bonn, Stuttgart, and other cities. They completed the University Library of Magdeburg (2003); the Welle department store in Bielefeld (2003); while more recent work includes an office building (Altstadt-Palais, Munich, 2008); additions and alterations to the Olympic Halls (Munich, 2008); ECE Stadtgalerie, Façade (Passau, 2005–08, published here); the Central Bus Terminal in Munich (2009); Chenshan Botanical Garden (Shanghai, China, 2009); and the Martinsried Campus (Munich, 2009). Current work includes a Youth Center and Hostel (Bad Cannstatt, 2010); the Archeological Museum in Chemnitz (2011); General Archive of Baden-Württemberg (Karlsruhe, 2012); and the extension for the 2nd Base of Operation of the Federal Ministry of Defense (Berlin, 2012), all in Germany unless stated otherwise. The firm, with offices in Munich and Stuttgart, currently employs 90 to 100 persons and includes Managing Partners Moritz Auer, Philipp Auer, Jörn Scholz, Achim Söding, and Stephan Suxdorf.

FRITZ AUER, 1933 in Tübingen geboren, wurde 1966 Teilhaber bei Behnisch & Partner und gründete 1980 sein Büro Auer+Weber. **CARLO WEBER** wurde 1934 in Saarbrücken geboren und studierte wie Auer an der Technischen Hochschule Stuttgart, bevor er an die École Nationale Supérieure des Beaux-Arts in Paris wechselte. Wie Auer wurde auch er 1966 Partner bei Behnisch & Partner. Das Büro war maßgeblich an Stadterneuerungsmaßnahmen in Bonn, Stuttgart und anderen Städten beteiligt und baute die Universitätsbibliothek Magdeburg (2003) und das Welle-Haus in Bielefeld (2003). Jüngere Projekte sind u. a. ein Bürogebäude (Altstadt-Palais, München, 2008), An- und Umbauten an den Olympiabauten (München, 2008), die Fassade der ECE-Stadtgalerie (Passau, 2005–08, hier vorgestellt), der Zentrale Omnibusbahnhof in München (2009), der Botanische Garten Chenshan (Shanghai, China, 2009) sowie der Campus Martinsried (München, 2009). Aktuelle Arbeiten des Büros sind u. a. ein Jugendzentrum und -hotel (Bad Cannstatt, 2010), das Archäologische Museum Chemnitz (2011), das Generallandesarchiv Baden-Württemberg (Karlsruhe, 2012) sowie die Erweiterung des zweiten Dienstsitzes des Bundesministeriums der Verteidigung in Berlin (2012). Die Firma unterhält Büros in München und Stuttgart und beschäftigt derzeit 90 bis 100 Mitarbeiter, darunter die geschäftsführenden Teilhaber Moritz Auer, Philipp Auer, Jörn Scholz, Achim Söding und Stephan Suxdorf.

FRITZ AUER, né à Tübingen, en Allemagne, en 1933, devient associé de l'agence Behnisch & Partner en 1966 et crée l'agence Auer+Weber en 1980. **CARLO WEBER** est né à Sarrebruck, en Allemagne, en 1934, et a également étudié à l'Université technique de Stuttgart, puis aux Beaux-Arts de Paris. Comme Auer, il devient associé de Behnisch & Partner en 1966. Ils ont beaucoup travaillé dans le domaine de la rénovation urbaine à Bonn, Stuttgart, et ailleurs. Ils ont réalisé la librairie universitaire de Magdeburg (2003) ; le grand magasin Welle de Bielefeld (2003), tandis que des projets plus récents incluent un immeuble de bureaux (Altstadt-Palais, Munich, 2008) ; des extensions et des modifications des salles olympiques de Munich (Munich, 2008) ; la façade du Centre commercial « ECE Stadtgalerie » (Passau, 2005–08, publié ici) ; la gare routière centrale de Munich (2009) ; le jardin botanique Chenshan (Shanghai, Chine, 2009) ; et le campus Martinsried (Munich, 2009). Leurs projets en cours incluent une auberge de jeunesse (Bad Cannstatt, 2010) ; le Musée archéologique de Chemnitz (2011) ; les Archives générales du Bade-Wurtemberg (Karlsruhe, 2012) ; et une extension pour la 2e base d'opération du ministère fédéral de la Défense (Berlin, 2012), tous situés en Allemagne sauf mention contraire. La société, avec ses bureaux à Munich et Stuttgart, emploie actuellement 90 à 100 personnes, incluant les associés Moritz Auer, Philipp Auer, Jörn Scholz, Achim Söding, et Stephan Suxdorf.

ECE STADTGALERIE

Passau, Germany, 2005–08

Address: Bahnhofstr. 1, 94032 Passau, Germany, +49 851 851 79 70, www.stadt-galerie-passau.de
Area: 5000 m² (façade). Client: ECE Project Management, Hamburg. Cost: € 4 million

The architects won a 2005 competition for this project, which consisted in rethinking the **FAÇADE OF THE ECE SHOPPING CENTER**, located near the center of Passau, a city of 50 000 inhabitants in Lower Bavaria. The concept seeks to integrate the rather large volume of the center into a smaller scale urban environment. Rather than employing a "traditional monolithic external wall," Auer+Weber resolved the issue by creating two layers—an internal functional skin and an external "display" layer. They explain: "In the direction of the inner city, the building skin demonstrates a clear plasticity with vertical emphasis. Alongside the railway the plasticity is held back for the benefit of a dynamic appearance and horizontal emphasis."

2005 gewann das Büro den Wettbewerb für dieses Projekt, bei dem es um die Neugestaltung der **FASSADE DES ECE-EINKAUFSZENTRUMS** ging. Das Zentrum liegt unweit der Stadtmitte von Passau, einer Stadt mit rund 50 000 Einwohnern in Niederbayern. Konzeptuell ging es dem Team darum, das eher großmaßstäbliche Volumen des Einkaufszentrums in sein kleinteiligeres urbanes Umfeld einzubinden. Statt eine „traditionelle monolithischen Außenwand" zu entwerfen, lösten Auer+Weber dieses Problem, indem sie zwei Schichten schufen – eine innere „Funktionsschicht" und eine äußere „Schauschicht". Sie führen aus: „In Richtung Innenstadt zeigt die Hüllschicht eine deutlich plastische Ausformung und betont die Vertikalität. Entlang der Bahnlinie wird die Plastizität zugunsten einer dynamischen und horizontalen Betonung zurückgenommen."

Les architectes ont remporté en 2005 un concours pour ce projet de conception d'une nouvelle **FAÇADE POUR LE CENTRE COMMERCIAL « ECE »**, proche du centre-ville de Passau, une agglomération de 50 000 habitants située en Basse-Bavière. Le concept vise à intégrer le volume assez imposant du centre dans un environnement urbain d'échelle moindre. Plutôt que d'utiliser le « traditionnel mur extérieur monolithique », Auer+Weber ont résolu le problème en créant deux couches – une peau interne fonctionnelle et une couche externe de « vitrine ». Ils expliquent qu'« en direction du centre-ville, la peau du bâtiment montre une plasticité accentuant clairement la verticalité. Le long de la voie ferrée, la plasticité est retenue au profit d'une apparence dynamique accentuant l'horizontalité ».

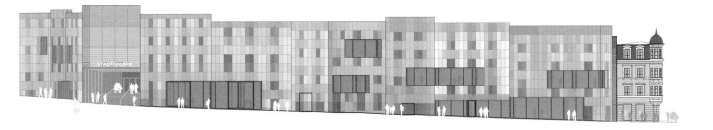

The drawing above and two photos show how the architects have given the ECE an appearance not unlike that of a row of houses, with varied color schemes and window placements.

Wie die Zeichnung oben und die beiden Abbildungen zeigen, gaben die Architekten dem ECE ein Erscheinungsbild, das einer Reihenhauszeile ähnelt. Unterschiedliche Farben und Fensterhöhen prägen das Bild.

Le dessin ci-dessus et les deux photos montrent comment les architectes ont donné à l'ECE l'apparence d'une rangée de maisons, en variant agencement des couleurs et emplacement des fenêtres.

b720 ARQUITECTOS

b720 Arquitectos
Tarradellas 123, 9ª
08029 Barcelona
Spain

Tel: +34 93 363 79 79
Fax: +34 93 363 01 39
E-mail: fermin.vazquez@b720.com
Web: www.b720.com

Fermín Vázquez Huarte-Mendicoa was born in Madrid in 1961. He is the Managing Partner of **b720 ARQUITECTOS**, a firm he created in 1997. He received his diploma in Architecture from the ETSA of Madrid. He has taught at the ETSA of Barcelona and the École d'Architecture et de Paysage of Bordeaux. He is a Professor at the European University of Madrid (UIM). b720 Arquitectos currently employs 60 people in offices in Barcelona and Madrid. Among its recently completed projects are the corporate headquarters of Indra (Barcelona, 2006); the America's Cup Building (Valencia, 2007); the renovation of Plaza del Torico (Teruel, 2006–07, published here); and La Mola, a hotel and conference center in Terrassa (Barcelona, 2008). Among current projects are the airport of Lleida (2009); the construction of a Casino (Lloret, Girona, 2010); the remodeling of the College of Quantity Surveyors of Alicante (completion date undefined); and social housing in Mieres (Asturias, completion date undefined), all in Spain. In 2008, b720 Arquitectos won the competition for the construction of the new Encants Market in Barcelona, an office tower in Seville, and the new World Trade Center of Igualada (Barcelona).

Fermín Vázquez Huarte-Mendicoa wurde 1961 in Madrid geboren. Er ist geschäftsführender Partner von **b720 ARQUITECTOS**, dem Büro, das er 1997 gründete. Sein Architekturdiplom erhielt er an der ETSA Madrid. Er nahm Lehraufträge an der ETSA Barcelona sowie der École d'Architecture et de Paysage in Bordeaux wahr und ist derzeit Professor an der Universidad Europea de Madrid (UEM). Gegenwärtig beschäftigt b720 Arquitectos 60 Mitarbeiter in seinen Büros in Barcelona und Madrid. Zu den unlängst fertiggestellten Projekten zählen die Hauptniederlassung von Indra (Barcelona, 2006), das America's-Cup-Gebäude (Valencia, 2007), die Sanierung der Plaza del Torico in Teruel (2006–07, hier vorgestellt) sowie La Mola, ein Hotel und Kongresszentrum in Terrassa (Barcelona, 2008). Aktuelle Projekte sind u. a. der Flughafen Lleida (2009), ein Kasino (Lloret, Girona, 2010), die Erweiterung des Colegio Oficial de Aparejadores y Arquitectos Técnicos de Alicante (Termin der Fertigstellung offen) sowie ein Projekt des sozialen Wohnungsbaus in Mieres (Asturien, Termin der Fertigstellung offen), alle in Spanien. 2008 gewann b720 Arquitectos die Wettbewerbe für den Neubau des Mercado dels Encants in Barcelona, ein Bürohochhaus in Sevilla sowie das neue World Trade Center in Igualada (Barcelona).

Fermín Vázquez Huarte-Mendicoa est né à Madrid en 1961. Il est associé gérant de **b720 ARQUITECTOS**, l'agence qu'il a créée en 1997. Il a obtenu son diplôme d'architecte à l'ETSA de Madrid. Il a enseigné à l'ETSA de Barcelone et à l'École d'architecture et de paysage de Bordeaux. Il est professeur à l'université européenne de Madrid (UIM). L'agence b720 Arquitectos emploie actuellement soixante personnes dans ses bureaux de Barcelone et Madrid. Ses projets récents incluent le siège de la société Indra (Barcelone, 2006) ; l'immeuble America's Cup (Valence, 2007) ; la rénovation de la Plaza del Torico à Teruel (2006–07, publié ici) ; et l'hôtel et Centre de conférences La Mola, à Terrassa (Barcelone, 2008). Ses projets en cours incluent l'aéroport de Lleida (2009) ; la construction d'un casino (Lloret, Gérone, 2010) ; la restructuration de l'École de métreurs-vérificateurs d'Alicante (date d'achèvement indéterminée) ; des logements sociaux à Mieres (Asturies, date d'achèvement indéterminée), tous situés en Espagne. En 2008, b720 Arquitectos a remporté le concours pour la construction du nouveau marché Del Encants, à Barcelone, pour une tour de bureaux à Séville, et pour le nouveau Centre de commerce international d'Igualada (Barcelone).

PLAZA DEL TORICO REFURBISHMENT

Teruel, Spain, 2006–07

Address: Plaza del Torico, 44001 Teruel, Spain
Area: 3722 m². Client: Sociedad Municipal Urban Teruel. Cost: €6.5 million

This project concerned the renovation of the 1799 square meters comprising the triangular area of the **PLAZA DEL TORICO**, and the 1047 square meters of arcades that surround it. Paving stones in basalt were replaced, and the use of existing old cisterns below grade for museum purposes envisaged. The architects explain: "The intervention focuses on the complete renovation of the appearance of the square, its pavement, porches and façades, with a carefully designed lighting system. In addition, the planned recovery for public use of the cisterns under the square, elements of great value and artistic heritage, is part of the scope of the work." 1230 LED lamps capable of changing color were embedded in the surface of the square. The lighting of the buildings around the square was put in place following directives of the European Union concerning low-energy usage and low maintenance. Below grade, natural stone was used.

Das Projekt umfasst die Sanierung der 1799 m² großen, dreieckigen Fläche der **PLAZA DEL TORICO** sowie der Arkaden, die den Platz säumen, mit einer Fläche von 1047 m². Die alten Pflastersteine aus Basalt wurden ersetzt und die Nutzung der unterirdischen historischen Zisternen unter dem Platz für Museumszwecke vorgesehen. Die Architekten erläutern: „Schwerpunkt der Intervention ist die umfassende Sanierung des Platzes in seinem gesamten Erscheinungsbild einschließlich der Pflasterung, Toreingänge und Fassaden durch ein detailliert durchgeplantes Beleuchtungssystem. Hinzu kommt die geplante Erschließung der Zisternen unter dem Platz für die Öffentlichkeit – Baudenkmäler von hohem künstlerischen Wert." 1230 LED-Leuchten, die ihre Farbe wechseln können, wurden in die Oberfläche des Platzes eingelassen. Die Beleuchtung der Bauten um den Platz herum entspricht den Vorgaben der Europäischen Union zu niedrigem Energieverbrauch und geringem Wartungsaufwand. In den unterirdischen Bereichen kam Naturstein zum Einsatz.

Ce projet de rénovation concernait les 1799 mètres carrés du triangle de la **PLAZA DEL TORICO** et les 1047 mètres carrés de galeries qui l'entourent. Les pavés de basalte ont été remplacés et d'anciennes citernes souterraines reconverties en musée. Selon les architectes, « l'intervention porte sur l'entière rénovation de l'aspect de la place, ses pavés, ses porches et façades, avec un système d'éclairage soigneusement conçu. De plus, le projet de restitution à un usage public des citernes sous la place, éléments de grande valeur patrimoniale et artistique, contribue à l'envergure du projet ». Mille deux cent trente ampoules LED (diodes électroluminescentes) de couleur changeante ont été encastrées dans la surface de la place. L'éclairage des bâtiments bordant la place est conforme aux directives de l'Union européenne concernant les économies d'énergie et d'entretien. En sous-sol, la pierre naturelle a été utilisée.

Night views put an emphasis on the lighting of the buildings. Both varied and attractive, this lighting follows European low-energy directives.

Nächtliche Ansichten heben besonders die Beleuchtung der Gebäude am Platz hervor. Das abwechslungsreiche und attraktive Lichtkonzept entspricht europäischen Energiesparvorschriften.

Des vues de nuit mettent en évidence l'éclairage des bâtiments. Cet éclairage, à la fois varié et attrayant, suit les directives européennes sur la consommation d'énergie.

The abstract pattern of lighting on the surface of the square itself is discreet but implies an idea of movement and the public use of the space.

Das abstrakte Lichtmuster im Bodenpflaster gibt sich diskret, deutet jedoch zugleich Bewegung und die öffentliche Nutzung des Platzes an.

Le motif d'éclairage abstrait sur le sol de la place suggère discrètement une idée de mouvement et d'un espace ouvert à tous.

BEHNISCH ARCHITEKTEN

Rotebühlstr. 163a
70197 Stuttgart
Germany

Tel: +49 711 607720
Fax: +49 711 6077299
E-mail: ba@behnisch.com
Web: www.behnisch.com

STEFAN BEHNISCH was born in 1957 in Stuttgart. He studied Philosophy at the Philosophische Hochschule der Jesuiten, Munich (1976–79), Economics at the Ludwig Maximilian University, Munich, and Architecture at the University of Karlsruhe (1979–87). He worked at Stephen Woolley & Associates (Venice, California, 1984–85), and has been a Principal Partner at Behnisch since 1989. Born in Manchester in 1966, **DAVID COOK** studied Architecture at the Polytechnic in Manchester and obtained his diploma at the University of East London in 1992. Since 1993, he has been working with Behnisch Architekten and, since 2006, has been a Partner in the office. Together with Stefan Behnisch and Martin Haas, he has been heading the practice Behnisch Architekten since 2006. **MARTIN HAAS** was born in 1967 in Waldshut. After working as a cameraman, he began studying Architecture at the Technical University of Stuttgart in 1988, where he obtained his diploma in 1995. He studied at South Bank University, worked with Alan Brookes Assoc. in London, and produced advertising films. In 1995, he started working with Behnisch Architekten and has been a Partner in the firm since 2006. Recent work includes Thermal Baths (Bad Aibling, 2007); the Römerbad Thermal Spa Extension (Bad Kleinkirchheim, Carinthia, Austria, 2006–07, published here); the Kovner Residence (Sebastopol, California, USA, 2008); and the Deutsches Meeresmuseum "Ozeaneum" (Stralsund, 2008), in Germany unless stated otherwise.

STEFAN BEHNISCH wurde 1957 in Stuttgart geboren. Er studierte Philosophie an der Philosophischen Hochschule der Jesuiten, München (1976–79), Wirtschaftswissenschaften an der Ludwig-Maximilians-Universität München und Architektur an der Universität Karlsruhe (1979–87). Er arbeitete für Stephen Woolley & Associates (Venice, Kalifornien, 1984–85) und ist seit 1989 Hauptgesellschafter von Behnisch Architekten. **DAVID COOK** wurde 1966 in Manchester geboren, studierte Architektur an der Polytechnischen Hochschule Manchester und machte sein Diplom 1992 an der University of East London. Seit 1993 ist er für Behnisch Architekten tätig und dort seit 2006 Partner. Seit 2006 leitet er das Büro mit Stefan Behnisch und Martin Haas. **MARTIN HAAS** wurde 1967 in Waldshut geboren. Nach anfänglicher Tätigkeit als Kameramann studierte er ab 1988 Architektur an der Technischen Hochschule Stuttgart, wo er 1995 sein Diplom machte. Er studierte an der South Bank University, arbeitete für Alan Brookes Assoc. in London und produzierte Werbefilme. Seit 1995 ist er für Behnisch Architekten tätig und seit 2006 Partner. Neuere Projekte sind u. a. die Thermalbäder in Bad Aibling (2007), die Erweiterung des Römerbads (Bad Kleinkirchheim, Kärnten, Österreich, 2006–07, hier vorgestellt), die Kovner Residence (Sebastopol, Kalifornien, 2008) sowie das Deutsche Meeresmuseum „Ozeaneum" (Stralsund, 2008).

STEFAN BEHNISCH est né en 1957 à Stuttgart. Il a étudié la philosophie à l'École supérieure de philosophie des Jésuites, à Munich (1976–79), l'économie à l'université Ludwig-Maximilians de Munich, et l'architecture à l'université de Karlsruhe (1979–87). Il a travaillé chez Stephen Woolley & Associates (Venice, Californie, 1984–85), et est associé principal de l'agence Behnisch depuis 1989. Né à Manchester en 1966, **DAVID COOK** a étudié l'architecture à l'École polytechnique de Manchester et a obtenu son diplôme à l'université de Londres-Est en 1992. Depuis 1993, il collabore avec Behnisch Architekten, dont il devient associé en 2006. Avec Stefan Behnisch et Martin Haas, il dirige le cabinet Behnisch Architekten depuis 2006. **MARTIN HAAS** est né en 1967 à Waldshut. Après avoir travaillé comme cameraman, il étudie l'architecture à l'Université technique de Stuttgart en 1988, où il obtient son diplôme en 1995. Il étudie à la South Bank University, travaille avec Alan Brookes Associates à Londres, et réalise des films publicitaires. Il commence en 1995 à collaborer avec Behnisch Architekten dont il devient associé en 2006. Leurs réalisations récentes incluent les thermes de Bad Aibling (2007) ; l'extension de l'établissement thermal Römerbad (Bad Kleinkirchheim, Kärnten, Autriche, 2006–07, publié ici) ; la résidence Kovner (Sebastopol, Californie, États-Unis, 2008) ; et le Musée océanographique de Stralsund (2008), toutes situées en Allemagne sauf mention contraire.

RÖMERBAD THERMAL SPA EXTENSION

Bad Kleinkirchheim, Carinthia, Austria, 2006–07

Address: Dorfstr. 74, 9546 Bad Kleinkirchheim, Austria, +43 240 82 82 301, www.therme-badkleinkirchheim.at
Area: 10 260 m². Client: Bad Kleinkirchheimer Thermen GmbH. Cost: €15 million

The **RÖMERBAD THERMAL SPA** opened in 1979 and was considered at the time to be an innovative departure in thermal spa architecture. The multistory main hall brought Roman baths to mind. Behnisch Architekten and five other architects were commissioned in 2005 to propose ways to renew the facility, and to add a wellness and sauna area, a rest room, a beauty area, and a children's space. Service spaces are concentrated on the northern side of the complex, while views of a stream and the mountains are privileged on the south. Thirteen new sauna and steam rooms were added in three different "landscape" configurations. The first of these, the Romanum, is on the lower level and "reflects the bathing culture of Ancient Rome." Near the entrance area, the Noricum "reflects the regional level of the spa—the water, forests and cliffs…" The so-called Maximum area is at the top of the spa, and is connected by a glazed spiral passage to the treatment area. Roof terraces are "integrated in the comprehensive graphic design of the roof as a fifth façade." A high atrium is included in the new wellness wing, while a sauna garden, new façades, and the general palette of materials and colors used harmonizes with the preexisting structure. The architects conclude: "As the name itself suggests, the atmosphere and ambience of this 'Roman Bath' is achieved not by merely ornamental means but by conscious abstraction, based on a limited number of essentially sculptural forms and colors."

Die Architektur des **RÖMERBADS** galt 1979 bei seiner Eröffnung als ausgesprochen innovativ für Thermalbäder dieser Art – mit seiner mehrstöckigen Haupthalle erinnerte es an römische Bäder. 2005 bat man Behnisch Architekten sowie fünf andere Teams um einen Entwurf zur Sanierung des Komplexes und zum Anbau eines Wellness- und Saunabereichs, eines Ruheraums, eines Kosmetik- und eines Kinderbereichs. Betriebsräume wurden an der Nordseite des Komplexes gebündelt, während sich im Süden Ausblicke zum Fluss und zu den Bergen bieten. 13 neue Sauna- und Dampfbadeinrichtungen wurden hinzugefügt und verteilen sich über drei verschiedene „Landschaften". Das Romanum liegt auf der untersten Ebene und „spiegelt die Badekultur des alten Rom". Das Noricum hingegen befindet sich unweit des Eingangs und reflektiert „den regionalen Kontext des Spas – Wasser, Wälder und Felsen ..." Das sogenannte Maximum schließlich liegt auf der obersten Ebene der Therme und ist durch eine verglaste Wendeltreppe mit den Behandlungsräumen verbunden. Dachterrassen wurden bei der betont grafischen Gestaltung des Dachs als fünfte Fassade integriert. Im neuen Wellnessbereich wurde ein hohes Atrium realisiert. Der Saunagarten, die neuen Fassaden und die allgemeine Farb- und Materialpalette harmonisieren mit dem bestehenden Altbau. Die Architekten fassen zusammen: „Wie schon der Name sagt, werden Atmosphäre und Flair des ‚Römerbads' nicht allein durch dekorative Elemente geschaffen, sondern durch bewusste Abstraktion, auf Grundlage einer begrenzten Anzahl im Grunde skulpturaler Formen und Farben."

L'ÉTABLISSEMENT THERMAL RÖMERBAD était considéré, à l'époque de son inauguration en 1979, comme une rupture innovante dans le domaine de l'architecture thermale. Le bâtiment principal de plusieurs étages évoquait les thermes romains. Behnisch Architekten et cinq autres architectes ont été invités, en 2005, à proposer un projet de rénovation de l'établissement, en y ajoutant un espace bien-être et sauna, des toilettes, un espace beauté, et un espace enfants. Les espaces de service sont concentrés dans la partie nord du complexe, tandis que la partie sud privilégie la vue sur un cours d'eau et les montagnes. Treize nouveaux saunas et bains de vapeur ont été rajoutés dans trois différentes configurations «paysagères». La première, le Romanum, situé au niveau inférieur, «évoque la culture des bains de la Rome antique». Situé à proximité de l'entrée, le Noricum «évoque l'aspect régional des thermes – l'eau, les forêts et les à-pics… ». Enfin, le Maximum, situé au niveau supérieur, est relié à l'espace de soins par un passage vitré en spirale. Des toits-terrasses sont «intégrés dans la conception globale du dessin du toit comme une cinquième façade… ». Un atrium élevé est inclus dans la nouvelle aile de l'espace bien-être, tandis que le jardin du sauna, les nouvelles façades et la gamme générale des matériaux et des couleurs utilisés s'harmonisent avec le bâtiment préexistant. Les architectes concluent ainsi : «Comme le suggère leur nom, l'atmosphère et l'ambiance de ces "bains romains" ne sont pas simplement créés par le décor, mais par une abstraction consciente fondée sur un nombre restreint de formes sculpturales et de couleurs. »

A site plan (right) and photos of the Spa suggest a careful integration of the architecture into the topography of the location. A section drawing (below) brings to mind the form of a cruise ship.

Wie der Lageplan (rechts) und Ansichten der Therme zeigen, wurde die Architektur einfühlsam in die örtliche Topografie integriert. Der Gebäudeschnitt (unten) erinnert an ein Kreuzfahrtschiff.

Un plan de situation (à droite) et des photos de l'établissement thermal suggèrent une intégration attentive de l'architecture dans la topographie du lieu. Une coupe (ci-dessous) évoque la forme d'un bateau de croisière.

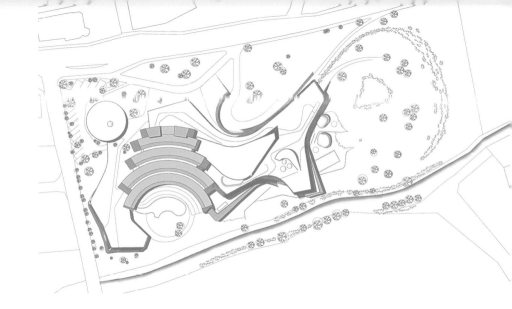

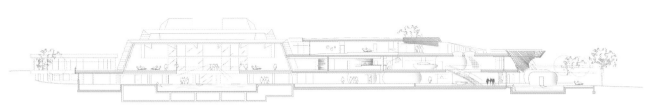

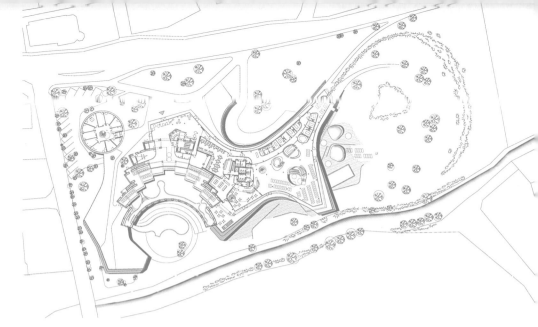

The sinuous curves of the baths and other architectural elements reinforce the impression that the building is almost carved out of its surroundings.

Die geschwungenen Formen der Becken und anderer architektonischer Elemente verstärken den Eindruck, das Gebäude sei geradezu aus seinem Umfeld herausgeschnitten worden.

Les courbes sinueuses des thermes et des autres éléments architecturaux renforcent l'impression d'un bâtiment presque sculpté dans son environnement.

BRUNO FIORETTI MARQUEZ

Bruno Fioretti Marquez Architekten
Erkelenzdamm 59–61
10999 Berlin
Germany

Tel: +49 30 616 57 80
Fax: +49 30 616 57 829
E-mail: post@bfm-architekten.de
Web: www.bfm-architekten.de

PIERO BRUNO was born in Trieste, Italy, in 1963. He graduated from the Istituto Universitario di Architettura Venezia (IUAV) in 1990. He worked in a number of architectural offices in Italy and Germany, before cofounding Bruno Fioretti Marquez Architects in 1995. **DONATELLA FIORETTI** was born in Savona, Italy, in 1962 and also graduated from the IUAV in 1990. She worked during that year in the atelier of Peter Zumthor (Haldenstein, Switzerland) and from 1991 to 1995 with Leon + Wohlhage (Berlin, Germany). **JOSÉ GUTIERREZ MARQUEZ** was born in Rosario, Argentina, in 1958 and graduated from the National University of Rosario in 1981, before also receiving a diploma from the IUAV in 1990. Their recent work includes the Ebracher Hof Library (Schweinfurt, 2005–07, published here); a mixed-use building in Schweinfurt (2007); a kindergarten (Cassarate, Switzerland, 2007–in planning); and an office building in Wesseling (2008–in planning), all in Germany unless stated otherwise.

PIERO BRUNO wurde 1963 in Triest, Italien, geboren. Sein Studium schloss er 1990 am Istituto Universitario di Architettura Venezia (IUAV) ab. Bevor er 1995 Bruno Fioretti Marquez Architekten gründete, war er für verschiedene Büros in Italien und Deutschland tätig. **DONATELLA FIORETTI** wurde 1962 in Savona, Italien, geboren und machte ihren Abschluss ebenfalls 1990 am IUAV. Noch im selben Jahr arbeitete sie für das Studio von Peter Zumthor (Haldenstein, Schweiz) sowie von 1991 bis 1995 bei Leon + Wohlhage (Berlin). **JOSÉ GUTIERREZ MARQUEZ** wurde 1958 in Rosario, Argentinien, geboren und schloss sein Studium 1981 an der Nationaluniversität von Rosario ab, bevor auch er 1990 einen Diplomabschluss an der IUAV machte. Jüngere Arbeiten sind u. a. die Stadtbücherei Ebracher Hof (Schweinfurt, 2005–07, hier vorgestellt), ein Wohn- und Geschäftshaus in Schweinfurt (2007), ein Kindergarten (Cassarate, Schweiz, 2007–) sowie ein Bürogebäude in Wesseling (2008–).

PIERO BRUNO est né à Trieste, en Italie, en 1963. Il obtient son diplôme à l'Institut universitaire d'architecture de Venise (IUAV) en 1990. Il travaille dans différents cabinets d'architectes, en Italie et en Allemagne, avant de cofonder Bruno Fioretti Marquez Architekten en 1995. **DONATELLA FIORETTI** est née à Savone, en Italie, en 1962 et obtient également son diplôme à l'IUAV en 1990. La même année, elle travaille dans l'atelier de Peter Zumthor (Haldenstein, Suisse) et, de 1991 à 1995, avec Leon + Wohlhage (Berlin, Allemagne). **JOSÉ GUTIERREZ MARQUEZ** est né en 1958 à Rosario, en Argentine, et obtient son diplôme à l'Université nationale de Rosario en 1981, puis un autre de l'IUAV en 1990. Leurs projets récents incluent la bibliothèque de l'Ebracher Hof (Schweinfurt, 2005–07, publié ici) ; un immeuble plurifonctionnel à Schweinfurt (2007) ; une école maternelle (Cassarate, Suisse, 2007– en cours) ; et un immeuble de bureaux à Wesseling (2008–), tous situés en Allemagne sauf mention contraire.

EBRACHER HOF LIBRARY

Schweinfurt, Germany, 2005–07

Address: Brückenstr. 29, 97421 Schweinfurt, Germany, +49 9721 51 79 60
www.swin.de/kommunen/ssw/bildung/stadtbuecherei_sw/Adresse.htm
Area: 1704 m². Client: City of Schweinfurt. Cost: € 6.5 million. Collaboration: S. Skiba, W. Vajen (Engineers)

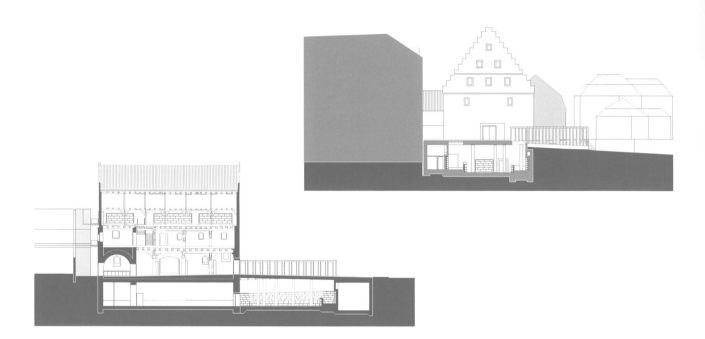

Schweinfurt is located in Bavaria and has a population of about 55 000 people. The city decided to transform a historic 15th-century barn erected for the storage of the tithe, into a city public library. The architects added an underground reading room with a "glass lantern" conceived to bring light into the spaces below grade. This element is visible from the street or the library square as a rather mysterious looking glazed band. It appears in the library square in front of the old structure. The architects also added a fire escape. They likewise worked on an office building located on the square, next to the library, which completes the composition, conceived as a new gate to Schweinfurt.

Die bayerische Stadt Schweinfurt mit rund 55 000 Einwohnern beschloss, einen alten Zehntspeicher aus dem 15. Jahrhundert in eine Stadtbücherei umzubauen. Die Architekten erweiterten das Gebäude um einen Lesesaal im Untergeschoss. Eine „Glaslaterne" lässt Licht in die dortigen Räume einfallen. Von der Straße sowie vom Vorplatz der Bücherei aus wirkt dieses Element wie ein geheimnisvolles Glasband, das vor dem Altbau angeordnet ist. Darüber hinaus ergänzten die Architekten das Gebäude um eine Feuertreppe. Außerdem entwarfen sie ein Wohn- und Geschäftshaus am selben Platz, unmittelbar neben der Bücherei. Es vervollständigt das Ensemble, das sich als neues Tor in die Schweinfurter Innenstadt zeigt.

Schweinfurt est une ville de Bavière de 55 000 habitants. La municipalité a décidé de convertir en bibliothèque publique une grange à dîme du XVᵉ siècle. Les architectes y ont ajouté une salle de lecture enterrée, pourvue d'un « lanterneau » conçu pour apporter de la lumière aux espaces en sous-sol. Depuis la rue ou la place de la bibliothèque, cet élément apparaît comme une bande de verre assez mystérieuse. Il est situé sur la place, devant l'ancien bâtiment. Les architectes ont également ajouté un escalier de secours. Ils sont aussi intervenus sur le bâtiment situé sur la place, à côté de la bibliothèque, et qui complète la composition, conçue comme une nouvelle porte de Schweinfurt.

Drawings show the relation of the new office building to the existing structure that was transformed into a library. The block-like form of the new structure represents a willful contrast to the older building.

Zeichnungen veranschaulichen das Zusammenspiel von neuem Bürohaus und Altbau, der zur Bibliothek umgebaut würde. Die blockhafte Gestalt des Neubaus ist ein bewusst gewählter Kontrast zum alten Baubestand.

Les dessins montrent la relation du nouvel immeuble de bureaux au bâtiment existant transformé en bibliothèque. Le cube de la nouvelle structure est en complet contraste avec le bâtiment ancien.

The façades of the Library and office building are seen in the image below. Reflections and light effects give a different impression of the buildings at night.

Im Bild unten die Fassade der Bibliothek und des Bürogebäudes. Spiegelungen und Lichteffekte lassen den Komplex bei Nacht ganz anders wirken.

Les façades de la bibliothèque et du nouveau bâtiment sont visibles sur la photo ci-dessous. La nuit, les effets de lumière et de reflets donnent une impression différente des bâtiments.

The underground reading room contrasts the old stone walls of the Library building with the warmth of wood finishings.

Im Lesesaal im Untergeschoss kontrastiert das alte Mauerwerk der Bücherei mit den warmtonigen Holzeinbauten.

La salle de lecture en sous-sol fait contraster les vieux murs en pierre de la bibliothèque avec les chaleureuses finitions en bois.

Another view of the reading room (right) and plans of the project, with the level below grade on the left.

Ein weiterer Blick in den Lesesaal (rechts) sowie zwei Grundrisse des Projekts. Links der Grundriss des Untergeschosses.

Une autre vue de la salle de lecture (à droite) et des plans du projet, dont celui du sous-sol à gauche.

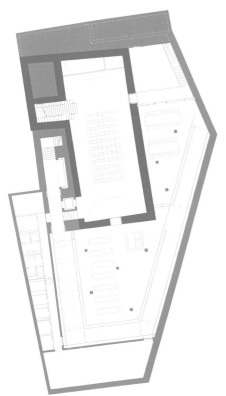

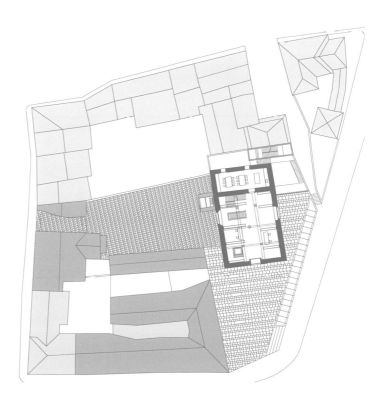

SANTIAGO CALATRAVA

Santiago Calatrava SA
Parkring 11
8002 Zurich
Switzerland

Tel: +41 1 204 50 00
Fax: +41 1 204 50 01
e-mail: admin.zurich@calatrava.com
Web: www.calatrava.com

Born in Valencia in 1951, **SANTIAGO CALATRAVA** studied Art and Architecture at the ETSA of Valencia (1968–73) and Engineering at the ETH in Zurich (doctorate in Technical Science, 1981). He opened his own architecture and civil engineering office the same year. Santiago Calatrava received the American Institute of Architects (AIA) 2005 Gold Medal. His built work includes Gallery and Heritage Square, BCE Place (Toronto, Canada, 1987); the Torre de Montjuic (Barcelona, Spain, 1989–92); the Kuwait Pavilion at Expo '92, Seville, and the Alamillo Bridge for the same exhibition (Seville, Spain); the Lyon Satolas TGV Station (Lyon, France, 1989–94); the Oriente Station in Lisbon (Portugal, 1998); the Valencia City of Science and Planetarium (Valencia, Spain, 1996–2000) and the Valencia Opera (2004); the Sondica Airport (Bilbao, Spain, 1990–2000); and a bridge in Orléans (France, 1996–2000). Other work includes the Tenerife Auditorium (Santa Cruz, Canary Islands, 2003); the Milwaukee Art Museum extension (Milwaukee, Wisconsin, USA, 2003); the Athens Olympic Sports Complex (Athens, Greece, 2004); the recently completed Quarto Ponte sul Canal Grande (Fourth Bridge on the Grand Canal, Venice, Italy, 1999–2006, published here); three bridges in Reggio Emilia (Reggio Emilia, Italy, 2002–07); and the Jerusalem Light Rail Train Bridge (Jerusalem, Israel, 2002–08). He is currently working on the Transportation Hub for the new World Trade Center site in New York.

SANTIAGO CALATRAVA wurde 1951 in Valencia geboren und studierte Kunst und Architektur an der ETSA in Valencia (1968–73) sowie Bauingenieurwesen an der ETH Zürich. 1981 mit der Promotion in Technischen Wissenschaften schloss er sein Studium ab. Im selben Jahr gründete er sein eigenes Büro als Architekt und Bauingenieur. 2005 wurde Calatrava mit der Goldmedaille des American Institute of Architects (AIA) ausgezeichnet. Zu seinen realisierten Projekten zählen der Gallery and Heritage Square, BCE Place (Toronto, Kanada, 1987), die Torre de Montjuic (Barcelona, 1989–92), der Landespavillon für Kuwait sowie die Alamillo-Brücke für die Expo '92 (Sevilla, Spanien), der TGV-Bahnhof Lyon Satolas (Lyon, 1989–94), der Bahnhof Oriente in Lissabon (1998), die Wissenschaftsstadt und das Planetarium in Valencia (1996–2000) sowie die Oper von Valencia (2004), der Flughafen Sondica (Bilbao, Spanien, 1990–2000) und eine Brücke in Orléans (Frankreich, 1996–2000). Weitere Arbeiten sind das Auditorium von Teneriffa (Santa Cruz, Kanarische Inseln, 2003), die Erweiterung des Milwaukee Art Museum (Milwaukee, Wisconsin, 2003), die Olympischen Sportanlagen in Athen (2004), die kürzlich eingeweihte Quarto Ponte sul Canal Grande (die vierte Brücke über den Canal Grande, Venedig, 1999–2006, hier vorgestellt), drei Brücken in Reggio Emilia (Italien, 2002–07) sowie eine Stadtbahnbrücke in Jerusalem (2002–08). Gegenwärtig arbeitet Calatrava am Verkehrsknotenpunkt für das neue World Trade Center in New York.

Né à Valence en 1951, **SANTIAGO CALATRAVA** étudie l'art et l'architecture à l'ETSA de Valence (1968–73) et l'ingénierie à l'ETH de Zurich (doctorat en sciences techniques, 1981). Il ouvre son premier cabinet d'architecture et de génie civil la même année. Santiago Calatrava reçoit la médaille d'or 2005 de l'American Institute of Architects (AIA). Ses réalisations incluent le complexe Gallery and Heritage Square, BCE Place (Toronto, Canada, 1987) ; la tour de télécommunications de Montjuic (Barcelone, Espagne, 1989–92) ; le pavillon du Koweït à l'Exposition universelle de Séville de 1992 et le pont Alamillo pour la même manifestation (Séville, Espagne) ; la gare TGV de Lyon Satolas (Lyon, France, 1989–94) ; la gare d'Oriente, à Lisbonne (Portugal, 1998) ; la Cité des sciences et le planétarium de Valence (Valence, Espagne, 1996–2000) et l'Opéra de Valence, dans la même ville (2004) ; l'aéroport Sondica (Bilbao, Espagne, 1990–2000) ; et un pont à Orléans (France, 1996–2000). D'autres projets incluent l'auditorium de Tenerife (Santa Cruz, îles Canaries, 2003) ; l'extension du Milwaukee Art Museum (Milwaukee, Wisconsin, États-Unis, 2003) ; le Complexe sportif olympique d'Athènes (Athènes, Grèce, 2004) ; le Quarto Ponte sul Canal Grande, récemment achevé (Quatrième pont sur le Grand Canal, Venise, Italie, 1999–2006, publié ici) ; trois ponts à Reggio Emilia (Reggio Emilia, Italie, 2002–07) ; et le pont de tramway de Jérusalem (Jérusalem, Israël, 2002–08). Il travaille actuellement sur la nouvelle gare centrale du site du World Trade Center à New York.

QUARTO PONTE SUL CANAL GRANDE

Venice, Italy, 1999–2006

Address: Piazzale Roma, 30135 Venice, Italy
Length: 94 meters. Client: Municipality of Venice. Cost: € 6.7 million

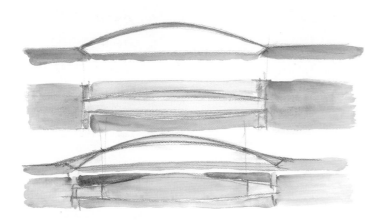

The extremely pure arch of the bridge is seen below at nightfall, spanning over the Grand Canal.

Der überaus schlichte Bogen der Brücke über den Canal Grande bei Anbruch der Nacht.

Ci dessous, l'arche très épurée de la passerelle vue au crépuscule, sur le Grand Canal.

Located near the main railway station of Venice, the bridge adds a much needed pedestrian route across the Grand Canal. Its modernity does not in any way conflict with neighboring buildings.

Durch die unweit des Bahnhofs von Venedig gelegene Brücke wurde ein dringend benötigter Fußgängerübergang über den Canal Grande geschaffen. Die Modernität des Bauwerks steht keineswegs im Widerspruch zur angrenzenden Bebauung.

Située à proximité de la gare centrale de Venise, la passerelle ajoute une voie piétonnière essentielle pour la traversée du Grand Canal. Sa modernité n'entre pas en conflit avec les bâtiments environnants.

The **QUARTO PONTE SUL CANAL GRANDE** pedestrian bridge is only the fourth bridge to be built over Venice's Grand Canal since the 16th century. Calatrava's new bridge, for which he was selected by a public commissioning process in November 1999, connects the Piazzale Roma bus station to the railway station. His design was approved in February 2001 and the project approved in April 2002, with a budget of 6.7 million euros. Conscious of the high visibility of this location and its historical significance, Calatrava says: "Care has been taken to integrate the bridge with the quays on either side. The steps and ramps are designed to add vitality to both sides of the canal, while the abutments (which are crescent-shaped) leave pedestrians free access to the quays. The areas at either end act as extensions of the bridge, creating new celebratory spaces for Venice. On the south side, the design also provides a new passage between Piazzale Roma and the mooring platforms for the ACTV water transport." The bridge is 94 meters long, with a central span of 81 meters. Its width varies, from 5.58 meters (at either foot) to 9.38 meters at the midpoint and it rises from a height of 3.2 meters at the foot to 9.28 meters at midpoint. The all-steel structural element consists of a central arch of a very large radius (180 meters), with two side arches and two lower arches.

Santiago Calatravas Fußgängerbrücke **QUARTO PONTE SUL CANAL GRANDE** ist tatsächlich erst die vierte Brücke, die seit dem 16. Jahrhundert über den Canal Grande gebaut wurde. Calatravas neue Brücke, ein Entwurf, mit dem er sich im November 1999 in einer öffentlichen Ausschreibung durchsetzen konnte, verbindet den Busbahnhof Piazzale Roma mit dem Bahnhof. Im Februar 2001 wurde der Entwurf befürwortet, das Projekt selbst im April 2002 mit einem Budget von 6,7 Millionen Euro genehmigt. Calatrava ist sich der Prominenz des Standorts und seiner historischen Bedeutung sehr wohl bewusst und merkt an: „Die Brücke wurde äußerst sorgsam an beide Uferseiten angebunden. Stufen und Rampen wurden so gestaltet, dass sie den Ufern entlang des Kanals zusätzliche Vitalität verleihen. Die halbmondförmigen Brückenpfeiler erlauben den Fußgängern freien Zugang zur Uferpromenade. Die Areale an beiden Brückenenden wirken wie eine Erweiterung des Bauwerks und schaffen zwei neue festliche Plätze in Venedig. Am Südufer entsteht zudem ein neuer Zugang zu den schwimmenden Haltestellen der ACTV-Wasserbusse." Die Brücke ist 94 m lang, ihre zentrale Spannweite beträgt 81 m. Die Breite reicht von 5,58 m (an den Brückenenden) bis zu 9,38 m in der Mitte, die Höhe von 3,2 m bis zu 9,28 m am Scheitelpunkt. Die Stahlkonstruktion basiert auf einem zentralen Bogen mit außergewöhnlich großem Radius (180 m) sowie zwei seitlichen und zwei niedrigeren Bögen.

Le **QUARTO PONTE SUL CANAL GRANDE**, passerelle sur le Grand Canal à Venise, est le quatrième pont à y être construit depuis le XVIe siècle. Le nouveau pont conçu par Calatrava, sélectionné par une procédure de commande publique en novembre 1999, relie la gare routière de Piazzale Roma à la gare ferroviaire. Son avant-projet a été approuvé en février 2001 et son projet final, d'un budget de 6,7 millions d'euros, en avril 2002. Conscient de la grande visibilité et de l'importance historique du lieu, Calatrava dit avoir pris soin «d'intégrer le pont aux quais de chaque côté. Les marches et rampes sont conçues pour dynamiser les deux rives du canal, tandis que les butées (en croissants) permettent aux piétons d'accéder librement aux quais. Les zones situées à chaque extrémité fonctionnent comme des extensions du pont, créant de nouveaux espaces festifs pour Venise. Du côté sud, le projet offre aussi un nouveau passage entre la Piazzale Roma et l'embarcadère des transports par eau de l'ACTV ». Le pont mesure 94 mètres de long, pour une portée centrale de 81 mètres. Sa largeur varie de 5,58 mètres (à chaque extrémité) à 9,38 mètres au point central et s'élève de 3,20 mètres à sa base et à 9,28 mètres au point central. La structure entièrement en acier se compose d'une arche centrale de rayon très large (180 mètres), de deux arches latérales et de deux arches plus basses.

As is usually the case, Santiago Calatrava gives an almost organic feel to his work, as seen here in the details of the abutment of the bridge, or even in its smooth, elegant arch.

Wie in den meisten Fällen verleiht Santiago Calatrava seinen Bauten eine geradezu organische Anmutung, hier zu sehen an den Details des Brückenaufgangs und dem sanften, eleganten Bogen der Brücke selbst.

Comme souvent, Santiago Calatrava donne une touche presque organique à sa création, comme on le voit ici dans les détails des butées de la passerelle, voire dans son arche lisse et élégante.

CANNON DESIGN

Cannon Design / 2170 Whitehaven Road
Grand Island, NY 14072 / USA
Tel: +1 716 773 6800 / Fax: +1 716 773 5909
E-mail: info@cannondesign.com / Web: www.cannondesign.com

Founded more than 60 years ago, **CANNON DESIGN** works with a staff of 750 people in the areas of architecture, engineering, and interior design. Robert J. Johnston is a Principal and National Sports Practice Leader for the firm. A captain of the Canadian lacrosse team for the 1978 Commonwealth Games, he received a Master's degree in Environmental Design from the University of Calgary. He was the Project Principal and Lead Planner for the Richmond Olympic Oval (Richmond, British Columbia, Canada, 2005–08, published here). Marion LaRue is a Principal and Operations Leader for Cannon Design. Her work has been concentrated in student life, wellness, sports, and recreational architecture. She received a B.Sc. in both Architecture and Environmental Science from the University of Waterloo. She was the Senior Project Manager for the Richmond Olympic Oval. Larry Podhora has 20 years of experience in the design of recreation centers. He received his M.Arch degree from the Bartlett School of Architecture, the University of London, as well as a B.Arch degree from the University of British Columbia, and was Architect of Record for the Richmond Olympic Oval. Recent projects by Cannon Design include Boston University, John Hancock Student Village (Boston, Massachusetts, 2005); Brigham and Women's Hospital, Shapiro Cardiovascular Center (Boston, Massachusetts, 2008); and University of California, San Diego, Price Center East (San Diego, California, 2008), all in the USA. Ongoing work includes the University Hospitals, Case Medical Center Cancer Hospital (Cleveland, Ohio, USA, 2010); King Faisal Specialist Hospital and Research Center (Riyadh, Saudi Arabia, 2011); and the M. D. Anderson Banner Cancer Center (Phoenix, Arizona, USA, 2011).

CANNON DESIGN, vor über 60 Jahren gegründet, beschäftigt rund 750 Mitarbeiter auf den Gebieten Architektur, Ingenieurwesen und Innenarchitektur. Robert J. Johnston, einer der Direktoren und Landessportchef des Büros, war bei den Commonwealth Games 1978 Kapitän der kanadischen Lacrosse-Mannschaft und schloss sein Studium mit einem Master in umweltverträglicher Planung an der Universität Calgary ab. Er war Projektleiter und Chefplaner beim Richmond Olympic Oval (Richmond, British Columbia, Kanada, 2005–08, hier vorgestellt). Marion LaRue ist Direktorin und Technische Unternehmensleiterin bei Cannon Design. Ihr Projektschwerpunkt sind primär Bildungs-, Wellness-, Sport- und Freizeiteinrichtungen. Sie schloss ihr Studium an der Universität Waterloo mit einem B. Sc. in Architektur und Umwelttechnik ab. Beim Richmond Olympic Oval zeichnete sie als leitende Projektmanagerin verantwortlich. Larry Podhora blickt auf 20 Jahre Erfahrung in der Gestaltung von Freizeiteinrichtungen zurück. Er absolvierte einen M. Arch. an der Bartlett School of Architecture der Universität von London sowie einen B. Arch. an der Universität von British Columbia. Podhora war zuständiger Architekt für das Richmond Olympic Oval. Jüngere Projekte von Cannon Design sind u. a. die John-Hancock-Studentensiedlung der Universität Boston (2005), das Shapiro-Herz-Kreislauf-Zentrum am Brigham and Women's Hospital (Boston, Massachusetts, 2008) und das Price Center East an der University of California (San Diego, Kalifornien, 2008), alle in den USA. Zu ihren aktuellen Projekten zählen die Case-Medical-Center-Krebsklinik der Universitätskliniken Cleveland (Cleveland, Ohio, 2010), die König-Faisal-Fachklinik und -Forschungseinrichtung (Riad, Saudi-Arabien, 2011) sowie das Krebszentrum M. D. Anderson Banner (Phoenix, Arizona, 2011).

Fondée il y a plus de soixante ans, l'agence **CANNON DESIGN** emploie une équipe de 750 personnes dans les domaines de l'architecture, de l'ingénierie et de l'architecture d'intérieur. Robert J. Johnston est entraîneur de l'équipe sportive de la firme. Capitaine de l'équipe canadienne de crosse aux Jeux du Commonwealth de 1978, il possède un Master en architecture bioclimatique de l'université de Calgary. Il était directeur de projet et urbaniste en chef de l'Anneau olympique de Richmond (Richmond, Colombie-Britannique, Canada, 2005–08, publié ici). Marion LaRue est directrice des opérations pour Cannon Design. Ses activités se sont concentrées sur la vie étudiante, le bien-être, le sport, et l'architecture de loisir. Elle est diplômée en architecture et en science environnementale de l'université de Waterloo. Elle était directrice principale du projet de l'Anneau olympique de Richmond. Larry Podhora a vingt ans d'expérience dans le domaine de l'architecture de loisir. Il a un master en architecture (M. Arch.) de la Bartlett School de l'université de Londres, ainsi qu'une licence en architecture de l'université de Colombie-Britannique (B. Arch.), et était architecte responsable du projet pour l'Anneau olympique de Richmond. Les récents projets de Cannon Design incluent le complexe John Hancock Student Village à l'université de Boston (Boston, Massachusetts, États-Unis, 2005); le Brigham et Women's Hospital du Shapiro Cardiovascular Center (Boston, Massachusetts, États-Unis, 2008); et le Centre étudiant Price Center East de l'université de Californie, à San Diego (San Diego, Californie, États-Unis, 2008), tous situés aux États-Unis. Ses projets en cours incluent les University Hospitals; le Case Medical Center Cancer Hospital (Cleveland, Ohio, États-Unis, 2010); l'extension du King Faisal Specialist Hospital and Research Center (Riyadh, Arabie saoudite, 2011); et le M. D. Anderson Banner Cancer Center (Phoenix, Arizona, États-Unis, 2011).

RICHMOND OLYMPIC OVAL

Richmond, British Columbia, Canada, 2005–08

Address: 6111 River Road, Richmond, BC V7C 0A2, Canada, +1 778 296 1400, www.richmondoval.ca
Area: 38 000 m². Client: City of Richmond. Cost: $153.38 million
Team: Larry Podhora (Architect of Record), Robert Johnston (Design Principal),
Marion LaRue (Senior Project Manager)

Completed well in advance of the 2010 Vancouver Winter Olympic Games, the Richmond Olympic Oval is both functional and elegant, making ample use of wood, for example.

Das Richmond Oval, mehr als zeitig vor den olympischen Winterspielen fertiggestellt, die 2010 in Vancouver ausgetragen werden, ist sowohl funktional als auch elegant. Holz kommt umfassend zum Einsatz.

Achevé très en avance pour les Jeux d'hiver 2010 de Vancouver, l'Anneau olympique de Richmond, à la fois fonctionnel et élégant, laisse la part belle au bois.

The **RICHMOND OLYMPIC OVAL** was built for the long-track speed-skating events to be held during the 2010 Olympic and Paralympic Winter Games. It is located on a 13-hectare site near the Fraser River and Vancouver International Airport. The Olympic configuration will see the Oval house a 400-meter speed-skating track and seating for about 8000 spectators. The building is naturally designed for summer indoor sports, such as running or basketball as well, and includes sport medicine and wellness areas, a fitness center, and a 1393-square-meter anti-doping laboratory for the Winter Games. The basic plan of the building is a straightforward rectangle, underlining its highly functional nature. The Oval is part of a waterfront urban development plan that includes a mixture of residential, commercial, and public facilities. The contribution of Cannon Design to this project assures that a high level of architectural quality is maintained even as the sporting objectives of the facility are fully achieved.

Das **RICHMOND OLYMPIC OVAL** wurde für die Eisschnelllaufwettkämpfe bei den Olympischen und Paralympischen Winterspielen 2010 gebaut. Der Komplex liegt auf einem 13 ha großen Areal unweit des Fraser River und des Flughafens von Vancouver. Für die Olympischen Spiele verfügt das Stadion über eine 400 m lange Eisschnelllaufstrecke und bietet 8000 Besuchern Platz. Dabei ist das Gebäude so angelegt, dass es ebenfalls für Hallensportarten wie Laufen oder Basketball genutzt werden kann. Darüber hinaus gibt es sportmedizinische und Wellnessbereiche, ein Fitnesscenter sowie ein 1393 m² großes Anti-Dopinglabor für die Winterspiele. Der Grundriss des Gebäudes ist ein einfaches Rechteck und betont dessen ausgeprägte Funktionalität. Der Komplex ist Teil einer städtebaulichen Ufererschließung, zu der auch Wohn-, Geschäfts- und öffentliche Bauten gehören. Der Beitrag von Cannon Design für dieses Projekt sorgt für ein hohes architektonisches Niveau und erfüllt zugleich die funktionalen Anforderungen, die an den Sportkomplex gestellt werden.

L'ANNEAU OLYMPIQUE DE RICHMOND a été construit pour les courses de patinage de vitesse longue piste des Jeux olympiques et paralympiques d'hiver. Il est implanté sur un site de 13 hectares proche du fleuve Fraser et de l'aéroport international de Vancouver. En configuration olympique, l'Anneau abritera une piste de patinage de vitesse de 400 mètres et près de 8000 spectateurs. Le bâtiment est naturellement conçu pour des sports d'été en salle, de la course à pied au basket, et comprend des installations de médecine du sport et de bien-être, un centre de culture physique, et un laboratoire antidopage de 1393 mètres carrés pour les Jeux d'hiver. Le plan du bâtiment est un simple rectangle, soulignant sa nature hautement fonctionnelle. L'Anneau fait partie d'un plan de développement urbain du bord de l'eau mêlant des équipements résidentiels, commerciaux et publics. La contribution de Cannon Design à ce projet témoigne qu'une haute qualité d'architecture est possible, tout en remplissant tous les objectifs sportifs de l'installation.

A general interior view showing the broad arch requiring no supporting columns and moveable bleachers in place for pre-Olympic events.

Eine Innenansicht zeigt den breiten Bogen, der keine Stützsäulen benötigt sowie mobile Tribünen, aufgebaut für vorolympische Veranstaltungen.

Vue générale montrant le grand arc sans colonne de soutien et les gradins mobiles mis en place pour les manifestations pré-olympiques.

The cantilevered canopies of the building are one of its most interesting architectural elements. To the right, an overall site plan showing the roof of the structure.

Die auskragenden Vordächer zählen zu den interessantesten architektonischen Elementen des Gebäudes. Rechts ein Lageplan des Geländes mit Dachaufsicht.

Les auvents en porte-à-faux du bâtiment constituent un de ses éléments architecturaux les plus intéressants. À droite, un plan d'ensemble du site montre le toit de la structure.

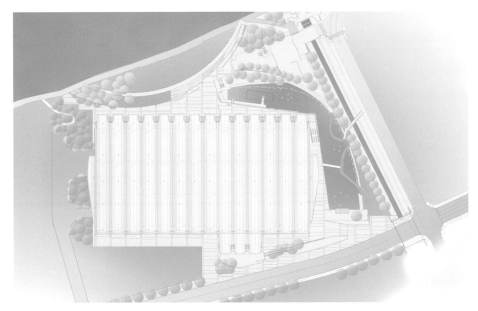

CEBRA

CEBRA a/s
Vesterbro Torv 1–3, 2.sal
8000 Aarhus C
Denmark

Tel: +45 87 30 34 39
Fax: +45 87 30 34 29
E-mail: cebra@cebra.info
Web: www.cebra.info

CEBRA is a Danish architectural firm located in Aarhus. The office was founded in 2001 by architects Mikkel Frost, Carsten Primdahl, and Kolja Nielsen. They have specialized in sustainable architecture. Today the office employs 20 people. Carsten Primdahl was born in 1970 in Aarhus, Denmark. He graduated from the Aarhus School of Architecture in 1998. Kolja Nielsen was born in 1968 in Hjørring, Denmark. He graduated from the Aarhus School of Architecture in 1996. Mikkel Frost was born in 1971 in Viby J, Denmark, and also graduated from Aarhus in 1996. CEBRA won the 2006 Golden Lion for the best national pavilion (Denmark) at the 10th International Architecture Biennale, Venice. Their Bakkegaard School (Gentofte, in collaboration with SRL Architects, 2003–05) was nominated for the Mies van der Rohe award in 2006. After completing the Gersonsvej Multipurpose Building (Gentofte, 2005–08, published here), CEBRA's current work includes Villa Strata, Apartments (Kolding, 2010); the KKG School (Hou, 2010); and the Isbjerget, Residence (Aarhus Harbour, in collaboration with JDS, SeARCH, and Louis Paillard, 2011), all in Denmark.

CEBRA ist ein dänisches Architekturbüro mit Sitz in Århus. Gegründet wurde die Firma 2001 von Mikkel Frost, Carsten Primdahl und Kolja Nielsen. Das Büro hat sich auf nachhaltige Architektur spezialisiert und beschäftigt heute 20 Mitarbeiter. Carsten Primdahl wurde 1970 in Århus geboren. 1998 schloss er sein Studium an der dortigen Hochschule für Architektur ab. Kolja Nielsen wurde 1968 in Hjørring, Dänemark, geboren. Er schloss sein Studium 1996 an der Hochschule für Architektur in Århus ab. Mikkel Frost wurde 1971 in Viby J, Dänemark, geboren. Auch er schloss sein Studium 1996 in Århus ab. 2006 wurde CEBRA mit dem Goldenen Löwen für den besten Landespavillon (Dänemark) auf der X. Architekturbiennale in Venedig ausgezeichnet. Im selben Jahr wurde das Büro für die Bakkegaard-Schule (Gentofte, in Zusammenarbeit mit SRL Architects, 2003–05) für den Mies-van-der-Rohe-Preis nominiert. Nach Fertigstellung des Gersonsvej Sport- und Freizeitzentrums (Gentofte, 2005–08, hier vorgestellt), arbeitet das Büro derzeit u. a. an den Villa-Strata-Apartments (Kolding, 2010), der KKG-Schule (Hou, 2010) sowie dem Wohnkomplex Isbjerget (Århus-Hafen, in Zusammenarbeit mit JDS, SeARCH und Louis Paillard, 2011), alle in Dänemark.

CEBRA est une agence d'architecture danoise basée à Aarhus. Le cabinet a été fondé en 2001 par les architectes Mikkel Frost, Carsten Primdahl et Kolja Nielsen, qui se sont spécialisés dans l'architecture durable. L'agence emploie aujourd'hui 20 personnes. Carsten Primdahl est né en 1970 à Aarhus, au Danemark. Il a obtenu son diplôme à l'École d'architecture d'Aarhus en 1998. Kolja Nielsen, né en 1968 à Hjørring, au Danemark, a obtenu son diplôme à l'École d'architecture d'Aarhus en 1996. Mikkel Frost, né en 1971 à Viby J, au Danemark, a également obtenu son diplôme à l'École d'architecture d'Aarhus en 1996. CEBRA a reçu le Lion d'or du meilleur pavillon étranger (Danemark) à la Biennale internationale d'architecture de Venise de 2006. Leur école Bakkegaard (Gentofte, en collaboration avec SRL Architects, 2003–05) a été sélectionnée pour le prix Mies van der Rohe 2006. Après avoir achevé l'immeuble plurifonctionnel Gersonsvej (Gentofte, 2005–08, publié ici), les projets de CEBRA en cours incluent l'ensemble d'appartements Villa Strata (Kolding, 2010) ; l'école KKG (Hou, 2010) ; et la résidence Isbjerget (Port d'Aarhus, en collaboration avec JDS, SeARCH, et Louis Paillard, 2011), tous situés au Danemark.

GERSONSVEJ MULTIPURPOSE BUILDING

Gentofte, Denmark, 2005–08

Address: Gersonsvej 41, 2900 Hellerup, Denmark, +45 39 98 59 91, www.hellerupfc.dk
Area: 2166 m². Client: Municipality of Gentofte. Cost: €9.632 million
Collaboration: Dorte Mandrup Architects

The architects were entrusted with the task of placing a sports and leisure facility together on the same relatively narrow site. They used the villa building type "interpreted according to specific technical requirements for each area," and extended and run together for the design as their concept sketch shows. "Niches or spaces" situated between indoor and outdoor areas are a feature of their scheme, as can be seen in the open, cagelike, house-shaped area for sports. The metallic, folded elements appear to be more opaque from the exterior and more open from the interior, where they look onto an inner garden. The high, bright spaces are rendered even more convivial with bright, colored furnishings.

Der Auftrag der Architekten lautete, eine kombinierte Sport- und Freizeiteinrichtung auf einem relativ schmalen Grundstück zu realisieren. Ausgehend vom Typus eines freistehenden Wohnhauses interpretierten sie den Bau „mit Blick auf die spezifischen technischen Anforderungen des jeweiligen Nutzungsbereichs". Sie vergrößerten den Gebäudetypus und führten ihn in einem Gesamtentwurf zusammen, wie die Konzeptskizze zeigt. Typisch für den Entwurf sind die „Nischen oder Räume", die formal zwischen Innen- und Außenbereich changieren, wie sich an den offenen, käfigähnlichen Sportanlagen zeigt, die aussehen wie Häuser. Die gefalzten Metallfassaden wirken nach außen vergleichsweise geschlossen, zum innen liegenden Garten hin jedoch offener. Durch das leuchtend bunte Mobiliar wirken die hohen, hellen Räume noch fröhlicher.

Les architectes avaient pour mission de placer des installations sportives et de loisir sur un même site relativement étroit. Ils ont utilisé des bâtiments de type villa « interprété selon les spécifications techniques requises pour chaque zone » en les étirant et les reliant pour leur projet, comme le montrent les esquisses du concept. « Des niches ou espaces », situés entre les espaces intérieurs et extérieurs, sont une des caractéristiques de leur projet, comme on peut le voir dans l'espace destiné au sport, ouvert, comme une cage en forme de maison. Les éléments métalliques pliés apparaissent plus opaques de l'extérieur et plus ouverts face à un jardin intérieur. Les espaces hauts et lumineux sont rendus encore plus conviviaux par le mobilier de couleurs vives.

The folded roofs of the building appear to be rather closed, a feeling obviated by the use of rooftop windows to bring in light.

Die gefalteten Dächer des Komplexes wirken recht geschlossen, Dachfenster mildern diesen Eindruck jedoch ab.

Les toits repliés du bâtiment semblent assez fermés, une impression corrigée par les fenêtres de toit qui apportent de la lumière.

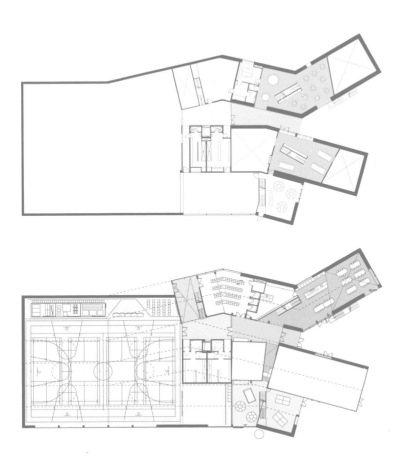

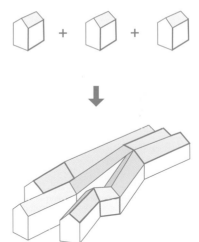

Plans and drawings show the
finger-like disposition of the different
elements of the program.

*Grundrisse und Zeichnungen
zeigen die wie Finger einer Hand
angeordneten verschiedenen
baulichen Elemente.*

*Les plans et dessins montrent la
configuration des différents éléments
de l'ensemble, disposés comme les
doigts de la main.*

Bright colors and ample light characterize the interiors of the structure, as would seem befitting of its use.

Kräftige Farben und großzügiger Lichteinfall prägen die Innenräume des Komplexes, was ihrer Nutzung entspricht.

Des couleurs vives et une grande luminosité caractérisent les intérieurs du bâtiment, comme il semble convenir à son usage.

DAVID CHIPPERFIELD

David Chipperfield Architects
1A Cobham Mews, Agar Grove
London NW1 9SB
UK

Tel: +44 20 72 67 9422
Fax: +44 20 71 7267 9347
E-mail: info@davidchipperfield.co.uk
Web: www.davidchipperfield.co.uk

Born in London in 1953, **DAVID CHIPPERFIELD** obtained his diploma in Architecture from the Architectural Association (AA, London, 1977). He worked in the offices of Norman Foster and Richard Rogers, before establishing David Chipperfield Architects (London, 1984). Built work includes the Arnolfini Arts Center (Bristol, UK, 1987); Toyota Auto (Kyoto, Japan, 1989–90); Matsumoto Corporation Headquarters (Okayama, Japan, 1990–92); Plant Gallery and Central Hall of the Natural History Museum (London, UK, 1993); Wagamama Restaurant (London, UK, 1995); River and Rowing Museum (Henley-on-Thames, UK, 1989–97); Kaistraße Studios (Dusseldorf, Germany, 1994–97); Landeszentralbank (Gera, Germany, 1994–2001); Figge Art Museum (Davenport, Iowa, USA, 1999–2005); housing in Villaverde (Madrid, Spain, 2000–05); Museum of Modern Literature (Marbach, Germany, 2002–06); and the America's Cup Building "Veles et Vents" (Valencia, Spain, 2005–06). Recently he has completed the Liangzhu Culture Museum (Hangzhou, China, 2003–08); Kivik Art Centre Pavilion (Kivik, Sweden, 2007–08, with Antony Gormley); the Neues Museum (Museum Island, Berlin, Germany, 1997–09); the Anchorage Museum at Rasmuson Center (Anchorage, Alaska, USA, 2003–09); and the design of numerous Dolce & Gabbana shops beginning in 1999. Underway is the Ansaldo City of Cultures (Milan, Italy, 2000–11); and the San Michele in Isola Cemetery (Venice, Italy, 1998–2013, published here).

DAVID CHIPPERFIELD, geboren 1953 in London, schloss sein Studium an der Architectural Association (AA) in London 1977 mit dem Diplom ab. Er arbeitete für Norman Foster und Richard Rogers, bevor er 1984 sein Büro David Chipperfield Architects in London gründete. Zu seinen gebauten Projekten zählen das Arnolfini Arts Center (Bristol, Großbritannien, 1987), Toyota Auto (Kioto, Japan, 1989–90), die Matsumoto-Hauptniederlassung (Okayama, Japan, 1990–92), die Pflanzenausstellung und Haupthalle des Natural History Museum (London, 1993), ein Wagamama Restaurant (London, 1995), das Fluss- und Rudermuseum (Henley-on-Thames, Großbritannien, 1989–97), ein Atelier- und Bürogebäude an der Kaistraße (Düsseldorf, 1994–97), der Umbau der ehemaligen Landeszentralbank Gera (1994–2001), das Figge Art Museum (Davenport, Iowa, 1999–2005), ein Wohnbauprojekt in Villaverde (Madrid, 2000–05), das Literaturmuseum der Moderne (Marbach, Deutschland, 2002–06) sowie das America's Cup Building „Veles et Vents" (Valencia, Spanien, 2005–06). Unlängst fertiggestellt wurden das Kulturmuseum Liangzhu (Hangzhou, China, 2003–08), der Kivik-Kunstpavillon (Kivik, Schweden, 2007–08, mit Antony Gormley), das Neue Museum (Museumsinsel, Berlin, 1997–09), das Anchorage-Museum im Rasmuson-Center (Anchorage, Alaska, 2003–09) sowie seit 1999 verschiedene Ladengeschäfte für Dolce & Gabbana. In Arbeit sind derzeit die Città della cultura in den ehemaligen Ansaldo-Werken (Mailand, 2000–11) sowie die Erweiterung des Friedhofs San Michele (Venedig, 1998–2013, hier vorgestellt).

Né à Londres en 1953, **DAVID CHIPPERFIELD** obtient son diplôme d'architecte à l'Architectural Association (AA, Londres, 1977). Il travaille dans les agences de Norman Foster et de Richard Rogers, avant de fonder David Chipperfield Architects (Londres, 1984). Ses projets réalisés incluent le Centre d'art Arnolfini (Bristol, Royaume-Uni, 1987) ; Toyota Auto (Kyoto, Japon, 1989–90) ; le siège de la compagnie Matsumoto (Okayama, Japon, 1990–92) ; la Galerie des plantes et le hall central du Musée d'histoire naturelle de Londres (Londres, Royaume-Uni, 1993) ; le restaurant Wagamama (Londres, Royaume-Uni, 1995) ; le musée de la Rivière et de l'Aviron (River and Rowing Museum, Henley-on-Thames, Royaume-Uni, 1989–97) ; l'immeuble Kaistraße Studios (Düsseldorf, Allemagne, 1994–97) ; la banque Landeszentralbank (Gera, Allemagne, 1994–2001) ; le Musée d'art Figge (Davenport, Iowa, États-Unis, 1999–2005) ; des logements à Villaverde (Madrid, Espagne, 2000–05) ; le Musée de la littérature moderne (Marbach, Allemagne, 2002–06) ; et l'immeuble de l'America's Cup « Veles et Vents » (Valence, Espagne, 2005–06). Récemment, il a achevé le musée de la Culture de Liangzhu (Hangzhou, Chine, 2003–08) ; le pavillon des arts de Kivik (Kivik, Suède, 2007–08, avec Antony Gormley) ; la restructuration du Neues Museum (Île aux musées, Berlin, Allemagne, 1997–09) ; le musée d'Anchorage au Centre Rasmuson (Anchorage, Alaska, États-Unis, 2003–09) ; et l'aménagement de nombreuses boutiques Dolce & Gabbana depuis 1999. Ses projets en cours incluent la Cité des cultures d'Ansaldo (Milan, Italie, 2000–11) ; et le cimetière de San Michele (Venise, Italie, 1998–2013, publié ici).

SAN MICHELE IN ISOLA CEMETERY

Venice, Italy, 1998–2013

Address: San Michele in Isola, 30121 Venice, Italy
Area: 66 000 m². Client: Comune di Venezia. Cost: not disclosed
Collaboration: Giuseppe Zampieri, Cristiano Billia, Carlo Gaspari

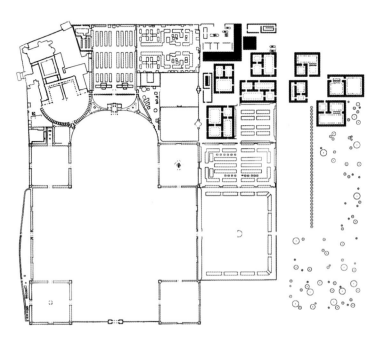

Much as he did in the Neues Museum in Berlin, Chipperfield contrasts old, brick walls with his own, more modern surfaces and materials. To the right, a plan shows the parts of the Cemetery that he has worked on.

Ganz wie bei seinem Ansatz für das Neue Museum in Berlin kontrastiert Chipperfield auch hier altes Mauerwerk mit eigenen, moderneren Oberflächen und Materialien. Rechts auf dem Grundriss zu sehen die Teile des Friedhofs, die Chipperfield bearbeitete.

Comme pour le Neues Museum à Berlin, Chipperfield fait contraster les vieux murs de briques avec ses propres surfaces et matériaux plus modernes. À droite, un plan montre les parties du cimetière sur lesquelles il est intervenu.

Set on an island located between Venice and Murano, the **SAN MICHELE CEMETERY** has been developed over a period of four centuries. With the aim of reconciling the exterior and interior appearances of the site, David Chipperfield is adding new courtyards and a chapel. The architect seeks "an organizational structure […] which groups the volumes together to form a greater sense of solidity. A first part of the project, the Courtyard of the Four Evangelists," opened in September 2007 with basalt cladding on its walls, and pavements inlaid with texts from the Evangelists. A black, exposed concrete colonnade is part of this phase, while the next part of the project, due for 2013 completion, calls for the creation of a new island, parallel to the existing cemetery with tomb buildings and gardens at the level of the water.

Der **FRIEDHOF SAN MICHELE** auf einer Insel zwischen Venedig und Murano hat eine 400-jährige Geschichte. Um das äußere und innere Erscheinungsbild des Ortes harmonisch zu verbinden, entschied sich David Chipperfield, den Komplex um neue Höfe und eine Kapelle zu erweitern. Dabei suchte der Architekt nach „einer räumlichen Organisation […], bei der die einzelnen Baukörper so gruppiert werden, dass sie größere Geschlossenheit vermitteln. Der erste Bauabschnitt, der Hof der Vier Evangelisten", wurde im September 2007 eröffnet. Die Mauern wurden mit Basalt verblendet, in die Böden wurden Zitate aus den Evangelien eingelassen. Auch eine schwarzer Kolonnade aus Sichtbeton ist Teil des ersten Bauabschnitts, während der zweite Teil (voraussichtliche Fertigstellung 2013) die Aufschüttung einer zusätzlichen Insel vorsieht, die neben dem bestehenden Friedhof liegen und Platz für Grabbauten und Parkanlagen bieten soll.

Situé sur une île entre Venise et Murano, le **CIMETIÈRE SAN MICHELE** existe depuis quatre siècles. Pour réconcilier les aspects extérieur et intérieur du site, David Chipperfield ajoute de nouvelles cours intérieures et une chapelle. L'architecte recherche « une structure organisationnelle […] qui regroupe les volumes pour créer une plus grande sensation de solidité. Une première phase du projet, la Cour des quatre évangélistes, a été achevée en septembre 2007, avec des murs revêtus de basalte, des pavements incrustés de textes des Évangiles et une colonnade en béton apparent noir. La seconde phase du projet, dont l'achèvement est prévu pour 2013, verra la création d'une nouvelle île, parallèle au cimetière existant, avec des jardins et les monuments funéraires au niveau de l'eau.

The sober, gray lines of Chipperfield's architecture are well suited to the function of these structures. Modernity seems to have no conflict with tradition in this instance.

Die nüchternen grauen Linien der Architektur Chipperfields scheinen der Funktion dieser Anlage stimmig zu entsprechen. Hier kommt es zu keinerlei Widerspruch zwischen Moderne und Tradition.

La sobriété des lignes grises de l'architecture de Chipperfield est en parfaite adéquation avec la fonction de ces bâtiments. La modernité ne semble, ici, pas entrer en conflit avec la tradition.

COOP HIMMELB(L)AU

Coop Himmelb(l)au / Wolf D. Prix / W. Dreibholz & Partner ZT GmbH
Spengergasse 37 / 1050 Vienna / Austria
Tel: +43 1 54 66 03 34 / Fax: +43 1 54 66 06 00
E-mail: office@coop-himmelblau.at / Web: www.coop-himmelblau.at

Wolf D. Prix, Helmut Swiczinsky, and Michael Holzer founded **COOP HIMMELB(L)AU** in 1968 in Vienna, Austria. In 1988, they opened a second office in Los Angeles. Wolf D. Prix was born in 1942 in Vienna, and educated at the Technical University, Vienna, at SCI-Arc, and at the Architectural Association (AA), London. Since 1993, he has been a Professor of Architecture at the University of Applied Arts in Vienna, Austria. Since 2003, he has been Head of the Institute for Architecture, the Head of Studio Prix, and serves as Vice Rector of the University. Wolfdieter Dreibholz was born in Vienna in 1941 and received a degree in Engineering and Architecture from the Technical University, Vienna, in 1966. He became CEO of COOP HIMMELB(L)AU Wolf D. Prix / W. Dreibholz & Partner ZT GmbH in 2004. Completed projects of the group include the master plan for Melun-Sénart (France, 1986–87); rooftop remodeling Falkestraße (Vienna, Austria, 1983/1987–88); East Pavilion of the Groninger Museum (Groningen, The Netherlands, 1990–94); remodeling of the Austrian Pavilion in the Giardini (Venice, Italy, 1995); UFA Cinema Center (Dresden, Germany, 1993–98); SEG Apartment Tower (Vienna, Austria, 1994–98); and EXPO.02, Forum Arteplage (Biel, Switzerland, 1999–2002). Recent work includes the Academy of Fine Arts (Munich, Germany, 1992/2002–05); the Akron Art Museum (Akron, Ohio, USA, 2001–07); BMW Welt (Munich, Germany, 2001–07); and the Central Los Angeles Area High School #9 for the Visual and Performing Arts (Los Angeles, California, USA, 2002–08, published here). Upcoming work includes the Dalian International Conference Center (Dalian, China, 2008–10); Busan Cinema Center (Busan, South Korea, 2005–11); Musée des Confluences (Lyon, France, 2001–13); and the European Central Bank (Frankfurt am Main, Germany, 2003–14).

Wolf D. Prix, Helmut Swiczinsky und Michael Holzer gründeten **COOP HIMMELB(L)AU** 1968 in Wien. 1988 eröffneten sie ein zweites Büro in Los Angeles. Wolf D. Prix wurde 1942 in Wien geboren und studierte an der Technischen Universität Wien, am SCI-Arc und der Architectural Association (AA) London. Seit 1993 ist er Professor für Architektur an der Universität für Angewandte Kunst in Wien, wo er seit 2003 zudem Leiter des Instituts für Architektur sowie des Studio Prix und Vizerektor der Universität ist. Wolfdieter Dreibholz wurde 1941 in Wien geboren und schloss sein Studium der Architektur und Bauingenieurwissenschaften 1966 an der Technischen Universität Wien ab. 2004 wurde er Geschäftsführer der Coop Himmelb(l)au Wolf D. Prix/W. Dreibholz & Partner ZT GmbH. Gebaute Projekte sind u. a. der Masterplan für Melun-Sénart (Frankreich, 1986–87), der Dachausbau Falkestraße (Wien, 1983/1987–88), der Ostpavillon des Groninger Museums (Niederlande, 1990–94), der Umbau des österreichischen Pavillons in den Giardini (Venedig, 1995), das UFA-Kinocenter (Dresden, 1993–98), das SEG-Apartmenthochhaus (Wien, 1994–98) sowie das Forum Arteplage, EXPO.02 (Biel, Schweiz, 1999–2002). Jüngere Arbeiten sind u. a. die Akademie der bildenden Künste (München, 1992/2002–05), das Akron Art Museum (Akron, Ohio, 2001–07), die BMW-Welt (München, 2001–07) und die Central Los Angeles Area High School #9 für bildende und darstellende Künste (Los Angeles, Kalifornien, 2002–08, hier vorgestellt). In Planung sind u. a. das Internationale Konferenzzentrum in Dalian (China, 2008–10), ein Kinocenter in Busan (Südkorea, 2005–11), das Musée des Confluences (Lyon, 2001–13) und die Europäische Zentralbank (Frankfurt am Main, 2003–14).

Wolf D. Prix, Helmut Swiczinsky, et Michael Holzer ont fondé **COOP HIMMELB(L)AU** en 1968 à Vienne, en Autriche. Ils ont ouvert une seconde agence à Los Angeles, en 1988. Wolf D. Prix est né en 1942 à Vienne, et a étudié à l'Université technique de Vienne, au SCI-Arc, et à l'Architectural Association (AA), à Londres. Depuis 1993, il est professeur d'architecture à l'Université des arts appliqués de Vienne, en Autriche. Depuis 2003, il est directeur de l'Institut d'architecture, directeur de l'atelier Studio Prix, et directeur adjoint de l'université. Wolfdieter Dreibholz est né en Vienne en 1941 et a obtenu un diplôme d'ingénierie et d'architecture à l'Université technique de Vienne, en 1966. Il est devenu directeur exécutif de Coop Himmelb(l)au Wolf D. Prix / W. Dreibholz & Partner ZT GmbH en 2004. Les projets réalisés du groupe incluent le plan directeur de Melun-Sénart (France, 1986–87) ; la restructuration d'un toit, Falkestraße (Vienne, Autriche, 1983/1987–88) ; le pavillon Est du musée de Groningue (Groningue, Pays-Bas, 1990–94) ; la restructuration du pavillon de l'Autriche dans les jardins de la Biennale (Venise, Italie, 1995) ; le complexe multisalle de cinéma UFA (Dresde, Allemagne, 1993–98) ; la tour d'appartements SEG (Vienne, Autriche, 1994–98) ; et le « Forum Arteplage » d'Expo.02 (Biel, Suisse, 1999–2002). Leurs projets récents incluent l'Académie des beaux-arts de Munich (Munich, Allemagne, 1992/2002–05) ; le Musée d'art d'Akron (Akron, Ohio, États-Unis, 2001–07) ; le complexe BMW Welt (Munich, Allemagne, 2001–07) ; et le Central Los Angeles Area High School #9 pour les arts visuels et les arts du spectacle (Los Angeles, Californie, États-Unis, 2002–08, publié ici). Les projets en cours incluent le Centre international de conférences de Dalian (Dalian, Chine, 2008–10) ; le Centre du cinéma de Pusan (Pusan, République de Corée, 2005–11) ; le musée des Confluences (Lyon, France, 2001–13) ; et le nouveau siège de la Banque centrale européenne (Francfort, Allemagne, 2003–14).

CENTRAL LOS ANGELES AREA HIGH SCHOOL #9 FOR THE VISUAL AND PERFORMING ARTS

Los Angeles, California, USA, 2002–08

Address: 450 N Grand Avenue, Los Angeles, CA, USA, +1 213 217 8600, www.central-lausd-ca.schoolloop.com
Area: 21 204 m². Client: LAUSD Los Angeles United School District CA USA
Cost: $171.9 million (including landscaping and outdoor pool). Project Partner: Karolin Schmidbaur

This project is part of the Los Angeles Unified School District (LAUSD) state bond-funded drive to have 155 new schools built by 2012. Located on a four-hectare site in downtown Los Angeles, it is on Grand Avenue, near the Disney Concert Hall by Frank O. Gehry and the Museum of Contemporary Art (Arata Isozaki). The High School includes a professional performing arts theater seating about 1000 people. The facility is designed for a total of 1800 students separated into four different academies, according to the discipline studied. The High School is made up of a total of seven buildings for the theater, classrooms, library, and cafeteria. The architects chose to design the buildings according to a "chess concept" that uses "architectural signs as symbols to communicate the commitment of the Los Angeles community to art." Thus, a tower shaped like the number "9" sits above the theater. A slanted, truncated cone is used for the library, while the functional classroom buildings create an orthogonal perimeter around interior courtyards. Large windows, in particular on Grand Avenue, allow visual continuity between the outside environment and the school. The main entrance of the school is located at the intersection of Grand Avenue and Cesar Chavez Street.

Das Projekt entstand auf Betreiben der Schulverwaltung von Los Angeles (Los Angeles Unified School District, LAUSD), die bis 2012 mithilfe von Anleihen 155 neue Schulen bauen will. Der Komplex liegt auf einem 4 ha großen Gelände in Downtown Los Angeles an der Grand Avenue, unweit der Disney Concert Hall von Frank Gehry und dem Museum of Contemporary Art von Arata Isozaki. Zur Schule gehört u. a. ein voll ausgestattetes Theater mit rund 1000 Plätzen. Die Gebäude sind für 1800 Schüler ausgelegt, die sich je nach Fachrichtung auf vier verschiedene Akademien verteilen. Der Komplex umfasst sieben Gebäude, in denen Theater, Klassenräume, eine Bibliothek und eine Cafeteria untergebracht sind. Die Architekten entschieden sich, das Ensemble nach dem „Schachprinzip" zu gestalten, „architektonische Zeichen werden als Symbole genutzt, um zu zeigen, wie sehr sich Los Angeles den Künsten verschrieben hat". So erhebt sich ein Turm in Form einer „9" über dem Theater. Ein schiefer, gekappter Kegel bietet Platz für die Bibliothek, während die Funktionsgebäude mit den Klassenräumen ein orthogonales Raster um die Innenhöfe herum bilden. Große Fenster, insbesondere zur Grand Avenue, schaffen eine visuelle Verknüpfung zwischen Umfeld und Schule. Der Haupteingang des Komplexes liegt an der Kreuzung Grand Avenue und Cesar Chavez Street.

Ce projet fait partie d'un programme subventionné par le Los Angeles Unified School District, visant à construire 155 nouvelles écoles d'ici 2012. Implanté sur Grand Avenue, dans le centre-ville, sur un terrain de quatre hectares proche du Disney Concert Hall de Frank Gehry et du Musée d'art contemporain (Arata Isozaki), l'école comprend un vrai théâtre de 1000 places. Le complexe est conçu pour un total de 1800 étudiants répartis entre quatre écoles, selon la discipline étudiée. L'école est constituée de sept bâtiments pour le théâtre, les salles de cours, la bibliothèque et la cafétéria. Les architectes ont conçu les bâtiments selon un « concept de damier » utilisant « des signes et symboles architecturaux pour communiquer l'attachement de la communauté de Los Angeles à l'art ». Ainsi, une tour en forme de chiffre « 9 » est posée au sommet du théâtre. Un cône oblique tronqué est utilisé pour la bibliothèque, tandis que les bâtiments fonctionnels des salles de cours créent un périmètre orthogonal autour de cours intérieures. De larges vitrages, en particulier sur Grand Avenue, permettent une continuité visuelle entre l'environnement extérieur et celui de l'école. L'entrée principale est située à l'intersection de Grand Avenue et de Cesar Chavez Street.

An aerial view (above right) shows the situation of the High School vis-à-vis downtown Los Angeles. To the right, the rather surprising forms of the complex.

Das Luftbild (oben rechts) veranschaulicht die Lage der Highschool unweit von Downtown Los Angeles. Rechts die erstaunlichen Formen des Komplexes.

Une vue aérienne (ci-dessus) montre la situation de l'école par rapport au centre de Los Angeles. À droite, les formes assez surprenantes du complexe.

Above, the theater seating 1,000 persons, and the library situated in the truncated cone form of the building.

Oben das Theater mit 1000 Plätzen und die Bibliothek, die im gekappten Kegel des Gebäudekomplexes untergebracht ist.

Ci-dessus, le théâtre de 1000 places et la bibliothèque située dans le bâtiment en forme de cône tronqué.

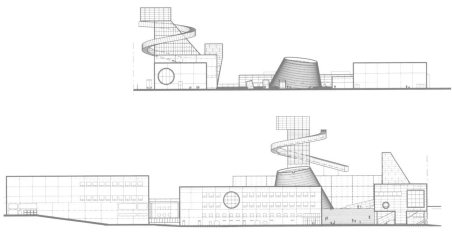

To the left, an angular metallic stairway recalls the forms of other work by the architects. To the right, elevations show the overall design seen from each side.

Die kantige Metalltreppe (links) erinnert an frühere Arbeiten der Architekten. Rechts Aufrisse, die den Entwurf von allen Seiten zeigen.

À gauche, un escalier métallique aux angles obliques rappelle les formes d'autres réalisations des architectes. À droite, des élévations montrent l'ensemble du projet vu de chaque côté.

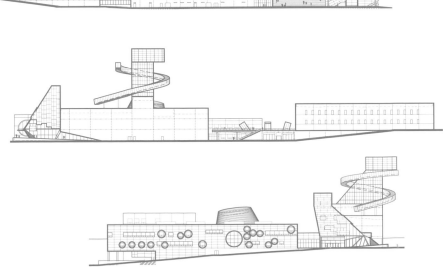

DILLER SCOFIDIO + RENFRO

Diller Scofidio + Renfro / 6 Cooper Square 5F
New York, NY 10003 / USA
Tel: +1 212 260 7971 / Fax: +1 212 260 7924
E-mail: disco@dsrny.com / Web: www.dsrny.com

ELIZABETH DILLER was born in Lodz, Poland, in 1954. She received her B.Arch degree from Cooper Union School of Arts in 1979. She is a Professor of Architecture at Princeton University. **RICARDO SCOFIDIO** was born in New York in 1935. He graduated from Cooper Union School of Architecture and Columbia University, where he is currently a Professor of Architecture. They founded Diller+Scofidio in 1979. **CHARLES RENFRO** became a partner in 2004. Renfro was born in Houston in 1964 and graduated from Rice University and Columbia. According to their own description: "DS+R is a collaborative, interdisciplinary studio involved in design, the visual arts and the performing arts. The team is primarily involved in thematically-driven experimental works that take the form of architectural commissions, temporary installations and permanent site-specific installations, multimedia theater, electronic media, and print." They completed the Seagram Building (New York, New York, 1998–99); the Blur Building (Expo 02, Yverdon-les-Bains, Switzerland, 2000–02); the Viewing Platforms at Ground Zero in Manhattan (New York, 2001); and the Institute of Contemporary Art in Boston (Massachusetts, 2004–06). Among current and ongoing work are the Lincoln Center projects in New York including the expansion of the Juilliard School of Music (2009); the renovation of Alice Tully Hall (New York, 2006–09, published here); the *Hypar* Restaurant (2010); the conversion of the High Line, a 2.4-kilometer stretch of elevated railroad into a New York City park (2009); and the Creative Arts Center at Brown University (Providence, Rhode Island, 2010), all in the USA unless stated otherwise.

ELIZABETH DILLER wurde 1954 in Lodz, Polen, geboren. 1979 schloss sie ihr Studium an der Cooper Union School of Arts mit einem B. Arch. ab. Sie ist Professorin für Architektur an der Universität Princeton. **RICARDO SCOFIDIO** wurde 1935 in New York geboren. Er absolvierte sein Studium an der Cooper Union School of Architecture und der Columbia University, wo er derzeit Professor für Architektur ist. Gemeinsam gründeten sie 1979 Diller+Scofidio. **CHARLES RENFRO** wurde 2004 Partner des Büros. Renfro wurde 1964 in Houston geboren und studierte an der Rice University und der Columbia University. Nach eigener Aussage ist „DS+R ein kooperatives, interdisziplinäres Studio, das in den Bereichen Architektur, bildende und darstellende Künste tätig ist. Das Team beschäftigt sich in erster Linie mit thematisch ausgerichteten, experimentellen Projekten, wobei es sich um architektonische Aufträge, temporäre Installationen und permanente, ortsspezifische Installationen handeln kann, um Multimediatheater, elektronische Medien und Publikationen." Abgeschlossene Projekte sind u. a. das Seagram Building (New York, 2000), das Blur Building (Expo 02, Yverdon-les-Bains, Schweiz, 2000–02), die Aussichtsplattformen für Ground Zero in Manhattan (New York, 2001) sowie das Institute of Contemporary Art in Boston (Massachusetts, 2004–06). Zu den aktuellen Arbeiten des Büros zählen die Projekte am Lincoln Center in New York, einschließlich der Erweiterung der Juilliard School of Music (2009), die Sanierung der Alice Tully Hall (New York, 2006–09, hier vorgestellt) und das *Hypar* Restaurant (2010), die Umnutzung der High Line, eines 2,4 km langen ehemaligen Hochbahnabschnitts als Parkanlage (New York, 2009) und schließlich das Creative Arts Center an der Brown University (Providence, Rhode Island, 2010).

ELIZABETH DILLER est née en Lodz, en Pologne, en 1954. Elle obtient son diplôme d'architecte (B. Arch.) à l'École des beaux-arts de la Cooper Union en 1979. Elle est professeur d'architecture à l'université de Princeton. **RICARDO SCOFIDIO** est né à New York en 1935. Il est diplômé de l'École d'architecture de la Cooper Union et de l'université Columbia, où il est actuellement professeur d'architecture. Ils ont fondé Diller+Scofidio en 1979. **CHARLES RENFRO** devient leur associé en 2004. Renfro est né à Houston en 1964 et est diplômé des universités Rice et Columbia. Selon leur propre description, « DS+R est un atelier en collaboration interdisciplinaire impliqué dans les domaines du design, des arts visuels et des arts du spectacle. L'équipe s'implique d'abord dans des projets thématiques expérimentaux, sous forme de commandes architecturales, d'installations temporaires et d'installations permanentes spécifiques à un site, de théâtre multimédia, d'édition électronique et papier ». Ils ont réalisé la tour Seagram (New York, 1998–99), le nuage « Blur » d'Expo.02 (Yverdon-les-Bains, Suisse, 2000–02), des plateformes d'observation sur le site de Ground Zero, à Manhattan (New York, 2001), et l'Institut d'art contemporain de Boston (Massachusetts, 2004–06). Parmi leurs projets en cours, on compte celui pour le Lincoln Center, à New York, dont l'extension de l'École de Musique Juilliard (2009) ; la rénovation de l'Alice Tully Hall (New York, 2006–09, publié ici) ; et le restaurant *Hypar* (2010) ; la conversion d'un tronçon long de 2,4 kilomètres d'une ligne de chemin de fer suspendue, la High Line, en un parc urbain (New York, 2009) ; et le Centre des arts créatifs de l'université Brown (Providence, Rhode Island, 2010), tous situés aux États-Unis, sauf mention contraire.

ALICE TULLY HALL

Lincoln Center, New York, New York, USA, 2006–09

Address: 1941 Broadway, New York, NY 10023, USA, +1 212 671 4050, www.lincolncenter.org
Area: 10 173 m². Client: Lincoln Center Development Project. Cost: not disclosed
Collaboration: FXFowle Architects

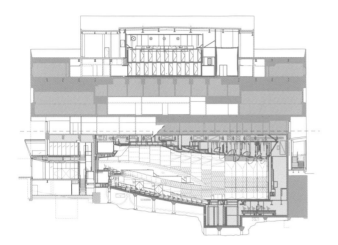
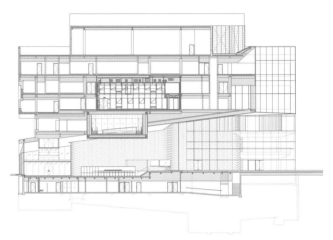

Part of an ongoing renovation project of Lincoln Center, New York's premier location for the performing arts, the **ALICE TULLY HALL** renovation participates in the architects' overall vision for the complex. "Rather than oppose the architectural strategies of the existing modern buildings, our design reinterprets the genetic code of the campus into a language that can speak to a diverse audience after several generations of social and political change," say the architects. Located beneath the Julliard School, the facility seats 1100 people. Diller Scofidio + Renfro stripped away the opaque elements of the structure, originally designed by Pietro Belluschi, to give Alice Tully Hall the Broadway visibility that it lacked. The visual and acoustic aspects of the hall were improved, for example by creating a "box-in-box" protection against the vibration caused by the nearby 7th Avenue subway line, or lining the inner surfaces with a "high-performance" wood that distributes sound evenly. Radiant heat and cooling systems, and a reconstruction of the Central Mechanical Plant that serves the 11 venues of Lincoln Center, contribute to a clear and present environmental awareness expressed in this project.

Als Teil einer nach wie vor andauernden Sanierung des Lincoln Center, New Yorks wichtigstem Spielort für darstellende Künste, veranschaulicht der Umbau der **ALICE TULLY HALL** die Vision der Architeken für den gesamten Komplex. Die Architekten erklären: „Statt sich als Gegenposition zur Architektur der bestehenden modernen Gebäude zu definieren, interpretiert unser Entwurf den genetischen Code des Campusensembles neu – auf eine Weise, die nach Generationen des sozialen und politischen Wandels ein breitgefächertes Publikum anspricht." Der unter der Juilliard School gelegene Saal fasst 1100 Besucher. Diller Scofidio + Renfro entfernten die massiven Wandelemente des ursprünglich von Pietro Belluschi entworfenen Baus und stellten so einen Blickkontakt zwischen der Alice Tully Hall und dem Broadway her, der vorher nicht gegeben war. Die visuellen und akustischen Qualitäten des Konzertsaals wurden verbessert, etwa durch die Konstruktion einer „Box in einer Box", die den Saal vor den Erschütterungen durch die nahe U-Bahn der 7th Avenue schützt, sowie die Verkleidung des Innenraums mit einem speziellen Holz, das für gleichmäßige Klangverteilung sorgt. Die Installation eines Fußbodenheizungs- und Kühlsystems ebenso wie die Sanierung der zentralen Haustechnikeinrichtungen, die sämtliche elf Spielstätten des Lincoln Center versorgen, zeugen vom ausgeprägten Umweltbewusstsein des Teams.

La transformation de l'**ALICE TULLY HALL** fait partie d'un projet de rénovation du Lincoln Center, le lieu le plus important de New York pour les arts du spectacle, et s'inscrit dans la vision d'ensemble des architectes pour le complexe. « Plutôt que d'opposer les stratégies architecturales des bâtiments modernes existants, notre projet réinterprète le code génétique du campus en un langage compréhensible par les divers publics, après plusieurs générations de changement politique et social », disent les architectes. Située sous l'École Juilliard, la salle peut accueillir 1100 spectateurs. Diller Scofidio + Renfro ont dépouillé le bâtiment de ses éléments opaques d'origine conçus par Pietro Belluschi, pour offrir à l'Alice Tully Hall la visibilité depuis Broadway qui lui faisait défaut. Les aspects visuels et acoustiques de la salle ont été améliorés, par exemple en créant une protection « box-in-box » contre les vibrations dues à la proximité de la ligne de métro de la 7ᵉ Avenue, ou en doublant les surfaces intérieures d'un bois « hautement performant » qui diffuse le son régulièrement. Des systèmes de chauffage et de refroidissement par rayonnement, et la reconstruction du bâtiment central des machines utilisé par les onze lieux du Lincoln Center, témoignent de la conscience écologique clairement exprimée dans ce projet.

Above, section drawings show the intervention of the architects on the preexisting building.

Querschnitte (oben) veranschaulichen die Eingriffe der Architekten in den bestehenden Gebäudekomplex.

Ci-dessus, des coupes montrent l'intervention des architectes sur le bâtiment préexistant.

Although it is a remake of the original Pietro Belluschi building, Alice Tully Hall stands out against Lincoln Center and the Upper West Side skyline of Manhattan.

Obwohl die Alice Tully Hall im Grunde ein Remake des Altbaus von Pietro Belluschi ist, hebt sie sich vom Lincoln Center und der Skyline der Upper Westside von Manhattan ab.

Nouvelle version du bâtiment d'origine de Pietro Belluschi, l'Alice Tully Hall se détache néanmoins sur le Lincoln Center et la silhouette de l'Upper West Side de Manhattan.

Where an enclosed, Modernist architecture existed, the architects have
created open, contemporary spaces.
To the right, the main concert hall.

Anstelle der früheren, geschlossenen
modernistischen Architektur gestalteten
die Architekten offene, zeitgenössische Räume. Rechts der große
Konzertsaal.

À la place de l'architecture moderniste
existante, enclavée, les architectes
ont créé des espaces contemporains
ouverts. À droite, la grande salle de
concert.

A café with high glazed walls opens out to the city, whereas Lincoln Center in general has always been rather closed and stony by comparison.

Ein Café mit hohen Glasfronten öffnet sich zur Stadt. Im Vergleich hierzu hatte sich das Lincoln Center bisher immer eher geschlossen und steinern präsentiert.

Avec ses hauts murs entièrement vitrés, ce café s'ouvre sur la ville, à la différence du Lincoln Center qui a toujours été assez froid et fermé.

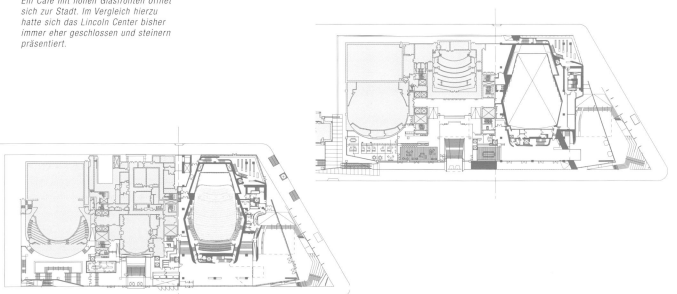

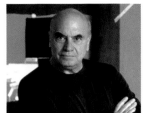

MASSIMILIANO AND DORIANA FUKSAS

Massimiliano and Doriana Fuksas / Piazza del Monte di Pietà 30
00186 Rome / Italy
Tel: +39 06 68 80 78 71 / Fax: +39 06 68 80 78 72
E-mail: office@fuksas.it / Web: www.fuksas.it

MASSIMILIANO FUKSAS was born in 1944 in Rome. He received his degree in Architecture at the "La Sapienza" University of Rome in 1969. He created Granma (1969–88) with Anna Maria Sacconi, and opened an office in Paris in 1989. He won the 1999 Grand Prix d'Architecture in France, and has written the architecture column of the Italian weekly *L'Espresso* since 2000. He was the Director of the 7th Architecture Biennale in Venice (1998–2000). He has worked with **DORIANA MANDRELLI FUKSAS** since 1985. She attended the Faculty of Architecture at the "La Sapienza" University of Rome and has been responsible for design in the firm since 1997. The presence in France of Massimiliano Fuksas was notably marked by his work at the Mediatheque in Rézé (1987–91); the National Engineering School in Brest (ENIB ISAMOR, 1990–92); the Maison des Arts at the Michel de Montaigne University in Bordeaux (1992–95); and the Maximilien-Perret High School Alfortville near Paris (1995–97). His Cor-ten steel entrance for the caves at Niaux (1988–93) shows, as did the Maison des Arts in Bordeaux, that Fuksas has a sustained interest in contemporary sculpture and art. More recently, Fuksas completed the Ferrari Research Center (Maranello, Italy, 2001–04); Fiera Milano (Rho-Pero, Milan, Italy, 2002–05); Zenith Strasbourg (Eckbolsheim, Strasbourg, France, 2003–07); Armani Ginza Tower (Tokyo, Japan, 2005–07); and the Church in Foligno (Italy, 2001–09, published here). Upcoming work includes the Peres Peace Center (Jaffa, Israel); Molas Golf Resort (Pula, Italy); Euromed Center in Marseille (France); and the French National Archives (Paris, France).

MASSIMILIANO FUKSAS wurde 1944 in Rom geboren und schloss sein Architekturstudium an der Universität Rom, La Sapienza, ab. Zusammen mit Anna Maria Sacconi gründete er das Büro Granma, das von 1969 bis 1989 bestand. 1989 eröffnete er ein neues Büro in Paris. 1999 wurde er in Frankreich mit dem Grand Prix d'Architecture ausgezeichnet, 1998 bis 2000 war er Direktor der VII. Architekturbiennale von Venedig (1998–2000) und schreibt seit 2000 eine Architekturkolumne für die italienische Wochenzeitschrift *L'Espresso*. Seit 1985 arbeitet er mit **DORIANA MANDRELLI FUKSAS** zusammen. Sie studierte ebenfalls Architektur an der La Sapienza in Rom und ist seit 1997 verantwortlich für die Entwürfe des Büros. In Frankreich machte sich Massimiliano Fuksas insbesondere mit Projekten wie der Mediathek in Rézé (1987–91) einen Namen sowie der Nationalen Hochschule für Bauingenieurwesen in Brest (ENIB ISAMOR, 1990–92), der Maison des Arts an der Universität Michel de Montaigne in Bordeaux (1992–95) und der Maximilien-Perret-Schule in Alfortville bei Paris (1995–97). Der aus Cor-Ten-Stahl gestaltete Eingangsbereich zu den Höhlen von Niaux (1988–93) belegt ebenso wie die Maison des Arts in Bordeaux Fuksas' anhaltendes Interesse an zeitgenössischer Skulptur und Kunst. In jüngerer Zeit konnte Fuksas das Ferrari-Forschungszentrum (Maranello, Italien, 2001–04), die Fiera Milano (Rho-Pero, Mailand, 2002–05), das Zenith Strasbourg (Eckbolsheim, Frankreich, 2003–07), den Armani Ginza Tower (Tokio, 2005–07) sowie die Kirche in Foligno (Italien, 2001–09, hier vorgestellt) fertigstellen. Geplante Projekte sind u. a. das Peres-Friedenszentrum (Jaffa, Israel), die Golfanlage Molas (Pula, Italien), das Euromed-Center in Marseille (Frankreich) sowie das französische Staatsarchiv (Paris).

MASSIMILIANO FUKSAS est né en 1944 à Rome. Il obtient son diplôme d'architecte à l'université de Rome La Sapienza en 1969. Il fonde Granma (1969–88) avec Anna Maria Sacconi, et ouvre un cabinet à Paris en 1989. En 1999, il gagne le grand prix d'Architecture de l'Académie des beaux-arts. Depuis 2000, il écrit la rubrique architecture de l'hebdomadaire italien *L'Espresso*. Il a été directeur de la VIIIᵉ Biennale d'Architecture de Venise (1998–2000). Il travaille avec **DORIANA MANDRELLI FUKSAS** depuis 1985. Celle-ci a étudié l'architecture à l'Université de Rome La Sapienza et est responsable de projets de l'agence depuis 1997. L'activité de Massimiliano Fuksas en France a notamment été marquée par la médiathèque de Rézé (1987–91), l'École nationale d'ingénieurs de Brest (ENIB ISAMOR, 1990–92), la Maison des arts de l'université Michel-de-Montaigne, à Bordeaux (1992–95), et le lycée Maximilien-Perret d'Alfortville, près de Paris (1995–97). L'entrée en acier Corten qu'il réalise pour les grottes de Niaux (1988–93) dénote, comme la Maison des arts de Bordeaux, l'intérêt constant de Fuksas pour l'art et la sculpture contemporains. Plus récemment, Fuksas a réalisé le Centre de recherches Ferrari (Maranello, Italie, 2001–04) ; la Foire de Milan (Rho-Pero, Milan, Italie, 2002–05) ; le Zénith de Strasbourg (Eckbolsheim, Strasbourg, France, 2003–07) ; la tour Armani Ginza (Tokyo, Japon, 2005–07) ; et la nouvelle église de Foligno (Italie, 2001–09, projet publié ici). Leurs projets en cours incluent la Maison de la paix Peres (Jaffa, Israël) ; le domaine de golf Molas (Pula, Italie) ; le Centre Euromed à Marseille (France) ; et le nouveau bâtiment des Archives nationales de France (Pierrefitte-sur-Seine, France).

CHURCH IN FOLIGNO
Foligno, Italy, 2001–09

Address: Via del Roccolo, 06034 Foligno, Italy
Area: 610 m² (church) and 1300 m² (parish complex). Client: Conferenza Episcopale Italiana
Cost: not disclosed

The architects won this project in a competition held in 2001 as a "sign of innovation that meets the latest international research, becoming a symbol of rebirth for the city after the earthquake." Foligno is located in the province of Perugia, in east central Umbria, and suffered a major earthquake in 1997. The actual Church building is made up of "two rectangles inserted into each other", while the Sacristy is a long, low, rectangular volume, also containing pastoral spaces, and a residence for the priest. The main volume is 30 x 22.5 meters and 25.8 meters high. A third volume connects the other two and contains a chapel for daily use. Massimiliano Fuksas describes "the suspension of a volume within another. Seeing through concrete to heaven, from outside, to inside, to outside." The artist Enzo Cucchi created a 13.5-meter-high cement and white Carrara marble sculpture for the exterior of the Church, called *Stele-Cross*. The painter Mimmo Paladino created a work called *14 Stations of the Cross*, and Fuksas Design designed the furniture and lighting.

Die Architekten gewannen 2001 den Wettbewerb für dieses Projekt. Ihr Entwurf wurde als ein „Zeichen für Innovation" verstanden, „das dem neuesten internationalen Forschungsstand entspricht und ein Symbol für die Wiedergeburt der Stadt nach dem Erdbeben ist". Foligno liegt in der Provinz Perugia, östlich von Zentralumbrien und wurde 1997 von einem schweren Erdbeben erschüttert. Der Kirchenbau selbst besteht aus „zwei ineinander verschachtelten Rechtecken", während die Sakristei als langgestreckter, niedriger rechteckiger Baukörper gestaltet wurde, in dem sich zudem Gemeinderäume sowie eine Wohnung für den Priester befinden. Der zentrale Baukörper misst 30 x 22,5 m und ist 25,8 m hoch. Ein drittes Bauteil verbindet die beiden anderen; dort ist außerdem eine Kapelle für tägliche Gottesdienste untergebracht. Massimiliano Fuksas spricht vom „Schweben des einen Volumens im anderen. Durch den Beton blickt man zum Himmel auf, von außen nach innen, von innen nach außen." Der Künstler Enzo Cucchi gestaltete eine 13,5 m hohe Skulptur aus Zement und weißem Carrara-Marmor für die Fassade der Kirche, das *Stele-Cross*. Der Maler Mimmo Paladino schuf *Die 14 Kreuzwegstationen*, während Fuksas die Gestaltung von Mobiliar und Leuchten übernahm.

Les architectes ont gagné ce projet dans un concours lancé en 2001 comme un « signe d'innovation à la pointe de la recherche internationale, devenant un symbole de la renaissance de la ville après le séisme ». Foligno est située dans la province de Pérouse, en Ombrie, dans l'Italie centrale, et a subi un important séisme en 1997. L'église actuelle est faite de « deux rectangles imbriqués l'un dans l'autre », tandis que la sacristie est un volume rectangulaire long et bas, comportant également des locaux paroissiaux et le presbytère. Le volume principal mesure 30 x 22,5 mètres pour une hauteur de 25,8 mètres. Un troisième volume relie les deux autres et contient une chapelle ordinaire. Massimiliano Fuksas décrit ainsi « la suspension d'un volume dans un autre. Voir à travers le béton vers le ciel, de l'extérieur, vers l'intérieur, vers l'extérieur ». L'artiste Enzo Cucchi a créé une sculpture en ciment et marbre blanc de 13,5 mètres de haut intitulée *Stele-Croce*. Le peintre Mimmo Paladino a créé les *14 Stations du chemin de croix*, et Fuksas Design a conçu le mobilier et les luminaires.

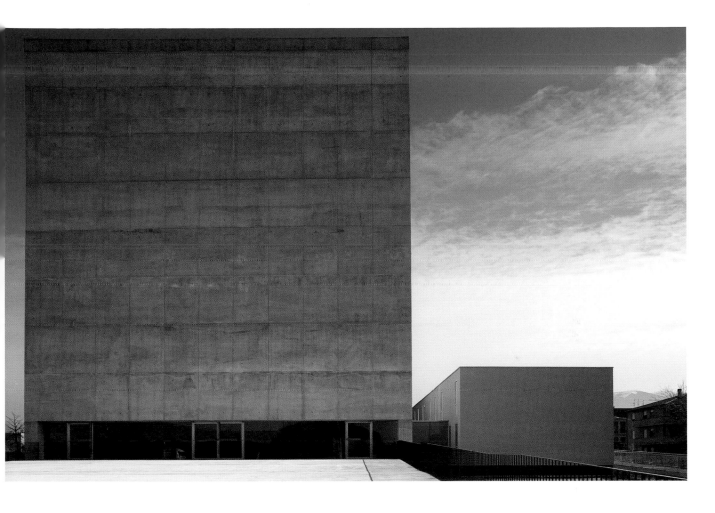

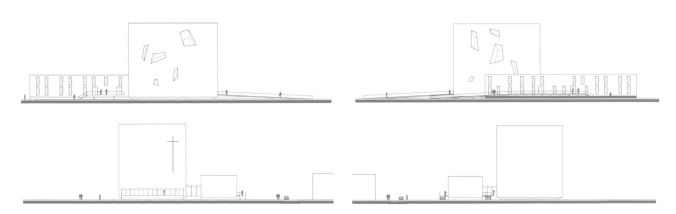

The Church stands out against a mountainous background. As the picture above and elevation drawings show, the basic form of the main structure is expressed as a weighty box that just barely lifts off the ground to allow for entry.

Die Kirche hebt sich deutlich vom Bergpanorama ab. Wie Foto (oben) und Aufrisse zeigen, ist das Hauptvolumen des Baus als massiver Kubus gestaltet, der sich nur soviel vom Boden löst, um den Zugang zu erlauben.

L'église se détache sur un arrière-plan montagneux. Comme le montrent la photo ci-dessus et les élévations, la forme de base du bâtiment principal est representée par un cube massif se détachant à peine du sol pour fournir un accès.

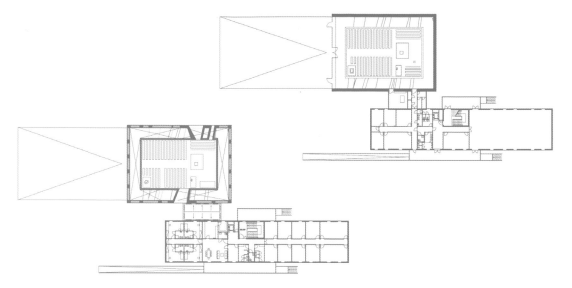

Plans show the main church and the connected pastoral and residence spaces. Inside, a feeling of weight seen in the exterior forms is alleviated by large, glazed openings.

Die Grundrisse zeigen den Hauptkirchenraum sowie die angeschlossenen Gemeinde- und Wohnräume. Im Innern des Gebäudes wird der äußere Eindruck der Massivität, durch großzügige Fensteröffnungen aufgelockert.

Les plans montrent l'église et les locaux paroissiaux et résidentiels qui lui sont rattachés. Les formes extérieures massives du bâtiment sont atténuées à l'intérieur par les larges ouvertures vitrées.

FRANK O. GEHRY

Gehry Partners, LLP / 12541 Beatrice Street
Los Angeles, CA 90066 / USA
Tel: +1 310 482 3000 / Fax: +1 310 482 3006

Born in Toronto, Canada, in 1929, **FRANK O. GEHRY** studied at the University of Southern California, Los Angeles (1949–51), and at Harvard (1956–57). Principal of Frank O. Gehry and Associates, Inc., Los Angeles, since 1962, he received the 1989 Pritzker Prize. Some of his notable projects are the Loyola Law School (Los Angeles, California, 1981–84); Norton Residence (Venice, California, 1983); California Aerospace Museum (Los Angeles, California, 1982–84); Schnabel Residence (Brentwood, California, 1989); Festival Disney (Marne-la-Vallée, France, 1989–92); Guggenheim Museum (Bilbao, Spain, 1991–97); the unbuilt Guggenheim Museum (New York, 1998–); and the Experience Music Project (Seattle, Washington, 1995–2000). Recent completed work includes the DG Bank Headquarters (Berlin, Germany, 2000); Fisher Center for the Performing Arts at Bard College (Annandale-on-Hudson, New York, 2002); Walt Disney Concert Hall (Los Angeles, California, 2003); and the Massachusetts Institute of Technology Stata Complex (Cambridge, Massachusetts, 2003). Recent and current work includes Maggie's Center (Dundee, Scotland, 1999–2003); Jay Pritzker Pavilion (Chicago, Illinois, 1999–2004); the Hotel Marques de Riscal (Elciego, Spain, 2003–06); InterActiveCorp Headquarters (New York, New York, 2003–07); the Art Gallery of Ontario Extension (Toronto, Canada, 2005–08); Serpentine Pavilion, Kensington Gardens (London, UK, 2008, published here); the Lou Ruvo Alzheimer's Institute (Las Vegas, Nevada, 2003–09); the Danske Hus, Danish Cancer Centre (Aarhus, Denmark, 2005–09); the Bridge of Life Museum (Panama City, Panama, 2000–10); and the New World Symphony (Miami, Florida, 2003–10), all in the USA unless stated otherwise.

FRANK O. GEHRY wurde 1929 in Toronto, Kanada, geboren und studierte an der University of Southern California, Los Angeles (1949–51), sowie in Harvard (1956–57). Seit 1962 ist Gehry Direktor von Frank O. Gehry and Associates, Inc., in Los Angeles und wurde 1989 mit dem Pritzker-Preis ausgezeichnet. Zu seinen bemerkenswertesten Projekten zählen die Loyola Law School (Los Angeles, 1981–84), die Norton Residence (Venice, Kalifornien, 1983), das California Aerospace Museum (Los Angeles, 1982–84), die Schnabel Residence (Brentwood, Kalifornien, 1989), Festival Disney (Marne-la-Vallée, Frankreich, 1989–92), das Guggenheim Museum Bilbao (Spanien, 1991–97), das nicht realisierte Guggenheim Museum New York (1998) sowie das Experience Music Project (Seattle, Washington, 1995–2000). Jüngere fertiggestellte Projekte sind u. a. die Zentrale der DG-Bank (Berlin, 2000), das Fisher Center for the Performing Arts am Bard College (Annandale-on-Hudson, New York, 2002), die Walt Disney Concert Hall (Los Angeles, 2003) und der Stata Complex am Massachusetts Institute of Technology (Cambridge, Massachusetts, 2003). Zu den aktuellen Arbeiten zählen Maggie's Center (Dundee, Schottland, 1999–2003), der Jay-Pritzker-Pavillon (Chicago, Illinois, 1999–2004), das Hotel Marques de Riscal (Elciego, Spanien, 2003–06), die Zentrale von InterActiveCorp (New York, 2003–07), die Erweiterung der Art Gallery of Ontario (Toronto, Kanada, 2005–08), der Serpentine Pavilion, Kensington Gardens (London, 2008, hier vorgestellt), das Lou-Ruvo-Alzheimer-Institut (Las Vegas, Nevada, 2003–09), das dänische Krebszentrum Danske Hus (Århus, Dänemark, 2005–09), das Bridge of Life Museum (Panama-Stadt, Panama, 2000–10) und schließlich die New World Symphony (Miami, Florida, 2003–10).

Né à Toronto, au Canada, en 1929, **FRANK O. GEHRY** étudie à l'université de Californie du Sud, à Los Angeles (1949–51) et à Harvard (1956–57). Directeur de Frank O. Gehry and Associates Inc., Los Angeles, depuis 1962, il reçoit le prix Pritzker 1989. Parmi ses projets remarqués, on compte la faculté de droit Loyola Law School (Los Angeles, Californie, 1981–84); la résidence Norton (Venice, Californie, 1983); le Musée de l'aérospaciale de Californie (Los Angeles, Californie, 1982–84); la résidence Schnabel (Brentwood, Californie, 1989); Disney Village (Marne-la-Vallée, France, 1989–92), le musée Guggenheim de Bilbao (Bilbao, Espagne, 1991–97); le musée Guggenheim non encore construit de New York (1998–); et le Centre culturel Experience Music Project (Seattle, Washington, 1995–2000). Ses réalisations récentes incluent le siège de la DG Bank (Berlin, Allemagne, 2000); le Centre Fisher pour les arts du spectacle àu Bard College (Annandale-on-Hudson, New York, 2002); la salle Walt Disney Concert Hall (Los Angeles, Californie, 2003); et le complexe universitaire Stata au Massachusetts Institute of Technology (Cambridge, Massachusetts, 2003). Ses projets récents incluent le dispensaire Maggie's Center (Dundee, Écosse, 1999–2003); le pavillon Jay Pritzker (Chicago, Illinois, 1999–2004); l'hôtel Marques de Riscal (Elciego, Espagne, 2003–06); le siège InterActiveCorp (New York, 2003–07); l'extension du Musée des beaux-arts de l'Ontario (Toronto, Canada, 2005–08); le pavillon Serpentine, Kensington Gardens (Londres, Royaume-Uni, 2008, publié ici); le Lou Ruvo Alzheimer's Institute (Las Vegas, Nevada, 2003–09); le Danske Hus, un centre de la Danish Cancer Society (Aarhus, Danemark, 2005–09); le musée de la Biodiversité de Panama (Panama City, Panama, 2000–10); et le New World Symphony (Miami, Floride, 2003–10), tous situés aux États-Unis sauf mention contraire.

SERPENTINE PAVILION

Kensington Gardens, London, UK, 2008

Area: 418 m². Client: Serpentine Gallery. Cost: not disclosed
Collaboration: Arup Nussli, Taylor Woodrow

This was the **2008 TEMPORARY PAVILION FOR THE SERPENTINE GALLERY** in Kensington Gardens, London—one of a series of prestigious commissions for ephemeral structures on the same location, with authors such as Oscar Niemeyer, Toyo Ito, and Álvaro Siza. It is a timber structure "that acts as an urban street connecting the park with the permanent gallery building." Glass canopies hang inside the structure for acoustics purposes. It was intended as a place for live performances with a capacity of about 275 spectators. Gehry explains: "The interplay between the exoskeleton of timber planks and the multiple glazed roof surfaces invokes imagery of striped park tent structures and catapults, capturing the visual energy of a place created from the juxtaposition of random elements." In a sense, the temporary nature and apparently random juxtaposition of its elements bring to mind the early work of Frank Gehry, before he called on sophisticated computer technology and cladding materials such as titanium. The Pavilion has now been installed at the Château La Coste near Aix-en-Provence, France.

Gehrys **TEMPORÄRER PAVILLON FÜR DIE SERPENTINE GALLERY** in Kensington Gardens, London, wurde 2008 realisiert – ein prestigeträchtiger Auftrag, der regelmäßig für einen temporären Bau an diesem Ort vergeben wird, bisher u. a. an Architekten wie Oscar Niemeyer, Toyo Ito oder Álvaro Siza. Gehrys Pavillon ist eine Holzkonstruktion, die „wie eine öffentliche Straße funktioniert und den Park und das permanente Galeriegebäude miteinander verbindet". Aus akustischen Gründen wurden Dachsegmente aus Glas in der Konstruktion abgehängt. Es sollten Liveveranstaltungen mit bis zu 275 Zuschauern stattfinden können. Gehry führt aus: „Das Zusammenspiel zwischen dem äußeren Skelett aus Holzbindern und der Vielzahl gläserner Dachsegmente erinnert an gestreifte Gartenzelte oder auch an Katapulte und symbolisiert die visuelle Energie eines Orts, der aus den Gegensätzen willkürlicher Elemente geboren wurde." In gewisser Weise knüpfen die temporäre Form und die scheinbar willkürliche Kombination gegensätzlicher Elemente an Gehrys Frühwerk an, an Zeiten, bevor er sich aufwendigen Computerprogrammen und Verblendmaterialien wie Titan zuwandte. Inzwischen wurde der Pavillon am Château La Coste unweit von Aix-en-Provence wieder aufgebaut.

C'était le **PAVILLON TEMPORAIRE 2008 DE LA SERPENTINE GALLERY**, dans Kensington Gardens, à Londres – un ensemble de commandes prestigieuses pour des bâtiments éphémères situés au même endroit, attribuées à des créateurs comme Oscar Niemeyer, Toyo Ito, et Álvaro Siza. C'est une structure de poutres « qui agit comme une rue reliant le parc avec le bâtiment permanent du musée ». Des toits en verre sont suspendus à l'intérieur pour les besoins de l'acoustique. Le bâtiment était destiné à des performances publiques pour environ 275 spectateurs. Gehry explique : « Le jeu entre l'exosquelette de planches de bois et les multiples surfaces de toiture vitrée évoque des images de tentes de jardin rayées et de balistes captant l'énergie visuelle d'une place créée par la juxtaposition aléatoire d'éléments. » La nature temporaire et la juxtaposition apparemment aléatoire de ces éléments rappellent les premières réalisations de Frank Gehry, avant qu'il ne recoure aux moyens sophistiqués de la technologie informatique et des matériaux de revêtement comme le titane. Le pavillon est maintenant installé en France, au Château La Coste, près d'Aix-en-Provence.

Drawings show the complexity of the structure with its sculptural elements enclosing an outdoor performance space.

Les dessins montrent la complexité de la structure, avec ses éléments sculpturaux enveloppant un espace de spectacles de plein air.

Zeichnungen veranschaulichen die Komplexität des Baus, dessen skulpturale Elemente eine Freiluftbühne rahmen.

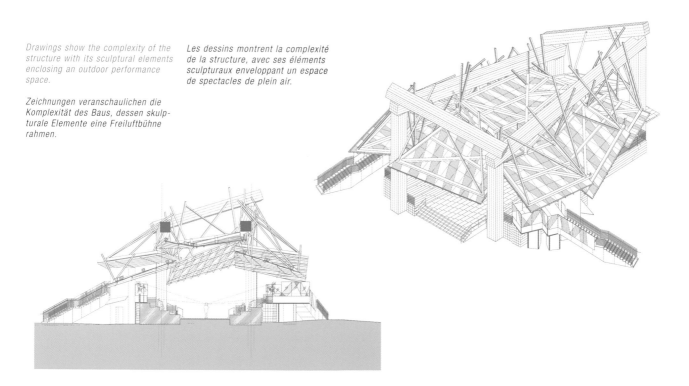

More like a vast contemporary sculpture than a building, the Pavilion has
all the hallmarks of a classic Frank
Gehry design.

*Der Pavillon wirkt eher wie eine zeit-
genössische Skulptur als ein Gebäude
und weist alle typischen Merkmale
eines Gehry-Entwurfs auf.*

*Le pavillon, qui ressemble plus à une
sculpture contemporaine monumentale qu'à un bâtiment, a toutes les
caractéristiques d'un classique de
Frank Gehry.*

The alternation of large openings and
the complex assembly of the roof
contrasts in the image to the right
with the more staid Georgian architecture of the Serpentine Gallery.

Der Wechsel zwischen großen Öffnungen und der komplexen Dachkonstruktion kontrastiert auf dem Bild
rechts auffällig mit der gesetzteren
georgianischen Architektur der Serpentine Gallery.

Les larges ouvertures alternées et
l'assemblage complexe de la toiture
contrastent, sur la photo de droite,
avec la sobriété de l'architecture
géorgienne de la Serpentine Gallery.

NICHOLAS GRIMSHAW

Grimshaw / 57 Clerkenwell Road / London EC1M 5NG / UK
Tel: +44 20 72 91 41 41 / Fax: +44 20 72 91 41 94
E-mail: communications@grimshaw-architects.com
Web: www.grimshaw-architects.com

A 1965 graduate of the Architectural Association (AA), **NICHOLAS GRIMSHAW** was born in 1939 in London. He created the firm Nicholas Grimshaw and Partners Ltd. in 1980, now known as Grimshaw. His numerous industrial/corporate/commercial structures include those built for Herman Miller in Bath (1976); BMW at Bracknell (1980); the furniture maker Vitra (Weil am Rhein, Germany, 1981); and the *Financial Times* in London in 1988. He also built the British Pavilion at the 1992 Universal Exhibition in Seville. One of his most visible works is the former International Terminal of Waterloo Station (London, 1988–93). Grimshaw currently employs over 200 staff with offices in London, New York, and Melbourne. Andrew Whalley, a Partner in the firm, was educated at the Mackintosh School of Architecture (B.Arch, 1984) and at the AA in London (1986). Vincent Chang, also a Partner, received his degrees at the Cambridge University School of Architecture (1988, 1991). Buildings include the Rolls Royce Manufacturing Plant and Head Office (West Sussex, UK, 2003); Zurich Airport (Zurich, Switzerland, 2003 and 2004); Sankei Nishi-Umeda Building (Osaka, Japan, 2004); University College London New Engineering Building (London, UK, 2005); Southern Cross Station (Melbourne, Australia, 2002–06, published here); Caixa Galicia Arts Foundation (A CoruÀa, Spain, 2006); University College London Cancer Institute, Paul O'Gorman Building (London, UK, 2007); Dubai Tower (design 2007); Amsterdam Bijlmer ArenA Station (Amsterdam, The Netherlands, 2002–07); Horno 3, Museo Del Acero (Monterrey, Mexico, 2006–07); London School of Economics New Academic Building (London, UK, 2004–08); and the Experimental Media and Performing Arts Center (EMPAC) (Troy, New York, USA, 2004–08, also published here).

NICHOLAS GRIMSHAW, 1939 in London geboren, schloss sein Studium 1965 an der dortigen Architectural Association (AA) ab. 1980 gründete er sein Büro Nicholas Grimshaw and Partners Ltd., heute bekannt als Grimshaw. Zu seinen zahllosen Fabrik-, Büro- und Gewerbebauten zählen Projekte für Herman Miller in Bath (1976), BMW in Bracknell (1980), den Möbelhersteller Vitra (Weil am Rhein, Deutschland, 1981) und die *Financial Times* in London (1988). Grimshaw realisierte auch den britischen Pavillon auf der Weltausstellung 1992 in Sevilla. Eine seiner bekanntesten Arbeiten ist das ehemalige Internationale Terminal an der Waterloo Station (London, 1988–93). Grimshaw beschäftigt derzeit rund 200 Mitarbeiter in seinen Büros in London, New York und Melbourne. Andrew Whalley, einer der Partner des Büros, studierte an der Mackintosh School of Architecture (B. Arch., 1984) und der AA in London (1986). Vincent Chang, ebenfalls Partner, machte seine Abschlüsse an der Architekturfakultät in Cambridge (1988, 1991). Zu den Bauten des Büros zählen die Werksanlagen und Geschäftszentrale von Rolls Royce (West Sussex, Großbritannien, 2003), der Flughafen Zürich (2003 und 2004), das Sankei Nishi-Umeda Building (Osaka, Japan, 2004), die neue Fakultät für Bauingenieurwesen am University College London (2005), die Southern Cross Station (Melbourne, Australien, 2002–06, hier vorgestellt), die Kunststiftung Caixa Galicia (A Coruña, Spanien, 2006), das Paul O'Gorman Building des Krebszentrums am University College London (2007), der Dubai Tower (Entwurf 2007), der Bahnhof Bijlmer ArenA (Amsterdam, 2002–07), Horno 3 am Museo del Acero (Monterrey, Mexiko, 2006–07), das New Academic Building an der London School of Economics (London, 2004–08) sowie das Zentrum für experimentelle Medien und darstellende Künste (EMPAC) in Troy (New York, 2004–08, ebenfalls hier vorgestellt).

Diplômé de l'Architectural Association (AA) en 1965, **NICHOLAS GRIMSHAW** est né en 1939 à Londres. Il fonde l'agence Nicholas Grimshaw and Partners Ltd. en 1980, maintenant connue sous le nom Grimshaw. Ses nombreux bâtiments industriels, de bureaux, ou commerciaux incluent ceux construits pour Herman Miller à Bath (1976) ; BMW à Bracknell (1980) ; le fabricant de meubles Vitra (Weil-am-Rhein, Allemagne, 1981) ; et le *Financial Times*, à Londres, en 1988. Il a également construit le Pavillon britannique de l'Exposition universelle de 1992 à Séville. Une de ses réalisations les plus connues est l'ancien terminal international la gare de Waterloo (Londres, 1988–93). Grimshaw emploie une équipe de 200 personnes dans ses bureaux de Londres, New York et Melbourne. Andrew Whalley, un associé de l'agence, a étudié à l'École d'architecture Mackintosh de Glasgow (B.Arch, 1984) et à l'AA de Londres (1986). Vincent Chang, également associé, est diplômé de l'École d'architecture de l'université de Cambridge (1988, 1991). Leurs projets réalisés incluent l'usine de fabrication et le siège de Rolls Royce (West Sussex, Royaume-Uni, 2003) ; l'aéroport de Zurich (Zurich, Suisse, 2003 et 2004) ; l'immeuble Sankei Nishi-Umeda (Osaka, Japon, 2004) ; le nouveau bâtiment de l'ingénierie au l'University College de Londres (2005) ; la gare de Southern Cross (Melbourne, Australie, 2002–06, publié ici) ; la Fundatión Caixa Galicia (La Corogne, Espagne, 2006) ; le bâtiment Paul O'Gorman, pour l'Institut du cancer du University College de Londres (UCL Cancer Institute 2007) ; la Dubai Tower (projet conçu en 2007) ; la gare Amsterdam Bijlmer ArenA (Amsterdam, 2002–07) ; Horno 3, le musée de l'Acier (Museo del Acero, Monterrey, Mexico, 2006–07) ; le nouveau bâtiment universitaire de la London School of Economics (Londres, Royaume-Uni, 2004–08) ; et l'Experimental Media and Performing Arts Center (EMPAC) (Troy, New York, 2004–08, également publié ici).

EXPERIMENTAL MEDIA AND PERFORMING ARTS CENTER (EMPAC)

Troy, New York, USA, 2004–08

Address: 110 8th Street, Troy, NY 12180, USA, +1 518 276 4135, www.empac.rpi.edu
Area: 19 120 m². Client: Rensselaer Polytechnic Institute. Cost: not disclosed
Collaboration: Davis Brody Bond Aedas (Architect of Record), Buro Happold (Engineer), Kirkegaard Associates (Acoustician),
Fisher Dachs Associates (Theater Design)

The Rensselaer Polytechnic Institute was established in Troy, New York, in 1824 by Stephen Van Rensselaer "for the purpose of instructing people […] in the application of science to the common purposes of life." The **EXPERIMENTAL MEDIA AND PERFORMING ARTS CENTER** is meant to be a nexus of technological and artistic innovation and optimized performance space, where the intersection of science and the arts is explored through sound, movement, and light." This new structure includes a 1200-seat concert hall, a 400-seat theater, two performance studios, and a dance studio. The campus radio station, editing rooms, and artist-in-residence studios are also part of the design, won by Grimshaw in an international competition. An atrium is the center of interaction between the various activities that are intentionally not separated, but rather allowed to go forward concurrently, a fact that made sound insulation an important feature in the design. Although its plan is essentially rectangular, the building features a subtle mixture of glazed, or wooden, surfaces, with a prominent pod clad in wood housing the main hall.

Das Rensselaer Polytechnic Institute wurde 1824 in Troy, New York, von Stephen Van Rensselaer gegründet, „um Menschen […] in der Anwendung der Wissenschaften auf allgemeine Bedürfnisse des täglichen Lebens zu unterrichten". Das **ZENTRUM FÜR EXPERIMENTELLE MEDIEN UND DARSTELLENDE KÜNSTE** will eine Begegnungsstätte technischer und künstlerischer Innovation sein und zugleich ein idealer Aufführungsort für darstellende Künste, an dem sich die Berührungspunkte von Naturwissenschaft und Künsten durch Klang, Bewegung und Licht ausloten lassen. Zum Neubau gehören ein Konzertsaal mit 1200 Plätzen, ein Theater mit 400 Plätzen, zwei Studiobühnen sowie eine Tanzbühne. Auch ein campuseigener Radiosender, Schneideräume und Ateliers für Gastkünstler sind Teil des Entwurfs, mit dem sich Grimshaw in einem internationalen Wettbewerb durchsetzen konnte. Zentraler Begegnungsort ist das Atrium, das zwischen den einzelnen Lehrbereichen liegt, die bewusst nicht getrennt wurden, sondern nebeneinander ihr Programm verfolgen – weshalb die Schallisolierung bei diesem Entwurf eine entscheidende Rolle spielt. Der Grundriss ist im Grunde rechteckig, der Bau zeichnet sich durch seine subtile Kombination aus Glas- und Holzflächen aus. Ein auffälliges, holzverschaltes Gehäuse dominiert die Haupthalle des Gebäudes.

Le Rensselaer Polytechnic Institute a été fondé à Troy, dans l'État de New York, en 1824 par Stephen Van Rensselaer «pour enseigner aux gens […] l'application de la science dans des usages de la vie courante». Le **CENTRE EMPAC (CENTRE POUR LES MÉDIAS EXPÉRIMENTAUX ET LES ARTS VIVANTS)** vise à «être un lien entre innovation technologique et artistique, et un espace de spectacle optimisé où les croisements entre sciences et arts sont explorés à travers le son, le mouvement et l'éclairage». Ce nouveau bâtiment comprend une salle de concert de 1200 places, un théâtre de 400 places, deux ateliers de théâtre et un atelier de danse. La station de radio du campus, des salles de montage et des ateliers-résidences d'artistes font également partie du projet remporté par Grimshaw à l'issue d'un concours international. Un atrium concentre les interactions des différentes activités intentionnellement non séparées, mais au contraire susceptibles de se poursuivre simultanément, ce qui fait de l'isolation phonique une caractéristique essentielle du projet. Bien que son plan soit fondamentalement rectangulaire, le bâtiment offre un mélange subtil de surfaces de verre et de bois, avec une coque proéminente de bois abritant la grande salle.

Images show the wooden pod housing the main, 1200-seat concert hall. The architect contrasts the use of wood cladding here with metal, stone, and glass.

Auf den Abbildungen der holzverschalte „pod", in dem der große Konzertsaal mit 1200 Plätzen untergebracht ist. Die Architekten setzen dem Holz hier Metall, Stein und Glas entgegen.

Les photos montrent l'enveloppe de bois abritant la salle de concert de 1200 places. Ici, l'architecte fait contraster le revêtement en bois avec le métal, la pierre et le verre.

Below, section drawings show the structure from either side, with the main concert hall visible at the lower right.

Die Querschnitte unten zeigen den Bau von beiden Seiten, der Konzertsaal ist unten rechts zu erkennen.

Ci-dessous, les coupes montrent chaque côté de la structure, avec la grande salle de concert visible en bas à droite.

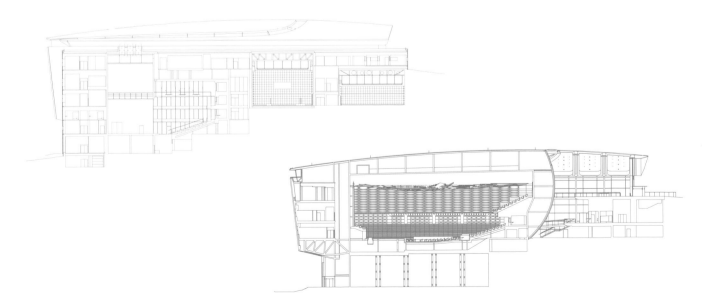

P 192.193

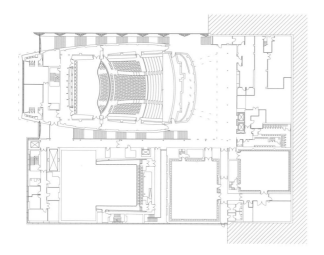
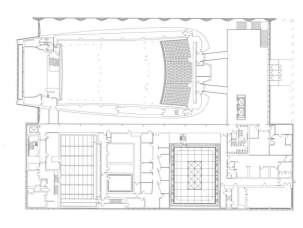

The concert hall (above) is seen in the upper part of the plans on the left page. The image to the left shows the variety given by Grimshaw to performance spaces within the complex.

Der Konzertsaal (oben) ist im oberen Bereich der Grundrisse auf der linken Seite zu sehen. Die Abbildung links belegt, wie abwechslungsreich Grimshaw die Bühnenräume im Komplex gestaltet hat.

La salle de concert (ci-dessus) est visible dans la partie supérieure des plans de la page de gauche. La photo à gauche montre la variété des espaces de spectacle insufflée par Grimshaw au sein du complexe.

SOUTHERN CROSS STATION

Melbourne, Australia, 2002–06

Address: 99 Spencer Street, Melbourne VIC 3000, Australia
Area: 245 729 m². Client: Leighton Contractors Pty Ltd. Cost: not disclosed
Collaboration: Daryl Jackson Pty Ltd (Joint Venture Architect), Leighton Contractors Pty Ltd (Main Contractor)

The former Spencer Street Station in Melbourne was the object of this project, intended to turn an existing facility into a "world-class interchange and new landmark for Melbourne" handling about 15 million travelers per year. The existing facility already dealt with regional and interstate rail and long-haul bus connections, as well as a bus link to the airport, due to become a rail connection. Occupying an area of 10.2 hectares, the overall project includes an office building and a retail plaza. The architect states: "The design is very open in plan, allowing good visibility across the station. The entire interchange is enclosed under a singular 'undulating blanket' roof form, which has been designed so that the two prevailing wind directions will naturally ventilate the internal volume."

Bei diesem Projekt ging es um die frühere Spencer Street Station in Melbourne, die „zum Umsteigebahnhof von Weltformat und zum neuen Wahrzeichen für Melbourne" werden sollte und jedes Jahr von über 15 Millionen Fahrgästen frequentiert wird. Der bestehende Bahnhof bündelte bereits den regionalen und überregionalen Schienenverkehr, den Fernreisebusverkehr sowie eine Busverbindung zum Flughafen, die mittelfristig auf die Schiene verlegt werden soll. Der Komplex mit einer Gesamtfläche von 10,2 ha umfasst auch ein Bürogebäude und ein Einkaufszentrum. Der Architekt erläutert: „Der Entwurf ist sehr offen gehalten und bietet großzügige Sichtachsen durch den Bahnhof. Der gesamte Publikumsverkehr ist unter einem einzigen, wie eine ‚Daunendecke' gewellten Dach zusammengefasst, das so konzipiert wurde, dass der Innenraum durch die zwei vorherrschenden Windrichtungen natürlich belüftet wird."

Ce projet avait pour objectif de convertir l'infrastructure existante de l'ancienne gare de Spencer Street à Melbourne en un « échangeur de niveau mondial et nouveau symbole pour Melbourne » où transitent annuellement une quinzaine de millions de voyageurs. L'infrastructure existante traitait déjà le trafic des lignes ferroviaires régionales et continentales, des lignes d'autocars long-courriers, ainsi que d'une navette de bus avec l'aéroport, devant être remplacée par une liaison par rail. Occupant une surface totale de 10,2 hectares, le projet comporte un immeuble de bureaux et un centre commercial. Les architectes déclarent : « Le projet a un plan très ouvert, permettant une bonne visibilité de la gare. L'échangeur est entièrement couvert d'une forme de toiture en » couverture ondoyante «, conçue de manière à ce que les flux d'air des deux directions prédominants ventilent naturellement le volume intérieur. »

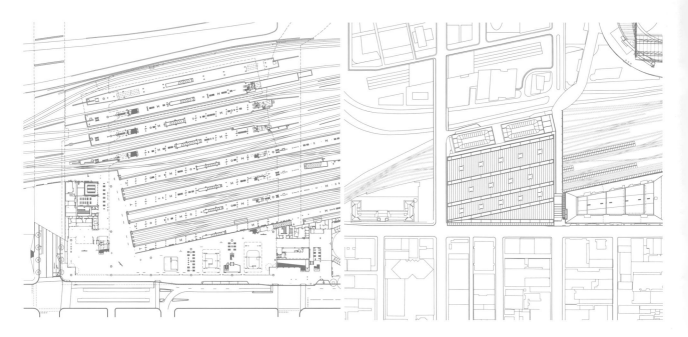

The undulating roof of the Station arches lightly over the tracks. Above, an overall plan of the facility.

Das geschwungene Dach des Bahnhofs wölbt sich mit großer Leichtigkeit über den Gleisen. Oben Grundrisse der Gesamtanlage.

Le toit ondoyant de la gare s'arque avec légèreté au-dessus des voies. Ci-dessus, un plan d'ensemble du complexe.

Airy, generous spaces characterize
public areas as well as the actual
track zone. To the right, an elevated
pod allows for movement and views
through the continuous open space of
the Station.

Öffentliche Bereiche wie Bahnsteige
wirken luftig und großzügig. Rechts
ein aufgeständerter „pod", der unge-
hinderte Bewegung und unverbaute
Blickachsen durch den Bahnhof
erlaubt.

Les zones publiques, comme celles
des voies proprement dites, se caractérisent par de généreux espaces
aérés. À droite, une enveloppe surélevée permet une circulation et une
vue ininterrompue dans l'espace
ouvert de la gare.

HERZOG & DE MEURON

Herzog & de Meuron / Rheinschanze 6
4056 Basel / Switzerland
Tel: +41 61 385 57 57 / Fax: +41 61 385 57 58
E-mail: info@herzogdemeuron.com

JACQUES HERZOG and **PIERRE DE MEURON** were both born in Basel in 1950. They received degrees in Architecture from the ETH in Zurich in 1975, after studying with Aldo Rossi, and founded their firm Herzog & de Meuron Architecture Studio in Basel in 1978. Harry Gugger and Christine Binswanger joined the firm in 1991, while Robert Hösl and Ascan Mergenthaler became Partners in 2004. Stefan Marbach became a Partner in 2006. Jacques Herzog and Pierre de Meuron won the 2001 Pritzker Prize, and both the RIBA Gold Medal and Praemium Imperiale in 2007. Their built work includes the Ricola Europe Factory and Storage Building in Mulhouse (France, 1993), and most notably they were chosen early in 1995 to design Tate Modern in London, the addition to the Tate Gallery for contemporary art, situated in the Bankside Power Station, on the Thames opposite Saint Paul's Cathedral, which opened in May 2000. In the near future, they will be engaged on building an extension to it. They were also short-listed in the competition for the new design of the Museum of Modern Art in New York (1997). More recently, they have built the Forum 2004 Building and Plaza (Barcelona, Spain, 2002–04); Allianz Arena (Munich, Germany, 2002–05); the de Young Museum (San Francisco, California, 2002–05); the Walker Art Center, Expansion of the Museum and Cultural Center (Minneapolis, Minnesota, 2003–05); the National Stadium, the Main Stadium for the Olympic Games in Beijing (China, 2008); the CaixaForum (Madrid, Spain, 2008); and TEA, Tenerife Espacio de las Artes (Santa Cruz de Tenerife, Canary Islands, Spain, 2003–08). Current work includes Vitrahaus, a new building to present Vitra's "Home Collection" on the Vitra campus in Weil am Rhein (Germany, 2009); the Elbe Philharmonic Hall in Hamburg (Germany, 2007–11, published here); and the Head Office for Roche Basel (Switzerland, projected completion 2011).

Sowohl **JACQUES HERZOG** als auch **PIERRE DE MEURON** wurden 1950 Basel geboren. Ihr Architekturstudium schlossen sie beide 1975 an der ETH Zürich ab, wo sie bei Aldo Rossi studierten, und gründeten 1978 ihr Büro Herzog & de Meuron in Basel. Harry Gugger und Christine Binswanger schlossen sich 1991 dem Büro an, Robert Hösl und Ascan Mergenthaler wurden 2004 Partner, zwei Jahre später Stefan Marbach. 2001 erhielten Jacques Herzog und Pierre de Meuron den Pritzker-Preis, 2007 die RIBA-Goldmedaille und den Praemium Imperiale. Zu ihren gebauten Projekten zählt das Europawerk und -lager von Ricola in Mulhouse (Frankreich, 1993), und das bekannteste Projekt des Büros ist fraglos der Anfang 1995 in Auftrag gegebene Entwurf für die Tate Modern, einen Erweiterungsbau für zeitgenössische Kunst der Londoner Tate Gallery. Der neue Standort im ehemaligen Elektrizitätswerk Bankside, einem Baudenkmal an der Themse gegenüber der Saint Paul's-Cathedral, konnte im Mai 2000 eröffnet werden. In näherer Zukunft wird das Büro einen weiteren Anbau realisieren. Auch beim Wettbewerb für die Umgestaltung des Museum of Modern Art in New York (1997) kamen Herzog & de Meuron auf die Shortlist. In jüngerer Zeit realisierte das Büro das Forum 2004, Gebäude und Vorplatz (Barcelona, 2002–04), die Allianz Arena (München, 2002–05), das De Young Museum (San Francisco, Kalifornien, 2002–05), die Erweiterung des Walker Art Center (Minneapolis, Minnesota, 2003–05), das Nationalstadion in Peking, Hauptaustragungsort der Olympischen Spiele 2008, das CaixaForum (Madrid, 2008) sowie das TEA, Tenerife Espacio de las Artes (Santa Cruz de Tenerife, Kanarische Inseln, Spanien, 2003–08). Aktuelle Projekte sind u. a. das VitraHaus, ein neuer Ausstellungsraum auf dem Vitra-Campus in Weil am Rhein (Deutschland, 2009), die Elbphilharmonie in Hamburg (2007–11, hier vorgestellt) sowie die Verwaltungszentrale von Roche (Basel, voraussichtliche Fertigstellung 2011).

JACQUES HERZOG et **PIERRE DE MEURON** sont tous deux nés à Bâle, en 1950. Ils obtiennent leur diplôme d'architecte à l'ETH de Zurich, en 1975, après avoir étudié avec Aldo Rossi, et fondé leur agence Herzog & de Meuron Architecture Studio à Bâle, en 1978. Harry Gugger et Christine Binswanger rejoignent l'agence en 1991, alors que Robert Hösl et Ascan Mergenthaler deviennent associés en 2004. Stefan Marbach devient associé en 2006. Jacques Herzog et Pierre de Meuron ont reçu le prix Pritzker 2001, ainsi que la médaille d'or du RIBA et le Praemium Imperiale, tous deux en 2007. Leurs réalisations incluent le Centre de stockage et production Ricola Europe, Mulhouse (France, 1993). Ils ont surtout été choisis pour le projet de la Tate Modern, extension de la Tate Gallery de Londres, dédiée à l'art contemporain, située dans l'ancienne centrale électrique Bankside Power Station, sur la Tamise, en face de la cathédrale Saint-Paul, et inaugurée en mai 2000. Ils vont prochainement en réaliser un agrandissement. Ils faisaient aussi partie des architectes sélectionnés pour le projet de rénovation du MoMA de New York (1997). Plus récemment, ils ont réalisé le Forum 2004 (Barcelone, 2002–04) ; le stade Allianz (Munich, 2002–05) ; le musée De Young (San Francisco, 2002–05) ; le Walker Art Center, extension du Musée et centre culturel de Minneapolis (Minneapolis, Minnesota, 2003–05) ; le Stade national, stade principal des Jeux olympiques de 2008 de Pékin ; le musée CaixaForum (Madrid, 2008) ; et le Centre d'arts Tenerife Espacio de las Artes (TEA) (Santa-Cruz de Tenerife, îles Canaries, Espagne, 2003–08). Leurs projets en cours incluent le nouveau bâtiment d'exposition de la « collection privée » de Vitra, sur le campus Vitra, à Weil-am-Rhein (Allemagne, 2009) ; la Philharmonie de l'Elbe, à Hambourg (2007–11, publié ici) ; et le siège de Roche, à Bâle (Suisse, achèvement prévu en 2011).

ELBE PHILHARMONIC HALL

Hamburg, Germany, 2007–11

Address: Am Kaiserkai, 20457 Hamburg, Germany, www.hamburg.de/elbphilharmonie
Area: 4214 m² (public space). Client: Freie und Hansestadt Hamburg. Cost: not disclosed
Collaboration: Ascan Mergenthaler (Partner), David Koch (Partner), Stefan Goeddertz (Associate),
Jürgen Johner (Associate), Nicholas Lyons (Associate), Stephan Wedrich (Associate)
Local Partner: Höhler + Partner Architekten und Ingenieure, Aachen, Germany

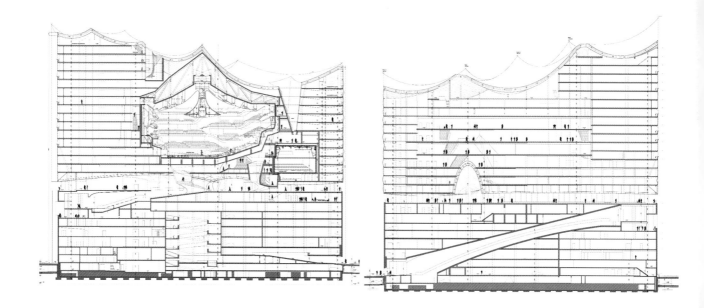

With 29 floors and a height for the **ELBE PHILHARMONIC HALL** of 110 meters, this is an imposing structure. The program includes a 2150-seat main auditorium, and a smaller 550-seat facility. A public plaza with covered terraces contains the main entrance, a reception and hotel lobby area, restaurants, cafés, a bar, ticketing areas, and a children's museum. The complex thus includes a 247-room five-star hotel and approximately 45 apartment units, ranging in size from 120 to 380 square meters. With its panoramic view of the city and harbor, the complex can best be described as a cultural center that also includes hotel and apartment areas. The architects state: "The new space that will emerge here is designed to emphasize the public and the musicians to such an extent that, together, they actually represent the architecture. This radical new architectural formulation of the Philharmonic building typology has been devised to capitalize on the unique quality of this unusual, new location in the city, a location that will substantially impact Hamburg in the 21st century." The new structure actually rests on top of a former cocoa bean warehouse called Kaispeicher A, built between 1963 and 1966. The architects have used this "robust, almost aloof" building as the foundation for the new Elbe Philharmonic complex.

Mit ihren 29 Stockwerken und einer Höhe von 110 m ist die **ELBPHILHARMONIE** ein imposanter Bau. Das Programm sieht einen großen Saal mit 2150 und einen kleinen Saal mit 550 Plätzen vor. An einer öffentlichen Plaza mit überdachten Terrassen liegen der Haupteingang, der Empfang und die Lobby eines Hotels, Restaurants, Cafés, eine Bar, der Kartenverkauf sowie ein Kindermuseum. Zum Komplex gehören ein Fünfsternehotel mit 247 Zimmern sowie rund 45 Wohnungen mit einer Fläche von 120 bis 380 m². Mit seinem Panoramablick über Stadt und Hafen lässt sich der Komplex am besten als Kulturzentrum mit Hotelbereich und Wohnflächen beschreiben. Die Architekten erläutern: „Der hier entstehende neue Ort wurde so geplant, dass Publikum und Musiker in einem Maß in den Mittelpunkt gerückt werden, dass sie im Grunde selbst zur Architektur werden lässt. Dieser radikal neue Architekturansatz, aus dem heraus die Typologie der Elbphilharmonie entwickelt wurde, profitiert außerordentlich von der Einzigartigkeit dieses ungewöhnlichen, neuen Standorts in der Stadt – einem Standort, der Hamburg im 21. Jahrhundert maßgeblich prägen wird." Der Neubau sattelt auf einem alten Kakaospeicher auf, dem sogenannten Kaispeicher A, der zwischen 1963 und 1966 erbaut wurde. Die Architekten nutzten diesen „massigen, geradezu erhabenen" Bau als Fundament für die neue Elbphilharmonie.

Avec ses 29 étages et ses 110 mètres de haut, la **PHILHARMONIE DE L'ELBE** est un bâtiment imposant. Le programme inclut un grand auditorium de 2150 places, et une salle plus petite de 550 places. Un espace public avec des terrasses couvertes accueille l'entrée principale, la réception et le hall de l'hôtel, des restaurants, des cafés, un bar, des billetteries et un musée pour enfants. Le complexe comprend donc un hôtel cinq étoiles de 247 chambres ainsi que 45 appartements de 120 à 180 mètres carrés. Avec une vue panoramique sur la ville et le port, le complexe peut être décrit comme un centre culturel englobant un espace hôtelier et un espace résidentiel. Comme le déclarent les architectes : « Le nouvel espace qui va émerger ici est conçu pour mettre en valeur le public et les musiciens de façon à ce qu'ensemble, ils deviennent eux-mêmes l'architecture. Cette approche architecturale radicalement nouvelle de la typologie des salles philharmoniques a été conçue pour tirer avantage des caractéristiques originales de sa nouvelle situation dans la ville, une situation qui aura un grand retentissement pour Hamburg au XXIe siècle. » Le nouveau bâtiment est en fait posé sur un ancien entrepôt de fèves de cacao nommé Kaispeicher A, construit entre 1963 et 1966. Les architectes ont utilisé cette structure « robuste, presque impersonnelle » comme substructure pour le nouveau complexe de la Philharmonie de l'Elbe.

An overall rendering of the building is seen above, with two section draw-ings opposite, showing that the unusual form of the exterior is echoed by the interior complexity of the structure.

Das Rendering des Gesamtkomplexes oben und die zwei Querschnitte gegenüber zeigen, dass die unge-wöhnlichen äußeren Formen im kom-plexen Innern des Gebäudes aufge-griffen werden.

Une représentation d'ensemble du bâtiment, ci-dessus, et deux coupes, page de gauche, montrant que la forme extérieure inhabituelle de la structure répond à sa complexité interne.

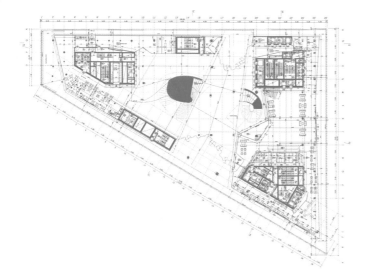

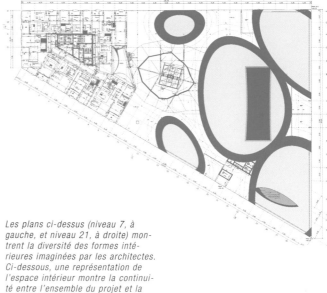

Above, plans (left, 8th level; right 22nd level) show the variety of interior forms imagined by the architects. Below, a rendering of interior space shows the continuity established with the overall architectural scheme and the design of the Philharmonic Hall.

Die Grundrisse (links 7. Obergeschoss, rechts 21. Obergeschoss) belegen die Vielfalt der von den Architekten entworfenen Innenräume. Unten ein Rendering des Innenraums, das die Kontinuität des architektonischen Gesamtkonzepts der Philharmonie deutlich werden lässt.

Les plans ci-dessus (niveau 7, à gauche, et niveau 21, à droite) montrent la diversité des formes intérieures imaginées par les architectes. Ci-dessous, une représentation de l'espace intérieur montre la continuité entre l'ensemble du projet et la salle philharmonique.

The main concert hall, seating 2,150 persons, has an unusual form that can be seen in the plans (left, 13th level; right, 12th level) below.

Der große Konzertsaal bietet 2150 Zuschauern Platz und ist ungewöhnlich geformt, wie auch die Grundrisse unten (links 12. Obergeschoss, rechts 11. Obergeschoss) zeigen.

La grande salle de concert, de 2150 places, est d'une forme inhabituelle, comme on peut le voir sur les plans (niveau 12, à gauche, et niveau 11, à droite) ci-dessous.

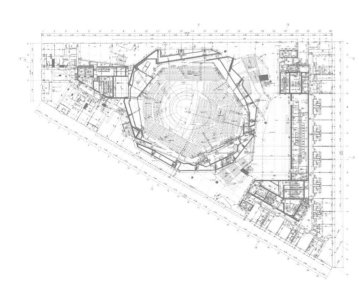

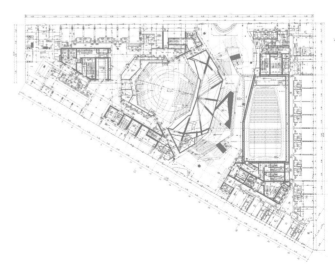

TOYO ITO

Toyo Ito & Associates, Architects
1–19–4 Shibuya, Shibuya-ku,
Tokyo 150–0002
Japan

Tel: +81 33 409 58 22
Fax: +81 33 409 59 69

Born in 1941 in Seoul, Korea, **TOYO ITO** graduated from the University of Tokyo in 1965 and worked in the office of Kiyonori Kikutake until 1969. He created his own office, Urban Robot (URBOT), in Tokyo in 1971, assuming the name of Toyo Ito Architect & Associates in 1979. He was awarded the Golden Lion for Lifetime Achievement from the 8th International Venice Architecture Biennale in 2002 and the RIBA Gold Medal in 2006. His completed work includes the Silver Hut (Nakano, Tokyo, 1982–84); Tower of the Winds (Yokohama, Kanagawa, 1986); Yatsushiro Municipal Museum (Yatsushiro, Kumamoto, 1988–91); a Public Kindergarten (Eckenheim, Frankfurt am Main, Germany, 1988–93); and the Elderly People's Home (1992–94) and Fire Station (1992–95), both located in the same city on the island of Kyushu. Other projects include his Nagaoka Lyric Hall (Nagaoka, Niigata, 1995–96); Odate Jukai Dome Park (Odate, 1993–97); and Ota-ku Resort Complex (Tobu-cho, Chiisagata-gun, Nagano, 1996–98), all in Japan. One of his most successful and widely published projects, the Mediatheque in Sendai, was completed in 2001, while in 2002 he designed a temporary pavilion for the Serpentine Gallery in London. More recently, he has completed TOD'S Omotesando Building (Shibuya, Tokyo, 2003–04); the Island City Central Park Grin Grin (Fukuoka, Fukuoka, 2004–05); Meiso no Mori Municipal Funeral Hall (Kakamigahara, Gifu, 2005–06); the Tama Art University Library (Hachioji City, Tokyo, 2005–07); and the Main Stadium for the World Games 2009 (Kaohsiung, Taiwan, 2006–09, published here).

TOYO ITO wurde 1941 in Seoul, Korea, geboren und schloss sein Studium 1965 an der Universität Tokio ab. Bis 1969 arbeitete er im Büro von Kiyonori Kikutake. Sein eigenes Büro Urban Robot (URBOT) gründete er 1971 in Tokio, seit 1979 firmiert es unter dem Namen Toyo Ito Architect & Associates. 2002 wurde er auf der Architekturbiennale in Venedig mit dem Goldenen Löwen für sein Lebenswerk ausgezeichnet, 2006 erhielt er die RIBA-Goldmedaille. Zu Itos Bauten gehören das Wohnhaus Silver Hut (Nakano, Tokio, 1982–84), der Turm der Winde in Yokohama, Kanagawa (Japan, 1986), das städtische Museum in Yatsushiro (Kumamoto, Japan, 1989–91), eine Kindertagesstätte in Frankfurt-Eckenheim (1988–93) sowie ein Seniorenwohnheim (1992–94) und eine Feuerwache (1992–95) auf der japanischen Insel Kyushu. Weitere Projekte sind die Nagaoka Lyric Hall (Nagaoka, Niigata, 1995–96), der Odate Jukai Dome Park (Odate, 1993–97) und die Ferienanlage Ota-ku (Tobu-cho, Chiisagata-gun, Nagano, 1996–98), alle in Japan. Eines seiner bekanntesten und meistpublizierten Projekte, die Mediathek in Sendai, konnte 2001 fertiggestellt werden, während er 2002 einen temporären Pavillon für die Serpentine Gallery in London entwarf. In jüngster Zeit realisierte er das Omotesando Building für Tod's (Shibuya-ku, Tokio, 2003–04), den Grin-Grin-Park auf Island City (Fukuoka, 2004–05), die Städtische Trauerhalle Meiso no Mori (Kakamigahara, Gifu, 2005–06), die Bibliothek der Kunsthochschule Tama (Hachioji, Tokio, 2005–07) sowie die Sportarena für die World Games 2009 (Kaohsiung, Taiwan, 2006–09, hier vorgestellt).

Né en 1941 à Séoul, en Corée du Sud, **TOYO ITO** obtient son diplôme à l'université de Tokyo en 1965 et travaille dans l'agence de Kiyonori Kikutake jusqu'en 1969. Il crée sa propre agence, Urban Robot (URBOT) à Tokyo, en 1971, et la renomme Toyo Ito Architect & Associates en 1979. Il a reçu un Lion d'or pour l'ensemble de son œuvre à la VIIIᵉ Biennale internationale d'architecture de Venise, en 2002, et la médaille d'or du RIBA, en 2006. Ses projets réalisés incluent Silver Hut (Nakano, Tokyo, 1982–84) ; la Tour des Vents (Yokohama, Kanagawa, 1986) ; le musée municipal de Yatsushiro (Yatsushiro, Kumamoto, 1988–91) ; une école maternelle (Eckenheim, Francfort, Allemagne, 1988–93) ; une maison de retraite (1992–94) et une caserne de pompiers (1992–95), tous deux situés dans la même ville de l'île de Kyushu. D'autres projets incluent une salle de spectacles à Nagaoka (Nagaoka, Niigata, 1995–96) ; le stade Odate Jukai Dome Park (Odate, 1993–97) ; et le complexe Ota-ku Resort (Tobu-cho, Chiisagata-gun, Nagano, 1996–98) ; tous situés au Japon. Un de ses projets le plus apprécié et le plus largement publié, la médiathèque de Sendai, a été achevé en 2001, tandis qu'en 2002, il concevait le pavillon temporaire de la Serpentine Gallery à Londres. Plus récemment, il a terminé le magasin TOD'S d'Omotesando (Shibuya-ku, Tokyo, 2003–04) ; le parc Grin Grin à Island City Central Park (Fukuoka, 2004–05) ; et le funérarium municipal Meiso no Mori (Kakamigahara, Gifu, Japon, 2005–06) ; la nouvelle bibliothèque de l'université d'art (Hachioji City, Tokyo, 2005–07) ; et le Stade principal pour les Jeux mondiaux 2009 (Kaohsiung, Taiwan, République de Chine, 2006–09, publié ici).

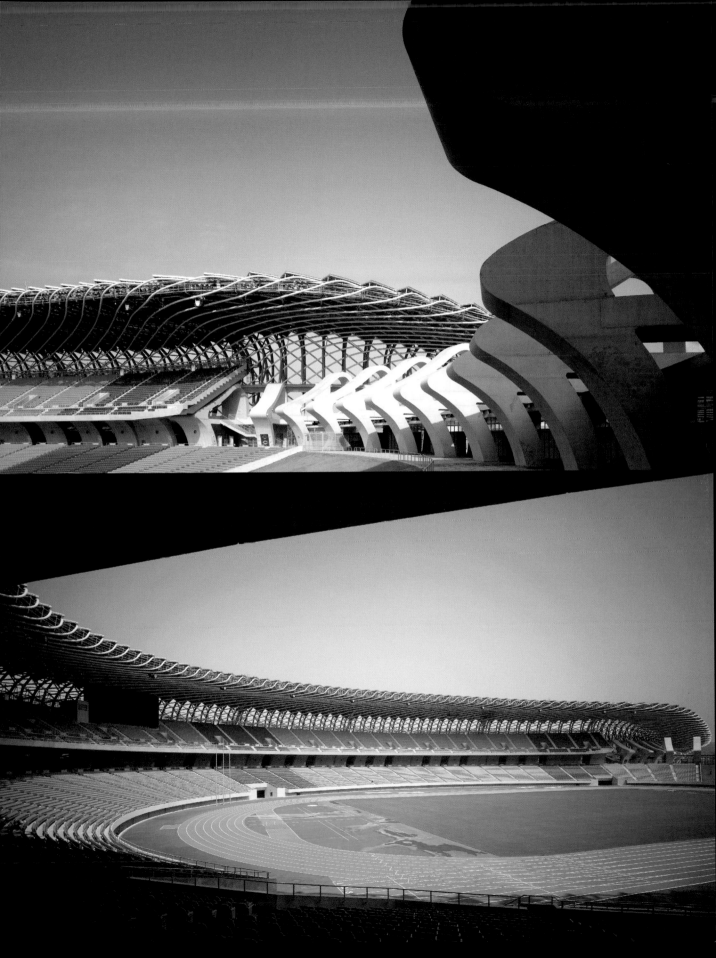

MAIN STADIUM
FOR THE WORLD GAMES 2009
Kaohsiung, Taiwan, 2006–09

Address: No. 200, Jhonghai Road, Zuoying District, Kaohsiung City 813, Taiwan, +886 7 954 0085
Area: 98 759 m². Clients: National Council on Physical Fitness and Sports (NCPFS), Executive Yuan /
Bureau of Public Works, City of Kaohsiung. Cost: € 103.33 million
Design Team: ITO TAKENAKA RLA Kaohsiung Main Stadium for 2009 World Games

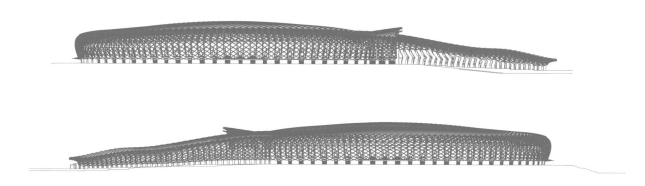

Kaohsiung is the second-largest city in Taiwan. The World Games are an international multiple-sport event, including sports that were not included in the Olympic Games, held once every four years. Kaohsiung was selected as the July 2009 venue. The stadium seats 40 000 people in its normal configuration and up to 55 000 for special occasions. A 22 000-square-meter roofing area is covered with solar cells mounted in laminated, tempered glass. A "Spiral Continuum" structure loops around the stadium, which is open on one side near the rapid transit (MRT) station and Zhong Hai Road, explaining the architects' idea of an "urban park." The basic form of the stadium is a regular oval, reaching a maximum height of 35 meters. The architect states: "The new Kaohsiung stadium embodies dynamic fluid movement like a vibrant body, and is expected to draw the city's attention as a hub of activities." The stadium does offer a particularly dynamic form, unexpected because of its open side and also because of the dramatic roof that sweeps over the spectator stands.

Kaohsiung ist die zweitgrößte Stadt Taiwans. Die World Games sind ein internationales Sportereignis mit Sportarten, die nicht bei den Olympischen Spielen vertreten sind, und findet alle vier Jahre statt. Kaohsiung wurde zum Austragungsort der Spiele im Juli 2009 bestimmt. Das Stadion bietet in seiner Standardkonfiguration Platz für 40 000 Besucher, bei Sonderveranstaltungen für bis zu 55 000 Besucher. Die 22 000 m² große Dachfläche ist mit Solarzellen bestückt, die in Verbundsicherheitsglas eingebettet sind. Eine durchgängige „Spirale" zieht sich um das gesamte Stadion herum, das sich an einer Seite zur nahe gelegenen MRT-Schnellbahnstation und zur Zhong Hai Road öffnet und damit das Konzept des Architekten von einem „urbanen Park" versinnbildlicht. Von seiner Grundform her ist das Stadion ein regelmäßiges Oval, das an seinem höchsten Punkt bis zu 35 m misst. Der Architekt führt aus: „Das neue Stadion in Kaohsiung ist Sinnbild einer dynamischen, fließenden Bewegung, wie die eines lebendigen Körpers und wird als Schauplatz unterschiedlichster Aktivitäten zum Anziehungspunkt für die ganze Stadt werden." Tatsächlich präsentiert sich das Stadion als besonders dynamische Form, die gerade mit ihrer offenen Seite überraschend wirkt, ebenso wie mit der dramatischen Dachkonstruktion, die über den Zuschauertribünen zu schweben scheint.

Kaohsiung est la deuxième plus grande ville de Taiwan. Les Jeux mondiaux sont une manifestation sportive pluridisciplinaire qui se déroule tous les quatre ans et comprend des disciplines non représentées aux Jeux olympiques. Kaohsiung a été sélectionnée comme ville d'accueil pour les Jeux de juillet 2009. Le stade offre 40 000 places dans sa configuration normale, et jusqu'à 55 000 pour des occasions spéciales. Une surface de toiture de 22 000 mètres carrés est recouverte de cellules photovoltaïques montées dans du verre trempé et feuilleté. Une structure en « continuum spiralé » fait une boucle autour du stade, ouvert du côté de la station de métro (MRT) et de Zhong Hai Road, explicitant l'idée de « parc urbain » de l'architecte. La forme de base du stade est un ovale régulier, d'une hauteur maximale de 35 mètres. L'architecte déclare que « le nouveau stade de Kaohsiung incarne le mouvement dynamique et fluide à la manière d'un corps plein de vie, et espère attirer l'attention sur la ville comme centre d'activités ». Le stade offre en effet une forme particulièrement dynamique, inattendue en raison de son côté ouvert et aussi de sa toiture spectaculaire qui s'étend au-dessus des tribunes des spectateurs.

Elevations show the progressively varying height of the structure, while the spectacular view to the right shows the end of the canopy structure over the stands.

Aufrisse veranschaulichen die verschiedenen Höhen des Komplexes, während die dramatische Ansicht rechts das Kopfende der Tribünendachkonstruktion zeigt.

Les élévations ci-dessus montrent la hauteur progressive du bâtiment, et la vue impressionnante de la page de droite, l'extrémité de la toiture au-dessus des tribunes.

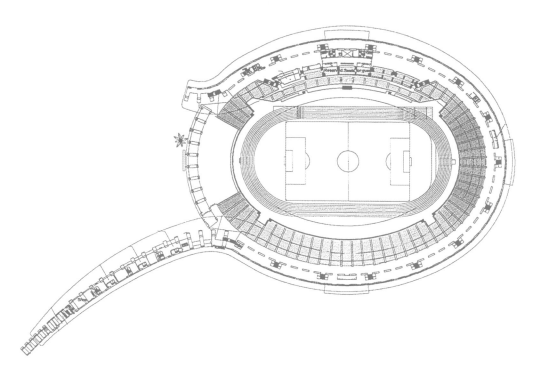

A plan shows the relatively simple oval shape of the Stadium. This simplicity is echoed in the curving, wrapping lines of the exterior structure seen below.

Der Grundriss belegt die vergleichsweise schlichte ovale Form des Stadions. Diese Schlichtheit findet sich in den geschwungenen Linien wieder, die sich um das Äußere des Gebäudes schmiegen (unten).

Un plan montre la forme ovale relativement simple du stade. Cette simplicité se retrouve dans les lignes incurvées qui enveloppent l'extérieur du bâtiment, visible ci-dessous.

The Stadium retains a light appearance that is not typical of such structures, even seen in this overall view (above). To the right, a site plan with the oval stadium in the center.

Das Stadion wirkt von großer Leichtigkeit, was für Bauten dieser Art eher untypisch ist und auf der Ansicht oben deutlich wird. Rechts ein Lageplan mit dem ovalen Stadion im Zentrum.

Le stade garde une apparence de légèreté, inhabituelle pour ce genre d'édifices, même lorsqu'il est vu dans sa totalité (ci-dessus). À droite, un plan de situation, avec le stade ovale au centre.

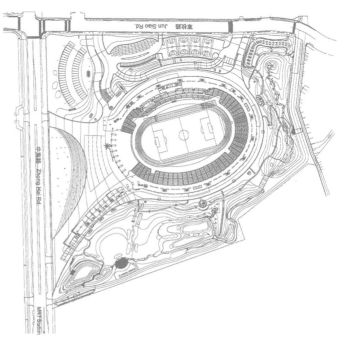

TAIJI KAWANO

Taiji Kawano Architects
2–13–11 Takasago
Katsushika
Tokyo 125–0054
Japan

Tel: +81 3 5668 4415
Fax: +81 3 5668 4415
E-mail: info@tk-arc.jp
Web: www.tk-arc.jp

TAIJI KAWANO was born in 1964 in Fukuoka. He received his Bachelor of Engineering degree from Kyushu University in 1988. He worked from 1990 to 2000 in the Kohyama Atelier and established his own firm, Taiji Kawano Architects, in 2001. He has been a Lecturer at the University of Tokyo since 2002. His work includes the I.S.S. Space Museum Project (Inabe, Mie, in collaboration with Yoshito Tomioka, 2001); CoCo Project (Kokonoe, Oita, 2002); J Panel Furniture (2003); Town House in Sendagi, Renovation (Bunkyo, Tokyo, 2005); Town House in Takasago (Katsushika, Tokyo, 2006); Yayoi Auditorium Annex, University of Tokyo (Bunkyo, Tokyo, 2007–08, published here); House at Niiza (Niiza, Saitama, 2008); and Ocha House, Ochanomizu University (Bunkyo, Tokyo, in collaboration with Nobihisa Motooka, 2009), all in Japan. Current work includes a New Dormitory for Ochanomizu University (Bunkyo, Tokyo, in collaboration with Nobihisa Motooka, 2011).

TAIJI KAWANO wurde 1964 in Fukuoka geboren. Sein Studium an der Universität Kyushu schloss er 1988 mit einem Bachelor in Ingenieurwissenschaften ab. Von 1990 bis 2000 arbeitete er im Atelier Kohyama und gründete 2001 sein eigenes Büro, Taiji Kawano Architects. Seit 2002 ist er Dozent an der Universität Tokio. Zu seinen Projekten zählen das I.S.S. Space Museum Project (Inabe, Mie, in Zusammenarbeit mit Yoshito Tomioka, 2001), das CoCo Project (Kokonoe, Oita, 2002), die Möbelserie „J Panel" (2003), die Sanierung eines Stadthauses in Sendagi (Bunkyo, Tokio, 2005), ein Stadthaus in Takasago (Katsushika, Tokio, 2006), der Anbau an das Yayoi-Auditorium der Universität Tokio (Bunkyo, Tokio, 2007–08, hier vorgestellt), ein Haus in Niiza (Niiza, Saitama, 2008) sowie das Haus Ocha an der Ochanomizu-Universität (Bunkyo, Tokio, in Zusammenarbeit mit Nobihisa Motooka, 2009), alle in Japan. Ein aktuelles Projekt ist das neue Wohnheim für die Ochanomizu-Universität (Bunkyo, Tokio, in Zusammenarbeit mit Nobihisa Motooka, 2011).

TAIJI KAWANO est né en 1964 à Fukuoka. Il obtient son diplôme d'ingénieur de l'université de Kyushu en 1988. Il travaille de 1990 à 2000 dans l'atelier Kohyama et fonde sa propre agence, Taiji Kawano Architects, en 2001. Il est maître de conférences à l'université de Tokyo depuis 2002. Ses projets réalisés incluent l'I.S.S. Space Museum Project (Inabe, Mie, en collaboration avec Yoshito Tomioka, 2001); CoCo Project (Kokonoe, Oita, 2002); le mobilier J Panel (2003); la rénovation d'un hôtel particulier à Sendagi, (Bunkyo, Tokyo, 2005); un hôtel particulier à Takasago (Katsushika, Tokyo, 2006); l'annexe de l'auditorium Yayoi de l'université de Tokyo (Bunkyo, Tokyo, 2007–08, publié ici); une maison à Niiza (Niiza, Saitama, 2008); et la maison expérimentale Ocha de l'université d'Ochanomizu (Bunkyo, Tokyo, en collaboration avec Nobihisa Motooka, 2009), tous situés au Japon. Ses projets en cours incluent une nouvelle résidence universitaire pour l'université d'Ochanomizu (Bunkyo, Tokyo, en collaboration avec Nobihisa Motooka, 2011).

YAYOI AUDITORIUM ANNEX

University of Tokyo, Bunkyo-ku, Tokyo, Japan, 2007–08

Address: 7–3–1 Hongo, Bunkyo-ku, Tokyo 113–8654, Japan
Area: 479 m². Client: University of Tokyo. Cost: not disclosed
Collaboration: Tomoya Nabeno (Staff), Masahiro Inayama (Structural Engineering),
Naoto Ando (Professor of Architecture, University of Tokyo)

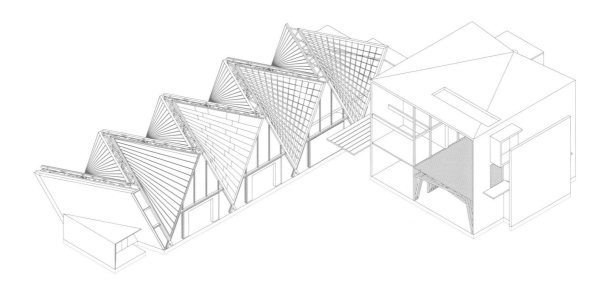

The repetitive folding form of the Annex again contrasts with the more blocky appearance of the earlier building. This is visible in both the drawing above and the photo.

Das repetitive Faltmuster des Anbaus steht im Kontrast zur eher kubischen Erscheinungsform des vorhandenem Gebäudes. Zeichnung (oben) und Foto zeigen dies deutlich.

La forme plissée répétitive de l'annexe contraste avec l'aspect plus cubique du bâtiment existant, comme on peut le voir sur le dessin ci-dessus et sur la photo.

This new Auditorium Annex is situated in a green zone of the University of Tokyo, on the north side of the front gate, near Hongo Street. The structure was situated to avoid cutting mature trees. The architect and client decided on a wood building, based on a hyperbolic paraboloid shell. Models in half scale and then on a full scale were made of the shell to find the appropriate ways to fix the plywood without causing it to twist. Exterior cladding is in sheet copper, ThermoWood (Japanese cedar), and plaster (FMX). Floors on the ground level are in polished concrete, while Japanese cedar is used on the upper level. Red cedar is used on walls and ceilings and, for other wall areas, Randomized Strand Board (Japanese cypress). The architect places a great deal of emphasis on the green, shaded surroundings. "If a lot of people experience the place as they would the shade of a tree in the forest that filters natural light, in the center of the city, that is great."

Der Hörsaalanbau liegt in einem Grünbereich der Universität Tokio, nördlich des Haupttors, unweit der Hongostraße. Die Lage des Baus wurde so gewählt, dass kein alter Baum gefällt werden musste. Architekt und Auftraggeber verständigten sich auf einen Holzbau aus einer hyperbolischen Parabolschale. Modelle in halber und schließlich in voller Größe wurden vorab gefertigt, um zu ermitteln, wie sich das Sperrholz fixieren lässt, ohne sich zu verdrehen. Die äußere Verschalung besteht aus Kupferplatten, ThermoWood (japanische Zeder) und Putz (FMX). Die Böden im Erdgeschoss sind aus poliertem Beton, im Obergeschoss kam japanische Zeder zum Einsatz. Für Wände und Decken wurde Rotzeder verwendet, für weitere Wandflächen RSB (japanische Zypresse). Besonderen Wert legte der Architekt auf das grüne, schattige Umfeld: „Es wäre schön, wenn viele Menschen diesen Ort wie den Schatten eines Baums im Wald erleben würden, der natürliches Licht filtert – und das mitten in der Stadt."

Cette nouvelle annexe de l'auditorium est implantée dans une zone verte de l'université de Tokyo, du côté nord du portail, près de la rue Hongo. Le bâtiment a été placé de manière à éviter de couper les arbres adultes. L'architecte et le client ont décidé d'un bâtiment en bois, basé sur le principe d'une coque en forme de paraboloïde hyperbolique. Des maquettes à demi-échelle, puis à l'échelle, ont été construites pour trouver la manière appropriée de fixer le contreplaqué sans le fausser. Les revêtements externes utilisent du cuivre en feuilles, du ThermoWood (cèdre du Japon), et de l'enduit (FMX). Les sols du rez-de-chaussée sont en béton poli, tandis que le cèdre du Japon est utilisé à l'étage. On a utilisé du cèdre rouge pour les murs et les plafonds, et pour d'autres surfaces de mur, des panneaux de particules à orientation aléatoire (cyprès du Japon). L'architecte attache beaucoup d'importance à l'environnement végétal ombragé. « Que beaucoup de gens puissent ressentir ce lieu au cœur de la ville comme la sensation procurée par l'ombre d'un arbre dans une forêt filtrant la lumière naturelle, en pleine ville, c'est formidable ! »

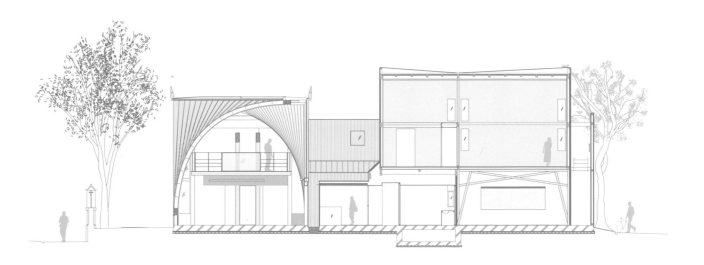

A section drawing above shows the relation of the Annex (left) to the original structure.

Der Querschnitt oben illustriert das Verhältnis zwischen Anbau (links) und vorhandenem Gebäude.

Une coupe, ci-dessus, montre la relation de l'annexe (à gauche) avec le bâtiment d'origine.

The structures have a light design
with wood as the dominant material.
Trees nearby contribute to the airi-
ness of the overall site.

Die Bauten wirken leicht, Holz ist das
prägende Material. Auch die Bäume
tragen zum luftigen Eindruck der
Gesamtanlage bei.

Les structures légères sont
construites essentiellement en bois.
La proximité des arbres contribue à
l'aspect aéré de l'ensemble du site.

The arching roof forms descend to floor level, leaving full-height glazed openings between each roof sequence. Below, the Annex is visible at the top of this site drawing.

Die gewölbeartigen Dachsegmente reichen bis auf den Boden herab. Zwischen den einzelnen Sequenzen sind raumhohe Glasfronten eingefügt. Auf dem Lageplan unten ist der Anbau im oberen Bereich zu erkennen.

Les voussures du toit descendent jusqu'au niveau du sol, avec des baies vitrées occupant toute la hauteur comprise entre les éléments de toiture consécutifs. Ci-dessous, l'annexe est visible en haut du plan de situation.

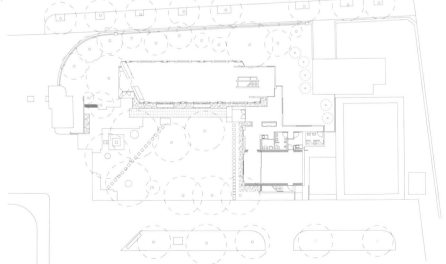

MARCIO KOGAN

Marcio Kogan
Alameda Tiete 505
04616–001 São Paulo, SP
Brazil

Tel: +55 11 3081 3522
Fax: +55 11 3063 3424
E-mail: info@marciokogan.com.br
Web: www.marciokogan.com.br

Born in 1952, **MARCIO KOGAN** graduated in 1976 from the School of Architecture at Mackenzie University in São Paulo. He received an IAB (Brazilian Architects Institute) Award for UMA Stores (1999 and 2002); Coser Studio (2002); Gama Issa House (2002); and Quinta House (2004). He also received the Record House Award for the Du Plessis House (2004) and the BR House (2005). In 2002, he completed a Museum of Microbiology in São Paulo and in 2003 he made a submission for the World Trade Center Site Memorial. He worked with Isay Weinfeld on the Fasano Hotel in São Paulo. He also participated with Weinfeld in the 25th São Paulo Biennale (2002) with the project for a hypothetical city named Happyland. Kogan is known for his use of boxlike forms, together with wooden shutters, trellises, and exposed stone. Amongst Kogan's recent residential projects are the Cury House (São Paulo, 2004–06); the E-Home, a "super-technological" house (Santander, Spain, 2007); an "extreme house" on an island in Paraty (Rio de Janeiro, Brazil, 2007); the Primetime Nursery (São Paulo, 2005–07, published here); the Warbler House (Los Angeles, California, 2008); a villa in Milan (Italy, 2008); and two other houses in Brasilia (Brazil). His office is also working on a "Green Building" in New Jersey (USA, 2008).

MARCIO KOGAN, geboren 1952, beendete sein Studium 1976 an der Fakultät für Architektur der Universität Mackenzie in São Paulo. Er erhielt Preise des IAB (Brasilianisches Institut für Architektur) für die UMA-Geschäfte (1999 und 2002), das Studio Coser (2002) sowie die Häuser Gama Issa (2002) und Quinta (2004). Für die Häuser Du Plessis (2004) und BR (2005) wurde ihm außerdem der Record House Award verliehen. 2002 konnte er das Museum für Mikrobiologie in São Paulo fertigstellen; 2003 gestaltete er einen Entwurf für die Gedenkstätte am ehemaligen World Trade Center. Mit Isay Weinfeld arbeitete er am Hotel Fasano in São Paulo (2001–03). Ebenfalls mit Weinfeld entwarf er die fiktive Stadt „Happyland" für die 25. Biennale von São Paulo (2002). Kogan ist bekannt für kastenartige Formen, in Kombination mit Holzläden, -gittern und offen liegendem Mauerwerk. Zu Kogans jüngeren Wohnbauten zählen das Haus Cury (São Paulo, 2004–06), das E-Home, ein „Hochtechnologiehaus" (Santander, Spanien, 2007), ein „extremes Haus" auf einer Insel in Paraty (Rio de Janeiro, Brasilien, 2007), der Kinderhort Primetime (São Paulo, 2005–07, hier vorgestellt), das Haus Warbler (Los Angeles, 2008), eine Villa in Mailand (2008) sowie zwei weitere Häuser in Brasília (Brasilien). Sein Büro arbeitet außerdem an einem „Grünen Haus" in New Jersey (USA, 2008).

Né en 1952, **MARCIO KOGAN** obtient son diplôme de l'École d'architecture de l'université Mackenzie, à São Paulo, en 1976. Il a reçu un prix de l'IBA (Institut brésilien d'architecture) pour les magasins UMA (1999 et 2002), le Studio Coser (2002), la maison Gama Issa (2002) et la maison Quinta (2004). Il a également reçu un Record House Award pour la maison Du Plessis (2004) et la maison BR (2005). En 2002, il termine le musée de microbiologie de São Paulo et soumet, en 2003, un projet pour le Mémorial du World Trade Center. Il a travaillé avec Isay Weinfeld sur l'hôtel Fasano, à São Paulo. Il a aussi participé avec Weinfeld à la 25e Biennale de São Paulo (2002), avec un projet pour une ville hypothétique nommée Happyland. Kogan est connu pour son utilisation de cubes, de stores en bois, de treillis et de pierre apparente. Parmi les récents projets d'habitation de Kogan, on compte la maison Cury (São Paulo, 2004–06) ; « E-Home », une maison « super-technologique » (Santander, Espagne, 2007) ; une maison « extrême » sur une île, à Parati (Rio de Janeiro, Brésil, 2007) ; une crèche Primetime Nursery (São Paulo, Brésil, 2005–07, publié ici); la maison Warbler (Los Angeles, Californie, 2008) ; une villa à Milan (Italie, 2008) ; et deux autres maisons à Brasilia (Brésil). Ses bureaux travaillent aussi sur un « immeuble écologique » dans le New Jersey (États-Unis, 2008).

PRIMETIME NURSERY

São Paulo, São Paulo, Brazil, 2005–07

Address: Rua General Jardim, 645 – Conj. 31, 01223–011 São Paulo, SP, Brazil
Area: 735 m². Client: Primetime Nursery. Cost: not disclosed
Collaboration: Lair Reis (Coauthor), Diana Radomysler, Regiane Leão (Interior Design Coauthors)

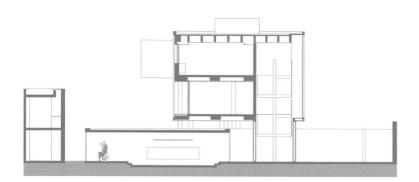

Mit seinen klaren Linien (Querschnitt oben) ist die Primetime Nursery nicht unmittelbar als Kindergarten erkennbar, solange man keinen der unten abgebildeten Spielbereiche sieht.

With its simple lines (seen in the section above) the Primetime Nursery is not readily identifiable as a nursery, unless play areas like the one below are visible.

Avec ses lignes simples (visibles dans la coupe ci-dessus) la crèche Primetime n'est pas immédiatement reconnaissable comme telle, à moins que des aires de jeu, comme ci-dessous, ne soient visibles.

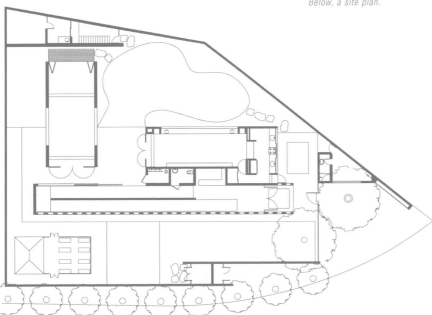

Above, the building is decidedly modern and open, with its yellow color suggesting a bright, happy use. Below, a site plan.

Das Gebäude ist unmissverständlich modern und offen gestaltet, die gelbe Farbe lässt auf eine helle, fröhliche Atmosphäre schließen. Unten ein Lageplan.

Ci-dessus, le bâtiment est résolument moderne et ouvert, et sa couleur jaune suggère une atmosphère lumineuse et joyeuse. Ci-dessous, un plan de situation.

As he often does, Marcio Kogan describes this project in a brief text, one that might have been written by his 18-month-old son. Writing about the **PRIMETIME NURSERY**, he says: "I found the place a little strange. I heard my daddy commenting that the building was modern architecture. I do not know what modern is. In fact, I do not know what architecture is." This approach shows the architect's attempt to be sensitive to the perceptions and needs of small children in such a school. His child (Gabriel) goes on to describe the "little round holes, like a cheese" that permeate the building, and the bright colors used in such elements as a suspended cube window that projects from the building's façade. "Above the entrance there is a hanging yellow box and I just don't know how it doesn't fall! Yellow is my favorite color," says Gabriel. Though an 18-month-old child might not have written any of this, Marcio Kogan does make his points: "I have a lot of fun with the windows that are really big and everything there has a lot of light. Some of the window frames are made of alveolar polycarbonate. Today I learned what an alveolar polycarbonate window frame is." The crisp, pure lines of the building are very much in the style of Marcio Kogan, with bright colors and a touch of humor that suit the specific use of the architecture well.

Marcio Kogan beschreibt sein Projekt wie so oft mit einem kleinen Text, den sein 18 Monate alter Sohn verfasst haben könnte. Über den **PRIMETIME-KINDER-GARTEN** schreibt er: „Mir kam dieser Ort ziemlich seltsam vor. Mein Daddy meinte, das Gebäude sei moderne Architektur. Ich weiß nicht, was modern ist. Ehrlich gesagt weiß ich noch nicht mal, was Architektur ist." Hier zeigt sich das Bemühen des Architekten, sich in die Wahrnehmung und Bedürfnisse kleiner Kinder in einem Kindergarten einzufühlen. Sein Sohn (Gabriel) berichtet weiter von „kleinen runden Löchern, wie bei einem Käse", die das Gebäude durchbohren, und den klaren Farben, die bei Elementen wie dem schwebenden Fensterkubus, der aus der Fassade des Gebäude herausragt, zum Einsatz kommen. „Über dem Eingang hängt eine gelbe Kiste, und ich weiß einfach nicht, warum sie nicht herunterfällt! Gelb ist meine Lieblingsfarbe", meint Gabriel. Auch wenn ein 18 Monate altes Kind kaum solche Texte verfassen dürfte, gelingt es Kogan auf diese Weise, sehr anschaulich zu sein: „Ich habe viel Spaß mit den Fenstern, die riesengroß sind. Alles hier ist so hell. Manche Fensterrahmen sind aus alveolarem Polycarbonat. Heute habe ich gelernt, was ein Fensterrahmen aus alveolarem Polycarbonat ist." Die klaren, puristischen Linien des Baus sind typisch für Kogans Stil, ebenso wie die klaren Farben und der Anflug von Humor, der bei dieser speziellen Art von Architektur zweifellos besonders passend ist.

Comme souvent, Marcio Kogan décrit son projet dans un texte bref, cette fois attribué à son fils âgé de 18 mois. À propos de la **CRÈCHE PRIMETIME**, il dit: «J'ai trouvé l'endroit un peu bizarre. J'ai entendu mon papa dire que ce bâtiment était de l'architecture moderne. Je ne sais pas ce que c'est, moderne. En fait, je ne sais pas ce que c'est, l'architecture.» Cette approche montre la tentative de l'architecte de se montrer sensible aux perceptions et aux besoins d'un jeune enfant dans un tel endroit. Son fils (Gabriel) continue à décrire les «petits trous ronds, comme un fromage» qui percent la façade du bâtiment, et les couleurs vives utilisées pour des éléments comme une fenêtre cube saillant de la façade du bâtiment. «Au-dessus de l'entrée, il y a un cube jaune suspendu et, je ne sais pas pourquoi, il ne tombe pas! le jaune est ma couleur préférée», dit Gabriel. Bien que rien de tout cela n'aurait pu être écrit par un enfant de 18 mois, Marcio Kogan est assez convaincant: «Je m'amuse beaucoup avec les fenêtres qui sont vraiment grandes et tout est plein de lumière. Certains châssis de fenêtres sont en polycarbonate alvéolaire. Aujourd'hui j'ai appris ce qu'était un châssis de fenêtre en polycarbonate alvéolaire.» Les lignes pures et nettes du bâtiment sont tout à fait dans le style de Marcio Kogan, avec des couleurs vives et une pointe d'humour qui convient bien à l'usage spécifique de cette architecture.

The activities of children do fit into the architecture well, but, on the whole, the Nursery looks as though it might serve other purposes just as readily.

Die Spielbereiche der Kinder fügen sich selbstverständlich in die Architektur, trotzdem wirkt das Gebäude, als ob es ebenso gut anderen Zwecken dienen könnte.

Les activités pour enfants s'intègrent bien à cette architecture, mais le bâtiment semble finalement pouvoir convenir aussi bien à d'autres usages.

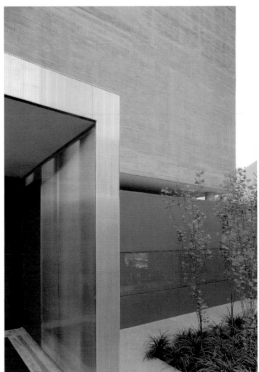

KUEHN MALVEZZI

Kuehn Malvezzi GmbH Architekten
Heidestr. 50
10557 Berlin
Germany

Tel: +49 30 39 80 68 00
Fax: +49 30 39 80 68 06
E-mail: info@kuehnmalvezzi.com
Web: www.kuehnmalvezzi.com

SIMONA MALVEZZI was born in Milan, Italy, in 1966. She received her degree in Architecture from the Politecnico di Milano (1987–94). She worked with Berni-Leroy (Milan, 1995–97) and with Hubmann & Vass (Vienna, Austria, 1998–2000), before cofounding Kuehn Malvezzi in 2001. **WILFRIED KUEHN** was born in Hamburg, Germany, in 1967. He also studied at the Politecnico di Milano and at the University of Lisbon (1886–1995). He worked in the office of Adolf Krischanitz (Vienna, 1995–2000), before the creation of Kuehn Malvezzi. **JOHANNES KUEHN** was born in Hamburg, Germany, in 1969. He studied at the Technical University Berlin and the University of Porto (1989–98). Kuehn Malvezzi designed the exhibition spaces for Documenta 11 in Kassel (2002); the extension to the Hamburger Bahnhof—Museum für Gegenwart for the Friedrich Christian Flick Collection (Berlin, 2004); and the Julia Stoschek Collection in Dusseldorf (2005–07, published here). They are currently converting the Baroque Unteres Belvedere (Lower Belvedere) in Vienna (Austria) into an exhibition venue for modern art, as well as designing an expansion to the Museum Berggruen in Berlin and new presentations of a number of historical collections, including the Liebieghaus Frankfurt, the Herzog Anton Ulrich-Museum in Braunschweig, the Kunstsammlung Nordrhein-Westfalen, and the Kunstgewerbemuseum Berlin, all in Germany unless otherwise stated.

SIMONA MALVEZZI wurde 1966 in Mailand geboren und schloss ihr Architekturstudium am Politecnico di Milano ab (1987–94). Sie arbeitete bei Berni-Leroy (Mailand, 1995–97) und Hubmann & Vass (Wien, 1998–2000), bevor sie 2001 an der Gründung von Kuehn Malvezzi beteiligt war. **WILFRIED KUEHN** wurde 1967 in Hamburg geboren. Auch er studierte am Politecnico di Milano sowie an der Universität Lissabon (1886–95). Vor der Gründung von Kuehn Malvezzi war er bei Adolf Krischanitz (Wien, 1995–2000) tätig. **JOHANNES KUEHN** wurde 1969 in Hamburg geboren. Er studierte an der Technischen Universität Berlin sowie der Universidade do Porto (1989–98). Kuehn Malvezzi gestaltete die Ausstellungsarchitektur der documenta 11 in Kassel (2002), entwarf den Anbau für die Friedrich Christian Flick Collection am Hamburger Bahnhof – Museum für Gegenwart (Berlin, 2004) sowie die Sammlung Julia Stoschek in Düsseldorf (2005–07, hier vorgestellt). Derzeit arbeitet das Büro am Umbau des barocken Unteren Belvedere in Wien zum Ausstellungsort für moderne Kunst sowie an einer Erweiterung des Museum Berggruen in Berlin und der Neupräsentation verschiedener historischer Kunstsammlungen, darunter am Liebighaus Frankfurt, dem Herzog Anton Ulrich Museum in Braunschweig, der Kunstsammlung Nordrhein-Westfalen und dem Kunstgewerbemuseum Berlin.

SIMONA MALVEZZI est née à Milan, en Italie, en 1966. Elle est diplômée en architecture de la Politecnico di Milano (1987–94). Elle a travaillé avec Berni-Leroy (Milan, 1995–97) et Hubmann & Vass (Vienne, 1998–2000), avant de participer à la création de Kuehn Malvezzi en 2001. **WILFRIED KUEHN** est né à Hambourg, en Allemagne, en 1967. Il a également étudié à la Politecnico de Milan et à l'université de Lisbonne (1886–1995). Il a travaillé dans l'agence d'Adolf Krischanitz (Vienne, 1995–2000) avant de créer Kuehn Malvezzi. **JOHANNES KUEHN** est né à Hambourg, en Allemagne, en 1969. Il a étudié à l'Université techinique de Berlin et à l'université de Porto (1989–98). Kuehn Malvezzi a conçu les espaces d'expositions de la Documenta 11 de Kassel (2002), l'extension du musée Hamburger Bahnhof–Museum für Gegenwart pour la collection Friedrich Christian Flick (Berlin, 2004), et la collection Julia Stoschek à Düsseldorf (2005–07, publié ici). Leurs projets en cours incluent la conversion du bâtiment baroque du musée du Belvédère (belvédère inférieur) de Vienne (Autriche) en un espace d'exposition d'art moderne ; l'extension du musée Berggruen à Berlin ; et la nouvelle présentation de plusieurs collections historiques, pour le musée Liebieghaus à Francfort ; le musée Herzog Anton Ulrich à Braunschweig ; le Kunstsammlung Nordrhein-Westfalen (collections de Rhénanie-du-Nord-Westphalie) à Düsseldorf ; et le Kunstgewerbemuseum (Musée des Arts décoratifs) à Berlin, tous situés en Allemagne sauf mention contraire.

JULIA STOSCHEK COLLECTION

Dusseldorf, Germany, 2005–07

Address: Schanzenstr. 54, 40549 Düsseldorf, Germany, +49 211 585 88 40, www.julia-stoschek-collection.net
Area: 3200 m². Client: Julia Stoschek. Cost: not disclosed
Project Architects: Jan Ulmer, Vincent Rahm, Michael Stoss, Roland Züger

The **JULIA STOSCHEK COLLECTION** was housed in an early 20th-century factory building. The architects were chosen for the renovation of the building as the result of a limited competition. Because of restrictions on the listed building, it was decided to maintain the original façade while gutting the interiors and rebuilding a new perimeter within the old walls. Kuehn Malvezzi sought to "neutralize the nostalgic effect of industrial architecture." They placed a glass box and panoramic terrace on top of the structure, replacing the original factory sign and giving a new identity to the building. Since the collection is made up largely of videos, the presentation relies on the creation of individual, soundproof spaces. A break in the floor slab between the first and second floors near the entrance allows visitors to visualize their itinerary in the building. The third and fourth floors, reaching a height of 12 meters, contain the home of Julia Stoschek and special-event spaces. Even the residential area is conceived as an exhibition space, where "pieces of furniture and works of art come together to create a complete installation." A six-meter-long table and large-scale sofa harmonize the furnishings of the residence with the large scale of the factory building. Simona Malvezzi explains that "white and dark grey in the upper levels continues below; the same colors and materials have been used in the exhibition spaces on the lower floors, homogenizing the public and private areas."

Die **SAMMLUNG JULIA STOSCHEK** ist in einem Fabrikgebäude des frühen 20. Jahrhunderts untergebracht. Die Architekten wurden im Rahmen eines einge-schränkten Wettbewerbs für die Sanierung ausgewählt. Aufgrund der Auflagen für das denkmalgeschützte Gebäude wurde die ursprüngliche Fassade beibehalten, das Innere des Baus jedoch entkernt und neue Wände in die alten Mauern der ehemaligen Fabrik eingezogen. Kuehn Malvezzi ging es darum, „die nostalgische Wirkung der Industriearchitektur zu brechen". Sie ersetzten das ursprüngliche Fabrikschild auf dem Bau durch eine Glasbox und eine Terrasse mit Panoramablick und gaben dem Gebäude so eine neue Identität. Da Videoarbeiten Schwerpunkt der Sammlung sind, ist die Präsentation der Werke auf separate, schallisolierte Räume angewiesen. Ein Durchbruch durch die Bodenplatte zwischen erstem und zweitem Stockwerk, unweit des Eingangs, ermöglicht den Besuchern, ihren Parcours durch das Gebäude visuell zu erfassen. In der dritten und vierten Ebene mit einer Raumhöhe von bis zu 12 m befinden sich die Wohnräume von Julia Stoschek sowie Räume für besondere Anlässe. Selbst der Wohnbereich ist wie ein Ausstellungsraum konzipiert, in dem sich „Möbelstücke und Kunstwerke zu einer Gesamtinstallation fügen". Ein 6 m langer Tisch und ein übergroßes Sofa harmonieren mit den Dimensionen des Fabrikgebäudes. Simona Malvezzi führt aus: „Das Weiß und Grau der oberen Ebenen setzt sich unten fort; in den Ausstellungsräumen der unteren Ebenen kamen dieselben Farben und Materialien zum Einsatz, sodass öffentliche und private Bereiche ein harmonisches Ganzes bilden."

LA COLLECTION JULIA STOSCHEK était hébergée dans une usine du début du XXᵉ siècle. Les architectes ont été sélectionnés pour rénover le bâtiment, à l'is-sue d'un concours restreint. En raison des restrictions imposées au bâtiment classé, il a été décidé de garder la façade d'origine, de dégarnir les intérieurs et de recons-truire un nouveau périmètre inclus dans des murs anciens. Kuehn Malvezzi a cherché à « neutraliser l'effet nostalgique de l'architecture industrielle ». Ils ont placé un cube de verre et une terrasse panoramique au sommet du bâtiment, remplacé l'enseigne d'origine de l'usine et donné une nouvelle identité au bâtiment. Puisque la col-lection est principalement constituée de vidéos, la présentation repose sur la création d'espaces individuels insonorisés. Une brèche dans le plancher entre le rez-de-chaussée et le premier étage, à proximité de l'entrée, permet au visiteur de visualiser son itinéraire dans le bâtiment. Les troisième et quatrième étages, d'une hauteur de 12 mètres, sont occupés par l'appartement de Julia Stoschek et des espaces réservés à des événements spéciaux. La zone d'habitation est elle-même conçue comme un espace d'exposition où « les meubles et les œuvres d'art sont réunis pour créer une installation achevée ». Une table de six mètres de long et un large canapé har-monisent l'ameublement de l'habitation avec l'échelle du bâtiment industriel. Simona Malvezzi explique que « le blanc et le gris foncé des étages supérieurs se retrou-vent plus bas ; la même palette de couleurs et de matériaux a été utilisée dans les espaces d'expositions des étages inférieurs, pour homogénéiser les parties publiques et privées ».

The architects' intervention is concentrated on the roof and upper levels (seen in the plans below and in the photos on both pages) of the existing factory structure.

Die Eingriffe der Architekten in die alte Fabrik konzentrieren sich besonders auf die Dachebene und die oberen Geschosse des Gebäudes (wie in den Grundrissen unten und den Abbildungen auf beiden Seiten zu sehen).

L'intervention de l'architecte s'est concentrée sur le toit et les niveaux supérieurs (visibles sur le plan ci-dessous et les photos des deux pages) de l'usine d'origine.

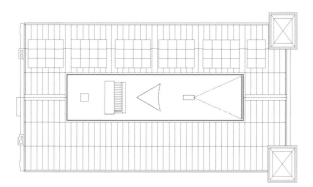

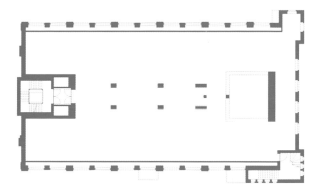

The architects have succeeded in creating modern forms within the volumes of the old factory. To the right, the uppermost levels.

Den Architekten gelang es, in den Räumen der alten Fabrik eine moderne Formensprache umzusetzen. Rechts die oberen Geschossebenen.

Les architectes ont réussi à créer des formes modernes dans les volumes de l'ancienne usine. À droite, les niveaux supérieurs.

LINE AND SPACE

Line and Space LLC
627 East Speedway
Tucson, AZ 85705
USA

Tel: +1 520 623 1313
E-mail: studio627@lineandspace.com
Web: www.lineandspace.com

Les Wallach was born in 1944 in Pittsburgh, Pennsylvania. He received degrees in both Engineering and Architecture from the University of Arizona (1967, 1974). He founded **LINE AND SPACE** in 1978 with an interest in environmentally responsible design. Henry Tom received his B.Arch degree from the University of Arizona in 1989, and started working with Line and Space in 1987. Robert Clements joined the firm in 1991, after receiving his B.Arch degree from the University of Arizona (1989). John Birkinbine, the youngest Principal at Line and Space, was made a partner in 2004. He received his B.Arch degree from the University of Arizona in 1994. Recent and current work includes the University of Arizona Helen S. Schaefer Poetry Center (Tucson, Arizona, 2002–07, published here); the Cesar Chavez Branch Library (Phoenix, Arizona, 2002–07); the Red Rock Canyon Visitor Center (Las Vegas, Nevada, 2009); Tianquin Bay Villas (Shenzhen, China, projected completion 2010); and the Mojave Discovery Center (Las Vegas, Nevada, projected completion 2011), all in the USA unless stated otherwise.

Les Wallach wurde 1944 in Pittsburgh, Pennsylvania, geboren. An der Universität von Arizona schloss er sein Studium in Bauingenieurwesen und Architektur ab (1967, 1974). 1978 gründete er **LINE AND SPACE** mit besonderem Augenmerk auf umweltgerechte Planung. Henry Tom beendete sein Studium 1989 an der Universität von Arizona mit einem B. Arch. und arbeitet seit 1987 bei Line and Space. Robert Clements schloss sich dem Büro 1991 an, nachdem er seinen B. Arch. 1989 an der Universität von Arizona absolviert hatte. John Birkinbine, jüngstes Mitglied der Leitung von Line and Space, wurde 2004 Partner. Er machte seinen B. Arch. 1994 an der Universität von Arizona. Jüngere und aktuelle Projekte sind u. a. das Helen S. Schaefer Poetry Center an der Universität von Arizona (Tucson, Arizona, 2002–07, hier vorgestellt), die Zweigbibliothek Cesar Chavez (Phoenix, Arizona, 2002–07), das Besucherzentrum im Red Rock Canyon (Las Vegas, Nevada, 2009), ein Villenkomplex in Tianquin Bay (Shenzhen, China, voraussichtliche Fertigstellung 2010) sowie das Mojave Discovery Center (Las Vegas, Nevada, voraussichtliche Fertigstellung 2011).

Les Wallach est né en 1944 à Pittsburgh, en Pennsylvanie. Il obtient ses diplômes d'ingénieur et d'architecte à l'université d'Arizona (1967, 1974). Il fonde **LINE AND SPACE**, en 1978, et privilégie des projets écologiquement responsables. Henry Tom obtient son diplôme d'architecte à l'université d'Arizona, en 1989, et commence à travailler avec Line and Space en 1987. Robert Clements rejoint l'agence en 1991, après avoir obtenu son diplôme d'architecte à l'université d'Arizona (1989). John Birkinbine, le plus jeune directeur de Line and Space, devient associé en 2004. Il a obtenu son diplôme d'architecte à l'université d'Arizona en 1994. Leurs projets récents incluent le Centre de la poésie Helen S. Schaefer de l'université d'Arizona (Tucson, Arizona, 2002–07, publié ici); la bibliothèque Cesar Chavez (Phoenix, Arizona, 2002–07); le Centre des visiteurs du Red Rock Canyon (Las Vegas, Nevada, 2009); Tianquin Bay Villas (Shenzhen, Chine, achèvement prévu en 2010); un Centre de découverte du désert Mojave (Las Vegas, Nevada, achèvement prévu en 2011), tous situés aux États-Unis sauf mention contraire.

UNIVERSITY OF ARIZONA
HELEN S. SCHAEFER POETRY CENTER

Tucson, Arizona, 2002–07

Address: 1508 East Helen Street, Tucson, AZ 85721–0150, USA,
+1 520 626 3765, www.poetrycenter.arizona.edu
Area: 1672 m². Client: University of Arizona. Cost: $68 million

The contemporary poetry collection of the University of Arizona is considered to be one of the best in the United States. This facility is intended for research, reading, teaching, and archiving related to this body of 50 000 works. Seeking to reconcile the expressed desires of users for both a solitary environment and one in which interaction with others is possible, the architects conceived a "progression toward solitude" in which the western area is occupied by an "active and noisy humanities seminar room" with transparent walls, and more intimate spaces, including a bamboo garden, to the east. Further, it was necessary to reconcile the use by the public and the academic community. Transition spaces modulate the uses and nature of the indoor and outdoor areas. The southern windows are protected from the strong sunlight by overhangs, while the western side has very little fenestration, to protect the interior from traffic noise. "On the east," the architects explain, "a 'binary wall' shades the building and bamboo garden while celebrating a line from a Richard Shelton poem ('…you shall learn the art of silence.'), with holes punched out in binary code."

Die Sammlung zeitgenössischer Lyrik an der Universität Arizona gilt als eine der besten der USA. Das Institut wird für Forschungsvorhaben genutzt, als Lesesaal, für Lehrveranstaltungen und als Archiv für den 50 000 Bände umfassenden Werkbestand. Um den Wunsch der Nutzer nach abgeschlossenen Arbeitsplätzen einerseits und Bereichen für die Kommunikation andererseits zu realisieren, entschieden sich die Architekten für eine „Progression der Einsamkeit". Dementsprechend gibt es im westlichen Bereich einen „Seminarraum für geräuschintensives geisteswissenschaftliches Arbeiten" mit transparenten Trennwänden, während im Osten ruhigere Bereiche liegen, wie etwa ein Bambusgarten. Darüber hinaus galt es, die Anforderungen öffentlicher und akademischer Nutzer in Einklang zu bringen. Übergangszonen vermitteln zwischen den unterschiedlichen Nutzungen sowie zwischen Innen- und Außenraum. Die südliche Fensterfront wird durch Auskragungen vor dem starken Sonnenlicht geschützt, während auf der Westseite kaum Fenster vorhanden sind, um den Innenraum vor Verkehrslärm abzuschirmen. „Im Osten", erklären die Architekten, „spendet eine ‚binäre Mauer' Schatten für Gebäude und Bambusgarten. In die Mauer ist ein Lochmuster eingearbeitet, das im Binärcode eine Zeile aus einem Gedicht Richard Sheltons (‚…you shall learn the art of silence') repräsentiert."

Le fonds de poésie contemporaine de l'université d'Arizona est considéré comme l'un des plus importants des États-Unis. Cette installation est destinée à la recherche, la lecture et l'archivage de ce fonds de 50 000 œuvres. Soucieux de répondre au désir, exprimé par les utilisateurs, d'un environnement qui soit à la fois solitaire et ouvert aux interactions avec les autres, les architectes ont conçu une « progression vers la solitude » allant de l'aile ouest occupée par une « salle de séminaires active et bruyante » dotée de murs transparents, vers des espaces plus intimes, dont un jardin de bambous, à l'est. De plus, il était nécessaire de concilier usage public et activités universitaires. Des espaces de transition modulent l'usage et la nature des espaces intérieurs et extérieurs. Les fenêtres du côté sud sont protégées du fort ensoleillement par des surplombs, tandis que le côté ouest possède peu de fenêtres pour protéger l'intérieur du bruit de la circulation. « À l'est », expliquent les architectes, « » un mur binaire « donne de l'ombre au bâtiment et au jardin de bambous, et » rend hommage à Richard Shelton par cette citation d'un de ses poèmes (…you shall learn the art of silence. « […vous apprendrez l'art du silence]) estampée en code binaire. »

Successive roof levels step up, with a large square opening corresponding to the central passage that cuts through the structure.

Die verschiedenen Dachniveaus sind treppenförmig gestaffelt. Eine großzügige Öffnung im Dach korrespondiert mit der das Gebäude durchschneidenden Haupterschließung.

Les toits s'échelonnent en hauteur et une grande ouverture carrée correspond au passage central traversant la structure.

Below, two section drawings and, above, a photo of the open passage demonstrating the interpenetration of exterior and interior spaces sought by the architects.

Unten zwei Querschnitte, oben ein Foto des Durchgangs, das die von den Architekten angestrebte Durchdringung von Außen- und Innenraum belegt.

Les deux coupes ci-dessous et la photo ci-dessus du passage ouvert montrent l'interpénétration des espaces intérieurs et extérieurs voulues par les architectes.

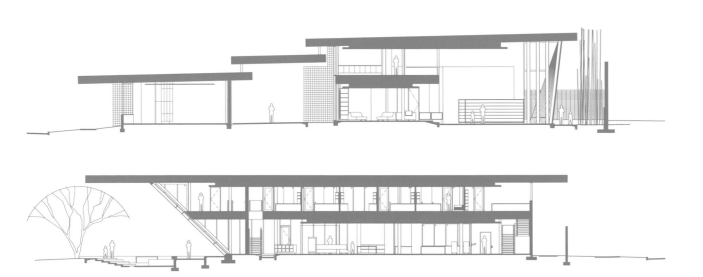

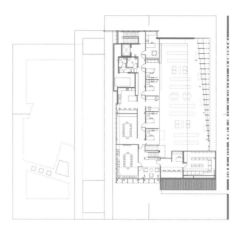

Above, left, a ground-level plan with the Humanities Seminar Room on the left, and the collection stacks on the right. Above, right, the level 2 plan with a number of offices and the open space above the stacks.

Oben ein Grundriss der Erdgeschossebene mit dem geisteswissenschaftlichen Seminarraum (links) und den Magazinen der Sammlungsbestände (rechts). Rechts oben ein Grundriss der zweiten Ebene mit Büroräumen sowie dem offenen Bereich über dem Freihandmagazin.

Ci-dessus à gauche, un plan du rez-de-chaussée, avec la salle de séminaires sur la gauche et les rayonnages de la collection sur la droite. Ci-dessus à droite, le plan du niveau 2 avec plusieurs bureaux et un espace ouvert au-dessus de la salle de rayonnages.

Above, the double-height stacks and reading space. Below, the seminar room and desks near the stacks.

Oben das Freihandmagazin mit doppelter Geschosshöhe und Leseecke. Unten der Seminarraum neben dem Magazin.

Ci-dessus, l'espace des rayonnages et de lecture sur deux niveaux. Ci-dessous, la salle de séminaires et des tables de bureau près des rayonnages.

LOCALARCHITECTURE

Localarchitecture
Côtes-de-Montbenon 30
Case Postale
1002 Lausanne
Switzerland

Tel: +41 21 320 06 86
E-mail: local@localarchitecture.ch
Web: www.localarchitecture.ch

Manuel Bieler, Antoine Robert-Grandpierre, and Laurent Saurer created **LOCALARCHITECTURE** in Lausanne, Switzerland, in 2002. Bieler was born in 1970 and received his degree in Architecture from the EPFL (Federal Polytechnic Institute, Lausanne) in 1996. He received a postgraduate diploma in the economy and management of construction from the EPFL in 2002. Antoine Robert-Grandpierre was born in 1972 and also received his degree in Architecture from the EPFL in 1996. Laurent Saurer, born in 1971, obtained his degree from the EPFL in 1998. They won Second Prize in the 2005 competition for the new Lausanne Museum of Modern Art. They have completed an opthamologist's office (Saint-Gallen, 2004); a widely published Cow Barn (Lignières, Neuchâtel, 2003–05); the Guyot House (Colombier, 2003–05); the Maison du Villaret (Colombier, 2004–05); the Temporary Chapel of St. Loup (Pompaples, 2008, published here); as well as housing in Corsy-sur-Lutry (Vaud, 2007–09), all in Switzerland. They are currently working on the Fédération Internationale de Motocyclisme (Mies 2006–), and the Verdeil Foundation / Pierrefleur School (Lausanne, 2006–), both in Switzerland.

Manuel Bieler, Antoine Robert-Grandpierre und Laurent Saurer gründeten ihr Büro **LOCALARCHITECTURE** 2002 in Lausanne. Bieler wurde 1970 geboren und schloss 1996 sein Architekturstudium an der EPFL (École Polytechnique Fédérale de Lausanne) ab. 2002 machte er sein Diplom in Bauökonomie und -management an der EPFL. Antoine Robert-Grandpierre wurde 1972 geboren und beendete sein Architekturstudium ebenfalls 1996 an der EPFL. Laurent Saurer, 1971 geboren, absolvierte 1998 seinen Studienabschluss an der EPFL. 2005 gewann das Team den zweiten Preis im Wettbewerb für den Neubau des Museums für moderne Kunst in Lausanne. Realisierte Projekte sind u. a. ein Ladenlokal für einen Augenoptiker (St. Gallen, 2004), ein vielfach publizierter Kuhstall (Lignières, Neuchâtel, 2003–05), das Haus Guyot (Colombier, 2003–05), die Maison du Villaret (Colombier, 2004–05), eine temporäre Kapelle in St. Loup (Pompaples, 2008, hier vorgestellt) sowie ein Wohnbauprojekt in Corsy-sur-Lutry (Waadt, 2007–09), alle in der Schweiz. Aktuell arbeitet das Büro an einem Projekt für die Fédération Internationale de Motocyclisme (Mies, seit 2006) sowie die Schule der Fondation Verdeil/Pierrefleur (Lausanne, seit 2006), beide in der Schweiz.

Manuel Bieler, Antoine Robert-Grandpierre et Laurent Saurer ont fondé **LOCALARCHITECTURE** à Lausanne, en Suisse, en 2002. Bieler, né en 1970, a obtenu son diplôme d'arcitecture à l'EPFL (École polytechnique fédérale de Lausanne) en 1996 ainsi qu'un diplôme de 3e cycle en économie et management de la construction de l'EPFL en 2002. Antoine Robert-Grandpierre, né en 1972, a également obtenu son diplôme d'architecte à l'EPFL en 1996. Laurent Saurer, né en 1971, a obtenu son diplôme de l'EPFL en 1998. Ils ont gagné le deuxième prix au concours pour le nouveau musée d'Art moderne de Lausanne en 2005. Ils ont réalisé un cabinet d'ophtalmologie (Saint-Gallen, 2004) ; une étable, largement publiée, à Lignières (Lignières, Neuchâtel, 2003–05) ; la maison Guyot (Colombier, 2003–05) ; la maison du Villaret (Colombier, 2004–05) ; une chapelle provisoire à Saint-Loup (Pompaples, 2008, publié ici) ; ainsi que deux immeubles d'habitation à Corsy-sur-Lutry (Vaud, 2007–09), tous situés en Suisse. Leurs projets en cours incluent le nouveau siège de la Fédération internationale de motocyclisme (Mies 2006) ; et la fondation de Verdeil, École Pierrefleur (Lausanne, 2006–), tous deux situés en Suisse.

TEMPORARY CHAPEL OF ST. LOUP

Pompaples, Switzerland, 2008

Area: 130 m². Client: Deaconesses of St. Loup. Cost: not disclosed
Collaboration: in association with Bureau d'architecture Danilo Mondada and Shel Hani Buri, Yves Weinand,
Architecture, Engineering, and Production Design

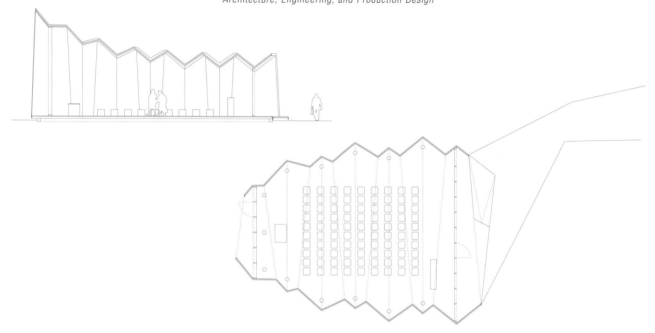

The architects were awarded the commission to renovate the home of the Community of the Deaconesses of St. Loup in the Canton of Vaud in 2007. Since this required that the facility be closed for 18 months, beginning in the summer of 2008, the architects proposed to erect a temporary chapel near the existing facilities. Localarchitecture is interested in wooden structures, and this one was designed using CAD software that was directly transferred to CNC milling to cut the four-centimeter-thick (walls) and six-centimeter-thick (roof) timber panels. Open at each end, the chapel is set directly on the ground, and is described by Localarchitecture as interpreting "the traditional layout of Protestant churches with their variations in width and height between transept and nave," and they explain that "the design creates a space whose horizontal and vertical dimensions vary via a series of origami-like folds that give rhythm to the interior and exterior of the building." Light is admitted in part through transparent plastic panels covered with fabric.

2007 erhielten die Architekten den Auftrag, das Mutterhaus der Diakonissengemeinschaft in St. Loup im Kanton Waadt zu sanieren. Da dies die Schließung der Einrichtung für 18 Monate ab Sommer 2008 bedeutete, schlugen die Architekten vor, eine temporäre Kapelle in der Nähe des Altbaus zu errichten. Localarchitecture beschäftigt sich mit Holzkonstruktionen und entwarf diesen Holzbau mithilfe von CAD, das unmittelbar auf eine CNC-Fräse übertragen wurde, mit der die 4 bzw. 6 cm starken Holzpaneele für die Wände und das Dach zugeschnitten wurden. Die an beiden Enden offene Kapelle steht unmittelbar auf der Erde und ist laut Localarchitecture eine Interpretation des „traditionellen Grundrisses protestantischer Kirchenbauten mit Höhen- und Breitenunterschieden zwischen Querhaus und Hauptschiff". Weiter führen sie aus: „Der Entwurf umreißt einen Raum, dessen horizontale und vertikale Abmessungen dank der origamiartigen Faltungen variieren, die dem Inneren und Äußeren des Gebäudes Rhythmus verleihen." Licht fällt teilweise durch transparente, stoffbespannte Kunststoffpaneele ein.

Les architectes ont remporté le projet de rénovation du bâtiment de la communauté des diaconesses de Saint-Loup, dans le canton de Vaud en 2007. Comme cela impliquait la fermeture du bâtiment pendant dix-huit mois, à partir de l'été 2008, les architectes ont proposé une chapelle provisoire près des installations existantes. Localarchitecture s'intéresse aux bâtiments en bois, et celui-ci a été conçu à l'aide d'un logiciel de CAO envoyant directement les données à la fraiseuse CNC pour la coupe des panneaux de bois de quatre centimètres (murs) et de six centimètres (toit) d'épaisseur. Ouverte à chaque extrémité, la chapelle est posée directement au sol, elle réinterprète, selon Localarchitecture « l'espace traditionnel des églises protestantes et les variations des largeurs et hauteurs de la nef, du transept jusqu'au chœur », et crée un espace « qui varie d'une échelle horizontale à une échelle verticale en passant par une succession de plis qui rythment les volumes intérieur et extérieur du bâtiment ». La lumière pénètre en partie par des panneaux de plastique transparent recouvert de textile.

Although the structure is meant to be temporary, its form echoes the much more permanent cliff behind the Community of the Deaconesses of St. Loup.

Obwohl es sich um einen temporären Bau handelt, wirkt er wie ein Echo der weitaus beständigeren Steilwand hinter dem Diakonissenmutterhaus von St. Loup.

Bien qu'il s'agisse d'un bâtiment provisoire, sa forme évoque la paroi rocheuse bien plus pérenne précaire, derrière la communauté des diaconesses de St-Loup.

An interior view, and a night image of the structure's low, open end.

Ein Blick in den Innenraum der Kapel-le und eine nächtliche Ansicht ihrer niedrigeren, transparenten Rückseite.

Une vue intérieure et une vue de nuit de l'extrémité basse et ouverte du bâtiment.

Based on an accordion-like folding of paper, the completed building nonetheless assumes a look of some permanence, and, in any case, remains quite original.

Das realisierte Gebäude basiert formal im Grunde auf einem zur Ziehharmonika gefalteten Blatt Papier. Dennoch wirkt es beständig und in jedem Fall außergewöhnlich.

Reproduisant la forme d'une feuille de papier pliée en accordéon, le bâtiment n'en revêt pas moins une certaine permanence et reste, en tout cas, vraiment original.

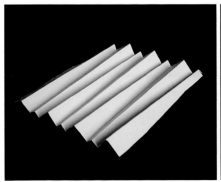

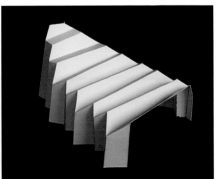

LUNDGAARD & TRANBERG

Lundgaard & Tranberg Arkitekter
Pilestræde 10, 3 sal
1112 Copenhagen K
Denmark

Tel: +45 33 91 07 17
Fax: +45 33 91 07 16
E-mail: mail@ltarkitekter.dk
Web: www.ltarkitekter.dk

LENE TRANBERG was born in 1956 in Copenhagen and received her degree from the Royal Danish Acadmey of Arts in 1984. Lundgaard & Tranberg Arkitekter was founded in 1984 by Lene Tranberg and **BOJE LUNDGAARD**. Aside from Lene Transberg, current partners of the firm are Erik Frandsen, Henrik Schmidt, Kenneth Warnke, Nicolai Richter-Friis, Peter Thorsen, and Trine Troelsen. Recent and current projects include Charlotte Gardens Service Center (Copenhagen, 2001–04); Copenhagen Business School "The Wedge" (Frederiksberg/Copenhagen, 2003–05); Tietgen Dormitory (Copenhagen, 2003–05); Ørestad Apartments (Copenhagen, 2005–06); The Royal Playhouse (Copenhagen, 2004–07, published here); The Lighthouse (Copenhagen, 2005–07); Harbor Isle Apartments (Copenhagen, 2005–08); Teglmose Grunden—housing project (Copenhagen, 2007–09); and SEB DOMICIL (Copenhagen, 2006–10), all in Denmark.

LENE TRANBERG wurde 1956 in Kopenhagen geboren und machte ihren Abschluss 1984 an der Königlich Dänischen Kunstakademie. Im selben Jahr gründete sie mit **BOJE LUNDGAARD** das Büro Lundgaard & Tranberg Arkitekter. Partner sind außerdem derzeit Erik Frandsen, Henrik Schmidt, Kenneth Warnke, Nicolai Richter-Friis, Peter Thorsen und Trine Troelsen. Jüngere und aktuelle Projekt sind u. a. das Servicecenter Charlotte Gardens (Kopenhagen, 2001–04), die Copenhagen Business School „The Wedge" (Frederiksberg/Kopenhagen, 2003–05), das Tietgen-Wohnheim (Kopenhagen, 2003–05), die Ørestad Apartments (Kopenhagen, 2005–06), das Königliche Schauspielhaus (Kopenhagen, 2004–07, hier vorgestellt), The Lighthouse (Der Leuchtturm, Kopenhagen, 2005–07), die Havneholmen Apartments (Kopenhagen, 2005–08), das Wohnbauprojekt Teglmose Grunden (Kopenhagen, 2007–09) sowie die dänische Zentrale der SEB-Bank (Kopenhagen, 2006–10).

LENE TRANBERG est née en 1956 à Copenhague et a obtenu son diplôme de l'Académie royale des beaux-arts du Danemark en 1984. L'agence Lundgaard & Tranberg Arkitekter a été fondée en 1984 par Lene Tranberg et **BOJE LUNDGAARD**. En dehors de Lene Transberg, les associés actuels de l'agence sont Erik Frandsen, Henrik Schmidt, Kenneth Warnke, Nicolai Richter-Friis, Peter Thorsen et Trine Troelsen. Leurs projets récents et en cours incluent la résidence hôtelière Charlottehaven (Copenhague, 2001–04) ; l'école de commerce The Wedge de Copenhague (Frederiksberg/Copenhague, 2003–05) ; la résidence universitaire de Tietgen (Copenhague, 2003–05) ; un immeuble d'appartements à Ørestad (Copenhague, 2005–06) ; le Théâtre royal de Copenhague (Copenhague, 2004–07, publié ici) ; l'ensemble d'appartements Fyrtårnet (Le phare) (Copenhague, 2005–07) ; l'ensemble d'appartements Havneholmen (Copenhague, 2005–08) ; un projet d'habitations à Teglmose Grunden (Copenhague, 2007–09) ; et le siège de la banque SEB (Copenhague, 2006–10), tous situés au Danemark.

THE ROYAL PLAYHOUSE
Copenhagen, Denmark, 2004–07

Address: Sankt Annæ Plads 36, 1250 Copenhagen, Denmark, +45 33 69 69 69, www.kglteater.dk
Area: 21 000 m². Client: Danish Ministry of Culture
Cost: € 70 million

The architects won the international competition for the design of the **ROYAL PLAYHOUSE** in 2002. The structure opened to the public in 2008. The Royal Playhouse is set at the juncture of the historic 18th-century Frederiksstaden area, the harbor, and the sea. The building is made up essentially of three elements—an oak deck promenade leading to the glass foyer; the primary theater spaces housed in a dark-brick masonry structure that "echoes the surrounding historic harbor warehouses"; and a glass-and-steel service level containing workspaces, administration, and areas for the actors. A copper-clad stage tower tops the design. The main auditorium, seating 650 people, is "circular and grotto-like [...] seemingly carved out of the masonry mass of the stage building," according to the architects. Seawater cooling with a heat pump and passive energy storage ensure that electricity for cooling will be 40 percent lower than in an ordinary building.

2002 gewann das Team den internationalen Wettbewerb für das **KÖNIGLICHE SCHAUSPIELHAUS**. Seit 2008 ist der Komplex für die Öffentlichkeit geöffnet. Das Königliche Schauspielhaus liegt zwischen dem historischen Frederiksstaden-Viertel aus dem 18. Jahrhundert, Hafen und Meer. Der Bau besteht im Wesentlichen aus drei Elementen – einer Terrassenpromenade aus Eichenholz, die Zugang zum verglasten Foyer bietet, den eigentlichen Theaterräumlichkeiten (untergebracht in einem dunklen Ziegelbau, der formal „an die umliegenden historischen Hafenspeicher anknüpft" sowie einer mit Stahl und Glas gebauten Serviceebene, in der sich Werkstätten, Verwaltung und Bereiche für die Schauspieler befinden. Ein kupferverblendeter Bühnenturm überragt den Entwurf. Der große Saal mit 650 Plätzen ist „rund und höhlenähnlich [...] und wirkt, als habe man ihn aus dem massiven Mauerwerk des Theatergebäudes herausgeschlagen", so die Architekten. Ein Seewasserkühlsystem sowie eine Wärmepumpe und ein Speicher für Passivenergie sorgen dafür, dass der Stromverbrauch zur Kühlung des Gebäudes 40 Prozent niedriger liegt als bei herkömmlichen Bauten.

Les architectes ont gagné le concours international pour la réalisation du **THÉÂTRE ROYAL** en 2002. Le bâtiment a été inauguré en 2008. Le Théâtre royal est implanté à la jonction du quartier historique du XVIIIᵉ siècle Frederiksstaden, du port et de la mer. Le bâtiment est essentiellement constitué de trois éléments : un pont-promenade en chêne menant au foyer vitré, les espaces du théâtre principal contenus dans une structure en maçonnerie de briques sombres qui « fait écho aux entrepôts environnants du port historique », et un étage de service en verre et acier, contenant des bureaux, l'administration et des espaces réservés aux acteurs. Revêtue de cuivre, une tour abritant la scène complète le bâtiment. Le grand auditorium, d'une jauge de 650 places est, selon les architectes, « circulaire et comme une grotte [...] semblant taillée dans la masse de maçonnerie du théâtre ». Un refroidissement par eau de mer, avec une pompe à chaleur et un stockage passif de l'énergie permettent une consommation électrique pour la climatisation réduite de 40% par rapport à un bâtiment ordinaire.

A harbor view with the Royal Playhouse standing out above neighboring buildings in the center of the image.

Hafenpanorama mit dem Königlichen Schauspielhaus in der Mitte, das sich von der nachbarschaftlichen Bebauung abhebt.

Une vue du port avec le Théâtre royal se détachant sur les immeubles voisins, au centre de la photo.

Above, the glazed bank of windows of the Playhouse stands out atop a series of thin columns, topped by a blank copper-clad block marking the stage. Below, a basic plan of the structure.

Das Fensterband des Schauspielhauses setzt sich auffällig von den darunter liegenden zierlichen Stützen ab und wird von einem schlichten kupferverblendeten Kubus überragt, in dem der Bühnenturm untergebracht ist. Unten ein Grundriss des Gebäudes.

Ci-dessus, la rangée de fenêtres vitrées se détachant au sommet d'une série de fines colonnes, est surmontée d'un cube aveugle revêtue en cuivre marquant l'emplacement de la scène du Théâtre royal. Ci-dessous, un plan du bâtiment.

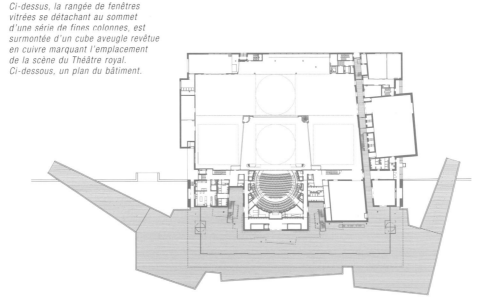

Seen from the side at night, the Playhouse assumes a lightness imparted by the broad, thin, central block that juts out toward the harbor. Below, the interior of the Playhouse.

Nächtlicher Blick auf die Seitenfront des Schauspielhauses. Durch das zum Hafen auskragende schmale Mittelband gewinnt der Bau an Leichtigkeit . Links eine Innenansicht des Theaterraums.

Vu de côté, la nuit, le Théâtre se pare d'une luminosité émise par la tranche large et plate du bloc central en saillie sur le port. À gauche, l'intérieur du théâtre.

Below, seating in the extended foyer area above the harbor. Right, a long narrow hall in the Playhouse.

Unton Sitzmöglichkeiten im großzügi gen Foyer über dem Hafen. Rechts ein langer schmaler Durchgang durch das Schauspielhaus.

Ci-dessous, des sièges dans le foyer s'étendant au-dessus du port. À droite, un étroit couloir dans le Théâtre.

FUMIHIKO MAKI

Maki and Associates / Hillside West Building C / 13–4 Hachiyama-cho
Shibuya-ku / Tokyo 150–0035 / Japan
Tel: +81 3 3780 3880 / Fax: +81 3 3780 3881

Born in Tokyo in 1928, **FUMIHIKO MAKI** received his B.Arch. degree from the University of Tokyo in 1952, and M.Arch degrees from the Cranbrook Academy of Art (1953) and the Harvard GSD (1954). He worked for Skidmore, Owings & Merrill in New York (1954–55) and Sert Jackson and Associates in Cambridge, Massachusetts (1955–58), before creating his own firm, Maki and Associates, in Tokyo in 1965. Notable buildings include the Fujisawa Municipal Gymnasium (Fujisawa, Kanagawa, 1984); Spiral (Minato-ku, Tokyo, 1985); Tepia (Minato-ku, Tokyo, 1989); Tokyo Metropolitan Gymnasium (Shibuya, Tokyo, 1990); and the Center for the Arts Yerba Buena Gardens (San Francisco, California, USA, 1993). The Hillside West buildings (completed in 1998) are part of his ongoing Hillside Terrace project. More recent and current work includes the Yokohama Bayside Tower (Yokohama, Kanagawa, 2003); TV Asahi Broadcast Center (Minato-ku, Tokyo, 2003); MIT Media Laboratory Expansion (Cambridge, Massachusetts, USA, 2004); National Language Research Institute (Tachikawa, Tokyo, 2004); Washington University Visual Arts and Design Center (Saint Louis, Missouri, 2004); Nakatsu City Museum (Nakatsu, Oita, 2005); and the Shimane Museum of Ancient Izumo (Izumo, Shimane, 2003–06), all in Japan unless stated otherwise. Having recently completed the Mihara Performing Arts Center (Mihara, Hiroshima, 2005–07, published here), and a building for the Aga Khan's Development Network in Ottawa (Canada, 2008), Fumihiko Maki is currently working on a tower for the United Nations in New York; a second tower in the area of the former World Trade Center in New York; and a new museum of Islamic art for the Aga Khan in Toronto (Canada).

FUMIHIKO MAKI wurde 1928 in Tokio geboren und schloss sein Studium 1952 mit einem B. Arch. an der Universität Tokio ab, dem M. Arch.-Abschlüsse an der Cranbrook Academy of Art (1953) und der Harvard GSD (1954) folgten. Er arbeitete für Skidmore, Owings & Merrill in New York (1954–55) und für Sert, Jackson and Associates in Cambridge, Massachusetts (1955–58), bevor er 1965 sein eigenes Büro, Maki and Associates, in Tokio gründete. Wichtige Bauten sind u. a. die städtische Sporthalle in Fujisawa (Fujisawa, Kanagawa, 1984), die Spirale (Minato-ku, Tokio, 1985), der Tepia-Pavillon (Minato-ku, Tokio, 1989), die städtische Sporthalle Tokio (Shibuya, Tokio, 1990) sowie das Kunstzentrum Yerba Buena Gardens (San Francisco, 1993). Die Hillside West Buildings (fertiggestellt 1998) entstanden als Teil des noch nicht fertiggestellten Hillside-Terrace-Projekts. Weitere jüngere und aktuelle Projekte sind der Yokohama Bayside Tower (Yokohama, Kanagawa, 2003), das Sendezentrum des Fernsehsenders Asahi (Minato-ku, Tokio, 2003), die Erweiterung des MIT-Medienlabors (Cambridge, Massachusetts, 2004), das Nationale Institut für Sprachforschung (Tachikawa, Tokio, 2004), das Zentrum für bildende Künste und Design der Universität Washington (St. Louis, Missouri, 2004), das Stadtmuseum in Nakatsu (Oita, 2005) sowie das Shimane-Museum des Izumo-Schreins (Izumo, Shimane, 2003–06), alle in Japan sofern nicht anders vermerkt. Nach der Fertigstellung des Zentrums für darstellende Künste in Mihara (Hiroshima, 2005–07, hier vorgestellt) und einem Gebäude für das Aga-Khan-Netzwerk für Entwicklungspolitik in Ottawa (Kanada, 2008) arbeitet Fumihiko Maki derzeit an einem Hochhaus für die Vereinten Nationen in New York, einem zweiten Hochhaus auf dem Gelände des ehemaligen World Trade Center in New York sowie an einem neuen Museum für islamische Kunst für die Aga-Khan-Stiftung in Toronto (Kanada).

Né à Tokyo en 1928, **FUMIHIKO MAKI** obtient une licence en architecture (B. Arch.) de l'université de Tokyo en 1952 et un master (M. Arch.) de la Cranbrook Academy of Art (1953) et de la GSD de l'université de Harvard (1954). Il a travaillé chez Skidmore, Owings & Merrill à New York (1954–55) et Sert Jackson and Associates à Cambridge, Massachusetts (1955–58), avant de fonder sa propre agence, Maki and Associates, à Tokyo, en 1965. Ses réalisations incluent notamment le gymnase municipal de Fujisawa (Fujisawa, Kanagawa, 1984) ; l'immeuble Spiral (Minato-ku, Tokyo, 1985) ; le siège de Tepia (Minato-ku, Tokyo, 1989) ; le complexe sportif Tokyo Metropolitan Gymnasium (Shibuya, Tokyo, 1990) ; et le Centre d'art contemporain Yerba Buena Gardens (San Francisco, Californie, États-Unis, 1993). Les immeubles Hillside West (achevés en 1998) font partie de son projet en cours pour Hillside Terrace. Ses projets réalisés plus récemment ou en cours incluent la Yokohama Bayside Tower (Yokohama, Kanagawa, 2003) ; le TV Asahi Broadcast Center (Minato-ku, Tokyo, 2003) ; l'extension du laboratoire des médias du MIT (Cambridge, Massachusetts, États-Unis, 2004) ; l'Institut national de recherche sur le langage (Tachikawa, Tokyo, 2004) ; le Visual Arts and Design Center de l'université Washington (Saint-Louis, Missouri, 2004) ; le musée de Nakatsu (Nakatsu, Oita, 2005) ; et le Shimane Museum of Ancient Izumo (Izumo, Shimane, 2003–06), tous situés au Japon sauf mention contraire. Après l'achèvement récent du Centre des arts du spectacle Popolo de Mihara (Mihara, Hiroshima, 2005–07, publié ici) et du Centre mondial du pluralisme, pour l'Aga Khan Development Network (Ottawa, Canada, 2008), Fumihiko Maki travaille actuellement sur la nouvelle tour du siège de l'ONU, à New York, une autre tour dans le quartier du World Trade Center à New York, et un nouveau musée d'art islamique pour les collections de l'Aga Khan à Toronto (Canada).

MIHARA PERFORMING ARTS CENTER

Mihara, Hiroshima, Japan, 2005–07

Address: 2–1–1 Miyaura, Mihara, Hiroshima, Japan
Area: 7421 m². Client: City of Mihara. Cost: ¥3.690 million. Collaboration: Hanawa Structural Engineers,
P. T. Morimura & Associates (Mechanical, Electrical), Nagata Acoustics

The city of Mihara (population 100 000) is located 70 kilometers east of Hiroshima. The site of the new **MIHARA PERFORMING ARTS CENTER** is in a park in the town. The Center has a rehearsal hall, practice room, a foyer, and main auditorium. "Given this condition," says Fumihiko Maki, "we created a design concept that expresses the building as a 'pavilion in the park.' A transparent foyer at the ground level gives the building a welcoming appearance and creates a direct dialogue between the interior and exterior activities. The foyer can be used independently for meetings, exhibitions, or for park goers to relax when the hall is not being used for large events. Small inner courtyards provide additional light to the foyer and, during favorable weather, can be opened for natural airflow." The building is characterized by the light elegance that is a mark of the work of the architect.

Mihara, eine Stadt mit 100 000 Einwohnern, liegt 70 km östlich von Hiroshima. Standort des neuen **ZENTRUMS FÜR DARSTELLENDE KÜNSTE** ist ein städtischer Park. Zum Zentrum gehören ein Probenraum, Trainingsräume, ein Foyer sowie ein großer Saal. „Wegen des Umfelds", erklärt Fumihiko Maki, „schufen wir einen Entwurf, der das Gebäude als 'Pavillon im Park' interpretiert. Durch sein transparentes Foyer im Erdgeschoss wirkt der Bau einladend, darüber hinaus entspinnt sich so ein direkter Dialog zwischen den Aktivitäten drinnen und draußen. Das Foyer lässt sich separat für Versammlungen oder Ausstellungen nutzen. Auch die Parkbesucher können sich hier entspannen, sofern das Foyer nicht für größere Veranstaltungen genutzt wird. Kleine Innenhöfe lassen zusätzliches Licht in das Foyer. Bei gutem Wetter können sie geöffnet werden und sorgen so für natürliche Belüftung." Der gesamte Komplex zeichnet sich durch jene leichte Eleganz aus, die typisch für das Werk des Architekten ist.

La ville de Mihara (100 000 habitants) est située à 70 kilomètres à l'est d'Hiroshima. Le site du nouveau **CENTRE DES ARTS DU SPECTACLE DE MIHARA** est dans un parc de la ville. Le centre est pourvu d'une salle de répétition, d'une salle d'entraînement, d'un foyer et d'un grand auditorium. « Étant données les conditions », dit Fumihiko Maki, « nous avons créé un concept de projet qui exprime le bâtiment comme un "pavillon dans le parc". » Un foyer transparent au rez-de-chaussée donne au bâtiment une apparence accueillante et crée un dialogue direct entre les activités intérieures et extérieures. Le foyer peut être utilisé indépendamment pour des réunions, des expositions, ou pour que les visiteurs du parc s'y détendent lorsque le hall n'est pas utilisé pour des manifestations importantes. Des courettes intérieures apportent un supplément de lumière au foyer et, lorsque le temps s'y prête, peuvent s'ouvrir pour créer une ventilation naturelle. » Le bâtiment se caractérise par l'élégante légèreté qui est la marque de l'œuvre de l'architecte.

The subtle lines and lightness of the Center are typical of the architecture of Fumihiko Maki. Here he alternates between a rectilinear base and the curving cupola marking the actual theater space.

Die unaufdringlichen Linien und die Leichtigkeit des Centers sind charakteristisch für die Architektur von Fumihiko Maki. Hier gestaltet er ein Wechselspiel zwischen geradlinigem Sockelgeschoss und geschwungener Kuppel, in der Bühnensäle untergebracht sind.

Les lignes subtiles et la légèreté du Centre sont caractéristiques de l'architecture de Fumihiko Maki. Ici, il passe d'une base rectangulaire à la coupole incurvée marquant l'emplacement du théâtre.

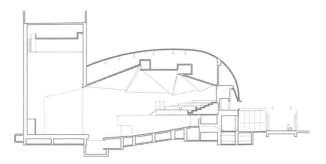

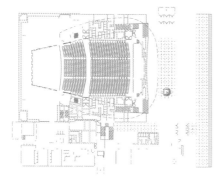

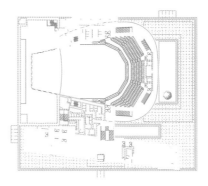

Plans of the complex show its essentially rectangular form with the main hall in the upper part of these drawings. Below, the warm, largely wood-clad interior of the hall.

Die Grundrisse zeigen die im Grunde rechteckige Form des Baus; im oberen Bereich der Zeichnungen der große Saal. Unten das warme, überwiegend holzverkleidete Interieur des Saals.

Des plans du complexe montrent sa forme essentiellement rectangulaire avec la grande salle dans leur partie supérieure. Ci-dessous, largement revêtu de bois, l'intérieur chaleureux de la salle.

The light, airy spaces that surround the hall, seen above, with their full-height glazing and rapport with nature—in the form of the sky or a single tree in a courtyard. Below, a rehearsal space.

Oben die hellen, luftigen Bereiche um den Bühnensaal mit ihrer deckenhohen Verglasung und ihrem klaren Bezug zur Natur – zum Himmel oder einem einzelnen Baum in einem der Innenhöfe. Unten ein Probenraum.

Vitrés sur toute leur hauteur, les espaces légers et aérés sont montrés ci-dessus dans leur relation avec la nature — le ciel et un arbre dans une cour intérieure. Ci-dessous, une salle de répétition.

MICHAEL MALTZAN

Michael Maltzan Architecture, Inc. / 2801 Hyperion Avenue, Suite 107
Los Angeles, CA 90027 / USA
Tel: +1 323 913 3098 / Fax: +1 323 913 5932
E-mail: info@mmaltzan.com / Web: www.mmaltzan.com

MICHAEL MALTZAN was born in 1959 in Levittown, New York. He holds both a B.F.A. and a B.Arch from the Rhode Island School of Design (1984, 1985) and an M.Arch degree from Harvard (1988). Since establishing his own firm in 1995, Michael Maltzan has been responsible for the design of a wide range of arts, educational, commercial, institutional, and residential projects, including the Mark Taper Center/Inner-City Arts campus (Phase I, Los Angeles, California, 1994); Harvard-Westlake School's Feldman-Horn Center for the Arts (North Hollywood, California, 1995); the Getty Information Institute Digital Laboratory (Brentwood, California, 1997); and the design of the Kidspace Children's Museum in Pasadena (California, 1998). Recent work includes MoMA QNS in Long Island City, which opened in June 2002 (New York); the new Sonoma County Museum in Santa Rosa (California, 2002); UCLA Hammer Museum in Los Angeles (California, 2003 and 2007); and the Biblioteca degli Alberi at the Giardini di Porta Nuova in Milan (Italy, 2004). More recently he has completed Ministructure No. 16 / Book Store for the Architecture Park in Jinhua (China, 2004–06); and the Inner-City Arts (Phase III, Los Angeles, California, 2008, published here). Current work includes the Fresno Metropolitan Museum (Fresno, California, 2005–); Jet Propulsion Laboratory Administration Complex (Pasadena, California, 2006–); the San Francisco State Creative Arts Center (San Francisco, California, 2008–); the Nine Muses Amphitheater and Pedestrian Bridge (New Orleans, Louisiana, 2008–); and the Chengdu Wide Horizon Development (Chengdu, China, 2009–), all in the USA unless stated otherwise.

MICHAEL MALTZAN wurde 1959 in Levittown, New York, geboren. Sein Studium schloss er mit einem B. F. A. und B. Arch. an der Rhode Island School of Design (1984, 1985) sowie einem M. Arch. in Harvard (1988) ab. Seit Gründung seines eigenen Büros 1995 hat Michael Maltzan eine breite Palette von Projekten im Bereich Kunst und Bildung, Gewerbe, öffentlicher Institutionen und Wohnbauten gestaltet. Hierzu zählen u. a. der Innenstadt-Kunstcampus des Mark Taper Center (1. Bauabschnitt, Los Angeles, 1994), das Feldman-Horn Center für Künste der Harvard-Westlake School (North Hollywood, Kalifornien, 1995), das Digitallabor des Getty Information Institute (Brentwood, Kalifornien, 1997) sowie die Gestaltung des Kidspace-Kindermuseums in Pasadena (Kalifornien, 1998). Jüngere Projekte sind das MoMA QNS in Long Island City, eröffnet im Juni 2002 (New York), das neue Sonoma County Museum in Santa Rosa (Kalifornien, 2002), das UCLA Hammer Museum in Los Angeles (2003 und 2007) sowie die Biblioteca degli Alberi in den Giardini di Porta Nuova in Mailand (2004). Unlängst fertiggestellt wurden Ministructure No. 16, eine Buchhandlung im Architekturpark in Jinhua (China, 2004–06), und der Innenstadt-Kunstcampus (3. Bauabschnitt, Los Angeles, 2008, hier vorgestellt). Aktuell in Arbeit sind das Fresno Metropolitan Museum (Fresno, Kalifornien, seit 2005), der Verwaltungskomplex des Jet Propulsion Laboratory (Pasadena, Kalifornien, seit 2006), das Creative Arts Center in San Francisco (seit 2008), das Nine Muses Amphitheater und eine Fußgängerbrücke (New Orleans, Louisiana, seit 2008) sowie das Erschließungsprojekt Wide Horizon in Chengdu (China, seit 2009).

MICHAEL MALTZAN est né en 1959 à Levittown, dans l'état de New York, aux États-Unis. Il est titulaire d'une licence en arts et d'une licence en architecture (B. Arch.) de la RISD, école de design de Rhode Island (1984, 1985) et d'un master en architecture (M. Arch.) de Harvard (1988). Depuis qu'il a fondé sa propre agence en 1995, Michael Maltzan a conçu une large gamme de projets destinés à des usages culturel, éducatif, commercial, institutionnel et d'habitation, dont le Centre Mark Taper, du campus Inner-City Arts (phase I, Los Angeles, Californie, 1994); le Centre pour les arts Feldman-Horn de l'Ecole Harvard-Westlake (North Hollywood, Californie, 1995); le Getty Information Institute Digital Laboratory (Brentwood, Californie, 1997); et le Kidspace Children's Museum, à Pasadena (Californie, 1998). Ses projets récents incluent le MoMA QNS, à Long Island, inauguré en 2002 (New York), le nouveau musée du comté de Sonoma, à Santa Rosa (Californie, 2002), le musée Hammer de l'UCLA, à Los Angeles (Californie, 2003 et 2007) et la Biblioteca degli Alberi dans les jardins de Porta Nuova, à Milan (Italie, 2004). Plus récemment, il a réalisé la Ministructure No16, une librairie pour le Parc d'architecture de Jinhua (Chine, 2004–06) et le campus Inner-City Arts (Phase III, Los Angeles, Californie, 2008, publié ici). Ses projets en cours incluent le Metropolitan Museum de Fresno (Fresno, Californie, 2005–); le complexe administratif de Jet Propulsion Laboratory (Pasadena, Californie, 2006–); le State Creative Arts Center de San Francisco (San Francisco, Californie, 2008–); un amphithéâtre et une passerelle dans le quartier des Neuf Muses (Nouvelle-Orléans, Louisiane, 2008–); et l'ensemble d'habitations Wide Horizon, à Chengdu (Chengdu, Chine, 2009–), tous projets situés aux États-Unis sauf mention contraire.

INNER-CITY ARTS

Los Angeles, California, 2008 (Phase III)

Address: 720 Kohler Street, Los Angeles, CA 90021–1518, USA, +1 213 627 9621, www.inner-cityarts.org
Area: 859 m² (Phase III). Client: Inner-City Arts. Cost: $9.2 million
Collaboration: Tim Williams (Project Director), Stacy Nakano (Project Manager)

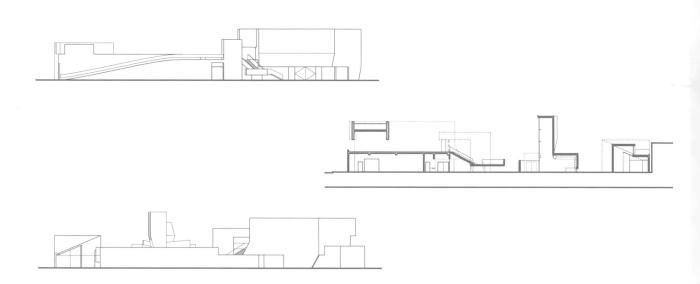

INNER-CITY ARTS provides a range of art facilities and services for Los Angeles youths. Phase I, completed in 1995 (with Marmol-Radziner Associates), includes a 1115-square-meter studio and support space surrounding the school's central outdoor courtyard. Phase II was completed in 2005, adding a larger studio space, kitchen, wood shop, and animation studios. Phase III, inaugurated in 2008, concerns a theater, visual-arts complex, performing-arts studios, parent-teacher resource center, gardens, and gathering spaces. Inner-City Arts is thus capable of handling over 16 000 students per year. The architects envisage the 4000-square-meter campus as a "village," where students gather in the central courtyard no matter what their activities. Its low profile and angled white forms make it stand out from the grayer urban environment, demonstrating that excellent architecture and an outstanding community project can find a common ground.

Der **INNENSTADT-KUNSTCAMPUS** (Inner-City Arts) bietet eine ganze Bandbreite von Kunsteinrichtungen und Angeboten für Jugendliche in Los Angeles. Zum 1995 abgeschlossenen ersten Bauabschnitt (mit Marmol-Radziner Associates) gehören ein 1115 m² großer Atelier- und Betreuungsbereich, der um den zentral gelegenen Innenhof des Komplexes angeordnet ist. Der zweite Bauabschnitt wurde 2005 fertiggestellt; hinzu kamen ein größerer Atelierbereich, eine Küche, eine Holzwerkstatt sowie Animationsstudios. Zum 2008 eingeweihten dritten Bauabschnitt gehören ein Theater, ein Bereich für bildende Künste, Studios für Tanz und Theater, ein Servicecenter für Eltern und Lehrer sowie Gärten und Aufenthaltsbereiche. Mit dieser Ausstattung kann der Kunstcampus jährlich bis zu 16 000 Kursteilnehmer betreuen. Die Architekten verstehen den 4000 m² großen Campus als „Dorf", in dessen zentralem Innenhof sich die Jugendlichen unabhängig von ihren jeweiligen Kursen treffen können. Mit seiner niedrigen Bauhöhe und den kantigen weißen Formen hebt sich der Komplex von seinem eher grauen urbanen Umfeld ab und stellt unter Beweis, dass exzellente Architektur und außergewöhnliche Sozialprojekte durchaus auf einen gemeinsamen Nenner zu bringen sind.

Le campus **INNER-CITY ARTS** propose une gamme d'équipements et d'enseignements artistiques pour les jeunes de Los Angeles. La phase I, achevée en 1995 (avec Marmol-Radziner Associates), comprend un atelier de 1115 mètres carrés et des espaces annexes autour de la cour centrale à ciel ouvert de l'école. La phase II, achevée en 2005, ajoute un espace d'atelier plus grand, une cuisine, un atelier bois, et des ateliers d'animation. La phase III, inaugurée en 2008, comprend un théâtre, un ensemble pour les arts visuels, des ateliers de théâtre, un centre de ressources parents/enseignants, des jardins et des espaces de réunions. Inner-City Arts a ainsi la possibilité d'accueillir plus de 16 000 élèves par an. Les architectes voient le campus de 4000 mètres carrés comme un « village » où les élèves se retrouvent dans la cour centrale, quelles que soient leurs activités. Sa silhouette basse et ses formes blanches et anguleuses le font ressortir de l'environnement urbain plus gris, et montre qu'une architecture d'excellence et un projet social exceptionnel peuvent se rencontrer.

The elevation drawings above and the images to the right show the low profile of Inner-City Arts and its village-like composition.

Das niedrige Profil des Komplexes und seine dorfähnliche Anlage zeigt sich in den Aufrissen oben und auf den Bildern rechts.

Les élévations ci-dessus et les photos à droite montrent la silhouette basse de l'Inner-City Arts et sa composition en village.

Enclosed courtyard spaces shield
common spaces from the street, but
the buildings themselves give little
hint of their use.

Innenhöfe schirmen die Gemein-
schaftsbereiche von der Straße ab.
Die Gebäude selbst lassen kaum
ahnen, wofür sie genutzt werden.

Les espaces des cours intérieures
protègent les espaces communs de la
rue, et les bâtiments eux-mêmes ne
laissent guère deviner leur usage.

The use of wood and generous interior spaces gives a warm, open feeling to the interior volumes seen here. Below, a plan of the entire complex.

Dank des Einsatzes von Holz und der großzügigen Räume wirken die Bauten innen sehr offen. Unten ein Grundriss der Gesamtanlage.

L'utilisation du bois et de généreux espaces donnent une atmosphère chaleureuse et accueillante aux volumes intérieurs vus ici. Ci-dessous, un plan de l'ensemble du complexe.

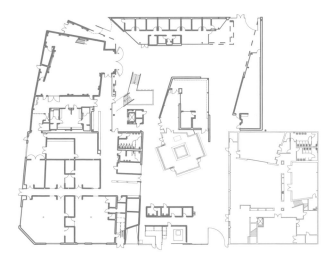

FRANCISCO MANGADO

Francisco Mangado
Vuelta del Castillo, 5 Ático
31007 Pamplona (Navarra)
Spain

Tel: +34 948 27 62 02
Fax: +34 948 17 65 05
E-mail: mangado@fmangado.com
Web: www.fmangado.com

FRANCISCO MANGADO was born in Estella, Navarra (Spain), in 1957 and obtained his degree in Architecture in 1981 from the School of Architecture of the University of Navarra. From the beginning of his career, Mangado combined academic duties with professional activity at his Pamplona studio. He has taught at the University of Navarra, University of Texas (Arlington), Harvard GSD, and the International University of Catalonia. His most significant projects include the "Baluarte" Auditorium and Congress Centre (Pamplona, Navarra, 2000–03); Dalí Square (Madrid, 2001–05); "Nueva Balastera" Soccer Stadium (Palencia, Castilla y León, 2005–06); Center for New Technologies (Santiago de Compostela, Galicia, 2005–07); Gamesa Eolica office building (Sarriguren, Navarra, 2005–07); swimming pools for the University of Vigo (Orense, Galicia, 2005–08); Spanish Pavilion Expo Zaragoza 2008 (Zaragoza, Aragon, 2006–08); high-performance Equestrian Center (Ultzama, Navarra, 2007–08); Ávila Municipal Congress and Exhibition Center (Castilla y León, 2004–09, published here); and the Museum of Archeology (Vitoria, Álava, 2004–09), all in Spain.

FRANCISCO MANGADO wurde 1957 in Estella, Navarra (Spanien), geboren und beendete sein Studium 1981 an der Architekturfakultät der Universität Navarra. Seit Beginn seiner Laufbahn verbindet Mangado seine akademische Tätigkeit mit seiner Arbeit in seinem Büro in Pamplona. Bislang hatte er Lehraufträge an der Universität Navarra, der Universität von Texas (Arlington), der Harvard GSD sowie der Internationalen Universität von Katalonien. Seine wichtigsten Projekte sind u. a. das Auditorium und Kongresszentrum Baluarte (Pamplona, Navarra, 2000–03), die Plaza de Dalí (Madrid, 2001–05), das Fußballstadion Nueva Balastera (Palencia, Castilla y León, 2005–06), das Zentrum für neue Technologien (Santiago de Compostela, Galizien, 2005–07), ein Bürogebäude für Gamesa Eolica (Sarriguren, Navarra, 2005–07), Schwimmbäder für die Universität Vigo (Orense, Galizien, 2005–08), der spanische Pavillon auf der Expo 2008 (Saragossa, Aragon, 2006–08), ein Profi-Trainingszentrum für Pferde (Ultzama, Navarra, 2007–08), das Städtische Kongress- und Messezentrum Ávila (Castilla y León, 2004–09, hier vorgestellt) sowie ein Archäologisches Museum (Vitoria, Álava, 2004–09), alle in Spanien.

FRANCISCO MANGADO est né à Estella, en Navarre (Espagne), en 1957 et a obtenu son diplôme d'architecte en 1981 à l'École d'architecture de l'université de Navarre. Dès le début de sa carrière, Mangado se partage entre son activité d'enseignant et ses activités professionnelles à son agence de Pampelune. Il a enseigné à l'université de Navarre, l'université du Texas (Arlington), au GSD d'Harvard et à l'université internationale de Catalogne. Ses projets les plus importants incluent l'auditorium et le Centre de congrès Baluarte (Pampelune, Navarra, 2000–03) ; la place Dalí (Madrid, 2001–05) ; le stade de football Nueva Balastera (Palencia, Castilla-León, 2005–06) ; le Centre des nouvelles technologies de Saint-Jacques-de-Compostelle (Galice, 2005–07) ; l'immeuble de bureaux Gamesa Eolica (Sarriguren, Navarra, 2005–07) ; une piscine pour l'université de Vigo (Ourense, Galice, 2005–08) ; le Pavillon espagnol de l'Expo 2008 de Saragosse (Saragosse, Aragon, 2006–08) ; le centre équestre d'Ultzama (Ultzama, Navarra, 2007–08) ; le Centre municipal de congrès et d'expositions d'Avila (Castille-León, 2004–09, publié ici) ; et le musée archéologique de Vitoria (Vitoria, Alava, 2004–09), tous situés en Espagne.

ÁVILA MUNICIPAL CONGRESS AND EXHIBITIONS CENTER

Ávila, Castilla y León, Spain, 2004–09

Address: Avenida de Madrid 102, 05001 Ávila, Spain, +34 920 27 08 38
Area: 18 944 m². Client: Ávila Town Hall, Junta de Castilla y León. Cost: € 36 million

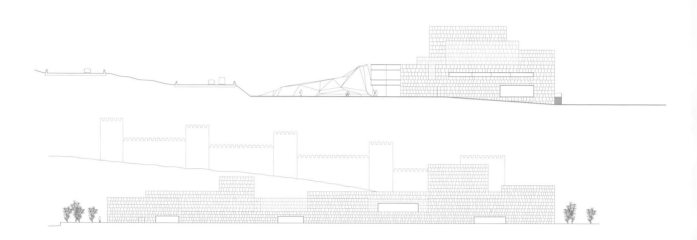

Elevations and photos give an idea of the scale of the Center and of its almost topographical composition.

Aufriss und Fotos vermitteln einen Eindruck der Dimensionen des Zentrums und seiner fast topografisch anmutenden Komposition.

Les élévations et les photos donnent une idée de l'échelle du centre et de sa composition presque topographique.

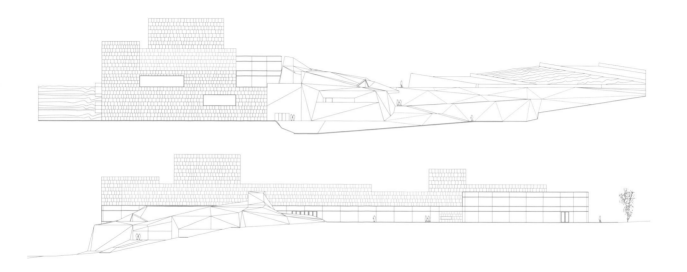

Francisco Mangado speaks of the "topographical, mineral compactness" of Ávila, "whose presence is revealed in a superb landscape sprinkled by granite stones that struggle to emerge and finally manage to do so in the artificial form of city walls. "Ávila itself," he says, "is a rock amid the harsh landscape surrounding it." It is a space at the foot of the city walls, once occupied by a river bed and then by a cattle market, where the architect was asked to place a congress and exhibition building. Because of the slope it is built on, and because of its own mineral, folded compactness as seen from some angles, the building holds its own while in no way overtly imposing its presence on the city and its walls. The complex is made up of two relatively distinct volumes—one that is orthogonal and elongated contains the auditoriums and main halls, while the less "even" one houses exhibition spaces. Access to all public spaces is through an entry square, while service areas are concentrated in the northern end of the buildings. The architect compares the whole to a "sculpture carved out of the terrain." Indeed, this structure demonstrates the highly innovative nature of contemporary Spanish architecture, which hopefully will survive the current economic downturn.

Francisco Mangado spricht von der „topografischen, mineralischen Dichte" Ávilas, einer Stadt, „deren Präsenz sich in einer fantastischen Landschaft entfaltet, in der immer wieder Granitfelsen zu finden sind, die mühsam nach oben zu streben scheinen, was ihnen schließlich in der kunstvollen Form der Stadtmauer gelingt". „Ávila selbst", so der Architekt, „ist ein Fels inmitten der rauen Landschaft." Der Architekt wurde beauftragt, auf einem Gelände unterhalb der Stadtmauern, wo früher ein Fluss-bett verlief und später ein Viehmarkt lag, ein Kongress- und Messezentrum zu bauen. Dank der Hanglage und seiner steinernen, gestauchten Kompaktheit, die aus ver-schiedenen Perspektiven höchst unterschiedlich wirkt, gelingt es dem Bau, sich zu behaupten, ohne dabei seine Präsenz der Stadt und ihren Mauern in aufdringlicher Weise aufzuzwingen. Der Komplex selbst besteht aus zwei deutlich unterscheidbaren Volumina – einem orthogonalen, länglichen Baukörper, in dem die Säle und Haupt-räume untergebracht sind, sowie einem weniger „geradlinigen" Baukörper für die Messeflächen. Zugang zu sämtlichen Bereichen bietet ein Vorplatz, während die Haus-technik primär im Nordteil der Bauten untergebracht ist. Der Architekt vergleicht das Gesamtensemble mit einer „Skulptur, die aus dem Baugrund herausgeschlagen wurde". Der Bau ist ein Beispiel für die höchst innovative zeitgenössische Architektur Spaniens, die hoffentlich die derzeitige Wirtschaftskrise überdauern wird.

Francisco Mangado parle de la « compacité topographique et minérale » d'Avila, « révélée par un paysage magnifique parsemé de rochers de granit qui luttent pour émerger et y parviennent finalement sous une forme artificielle dans les remparts ». « Avila », dit-il, « est elle-même un roc dans le paysage rude qui l'entoure ». C'est dans un ancien lit de rivière, autrefois occupé par un marché aux bestiaux, que l'architecte devait implanter un Centre de congrès et d'expositions. En raison, à la fois de la pente sur laquelle il est construit, et de sa propre compacité minérale et plissée selon certains angles de vue, le bâtiment affirme sa présence, sans l'imposer osten-siblement à la ville et à ses remparts. Le complexe comprend deux volumes relativement distincts – l'un orthogonal et allongé abrite les auditoriums et les grandes salles, tandis que l'autre, moins « régulier », abrite les espaces d'expositions. L'accès du public se fait en passant par une place, tandis les zones de services sont concentrées à l'extrémité nord des bâtiments. L'architecte compare le tout à « une sculpture taillée dans le relief ». Ce bâtiment démontre la nature hautement novatrice de l'archi-tecture espagnole contemporaine, qu'on souhaite voir surmonter la crise économique actuelle.

The architect presents a willful contrast between the orthogonal auditorium and main hall building (visible at the top of the plan to the right) and the more folded exhibition space seen at the bottom of the drawing.

Der Architekt schafft bewusste Kontraste zwischen dem rechtwinkligen Hauptgebäude mit Auditorium und großem Saal (auf dem Grundriss rechts im oberen Bereich erkennbar) und dem „gefaltet" wirkenden Messebereich unten auf dem Grundriss.

L'architecte crée un contraste délibéré entre le bâtiment orthogonal accueillant l'auditorium et la grande salle (visible sur la partie supérieure du plan à droite) et l'espace d'exposition plus plissé, visible sur la partie inférieure.

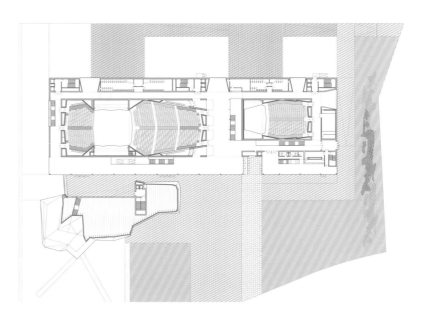

GIANCARLO MAZZANTI

Giancarlo Mazzanti & Arquitectos Ltda.
Calle 29 6–94 OF. 401
Bogotá
Colombia

Tel: +57 1 232 6309
E-mail: mazzanti.arquitectos@gmail.com
Web: www.giancarlomazzanti.com

GIANCARLO MAZZANTI SIERRA was born in 1963 in Barranquilla, Colombia. He received a diploma in Architecture from the Javeriana University (Bogotá, 1989) and completed postgraduate studies in the history and theory of architecture at the University of Florence (Italy, 1999). Built work includes the International Convention Center (Medellín, 2002); the Ordoñez House (Bogotá, 2007); as well as the Santo Domingo Library Park (Medellín, 2006–07, published here). His recent and current work includes Four Arenas for the South American Games (Medellín, 2008); Tulio Ospina Park (Medellín, 2008, under development); and the Museum of Modern Art of Barranquilla (Barranquilla, 2008, also under development).

GIANCARLO MAZZANTI SIERRA wurde 1963 in Barranquilla, Kolumbien, geboren. Sein Diplom in Architektur machte er 1989 an der Javeriana-Universität in Bogotá und schloss 1999 einen Aufbaustudiengang in Architekturgeschichte und -theorie an der Universität Florenz ab. Zu seinen realisierten Projekten zählen das Internationale Messezentrum (Medellín, 2002), das Haus Ordoñez (Bogotá, 2007) sowie die Biblioteca España in Santo Domingo Savio (Medellín, 2006–07, hier vorgestellt). Jüngere und aktuelle Projekte sind u. a. die vier Arenen für die Südamerikaspiele (Medellín, 2008), der Parque Tulio Ospina (Medellín, 2008, in Arbeit) sowie das Museum für moderne Kunst in Barranquilla (2008, ebenfalls in Arbeit).

GIANCARLO MAZZANTI SIERRA est né en 1963 à Barranquilla, en Colombie. Il est diplômé en architecture de l'université Javeriana (Bogotá, 1989) et a étudié l'histoire et la théorie de l'architecture à l'université de Florence (Italie, 1999). Ses réalisations incluent le Centre international de convention de Medellín (Medellín, 2002), la maison Ordoñez (Bogotá, 2007), ainsi que la bibliothèque publique du parc Santo Domingo Savio (Medellín, 2006–07, publié ici). Ses projets récents et en cours incluent quatre stades pour les Jeux sud-américains de 2008 (Medellín, 2008) ; le parc Tulio Ospina (Medellín, 2008, en cours de développement) ; et le Musée d'art moderne de Barranquilla (Barranquilla, 2008, également en cours de développement).

SANTO DOMINGO LIBRARY PARK

Santo Domingo Savio, Medellín, Colombia, 2006–07

Address: Carrera 33B, #107A-100, Medellín, Colombia, +57 4 385 7598, www.reddebibliotecas.org.co
Area: 2960 m². Client: EDU (Empresa de Desarrollo Urbano), City of Medellín. Cost: $3.039 million
Collaboration: Andrés Sarmiento, Juan Manuel Gil, Fredy Pantoja

A plan and images such as the one on the previous double page show how the structure sits above Medellin, offering views of the city, but also more sheltered spaces marked by exterior wooden decks.

Der Lageplan und das Panorama auf der vorherigen Doppelseite verdeutlichen die Lage des Komplexes über Medellín mit Blick auf die Stadt. Doch es gibt auch geschütztere Bereiche wie etwa die Holzterrassen.

Un plan et des photos comme celle de la double-page précédente montrent comment le bâtiment surplombe Medellin, et offre une vue sur la ville, ainsi que des espaces plus abrités signalés par des planchers extérieurs en bois.

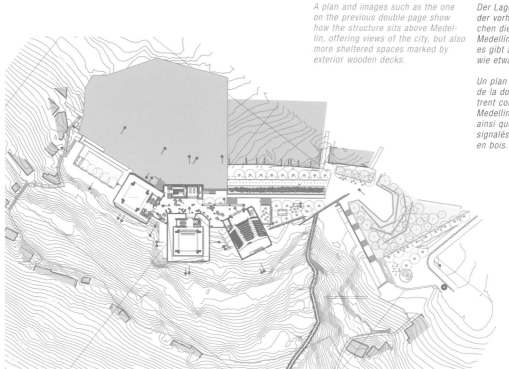

Even though the city is a constant
presence around the Library, it does
offer both a change of scale and of
atmosphere as compared to the surrounding architecture.

Obwohl die Stadt immer präsent ist,
hebt sich der Komplex durch seine
Größe und Atmosphäre von der
Bebauung der Nachbarschaft ab.

Même si la présence de la ville est
constamment perceptible autour de la
bibliothèque, celle-ci offre un vrai
changement d'échelle et d'ambiance
comparée à l'architecture environnante.

Located on a hillside that was the site of substantial violence in the 1980s because of drug traffic, this project is part of the government's master plan to give "equal economic and social opportunities to the population." The program called for a library, classrooms, administrative offices, and an auditorium in a single structure. The architects proposed a common platform joining the different facilities, and sought to echo the mountainous terrain of the landscape, through the "construction of a topography that belongs to the valley." The building is "folded and cut like the mountains that surround it," and its three volumes in dark brick set on the common platform give it the look of a group of structures more than a single one. Visible from a large part of the city, the project, which has drawn numerous tourists, is intended as a symbol of the new Medellín. The architect concludes: "In addition to making an icon, the first premise was to develop a building that, through its interior design, could decontextualize the individual from the poverty that surrounds him, creating a warm atmosphere based on natural light, generating atmosphere for study and reading. This is the reason why the building takes a timid look into the city through the small windows that show the relation with the valley, letting light enter from the top of the building."

Das auf einen Hügel gebaute Projekt liegt in einer Gegend, die in den 1980er Jahren durch Gewalt, hervorgerufen durch den Drogenhandel, erschüttert wurde. Der Komplex entstand im Rahmen eines Regierungsprogramms, das „der Bevölkerung gleiche wirtschaftliche und soziale Bedingungen" ermöglichen will. Vorgesehen waren eine Bibliothek, Klassenräume, Büros für die Verwaltung und ein Auditorium. Die Architekten schlugen eine gemeinsame Plattform vor, die alle Einrichtungen miteinander verbinden sollte. Dabei ging es ihnen darum, die Berglandschaft der Gegend aufzugreifen und „eine Topografie" zu bauen, „die einen klaren Bezug zum Tal hat". Der Komplex ist „gefaltet und zerklüftet, wie die Berge, die ihn umgeben". Die drei Volumina aus dunklem Ziegel, platziert auf der gemeinsamen Plattform, wirken eher wie ein Ensemble als ein einzelnes Gebäude. Das Projekt, das zahlreiche Touristen anzieht, ist von vielen Punkten der Stadt aus sichtbar und soll zum Wahrzeichen eines neuen Medellín werden. Der Architekt fasst zusammen: „Neben unserem Wunsch, ein Wahrzeichen zu schaffen, ging es zunächst darum, ein Bauwerk zu entwickeln, das durch die Innenraumgestaltung den Einzelnen aus dem Kontext der ihn umgebenden Armut herauslöst und das mithilfe des natürlichen Lichts eine warme Atmosphäre schafft, die zum Lernen und Lesen einlädt. Deshalb bietet das Bauwerk durch seine kleinen Fenster, die eine Beziehung zum Tal andeuten, nur eingeschränkte Blicke auf die Stadt, während das Licht stattdessen von oben in das Gebäude einfällt."

Implanté sur un site à flanc de côteau, dans une zone dévastée par la violence liée au trafic de drogue dans les années 1980, ce projet fait partie d'un plan directeur gouvernemental destiné à donner « une égalité de chances économique et sociale à la population ». Le programme prévoyait une bibothèque, des salles de cours, des bureaux administratifs et un auditorium réunis dans un même bâtiment. Les architectes ont proposé une plate-forme réunissant différents équipements, en cherchant à répondre au paysage montagneux par « la construction d'une topographie propre à la vallée ». Le bâtiment est « plissé et découpé comme les montagnes environnantes », et ses trois volumes en briques noires posés sur la plateforme donnent plus l'impression de bâtiments séparés que d'une structure unique. Visible d'une grande partie de la ville, le projet, qui attire de nombreux touristes, se veut un symbole du renouveau de Medellín. Les architectes concluent ainsi : « En plus d'en faire un symbole, le postulat était de développer un bâtiment qui, par son architecture intérieure, puisse extraire l'individu du contexte de pauvreté qui l'entoure, en créant une atmosphère chaleureuse basée sur la lumière naturelle et en générant une atmosphère propice à l'étude et à la lecture. C'est pour cette raison que le bâtiment jette un regard timide vers la ville à travers les petites fenêtres qui montrent la relation avec la vallée et laissent entrer la lumière par le haut de l'édifice. »

MGM ARQUITECTOS

MGM Arquitectos
C/ Murillo 4
41001 Seville
Spain

Tel: +34 954 56 41 14
E-mail: mgm@morales-giles-mariscal.com
Web: www.morales-giles-mariscal.com

JUAN GONZÁLEZ MARISCAL was born in Seville in 1961 and graduated from the ETSA Seville in 1986. **JOSÉ MORALES SÁNCHEZ** was born in 1959 and obtained his degree in Architecture from the ETSA (Seville, 1985), and his doctorate from the same institution in 1988. He has been a full Professor in the Architectural Projects Department (ETSA Seville) since 2004. **SARA DE GILES DUBOIS** was born in 1972 and obtained a degree in architecture from the ETSA Seville in 1998. Sara de Giles Dubois has been an Associate Professor in the Architectural Projects Department (ETSA Seville) since 1999. José Morales and Juan González Mariscal worked together beginning in 1987. Sara de Giles Dubois joined them as a Partner in MGM in 1998. Their work includes the Herrera House in the historic center of Garrobo (Seville, 1996–99); a New Education Institute (Galisteo, Cáceres, 2004–06, published here); a New Theatrical Space (Nijar, Almería, 2006, also published here); rehabilitation and extension of the Ramos Carrion Theater (Zamora, 1995–2008); and the construction of 140 social housing units ("Europan 5," Ceuta, Mount Hacho, 1998–2008), all in Spain.

JUAN GONZÁLEZ MARISCAL wurde 1961 in Sevilla geboren und schloss sein Studium 1986 an der ETSA Sevilla ab. **JOSÉ MORALES SÁNCHEZ** (geboren 1959) beendete sein Architekturstudium 1985 an derselben Hochschule, wo er 1988 auch promovierte. Seit 2004 ist er ordentlicher Professor an der dortigen Architekturfakultät. **SARA DE GILES DUBOIS** wurde 1972 geboren und schloss ihr Architekturstudium 1998 ebenfalls an der ETSA Sevilla ab. Seit 1999 ist sie Lehrbeauftragte der dortigen Architekturfakultät. José Morales und Juan González Mariscal arbeiten bereits seit 1987 zusammen. Sara de Giles Dubois schloss sich ihnen 1998 als Partnerin an. Zu ihren Projekten zählen das Haus Herrera in der historischen Altstadt von Garrobo (Sevilla, 1996–99), das Bildungsinstitut in Galisteo (Cáceres, 2004–06, hier vorgestellt), ein Kulturzentrum (Nijar, Almería, 2006, ebenfalls hier vorgestellt), die Sanierung und Erweiterung des Ramos-Carrion-Theaters (Zamora, 1995–2008) sowie der Bau von 140 Sozialwohnungen „Europan 5" (Ceuta, Monte Hacho, 1998–2008).

JUAN GONZÁLEZ MARISCAL est né à Séville en 1961 et a obtenu son diplôme de l'ETSA de Séville en 1986. **JOSÉ MORALES SÁNCHEZ**, né en 1959, est diplômé en architecture de l'ETSA (Séville, 1985). Il a obtenu un doctorat de la même école en 1988. Il est directeur titulaire du département des projets d'architecture (ETSA de Séville) depuis 2004. **SARA DE GILES DUBOIS**, née en 1972, a obtenu son diplôme de l'ETSA de Séville en 1998. Elle est professeur associée au département des projets d'architecture (ETSA Séville) depuis 1999. José Morales Sánchez et Juan González Mariscal travaillent ensemble depuis 1987. Sara de Giles Dubois devient associée de MGM en 1998. Leurs réalisations incluent la maison Herrera dans le centre historique de Garrobo (Séville, 1996–99) ; une nouvelle école à Galisteo (Galisteo, Cáceres, 2004–06, publié ici) ; un nouveau théâtre à Nijar (Nijar, Almería, 2006, également publié ici) ; la rénovation et l'extension du Théâtre Ramos Carrion (Zamora, 1995–2008) ; et la construction d'un ensemble de 140 logements sociaux (Europan 5, Ceuta, Mont Hacho, 1998–2008).

NEW EDUCATION INSTITUTE

Galisteo, Cáceres, Spain, 2004–06

Address: C/ Constitución S/N, 10691 Galisteo, Spain, +34 927 01 72 00
Area: 3132 m². Client: Consejería de Educación, Ciencia y Tecnología de la Junta de Extremadura.
Cost: € 1.612 million. Collaboration: Carlos Morales

The site offers views of the historic center of Galisteo. The main access to the building, whose height does not exceed 7.2 meters, is located on the western side. The structure contains administrative offices and spaces for the teachers, a communications center, classrooms and workshops, patios and lockers, and a sports area. These areas are connected by a covered corridor that crosses through the building from north to south. The sports area is set to the north. Workshop and classroom areas are associated with patios that are "connected with the landscape through a discontinuous façade." The administrative offices and spaces for teachers are on the upper level, near the main access, allowing for visits that do not cross through the student areas. The school is characterized by a strict, modern appearance, which nonetheless allows light and views of the city to penetrate its façades.

Das Grundstück bietet Ausblick auf das historische Zentrum von Galisteo. Hauptzugang zum Gebäude, das nur 7,2 m hoch ist, erfolgt von westlicher Seite. Im Bau selbst befinden sich Büros und Lehrerzimmer, ein Computerzentrum, Klassenräume und Werkstätten, Höfe und Schließfächer sowie ein Sportbereich. Ein überdachter Gang, der sich von Norden nach Süden durch das Gebäude zieht, verbindet die Areale. Der Sportbereich orientiert sich nach Norden. Werkstätten und Klassenräume sind an Höfe angebunden, die durch „eine aufgebrochene Fassade an die Landschaft anknüpfen". Büros und Lehrerzimmer befinden sich im Obergeschoss unweit des Haupteingangs, sodass Besucher nicht erst den Klassenraumtrakt durchqueren müssen. Die Schule wirkt streng und modern, lässt durch ihre transparente Fassade jedoch Licht einfallen und bietet Ausblicke auf die Stadt.

Le site offre des points de vue sur le centre historique de Galisteo. L'entrée principale du bâtiment, dont la hauteur n'excède pas 7,20 mètres, est située du côté ouest. Le bâtiment comprend des bureaux et des espaces pour les enseignants, un centre de communication, des salles de classe et ateliers, des patios et des vestiaires, et une aire de sports. Ces différentes zones sont reliées par une galerie qui traverse les bâtiments du nord au sud. La zone de sport est située au nord. Les zones des ateliers et salles de classe sont connectées par des patios «reliés au paysage à travers une façade discontinue». Les bureaux administratifs et les locaux réservés aux enseignants sont situés à l'étage, près de l'entrée principale, pour permettre l'accès des visiteurs sans passer par les zones des élèves. L'école se caractérise par une apparence stricte et moderne laissant néanmoins la lumière et des perspectives sur la ville pénétrer ses façades.

With its very long, low profile, the Institute appears to sit lightly on the flat landscape.

Dank seines langgestreckten, niedrigen Profils scheint das Institut ganz leicht auf der flachen Landschaft aufzusitzen.

Avec sa très longue silhouette basse, l'école semble délicatement posée sur le terrain plat.

Though it appears rather monolithic from some angles, the Institute is in fact varied in its composition and relation to the environment.

Obwohl das Institut aus einigen Blickwinkeln geradezu monolithisch wirkt, ist der Bau tatsächlich recht ab-wechslungsreich in seiner Komposition und den Bezügen zur Landschaft.

Bien qu'assez monolithique sous certains angles, l'école varie en fait dans sa composition et sa relation à l'environnement.

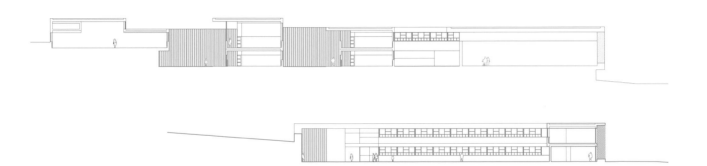

The low profile seen from the
exterior generates spaces within the
complex that are equally rectilinear,
but also open to the sky, as seen
on this page.

Das niedrige Profil des Gebäudes
schafft im Innern Räume, die ebenso
rechtwinklig sind, sich aber zum
Himmel hin öffnen, wie auf dieser
Seite zu sehen.

La silhouette basse, vue de
l'extérieur, génère, à l'intérieur du
complexe, des espaces tout aussi
rectilignes mais également ouverts
sur le ciel, comme on le voit ici.

Plans show that the architecture is actually more complex than most photos show, with its angled and varied composition.

Die Grundrisse belegen, dass die Architektur dank ihrer schiefwinkligen, abwechslungsreichen Komposition wesentlich komplexer ist, als die meisten Aufnahmen ahnen lassen.

Avec sa composition variée et en angles, l'architecture que révèlent ces plans, apparaît plus complexe que les photos ne le laissent croire.

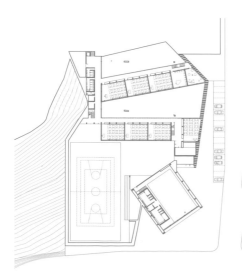

NEW THEATRICAL SPACE IN NIJAR

Almería, Spain, 2006

Address: Calle del Parque, 04100 Nijar, Spain
Area: 2054 m². Client: Consejería de Cultura de la Junta de Andalucía y Ayuntamiento de Nijar
Cost: €2.360 million

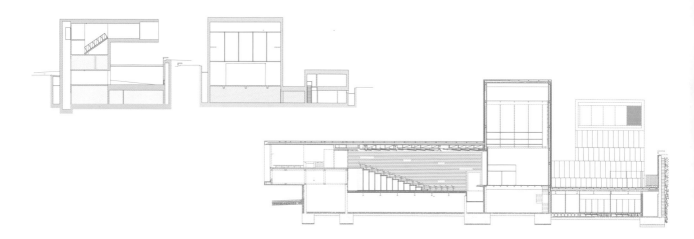

The building stands out from its dry environment, glowing from within at night. Elevations on the left page show the placement of the theater within the overall structure.

Das Gebäude hebt sich von seiner trockenen landschaftlichen Umgebung ab und leuchtet nachts von innen. Aufrisse auf der linken Seite veranschaulichen die Lage des Theatersaals innerhalb des Komplexes.

La construction émerge de l'environnement aride, illuminée de l'intérieur dans la nuit. Les élévations, page de gauche, montrent la disposition du théâtre dans la structure d'ensemble.

This site, previously occupied by terraced orchards, is barely visible from the street. The architects sought to integrate the terraced topography into their project. They were asked to create an exhibition pavilion, a flexible-use theater, studios for music, and rehearsal rooms. These functions are joined together at the lowest level, but emerge separately on the site. A "moat" surrounds the structure whose most visible material is aluminum panel. The elements of the design were considered as being tubular volumes in which different functional packages are inserted. The boxes created by the architects have bright colors within, but offer a relatively blank, metallic aspect from most exterior vantage points. "We wanted the building life to be understood by going from one side to the other," say the architects. "We hope that echoes and bodies run between the two volumes, through the space through which the landscape or the torrid shadows of the hot summer of Almería penetrate."

Das Grundstück, auf dem früher Obstterrassen lagen, ist von der Straße kaum einsehbar. Die Architekten bemühten sich, die Terrassen in das Projekt zu integrieren. Laut Auftrag sollten ein Pavillon für Ausstellungen, eine Mehrzweckbühne, Musikstudios und Probenräume realisiert werden. Die Funktionsbereiche sind im Untergeschoss miteinander verbunden, erheben sich jedoch separat auf dem Gelände. Ein „Wallgraben" umzieht den Komplex, dessen auffälligstes Material Aluminiumpaneele sind. Die einzelnen Elemente des Entwurfs wurden als schlauchartige Volumina konzipiert, in welche die unterschiedlichen Funktionen integriert wurden. Die von den Architekten gestalteten Boxen sind innen leuchtend farbig gestrichen, geben sich nach außen jedoch eher monochrom bzw. metallisch. „Wir wollten, dass sich das ‚Leben' des Baus nach und nach beim Gang um den Komplex erschließt", erklären die Architekten. „Wir hoffen, dass zwischen den Baukörpern ein Echo entsteht, dass sich Menschen in diesem Zwischenraum bewegen, der von der Landschaft und den Schatten der sengenden Sommer Almerías durchdrungen wird."

Ce site, précédemment occupé par un verger en terrasses, est difficilement visible de la rue. Les architectes ont cherché à intégrer la topographie en terrasses à leur projet. On leur demandait de créer un pavillon d'exposition, un théâtre modulable, des studios de musique et des salles de répétition. Ces fonctions sont réunies au niveau inférieur, mais émergent séparément sur le site. Une « douve » entoure le bâtiment dont le matériau le plus visible est le panneau d'aluminium. Les éléments du projet ont été considérés comme des volumes tubulaires dans lesquels venaient s'insérer différents ensembles fonctionnels. L'intérieur des caissons créés par les architectes est vivement coloré, mais ils apparaissent relativement neutres et métalliques de la plupart des points de vue extérieurs. « Nous voulions que la vie du bâtiment prenne son sens en le traversant d'un côté à l'autre », disent les architectes. « Nous souhaitons que les échos et les corps courent entre les deux volumes, à travers l'espace où pénètrent le paysage et les ombres de l'été torride d'Almeria. »

Below, the main theater space with an abstract, colorful décor that contrasts with the austerity of the exterior.

Unten der große Theatersaal mit seiner abstrakten, farbenfrohen Wandbemalung, die einen Kontrast zum strengen Außenbau bildet.

Ci-dessous, l'espace de la grande salle, avec son décor abstrait et coloré, contraste avec l'austérité de l'extérieur.

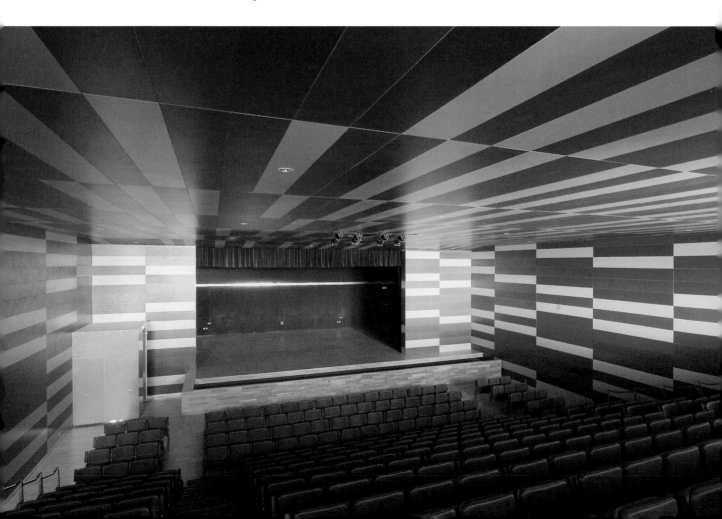

Generous glazing offers views of the
city. The architects employ a variety
of colors inside the building, but
insist on strict, sharp forms.

Großzügige Glasfronten geben den
Blick auf die Stadt frei. Die Architek-
ten arbeiteten mit einer ganzen
Bandbreite von Farben im Innern des
Gebäudes, blieben aber konsequent
bei strengen, scharfkantigen Formen.

Les vitrages généreux offrent de
larges vues sur la ville. Les architectes emploient des couleurs variées
tout en s'appuyant sur des formes
strictes et pures.

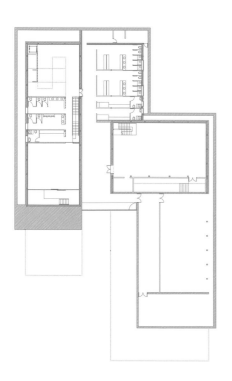

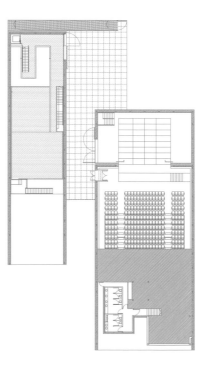

Plans show the orthogonal composition, while photos again emphasize the somewhat surprising use of bright colors on the almost abstract interiors.

Die Grundrisse veranschaulichen die Rechtwinkligkeit der Komposition, während die Fotos einmal mehr den beinahe überraschenden Einsatz kräftiger Farben in den geradezu abstrakt wirkenden Innenräumen belegen.

Les plans montrent la composition orthogonale, tandis que les photos mettent à nouveau l'accent sur l'utilisation assez surprenante de couleurs vives dans des intérieurs presque abstraits.

MIRALLES TAGLIABUE – EMBT

Miralles Tagliabue Arquitectes Associats – EMBT
Passatge de la Pau, 10 bis. pral.
08002 Barcelona / Spain

Tel: +34 934 12 53 42 / Fax: +34 934 12 37 18
E-mail: publicacio@mirallestagliabue.com
Web: www.mirallestagliabue.com

Born in Barcelona in 1955, Enric Miralles received his degree from the ETSA in that city in 1978. He died in 2001. He formed a partnership with Carme Pinós in 1983, and won a competition for the Igualada Cemetery Park on the outskirts of Barcelona in 1985 (completed in 1992). Contrary to the minimalism of other local architects like Viaplana and Piñón, with whom he worked from 1974 to 1984, or Estève Bonnel, Miralles was known for the exuberance of his style. While interested in deconstruction as it is applied to literature, Miralles was skeptical about its application to architecture. His work includes the Olympic Archery Ranges (Barcelona, 1989–91); the La Mina Civic Center (Barcelona, 1987–92); the Morella Boarding School (Castelló, 1986–94); and the Huesca Sports Hall (Huesca, 1988–94), all in Spain. The most visible recent project of the firm was the Scottish Parliament (Edinburgh, Scotland, 1998–2004). Benedetta Tagliabue was born in Milan, Italy, and graduated from the IUAV in Venice in 1989. She studied and worked in New York (with Agrest & Gandelsonas) from 1987 to 1989. She worked for Enric Miralles, beginning in 1992, first becoming a Partner, then leading the studio after his death. **EMBT** completed the Rehabilitation of the Santa Caterina Market (Barcelona, 1997–2005); the Principal Building for the University Campus (Vigo, 2006); headquarters for Gas Natural (Barcelona, 2007); the Public Library (Palafolls, 1997–2007, published here); and a stage set for the Merce Cunningham Dance Company (Barcelona, 2009), all in Spain.

Enric Miralles wurde 1955 in Barcelona geboren und schloss sein Studium 1978 an der ETSA Barcelona ab. Er starb 2000. Miralles hatte 1983 gemeinsam mit Carme Pinós ein Büro gegründet, mit dem sie 1985 den Wettbewerb für die Friedhofsanlage in Igualada am Stadtrand von Barcelona gewannen (fertiggestellt 1992). Im Gegensatz zum Minimalismus anderer Architekten aus Barcelona, etwa Viaplana und Piñón, mit denen er von 1974 bis 1984 zusammengearbeitet hatte, oder Estève Bonnel, war Miralles für seinen extravaganten Stil bekannt. Obwohl er sich durchaus für den Dekonstruktivismus in der Literatur interessierte, war er skeptisch, was dessen Anwendung in der Architektur anging. Zu seinen Projekten zählen die Olympische Bogenschießanlage (Barcelona, 1989–91), das Stadtteilzentrum in La Mina (Barcelona, 1987–92), ein Internat in Morella (Castelló, 1986–94) sowie das Sportzentrum in Huesca (Huesca, 1988–94), alle in Spanien. Das bekannteste Projekt von Miralles Tagliabue in jüngerer Zeit ist das Schottische Parlament (Edinburgh, 1998–2004). Benedetta Tagliabue wurde in Mailand geboren und schloss ihr Studium 1989 am IUAV in Venedig ab. Von 1987 bis 1989 studierte und arbeitete sie in New York (bei Agrest & Gandelsonas). Ab 1992 kooperierte sie mit Enric Miralles, wurde dann Partnerin und leitet das Büro seit dem Tod von Miralles. **EMBT** betreute den Umbau der Markthalle Santa Caterina (Barcelona, 1997–2005), das Hauptgebäude auf dem Universitätscampus von Vigo (2006), die Zentrale von Gas Natural (Barcelona, 2007), die Bibliothek in Palafolls (1997–2007, hier vorgestellt) sowie ein Bühnenbild für die Merce Cunningham Dance Company (Barcelona, 2009), alle in Spanien.

Né à Barcelone en 1955, Enric Miralles y a obtenu son diplôme de l'ETSA en 1978. Il est décédé en 2001. Il s'est associé avec Carme Pinós en 1983, et a gagné le concours pour le parc du nouveau cimetière d'Igualada, dans les environs de Barcelone en 1985 (terminé en 1992). Au contraire du minimalisme adopté par les autres architectes locaux, comme Viaplana et Piñón avec qui il a travaillé de 1974 à 1984, ou encore Estève Bonnel, Miralles était réputé pour son style exubérant. Bien qu'intéressé par le déconstructivisme appliqué à la littérature, Miralles était sceptique quant à son application en architecture. Ses projets réalisés incluent le terrain de tir à l'arc des Jeux olympiques de Barcelone (Barcelone, 1989–91) ; le Centre social de La Mina (Barcelone, 1987–92) ; un pensionnat à Morella (Castelló, 1986–94) ; et la salle de sports de Huesca (Huesca, 1988–94), tous situés en Espagne. Son projet récent le plus connu est le Parlement écossais (Édimbourg, Écosse, 1998–2004). Benedetta Tagliabue est née à Milan, en Italie, et a obtenu son diplôme de l'IUAV de Venise, en 1989. Elle a étudié et travaillé à New York (avec Agrest & Gandelsonas) de 1987 à 1989. Elle a commencé à travailler pour Enric Miralles en 1992, d'abord comme associée, puis a pris la direction de l'agence après sa mort. **EMBT** a réalisé la réhabilitation du marché Santa Caterina (Barcelone, 1997–2005) ; le bâtiment de la Direction du campus universitaire (Vigo, 2006) ; le siège de Gas Natural (Barcelone, 2007) ; la bibliothèque municipale de Palafolls (Palafolls, 1997–2007, publié ici) ; et une scénographie pour la Merce Cunningham Dance Company (Barcelone, 2009), tous projets situés en Espagne.

PUBLIC LIBRARY

Palafolls, Spain, 1997–2007

Address: Parc de les Esplanes s/n, 08389 Palafolls, Spain, +34 937 652 834
Area: 714 m². Client: City of Palafolls. Cost: € 1.15 million

This project, which took over ten years to complete, was initiated by Enric Miralles, who wrote (in 1997): "We have tried in different ways to give the library an appearance of a labyrinth, a series of rooms and gardens put together in a nonlinear way. The building is an experiment that shows every part of the development of the project, its continuing changes and variations, as well as the authority of accepting the final result..." Ten years later, describing the process of gestation that went into the project, Benedetta Tagliabue wrote: "The walls are converted into lines that lead people from the outside to the inside and vice versa, forming secret patios where you can bring books and find a tree under which to sit and read as in the ancient gardens... The only real and massive wall of the library is the dividing line between the inside and the outside, this line is 'the door' of the library and it is for us a true sensory processing machine..." Rising up out of the red earth with its gray arching roofs, the Library does have something of a living creature about it, a complexity that surely is, as Tagliabue insists, born of the long period between the initial project and this final, surprising result.

Das Projekt, dessen Realisierung über zehn Jahre in Anspruch nahm, wurde von Enric Miralles initiiert, der 1997 schrieb: „Wir haben auf verschiedene Weise versucht, die Bibliothek wie ein Labyrinth zu gestalten, eine Abfolge von Räumen und Gärten, die nicht linear aneinandergefügt wurden. Das Gebäude ist ein Experiment; hier sind alle Entwicklungsphasen des Projekts, seine Veränderungen und Variationen ablesbar; dennoch besitzt es die Größe, das Endergebnis zu akzeptieren ..." Zehn Jahre später beschrieb Benedetta Tagliabue den Reifungsprozess, der das Projekt prägte: „Die Wände wurden zu Linien, die die Besucher von außen nach innen (und umgekehrt) leiten, durch sie entstehen verborgene Innenhöfe, in die man seine Bücher tragen darf, wo man einen Baum findet, unter dem man sitzen und lesen kann, wie in den Gärten früherer Zeiten ... Die einzig wirklich massive Wand der Bibliothek ist die Trennwand zwischen innen und außen. Diese Linie bildet die eigentliche ‚Tür' zur Bibliothek. Für uns ist sie eine sinnesverarbeitende Maschine ..." Mit ihren grauen gewölbten Dächern erhebt sich die Bibliothek über dem roten Erdboden und mutet dabei fast wie ein lebendiges Wesen an. Diese Komplexität erklärt sich zweifellos, wie Tagliabue betont, aus der langen Zeitspanne, die zwischen dem ursprünglichen Entwurf und dem überraschenden Ergebnis liegt.

Ce projet, achevé en dix ans, a été commencé par Enric Miralles, qui écrivait (en 1997) : « Nous avons essayé plusieurs solutions pour donner à la bibliothèque l'apparence d'un labyrinthe, une suite de salles et de jardins réunis d'une façon non linéaire. Le bâtiment est une expérience qui montre toutes les phases de développement du projet, ses changements continus et ses variations, ainsi que la volonté d'accepter le résultat final ... ». Dix ans plus tard, décrivant le processus de gestation du projet, Benedetta Tagliabue écrivait : « Les murs sont convertis en lignes qui conduisent les gens de l'extérieur à l'intérieur et vice versa, en formant des patios secrets où vous pouvez apporter des livres et trouver un arbre sous lequel vous asseoir pour lire, comme dans les jardins antiques ... Le seul mur réel et massif de la bibliothèque est la ligne divisant l'intérieur et l'extérieur, cette ligne est la » porte « de la bibliothèque et c'est pour nous une vraie machine sensorielle ... » S'élevant de la terre rouge avec ses toits gris cintrés, la bibliothèque a assurément quelque chose d'une créature vivante, une complexité née, comme Tagliabue le souligne, de la longue période entre le projet initial et son surprenant résultat final.

The unusual appearance of the Library suggests more of a continuous, earth-bound movement than a more conventional, geometric architecture.

Das ungewöhnliche Erscheinungsbild der Bibliothek lässt eher an natürliche Erdbewegungen denken als an konventionelle, geometrische Architektur.

L'aspect inhabituel de la bibliothèque suggère plus un mouvement naturel continu qu'une architecture géométrique conventionnelle.

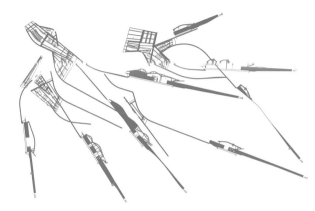

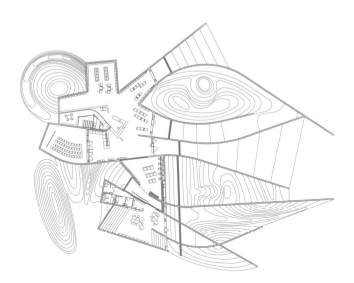

Plans and an overall image emphasize the curvature and wave like
movement of the roof design and the
actual volumes of the library.

Grundrisse und eine Aufnahme der
Gesamtanlage lassen die geschwungenen Linien und wellenförmige
Dynamik der Dächer und Baukörper
der Bibliothek besonders deutlich
werden.

Les plans et la photo d'ensemble
mettent l'accent sur les courbures et
les mouvements ondulants des toits
et sur les volumes de la bibliothèque.

Interiors are utilitarian, with beams and columns in evidence, and natural light coming in through the variously shaped windows.

Die Innenräume sind zweckmäßig gehalten, Träger und Stützen sind offen sichtbar, durch die unterschiedlich geformten Fenster fällt Tageslicht ein.

Les intérieurs sont fonctionnels, avec des poutres et colonnes visibles et un éclairage naturel fourni par des fenêtres de différentes formes.

RAFAEL MONEO

Rafael Moneo / Cinca 5 / 28002 Madrid / Spain
Tel: +34 91 564 22 57 / Fax: +34 91 563 52 17
E-mail: r.moneo@rafaelmoneo.com

RAFAEL MONEO was born in Tudela, Navarra (Spain), in 1937. He graduated from the ETSA in Madrid in 1961. The following year, he went to work with Jørn Utzon in Denmark. Rafael Moneo has taught extensively at the ETSA in Madrid and Barcelona. He was chairman of the Department of Architecture at Harvard GSD from 1985 to 1990. He won the 1996 Pritzker Prize, and the 2003 RIBA Gold Medal. His work includes the National Museum of Roman Art (Mérida, 1980–86); the San Pablo Airport Terminal in Seville (1989–91) built for Expo '92; the Atocha railway station in Madrid (1991); the Miró Foundation in Palma (1992); the interior architecture of the Thyssen-Bornemisza Collection in Madrid (1992); the Davis Museum at Wellesley College (Wellesley, Massachusetts, USA, 1993); Potsdamer Platz Hotel and Office Building (Berlin, Germany, 1993–98); Murcia Town Hall (Murcia, 1995–98); Kursaal Auditorium and Congress Center (San Sebastián, Guipúzcoa, 1990–99); the Cathedral of Our Lady of the Angels (Los Angeles, California, USA, 1996–02). He has also worked recently on an extension of the Prado Museum (Madrid, 2001–06); the Chace Student Center for the Rhode Island School of Design (Providence, Rhode Island, USA, 2000–08); Laboratory for Interface and Engineering at Harvard (Cambridge, Massachusetts, USA, 2000–08); the University of Deusto Library (Bilbao, 2001–08, published here); the Museum of the Roman Theater (Cartagena, 2002–08); and a laboratory for the Novartis Campus (Basel, Switzerland, 2009), all in Spain unless stated otherwise. He is presently working on the Northwest Science Building for Columbia University (New York, USA); and the Princeton University Neuroscience and Psychology Building (New Jersey, USA).

RAFAEL MONEO wurde 1937 in Tudela, Navarra (Spanien), geboren. Sein Studium schloss er 1961 an der ETSA Madrid ab. Im darauffolgenden Jahr ging er nach Dänemark, um für Jørn Utzon zu arbeiten. Rafael Moneo lehrte lange Zeit an der ETSA in Madrid sowie in Barcelona. Von 1985 bis 1990 war er Dekan der Architekturfakultät der Harvard GSD. 1996 wurde er mit dem Pritzker-Preis ausgezeichnet, 2003 mit der RIBA-Goldmedaille. Zu seinen Arbeiten zählen das Museum für römische Kunst (Mérida, 1980–86), das Terminal am San-Pablo-Flughafen in Sevilla, gebaut für die Expo '92 (1989–91), der neue Bahnhof Atocha in Madrid (1991), die Miró-Stiftung in Palma (1992), die Innenarchitektur der Sammlung Thyssen-Bornemisza in Madrid (1992), das Davis Museum am Wellesley College (Wellesley, Massachusetts, 1993), ein Hotel und Bürogebäude am Potsdamer Platz (Berlin, 1993–98), das Rathaus in Murcia (1995–98), das Kongresszentrum „Kursaal" (San Sebastián, Guipúzcoa, 1990–99) und die Kathedrale Our Lady of the Angels (Los Angeles, 1996–2002). Unlängst arbeitete er an einer Erweiterung des Prado (Madrid, 2001–06), dem Chace-Studentenzentrum an der Rhode Island School of Design (Providence, Rhode Island, 2000–08), dem Laboratory for Interface and Engineering in Harvard (Cambridge, Massachusetts, 2000–08), der Bibliothek der Universität Deusto (Bilbao, 2001–08, hier vorgestellt), dem Museum des römischen Theaters von Cartagena (Spanien, 2002–08) sowie einem Labor auf dem Novartis Campus (Basel, 2009). Derzeit in Arbeit ist das Northwest Science Building für die Columbia University (New York) sowie ein Gebäude für Neurowissenschaften und Psychologie an der Universität Princeton (New Jersey).

RAFAEL MONEO est né à Tudela, en Navarre (Espagne), en 1937. il obtient son diplôme de l'ETSA à Madrid, en 1961. L'année suivante, il part travailler avec Jørn Utzon au Danemark. Rafael Moneo a beaucoup enseigné à l'ETSA de Madrid et de Barcelone. Il a été président du département d'architecture à la GSD de Harvard, de 1985 à 1990. Il a gagné le prix Pritzker 1996 et la médaille d'or du RIBA 2003. Ses réalisations incluent le Musée national d'art romain (Mérida, 1980–86) ; le terminal de l'aéroport San Pablo de Séville (1989–91) construit pour Expo 92 ; la gare d'Atocha à Madrid (1991) ; la Fondation Miró à Palma de Majorque (1992) ; l'architecture intérieure du musée Thyssen-Bornemisza à Madrid (1992) ; le musée Davis du Wellesley College (Wellesley, Massachusetts, États-Unis, 1993) ; un hôtel et un immeuble de bureaux sur la Potsdamer Platz (Berlin, Allemagne, 1993–98) ; la mairie de Murcia (Murcia, 1995–98) ; l'auditorium et le Centre de congrès du Kursaal, à Saint-Sébastien (Guipúzcoa, 1990–99) ; la cathédrale Notre-Dame-des-Anges, à Los Angeles (Los Angeles, Californie, États-Unis, 1996–02). Ses réalisations récentes incluent l'extension du musée du Prado (Madrid, 2001–06) ; le Centre étudiant Chace, pour l'École de design de Rhode Island (Providence, Rhode Island, États-Unis, 2000–08) ; le Laboratory for Interface and Engineering d'Harvard (Cambridge, Massachusetts, États-Unis, 2000–08) ; la bibliothèque de l'université de Deusto (Bilbao, 2001–08, publié ici) ; le Musée du théâtre romain (Cartagène, 2002–08) ; et un laboratoire sur le campus Novartis (Bâle, Suisse, 2009), toutes situées en Espagne sauf mention contraire. Il travaille actuellement sur un nouveau bâtiment des sciences (Northwest Science Building) pour l'université Columbia (New York) et un nouveau bâtiment des Neurosciences et Psychologie (Neuroscience and Psychology Building) pour l'université de Princeton (New Jersey, États-Unis).

UNIVERSITY OF DEUSTO LIBRARY

Bilbao, Spain, 2001–08

Address: Avenida de las Universidades 24, 48007 Bilbao, Spain, +34 94 413 90 00, www.biblioteca.deusto.es
Area: 19 000 m². Client: Deusto University. Cost: not disclosed
Project Architect: Valerio Canals Revilla

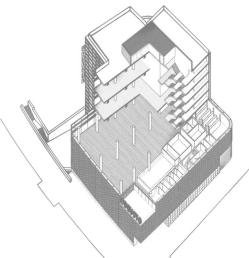

Rafael Moneo says that it is difficult to imagine a better location for a new building in Bilbao, near Frank Gehry's Guggenheim Bilbao, as befits a structure intended for a university that has played a key role in the life of the city. Cesar Pelli laid out the urban plan for the area. The architect, however, considered the proximity of the Gehry building and the tight schedule for construction to be difficulties that he had to overcome. Moneo had no desire to try to compete with Gehry, but he did wish to give the university library the stature that it deserved. He selected a monochromatic, neutral presence in contrast with the "brightness of the Guggenheim," and to better integrate the building into a neighboring park. Rounded corners on two sides mark this "translucent solid." A large notch marks one corner of the building, where an illuminated sign signals the name of Deusto. A parking lot for 74 vehicles is located below grade, while the first three floors each offers a surface of 1699 square meters. A main staircase open to a skylight and interior patio connects all the floors and mezzanines of the library. Moneo's subtlety and intelligence mark this structure as a counterpoint to the exuberance of Gehry.

Rafael Moneo zufolge lässt sich kaum ein besserer Standort für einen Neubau in Bilbao denken, als in der Nähe von Frank Gehrys Guggenheim Museum – zumal für eine Universität, die eine Schlüsselrolle im Leben der Stadt spielt. Die stadtplanerische Gestaltung des Viertels lag bei Cesar Pelli. Moneo empfand die Nähe zu Gehrys Gebäude und den engen Zeitplan zunächst als Hindernisse, die es zu überwinden galt. Zwar wollte er keineswegs mit Gehry konkurrieren, sehr wohl aber der Universitätsbibliothek ein angemessenes Profil geben. Im Gegensatz zum „Glanz des Guggenheim" entschied er sich für eine monochrome, neutrale Gestalt, die zudem besser mit dem benachbarten Park harmoniert. Der „transluzente Körper" hat an zwei Seiten auffällig gerundete Ecken. Ein tiefer Einschnitt markiert eine Ecke des Gebäudes; hier ist auf einem Leuchtschild der Name Deusto zu lesen. Im Untergeschoss befinden sich Parkplätze für 74 Fahrzeuge, die drei Obergeschosse haben jeweils eine Fläche von 1699 m². Eine Haupttreppe, die sich zum Oberlicht und zum Innenhof hin öffnet, verbindete sämtliche Geschossen und Zwischengeschosse der Bibliothek. Moneos Subtilität und Intelligenz sind in diesem Bauwerk spürbar und lassen es zum Kontrapunkt zu Gehrys Opulenz werden.

Rafael Moneo dit qu'il est difficile d'imaginer, pour un nouveau bâtiment destiné à une université ayant joué un rôle important dans le développement de Bilbao, un meilleur emplacement que celui-ci, proche du musée Guggenheim de Frank Gehry. Cesar Pelli a conçu le plan directeur de cette zone. L'architecte considérait toutefois la proximité du bâtiment de Gehry et les contraintes du programme comme des difficultés à surmonter. Moneo ne cherchait pas à entrer en compétition avec Gehry, mais souhaitait donner à la bibliothèque universitaire la stature qu'elle mérite. Il a opté pour une présence monochrome et neutre, contrastant avec « l'éclat du Guggenheim », et une meilleure intégration du bâtiment dans l'environnement du parc voisin. Deux coins arrondis caractérisent ce « solide translucide ». Une large encoche entaille un coin du bâtiment où une enseigne lumineuse affiche le nom Deusto. Un parking de 74 places est situé en sous-sol, tandis que les trois premiers niveaux font chacun 1699 mètres carrés. Un escalier principal à ciel ouvert et un patio relient les étages et mezzanines de la bibliothèque. L'habileté et la subtilité de Moneo marquent ce bâtiment en contrepoint de l'exubérance de Gehry.

An axonometric drawing and photos show the overall forms of the Library, which is within sight of Frank Gehry's Guggenheim Bilbao (photo above).

Axonometrie und Fotos dokumentieren die Form der Bibliothek, die in Sichtweite von Frank Gehrys Guggenheim Bilbao gelegen ist (Foto oben).

L'axonométrie et les photos montrent les formes d'ensemble de la bibliothèque visible depuis le musée Guggenheim de Bilbao de Frank Gehry (photo ci-dessus).

A plan shows that the building is somewhat angled in response to its site. A cafeteria space (below) has generous, high spaces and natural light.

Der Grundriss zeigt, dass das Gebäude dem Grundstück entsprechend leicht abgeschrägt wurde. Die Caféteria (unten) ist großzügig, hat hohe Decken und wird mit Tageslicht versorgt.

Le plan montre les angles un peu obliques du bâtiment, faisant écho au site. Une cafétéria (ci-dessous) bénéficie de hauts espaces généreux et d'une lumière naturelle.

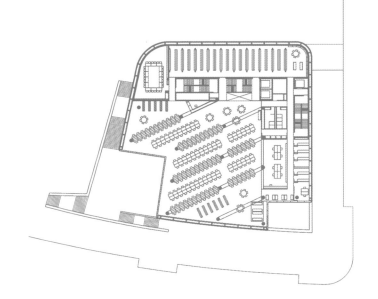

Reading spaces are aligned in
efficient rows, as is the overhead
lighting, but spaces like the one
to the right are ample and airy.

Die Leseplätze sind effizient zu
Reihen angeordnet und beleuchtet,
Bereiche wie rechts im Bild jedoch
wirken großzügig und luftig.

Les espaces de lecture sont alignés
en rangées fonctionnelles, tout
comme les éclairages de plafond,
mais les espaces comme celui de
droite sont généreux et aérés.

MONEO BROCK STUDIO

Moneo Brock Studio
Fco. de Asís Méndez
Casariego 7, bajo
28002 Madrid / Spain

Tel: +34 91 56 38 05
E-mail: contact@moneobrock.com
Web: www.moneobrock.com

Belén Moneo Feduchi and Jeff Brock formed **MONEO BROCK STUDIO** in 1993 in New York. At the same time, they worked for the studio of Rafael Moneo. In December of 1993, they moved for two years to Stockholm, where they directed the project of the New Museums of Modern Art and Architecture. At the end of 2001, the office moved to Madrid. Belén Moneo Feduchi, the daughter of Rafael Moneo, grew up in Madrid, and graduated from Harvard College in 1988. She attended Columbia University's Graduate School of Architecture, Planning, and Preservation and received an M.Arch degree in 1991. Between graduating and starting Moneo Brock Studio, she worked for Smith-Miller+Hawkinson Architects in New York. Jeff Brock attended Princeton College, where he majored in Architecture. In 1985, he moved to New York City and began work with Robert Marino Architect. After three years at this office, he attended Columbia University's Graduate School of Architecture, Planning, and Preservation and received an M.Arch degree in 1991. Their projects include the Thermal Baths (Panticosa, Huesca, 2002–08, published here); a Country House (El Escorial, Madrid, 2002–08); Gas Station (San Agustin de Guadalix, (Madrid, 2004–08); Glass Pavilion and Park (Cuenca, 2005–); and the Museum Fundacion Telefonica (Gran Via, Madrid, 2008–). Work with Rafael Moneo includes the Cranbrook Academy of Art Studio Building (Bloomfield Hills, Michigan, 1997–2002); and the Columbia University Interdisciplinary Science Building (New York, 2005–), both in the USA.

Belén Moneo Feduchi und Jeff Brock gründeten das **MONEO BROCK STUDIO** 1993 in New York. Beide waren damals noch für Rafael Moneo tätig. Im Dezember 1993 zogen sie für zwei Jahre nach Stockholm, wo sie die Leitung für das Doppclprojckt Museum für Moderne Kunst und Architekturmuseum innehatten. Ende 2001 zog das Büro nach Madrid. Belén Moneo Feduchi, Tochter von Rafael Moneo, wuchs in Madrid auf und studierte bis 1988 am Harvard College. Anschließend absolvierte sie einen Aufbaustudiengang in Architektur, Bauplanung und Denkmalschutz an der Columbia University, den sie 1991 mit einem M. Arch. abschloss. Danach war sie bis 1993 für Smith-Miller+Hawkinson Architects in New York tätig. Jeff Brock studierte am Princeton College, wo er seinen Abschluss in Architektur machte. 1985 zog er nach New York und arbeitete für Robert Marino. Nach dreijähriger Tätigkeit absolvierte auch er den Aufbaustudiengang in Architektur, Bauplanung und Denkmalschutz an der Columbia University, den er ebenfalls 1991 mit einem M. Arch. abschloss. Zu den Projekten des Teams zählen ein Thermalbad (Panticosa, Huesca, 2002–08, hier vorgestellt), ein Landhaus (El Escorial, Madrid, 2002–08), eine Tankstelle (San Agustin de Guadalix, Madrid, 2004–08), ein Glaspavillon und Park (Cuenca, 2005–) sowie das Museum Fundación Telefonica (Madrid, 2008–). Gemeinsam mit Rafael Moneo realisierten sie u. a. das Atelierhaus der Cranbrook Academy of Art (Bloomfield Hills, Michigan, 1997–2002) sowie das Gebäude für Interdisziplinäre Wissenschaften an der Columbia University (New York, 2005–).

Belén Moneo Feduchi et Jeff Brock ont fondé **MONEO BROCK STUDIO** en 1993 à New York, tout en travaillant dans l'agence de Rafael Moneo. En décembre 1993, ils s'installent pour deux ans à Stockholm où ils développent le projet du nouveau Musée d'art moderne et d'architecture. Fin 2001, ils s'installent à Madrid. Belén Moneo Feduchi, fille de Rafael Moneo, a grandi à Madrid. Elle obtient son diplôme d'Harvard en 1988 et continue ses études à l'École supérieure d'architecture, d'aménagement et de conservation de l'université Columbia, où elle obtient un master en architecture (M. Arch.) en 1991. Entre l'obtention de son diplôme et la création de Moneo Brock Studio, elle travaille pour Smith-Miller+Hawkinson Architects à New York. Jeff Brock a étudié à Princeton où il s'est spécialisé en architecture. En 1985, il s'installe à New York et commence à travailler chez Robert Marino Architect. Après trois années dans cette agence, il étudie à l'École supérieure d'architecture, d'aménagement et de conservation de l'université Columbia et obtient un master en architecture (M. Arch.) en 1991. Leurs réalisations incluent les thermes de Panticosa (Huesca, 2002–08, publié ici) ; une maison de campagne (El Escorial, Madrid, 2002–08) ; une station-service (San Agustin de Guadalix, Madrid, 2004–08) ; le parc et le pavillon de verre de Cuenca (2005–) ; et le musée de la Fundación Telefónica sur la Gran Via à Madrid (2008–). Leurs réalisations avec Rafael Moneo incluent le bâtiment des ateliers de l'Académie des beaux-arts Cranbrook à Bloomfield Hills (Michigan, États-Unis, 1997–2002) ; et le bâtiment des sciences interdisciplinaires de l'université Columbia à New York (2005–).

THERMAL BATHS

Panticosa, Huesca, Spain, 2002–08

Address: Ctra. Del Balneario km 10, 22650 Panticosa, Spain, +34 902 25 25 22, www.panticosa.com
Area: 7250 m². Client: Aguas de Panticosa. Cost: not disclosed
Collaboration: Iñigo Cobeta

The **THERMAL BATHS OF PANTICOSA** are located in the Valle del Tena in the Pyrenees of the Aragon region of Spain. The architects sought to provide a "balanced response to the natural setting on the one hand and to the urbanized context on the other." Municipal rules required that a good part of the allotted floor area be located below grade. The program includes thermal pools, a gymnasium, treatment rooms, and various spaces for recreation and relaxation. Windows are positioned to allow a close connection to the mountainous landscape. Pools and saunas are located on the main level, with one exterior and three interior hot pools, Turkish baths, cold baths, ice baths, saunas, showers, foot baths, relaxation areas, and juice bars. The architects explain: "The façade is built of a custom-made glass block, trapezoidal in section, acid-etched both inside and out. This block's form was designed to accentuate the curvilinear aspect of the façade, the overlapping of each block course over the one below creating a shadow line that reiterates the planimetric curve of the façade."

Die **THERMALBÄDER VON PANTICOSA** liegen im Valle del Tena in den Pyrenäen, mitten in der spanischen Region Aragon. Den Architekten ging es darum, eine „ausgewogene Antwort auf die landschaftliche Umgebung einerseits und das verstädterte Umfeld andererseits" zu finden. Den örtlichen Bauvorgaben zufolge musste ein Großteil der Nutzfläche im Untergeschoss untergebracht werden. Zum Programm gehören ein Thermalschwimmbecken, eine Sporthalle, Behandlungsräume sowie verschiedene Bereiche zur Erholung und Entspannung. Die Anordnung der Fenster schafft einen engen Bezug zur Berglandschaft. Die Schwimmbecken und Saunen liegen im Hauptgeschoss, darunter ein Außen- und drei Innenthermalbecken, türkische Bäder, Kaltwasser- und Eiswasserbecken, Saunen, Duschen, Fußbäder, Entspannungszonen und Saftbars. Die Architekten führen aus: „Die Fassade wurde mit einem maßgefertigten Glasbaustein mit trapezförmigem Zuschnitt errichtet, der innen und außen säuregeätzt ist. Die Grundform der Bausteine unterstreicht den Schwung der Fassade. Dadurch dass die Bausteine Reihe für Reihe weiter auskragen, entsteht eine Schattenlinie, die die planimetrische Kurve der Fassade betont".

LES THERMES DE PANTICOSA sont situés dans la vallée de Tena, dans les Pyrénées aragonaises, en Espagne. Les architectes ont cherché à fournir une « réponse équilibrée entre site naturel et environnement urbain ». La réglementation municipale a contraint à placer en sous-sol une bonne partie de la surface allouée. Le programme comprend des piscines thermales, un gymase, des salles de traitement et divers espaces de loisir et de détente. L'emplacement des fenêtres permet une étroite relation avec le paysage montagneux. Au niveau principal, on trouve les piscines et saunas, avec un bain chaud à l'extérieur et trois à l'intérieur, les hammams, les bains froids, les bains glacés, les saunas, les douches, les bains de pieds, les aires de détente et les bars à jus de fruits. Les architectes expliquent : « La façade est constituée de briques de verre fabriquées sur mesure, de section trapézoïdale, gravées sur les faces interne et externe. La forme de ces briques a été conçue pour accentuer l'aspect curviligne de la façade, le chevauchement de chaque rang sur le rang inférieur créant une ligne d'ombre qui reprend la planimétrie incurvée de la façade. »

The Thermal Baths are backed into their rugged mountainous setting, as the plans, below, show. The glass block façade does not conflict with neighboring architecture, but does stand apart.

Die Therme wird von der zerklüfteten Berglandschaft eingerahmt, wie die Grundrisse unten belegen. Die Glasbausteinfassade steht nicht im Widerspruch zur baulichen Umgebung, sondern hebt sich vielmehr von ihr ab.

Les thermes sont adossés à un site montagneux accidenté, comme le montrent les plans ci-dessous. La façade en briques de verre se détache de l'architecture environnante, sans entrer en conflit avec elle.

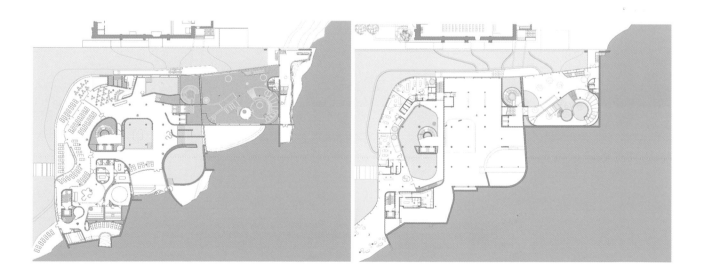

Interior spaces offer glimpses of the mountain environment and echo the curvature of the façades.

Die Innenräume erlauben hier und da einen Blick auf die bergige Umgebung und greifen die geschwungene Kontur der Fassade auf.

Les espaces intérieurs laissent entrevoir l'environnement montagneux et répondent aux courbures des façades.

Atmospheres vary within the complex according to the types of baths. The interior architecture deploys a certain complexity with an emphasis on curves.

Die Stimmung der einzelnen Bereiche variiert je nach Art der Thermalbäder. Die Innenarchitektur ist vergleichs- weise komplex und betont die geschwungenen Formen.

L'atmosphère varie à l'intérieur du complexe, selon les types de bains. L'architecture intérieure affiche une certaine complexité, mettant l'accent sur les courbes.

ALBERTO NICOLAU

Alberto Nicolau Arquitectos
c/ Justiniano 3, 3° I
28004 Madrid
Spain

Tel/Fax: +34 91 308 51 77
E-mail: albertonicolau@gmail.com

ALBERTO NICOLAU was born in Madrid in 1967. He received his degree in Architecture from the ETSA Madrid (ETSAM, 1995). During his studies he was an intern in the office of Alison and Peter Smithson (1991). Subsequent to his graduation, he worked with Foster and Partners (London, 1995–97), and then with Rafael Moneo (1997–2003), where he was assigned to the Our Lady of the Angels Cathedral in Los Angeles. He founded his own practice in Madrid in 2002. He has been a Design Lecturer at the ETSAM since that date. His work includes the Valdesanchuela Swimming Pool (Valdemoro, Madrid, 2006–07, published here); housing in Spuimarkt (The Hague, The Netherlands, with Rafael Moneo, 2007); and a Truck Maintenance Garage (Valdemoro, Madrid, with **FERNANDO IZNAOLA**, 2007–08). Projects under construction include the Leonor González Housing Estate (Valiecas, Madrid, with F. Iznaola).

ALBERTO NICOLAU wurde 1967 in Madrid geboren. Sein Architekturstudium an der ETSA Madrid (ETSAM) schloss er 1995 ab. Während seines Studiums absolvierte er ein Praktikum bei Alison and Peter Smithson (1991). Im Anschluss an sein Diplom war er für Foster and Partners (London, 1995–97) und für Rafael Moneo tätig (1997–2003), wo er an der Planmung der Kathedrale Our Lady of the Angels in Los Angeles arbeitete. Sein eigenes Büro gründete er 2002 in Madrid. Seither lehrt er auch als Dozent für Entwerfen an der ETSAM. Zu seinen Projekten zählen das Schwimmbad in Valdesanchuela (Valdemoro, Madrid, 2006–07, hier vorgestellt), ein Wohnbauprojekt am Spuimarkt (Den Haag, mit Rafael Moneo, 2007) sowie eine Lkw-Werkstatt (Valdemoro, Madrid, mit **FERNANDO IZNAOLA**, 2007–08). Im Bau befindet sich u. a. die Wohnsiedlung Leonor González (Vallecas, Madrid, ebenfalls mit Fernando Iznaola).

ALBERTO NICOLAU est né à Madrid en 1967. Il est diplômé d'architecture de l'ETSA de Madrid (ETSAM, 1995). Au cours de ses études, il fait un stage à l'agence d'Alison et de Peter Smithson (1991). Après son diplôme, il travaille avec Foster and Partners (Londres, 1995–97), puis avec Rafael Moneo (1997–2003) où il est affecté au projet de la cathédrale Notre-Dame-des-Anges de Los Angeles. Il fonde sa propre agence à Madrid, en 2002. Il est chargé de cours à l'ETSAM depuis cette date. Ses réalisations incluent la piscine municipale Valdesanchuela (Valdemoro, Madrid, 2006–07, publié ici); des logements à Spuimarkt (La Haye, Pays-Bas, avec Rafael Moneo, 2007); et un garage d'entretien pour poids lourds (Valdemoro, Madrid, avec **FERNANDO IZNAOLA**, 2007–08). Ses projets en cours de construction incluent le lotissement Leonor González (Valiecas, Madrid, avec Fernando Iznaola).

VALDESANCHUELA SWIMMING POOL

Valdemoro, Madrid, Spain, 2006–07

Address: Calle Valdesanchuela, 28340 Valdemoro, Spain
Area: 5256 m². Client: Valdemoro Town Hall. Cost: € 6.745 million

"I have always enjoyed looking up from under water at the reflection of light going through its surface," says Alberto Nicolau. "The undulations of the water surface generate a crucible of blues and glitters I've always found mesmerizing." It was on this basis that the architect imagined the **VALDESANCHUELA SWIMMING POOL** "as if it were a series of waves." This metaphor is visible both inside the structure and from the exterior. The main area is formed by a series of parallel, curved strips with "fishlike shaped panes of polycarbonate" between them. The south façade of the building is transparent, allowing users to see the garden and park beyond. The areas around the facility are planted with maples and Ginkgo Biloba trees. Glowing from the inside at night, the Swimming Pool is visible from a nearby highway. Visitors cannot see the pool from the entrance, but they do notice the curving ceiling of the pool before ascending a set of stairs and discovering the main space.

„Ich habe schon immer gern durch die Wasseroberfläche nach oben geschaut, auf die Lichtreflexe, die sich im Wasser brechen", erzählt Alberto Nicolau. „Die Wellen der Wasseroberfläche lassen eine Mischung aus Blautönen und Glanzlichtern entstehen, die mich schon immer fasziniert hat." Diese Erfahrung wurde zum Ausgangspunkt für den Entwurf des **SCHWIMMBADS IN VALDESANCHUELA**, das „wie eine Reihe von Wellen" wirkt. Diese Metapher wird sowohl im Innern des Gebäudes als auch außen sichtbar. Der Hauptraum besteht aus einer Reihe parallel verlaufender, geschwungener Längssegmente, in die „fischförmige Scheiben aus Polycarbonat" eingelassen sind. Die Südfassade des Gebäudes ist transparent und ermöglicht den Badegästen Ausblicke in den Garten und den dahinterliegenden Park. Um den Komplex herum wurden Ahorne und Ginkgobäume gepflanzt. Das nachts von innen leuchtende Schwimmbad ist auch von der nahe gelegenen Autobahn sichtbar. Für Besucher ist das Becken vom Eingang zunächst nicht einsehbar, allerdings können sie die geschwungene Decke wahrnehmen, noch bevor sie die Treppe hinaufsteigen und sich der Hauptraum erschließt.

« J'ai toujours aimé regarder sous l'eau les réflexions de la lumière traversant la surface », dit Alberto Nicolau. « Les ondulations de la surface de l'eau génèrent un creuset de bleu et de paillettes que j'ai toujours trouvé fascinant. » C'est sur cette base que l'architecte a imaginé la **PISCINE VALDESANCHUELA**, « comme une série de vagues ». On retrouve cette métaphore à l'intérieur comme à l'extérieur du bâtiment. La zone principale est formée d'une série de bandes parallèles incurvées, reliées par des « panneaux de polycarbonate pisciformes ». La façade sud transparente de l'édifice permet aux usagers de voir le jardin et le parc au-delà. Les espaces autour du bâtiment sont plantés d'érables et de Ginkgo biloba. Illuminée de l'intérieur la nuit, la piscine est visible depuis l'autoroute proche. Si les visiteurs ne voient pas la piscine depuis l'entrée, ils en remarquent le plafond incurvé, avant de gravir une volée de marches pour découvrir l'espace principal.

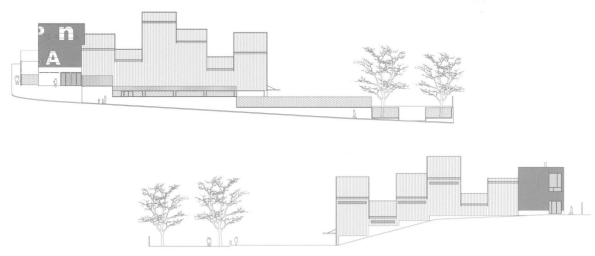

From the street side (left) the building presents largely blank volumes
identified by the super-scale graph-
ics. From the opposite side, the
great, glazed arch presents a clear
contrast.

Zur Straßenseite hin (links) präsentiert sich der Bau vorwiegend als
schmuckloses Volumen, dessen Funktion die übergroßen Buchstaben verraten. Auf der gegenüberliegenden
Seite bildet die große geschwungene
Glasfront einen deutlichen Kontrast.

Depuis la rue (à gauche), le bâtiment
présente des volumes en grande
partie aveugles identifiés par des
graphismes géants. Du côté opposé,
la grande arche vitrée offre un net
contraste.

P 308.309

The wavelike form of the roof of the structure is visible in the elevation below and the section drawing on the right page.

Die Wellenform des Dachs wird im Aufriss unten und der Schnittzeichnung auf der rechten Seite deutlich sichtbar.

La forme ondoyante du toit du bâtiment est visible sur l'élévation ci-dessous et sur la coupe, page de droite.

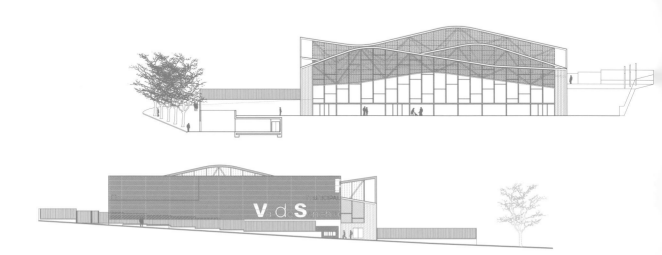

The curvature of the roof is echoed inside the main swimming-pool area.

Die geschwungene Kontur des Dachs ist auch im Innenraum des Schwimmbads erkennbar.

La courbure du toit se répercute à l'intérieur de la zone du grand bassin.

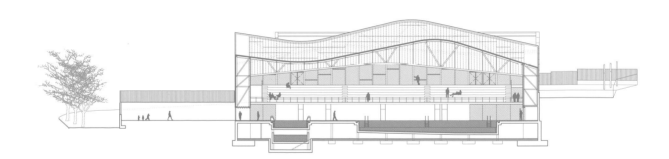

Concert House, Danish Radio ▶

JEAN NOUVEL

Ateliers Jean Nouvel / 10 Cité d'Angoulème / 75011 Paris / France
Tel: +33 1 49 23 83 83 / Fax: +33 1 43 14 81 10
E-mail: info@jeannouvel.fr / Web: www.jeannouvel.com

Born in 1945 in Fumel, France, **JEAN NOUVEL** studied in Bordeaux and then at the Paris École des Beaux-Arts (1964–72). From 1967 to 1970, he was an assistant of Claude Parent and Paul Virilio. In 1970, he created his first office with François Seigneur. Jean Nouvel received the RIBA Gold Medal in 2001. His first widely noticed project was the Institut du Monde Arabe (Paris, 1981–87, with Architecture Studio). Other works include his Nemausus Housing (Nîmes, 1985–87); Lyon Opera House (1986–93); Vinci Conference Center (Tours, 1989–93); Euralille Shopping Center (Lille, 1991–94); Fondation Cartier (Paris, 1991–94); Galeries Lafayette (Berlin, 1992–95), all in France unless stated otherwise. His unbuilt projects include the 400-meter-tall "Tour sans fin," La Défense (Paris, 1989); Grand Stade for the 1998 World Cup (Paris, 1994); and Tenaga Nasional Tower (Kuala Lumpur, 1995). In 2003, Jean Nouvel won a competition sponsored by the Aga Khan Trust for Culture for the design of the waterfront Corniche in Doha (Qatar), and was called on to design the new Guggenheim Museum in Rio de Janeiro (Brazil). His major completed projects since 2000 are the Music and Conference Center (Lucerne, Switzerland, 1998–2000); the Agbar Tower (Barcelona, Spain, 2001–03); social housing at the Cité Manifeste (Mulhouse, France, 2004); the extension of the Reina Sofia Museum (Madrid, Spain, 1999–2005); the Quai Branly Museum (Paris, France, 2001–06); an apartment building in SoHo (New York, New York, USA, 2006); and the Guthrie Theater (Minneapolis, Minnesota, USA, 2006). Current projects also include Les Bains des Docks (Le Havre, France, 2006–08, published here); the city hall in Montpellier (France, 2002–09); Concert House, Danish Radio (Copenhagen, Denmark, 2003–09, also published here); the new Philharmonic Hall in Paris (France); and the Louvre Abu Dhabi (UAE).

JEAN NOUVEL, geboren 1945 in Fumel, Frankreich, studierte zunächst in Bordeaux und anschließend an der Pariser École des Beaux-Arts (1964–72). Von 1967 bis 1970 war er Assistent von Claude Parent und Paul Virilio. 1970 gründete er sein erstes Büro mit François Seigneur. 2001 wurde er mit der RIBA-Goldmedaille ausgezeichnet. Sein erstes weithin bekannt gewordenes Projekt war das Institut du Monde Arabe (Paris, 1981–87, mit Architecture Studio). Weitere Arbeiten sind u. a. das Wohnbauprojekt Nemausus (Nîmes, 1985–87), die Oper in Lyon (1986–93), das Konferenzzentrum Vinci (Tours, 1989–93), das Einkaufszentrum Euralille (Lille, 1991–94), die Fondation Cartier (Paris, 1991–94) und die Galeries Lafayette (Berlin, 1992–95). Zu seinen nicht realisierten Bauten zählen der 400 m hohe „Tour sans fin" (Turm ohne Ende), La Défense (Paris, 1989), das Grand Stade für die Fußballweltmeisterschaften 1998 (Paris, 1994) sowie der Tenaga Nasional Tower (Kuala Lumpur, 1995). 2003 gewann Jean Nouvel einen Wettbewerb des Aga Khan Trust for Culture für eine Küstenstraße in Doha (Katar) und erhielt den Auftrag, das neue Guggenheim Museum in Rio de Janeiro zu entwerfen. Seine bedeutendsten realisierten Projekte seit 2000 sind das Kultur- und Kongresszentrum Luzern (Schweiz, 1998–2000), der Agbar-Turm (Barcelona, 2001–03), Sozialbauwohnungen in der Cité Manifeste (Mulhouse, Frankreich, 2004), die Erweiterung des Museums Reina Sofia (Madrid, 1999–2005), das Museum am Quai Branly (Paris, 2001–06), ein Apartmenthaus in SoHo (New York, 2006) sowie das Guthrie-Theater (Minneapolis, Minnesota, 2006). Zu den aktuellen Arbeiten gehören Les Bains des Docks (Le Havre, 2006–08, hier vorgestellt), das Rathaus in Montpellier (2002–09), das Konzerthaus für den dänischen Rundfunk (Kopenhagen, 2003–09, ebenfalls hier vorgestellt), die neue Philharmonie in Paris sowie der Louvre Abu Dhabi (VAE).

Né en 1945 à Fumel, en France, **JEAN NOUVEL** a étudié à Bordeaux, puis à l'École des beaux-arts de Paris (1964–72). De 1967 à 1970, il est assistant de Claude Parent et Paul Virilio. En 1970, il fonde sa première agence avec François Seigneur. Jean Nouvel a reçu la médaille d'or du RIBA en 2001. Sa première réalisation majeure reconnue a été l'Institut du monde arabe (Paris, 1981–87, avec Architecture Studio). Ses autres réalisations incluent l'ensemble de logements Nemausus (Nîmes, 1985–87) ; l'Opéra de Lyon (1986–93) ; le Centre de congrès Vinci (Tours, 1989–93) ; le Centre commercial Euralille (Lille, 1991–94) ; la Fondation Cartier (Paris, 1991–94) et les Galeries Lafayette (Berlin, 1992–95), toutes situées en France sauf mention contraire. Ses projets non réalisés incluent la « Tour sans fin » de La Défense, haute de 400 mètres (Paris, 1989) ; le Stade de France pour la Coupe du monde 1998 (Paris, 1994) ; et la tour Tenaga Nasional (Kuala Lumpur, 1995). En 2003, Jean Nouvel gagne un concours parrainé par l'agence de l'Aga Khan pour la Culture (Aga Khan Trust for Culture) pour l'aménagement du front de mer de la Corniche à Doha (Qatar), et est appelé à concevoir le nouveau musée Guggenheim à Rio de Janeiro (Brésil). Ses projets réalisés les plus importants depuis 2000 sont le Palais de la culture et des congrès de Lucerne (Suisse, 1998–2000) ; la tour Agbar à Barcelone (Espagne, 2001–03) ; des logements sociaux à la Cité Manifeste de Mulhouse (France, 2004) ; l'extension du musée Reina Sofia à Madrid (Espagne, 1999–2005) ; le musée du quai Branly à Paris (France, 2001–06) ; un immeuble d'appartements à SoHo (New York, 2006) ; et le Théâtre Guthrie à Minneapolis (Minnesota, États-Unis, 2006). Ses projets en cours incluent également Les Bains des Docks (Le Havre, France, 2006–08, publié ici) ; la nouvelle mairie de Montpellier (France, 2002–09) ; la salle de concert de la radio danoise à Copenhague (Danemark, 2003–09, également publié ici) ; la nouvelle Philharmonie de Paris (France) ; et le musée du Louvre Abou Dhabi (EAU).

CONCERT HOUSE, DANISH RADIO

Copenhagen, Denmark, 2003–09

*Address: Emil Holms Kanal 20, 0999 Copenhagen C, Denmark, +45 35 20 30 40, www.dr.dk/Koncerthuset
Area: 25 000 m². Client: DR Denmarks Radio. Cost: not disclosed
Team: Stephan Zopp, Brigitte Metra, Frédérique Monjanel*

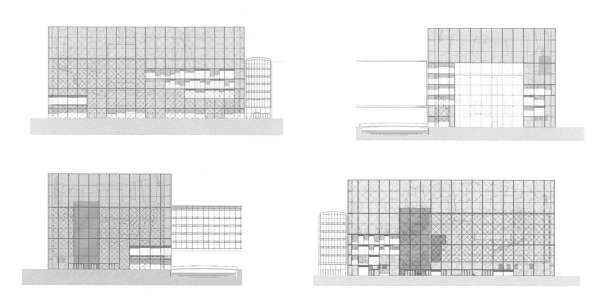

"In an uncertain future," writes Jean Nouvel, "our only choice is to respond using the positive force of uncertainty: mystery—mystery that is never far from seduction and thus, attraction." It is thus that he created a "mysterious parallelepiped" for the new **DANISH RADIO CONCERT HOUSE** in Copenhagen. The architect explains that the interior is like a street lined with shops, running along an urban canal. A covered square lies beneath the wood-clad concert hall. Nouvel is no stranger to the "spatial labyrinth," and in this instance he describes the interior as "Piranesian." In terms of more recent architecture, Nouvel evokes the spirit of the Danish architect Theodor Lauritzen and Hans Scharoun. The shimmering, blue, partially translucid façades of the building can be used at night to project images, and Nouvel's dark spaces spring to life with lights and mixed signs from the worlds of commerce and music.

„Angesichts einer unsicheren Zukunft", schreibt Jean Nouvel, „haben wir nur die Wahl, uns die positive Energie dieser Unsicherheit zunutze zu machen: das Geheimnis – ein Geheimnis, das nie weit davon entfernt ist, zu verführen und deshalb fasziniert." Deshalb entwarf Nouvel ein „geheimnisvolles Parallelepiped" für das neue **KONZERTHAUS DES DÄNISCHEN RUNDFUNKS** in Kopenhagen. Wie der Architekt erläutert, erinnert das Innere des Baus an eine von Geschäften gesäumte Straße an einem Kanal. Unterhalb des holzverkleideten Konzertsaals liegt eine überdachte Lobby. Nouvel ist das Konzept des „räumlichen Labyrinths" nicht fremd; in diesem Fall beschreibt er den Innenraum als „piranesisch". Blickt man auf die jüngere Architekturgeschichte zurück, so knüpft Nouvel hier an den Geist des dänischen Architekten Theodor Lauritzen oder an Hans Scharoun an. Auf die schimmernde, blaue, z. T. transparente Fassade des Baus lassen sich nachts Bilder projizieren: Dann erwachen Nouvels dunkle Räume durch die Lichter und die verschiedensten Zeichen aus der Welt der Werbung und Musik zum Leben.

« Au futur incertain », écrit Jean Nouvel, « on ne peut répondre que par la force positive de l'incertitude : le mystère. Le mystère qui n'est jamais loin de la séduction, donc de l'attractivité. » C'est ainsi qu'il a créé un « parallélépipède mystérieux » pour la nouvelle **SALLE DE CONCERT DE LA RADIO DANOISE** à Copenhague. L'architecte explique que l'intérieur est comme une rue bordée de commerces, suivant un canal urbain. Une place couverte s'étend sous la salle revêtue de bois. Nouvel s'y connaît en « labyrinthes spatiaux », et dans ce cas, il décrit l'intérieur comme « piranésien ». En termes d'architecture plus récente, Nouvel évoque l'esprit de l'architecte danois Theodor Lauritzen et de Hans Scharoun. Les façades chatoyantes, bleues et partiellement translucides, peuvent être utilisées la nuit pour y projeter des images, et les espaces sombres de Nouvel prennent vie avec les lumières et le mélange des signes du monde du commerce et de celui de la musique.

Although elevations of the building show its fundamentally rectilinear form, photos at night (right) translate an almost evanescent blue presence.

Zwar belegen die Aufrisse die primär rechtwinklige Form des Baus, dennoch vermitteln die Nachtaufnahmen (rechte Seite) fast den Eindruck eines sich auflösenden blauen Körpers.

Bien que les élévations du bâtiment montrent sa forme essentiellement rectiligne, celle-ci se traduit dans les photos de nuit (page de droite) par une présence bleue presque évanescente.

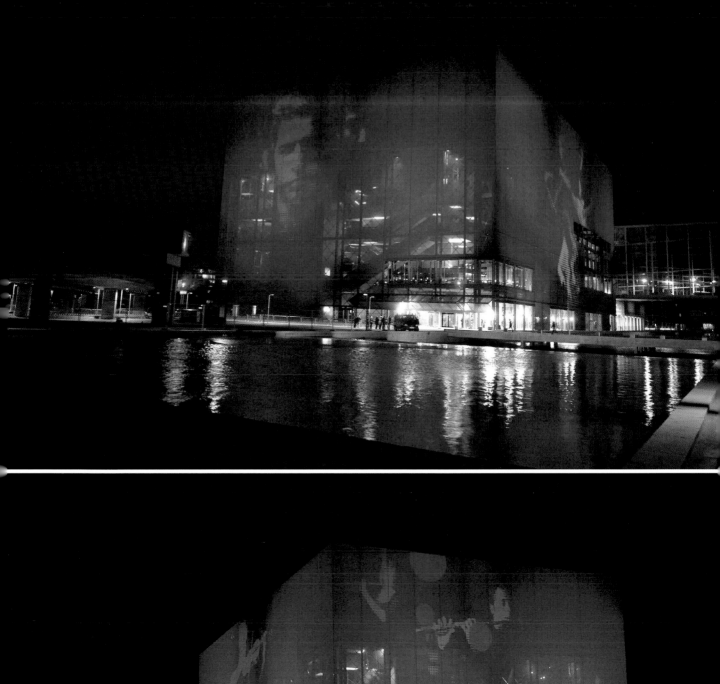

Concrete and glass are the main materials visible in this interior view at night, where colored lights enliven the space.

Beton und Glas sind die dominieren-den Materialien auf diesen nächtlichen Innenansichten. Farbiges Licht belebt die Räume.

Le béton et le verre sont les principaux matériaux visibles dans cette vue intérieure de nuit, où les éclairages colorés animent l'espace.

Interior volumes are generous for the most part, with unexpected lighting patterns visible, for example, on the escalators (right).

Die Innenräume sind zumeist großzügig bemessen. Überraschende Lichtmuster zeichnen sich unter anderem auf den Rolltreppen ab (rechts).

Les volumes intérieurs sont généreux pour la plupart, avec des motifs lumi-neux inattendus, par exemple sur les escaliers roulants (à droite).

Above, the main concert hall, which sits above an enclosed public square (below).

Oben der große Konzertsaal, der über einem umbauten öffentlichen Platz liegt (unten).

Ci-dessus, la grande salle de con-cert, située au-dessus d'une place publique intérieure (ci-dessous).

A plan shows the irregular form
of the concert hall. Below a recording
studio.

*Der Grundriss veranschaulicht die
unregelmäßigen Formen des Konzertsaals. Unten ein Aufnahmestudio.*

*Un plan montre la forme irrégulière
de la grande salle de concert.
Ci-dessous, un studio d'enregistrement.*

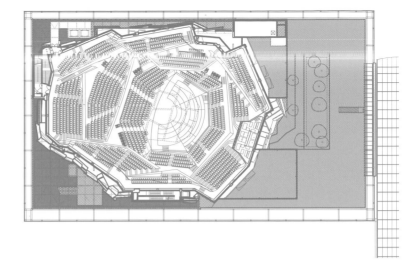

LES BAINS DES DOCKS

Le Havre, France, 2006–08

Address: Quai de la Réunion, 76600 Le Havre, France, +33 2 32 79 29 55,
www.vert-marine.com/les-bains-des-docks-le-havre-76
Area: 8600 m². Client: Mairie du Havre, CODAH. Cost: not disclosed
Collaboration: Mirco Tardio

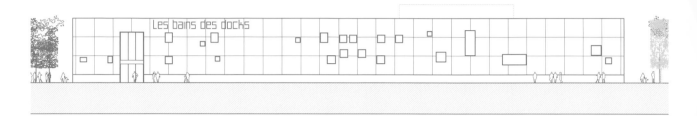

With a long history of port activity, today substantially reduced, Le Havre has undertaken a careful examination of it dockside areas, under the name Port 2000. Facilities such as the Chamber of Commerce, hotels, residences, a clinic, offices, and retail spaces are in the Works for these spaces, in the hope of bringing the port back to life. A new marina for 300 to 600 private boats provided the occasion for the conversion of the Bassin de la Citadelle, where restaurants, discothèques, and cafés are installed, also to be the location for an aquatic center with a 50-meter-long exterior pool, an interior/exterior pool and a bath therapy facility. A lobby with access to locker rooms is at ground level. Above, the pools are located near the administrative offices, a cafeteria, and a cardio-training area. Though other buildings are planned for the area, for the moment, the dark exterior volumes of the center give way to interior spaces made up of a surprising assembly of white geometric elements, a kind of interior world where water and relaxation are the rule.

Le Havre blickt auf eine lange Hafengeschichte zurück. Doch angesichts der stark reduzierten Hafentätigkeit musste sich die Stadt ausführlich mit der künftigen Nutzung dieser Areale auseinandersetzen. Das „Port 2000" genannte Programm sieht vor, Einrichtungen wie die Handelskammer, Hotels, Wohnungen, ein Krankenhaus, Büro- und Gewerbeflächen anzusiedeln, um die Gegend neu zu beleben. Ein neuer Jachthafen für 300 bis 600 Boote gab Anlass zum Umbau des Bassin de la Citadelle, wo es bereits Restaurants, Diskotheken und Cafés gab. Hier sollte ein Aquazentrum mit einem 50-m-Freibad, kombinierten Innen- und Außenbecken sowie Aquatherapieeinrichtungen entstehen. Die Eingangshalle mit Zugang zu den Schließfächern befindet sich im Erdgeschoss. Darüber liegen die Schwimmbecken sowie die Büros, eine Cafeteria und ein Bereich für Ausdauertraining. Obwohl geplant ist, weitere Bauten in der Gegend anzusiedeln, befindet sich hier derzeit nur Nouvels nach außen hin dunkles Aquazentrum, dessen Innenräume von einer überraschenden Kombination weißer geometrischer Formen gebildet werden. Die Innenwelt des Baus wird von Wasser und Entspannung bestimmt.

Avec une longue histoire d'activité portuaire, aujourd'hui fortement réduite, Le Havre a entrepris un examen minutieux des quartiers des quais à travers un projet intitulé «Port 2000». Des équipements comme la chambre de commerce, des hôtels, des logements, une clinique, des bureaux et des commerces font partie des grands travaux destinés à revitaliser le port. Une nouvelle marina pour 300 à 600 bateaux a fourni l'occasion d'une reconversion du bassin de la Citadelle, où se sont installés des restaurants, des discothèques et des cafés, qui devient aussi l'emplacement d'un centre aquatique avec une piscine à ciel ouvert de 50 mètres, une piscine couverte/découverte et un équipement de balnéothérapie. Un hall donnant accès aux vestiaires est situé au rez-de-chaussée. Au-dessus, les piscines sont situées près des bureaux administratifs, d'une cafétéria, et d'un espace de cardio-training. Bien que d'autres bâtiments soient planifiés dans cette zone, pour le moment, les volumes extérieurs sombres laissent place à des espaces intérieurs constitués d'un assemblage surprenant d'éléments géométriques blancs, une sorte de monde intérieur où l'eau et la détente sont la règle.

Seen from across the water, or in the elevation drawing above, the Bains structure resembles a warehouse, but its interior spaces are much more unexpected (right page).

Der Blick über das Wasser und der Aufriss oben lassen Les Bains fast wie eine Lagerhalle wirken. Im Innern jedoch präsentieren sich die Räume überraschend anders (rechte Seite).

Vu de l'autre côté du bassin des Docks ou dans l'élévation ci-dessus, le bâtiment des Bains ressemble à un entrepôt, mais ses espaces intérieurs sont beaucoup plus inattendus (page de droite).

Within a strictly rectangular plan,
the architect places the mostly-white
bath areas with their unexpected
cut-outs and views to other spaces.

*Im streng rechtwinkligen Grundriss
platzierte der Architekt die vorwiegend
weiß gehaltenen Badezonen mit
etlichen überraschenden Einschnitten
und Durchblicken in andere Bereiche.*

*C'est à l'intérieur d'un plan
strictement rectangulaire que l'architecte place des zones de baignade en
grande partie blanches, avec des
découpes inattendues et des vues
sur les autres espaces.*

A bathing area for children is placed next to a red seating area, contrasting with the mostly white environment. A waterfall and the orchestration of the volumes enliven the actual bath spaces.

Der Badebereich für Kinder liegt neben einer in Rottönen gehaltenen Ruhezone, die einen Kontrast zum zumeist weißen Umfeld bildet. Belebt wird der Schwimmbereich durch die Anordnung der einzelnen Volumina und einen Wasserfall.

Une zone de baignade pour enfants est située près d'un coin de repos rouge contrastant avec l'environnement majoritairement blanc. Une chute d'eau et l'agencement des volumes animent les espaces de baignade.

ONL

ONL [Oosterhuis_Lénárd] / Essenburgsingel 94c / 3022 EG Rotterdam / The Netherlands
Tel: +31 10 244 70 39 / Fax: +31 10 244 70 41
E-mail: oosterhuis@oosterhuis.nl / Web: www.oosterhuis.nl

ONL is described as a "multidisciplinary architectural firm where architects, visual artists, web designers, and programmers work together and join forces." Kas Oosterhuis was born in Amersfoort (The Netherlands) in 1951. He studied architecture at the Technical University in Delft (1970–79) and was a Unit Master at the Architectural Association (AA) in London in 1987–89. He has been a Professor at the Technical University in Delft since 2000. He is a member of the board of the Witte de With Museum in Rotterdam. He has built the Salt Water Pavilion (Neeltje Jans, Zeeland, 1994–97); the Multimedia Pavilion (North Holland Floriade, 2000–01); and Headquarters for True Colors (Utrecht, 2000–01). Ilona Lénárd is the other Principal of ONL [Oosterhuis_Lénárd]. A visual artist, she was born in Hungary, and then lived and worked in the Atelier Theo van Doesburg in Meudon, France (1988–89). She has worked with Kas Oosterhuis on various projects that involve a fusion of art and architecture. One notable recent project is the WTC 911, which proposes a "self-executable and programmable hi-res building that reconfigures its shape, content, and character during one year of its life cycle." Other work includes 9 Variomatic catalogue houses (Deventer, 2000); TT monument (Assen, 2000); and an Acoustic Barrier (Leidsche Rijn, Utrecht, 2002), all in the Netherlands. Oosterhuis has also worked on sophisticated projects that use engineering or game software to develop new types of space. ONL's "Protospace" project at the TU Delft involves creating virtual, interactive architecture. Their Acoustic Barrier, Ekris Showroom, and Hessing Cockpit (Leidsche Rijn Utrecht, 2000–05) developed the theme of a combined automotive sales facility and sound barrier. They are currently involved on the Space Xperience Center, Hato Airport (Curaçao, Netherlands Antilles, 2011–12, published here).

ONL versteht sich als „multidisziplinäres Architekturbüro, in dem Architekten, bildende Künstler, Webdesigner und Programmierer zusammenarbeiten und ihre Kräfte bündeln". Kas Oosterhuis wurde 1951 in Amersfoort (Niederlande) geboren. Er studierte Architektur an der Technischen Universität Delft (1970–79) und war von 1987 bis 1989 Unit Master an der Architectural Association (AA) in London. Seit 2000 ist er Professor an der Technischen Universität Delft. Darüber hinaus ist er Vorstandsmitglied des Museums Witte de With in Rotterdam. Zu seinen gebauten Projekten zählen ein Salzwasserpavillon (Neeltje Jans, Zeeland, 1994–97), ein Multimediapavillon (Noord-Holland Floriade, 2000–01) und die Geschäftszentrale für True Colors (Utrecht, 2000–01). Zweite Leiterin von ONL [Oosterhuis_Lénárd] ist Kas Oosterhuis Lénárd. Die bildende Künstlerin wurde in Ungarn geboren und lebte und arbeitete im Atelier Theo van Doesburg in Meudon, Frankreich (1988–89). Mit Kas Oosterhuis kooperierte sie bei zahlreichen Projekten an der Schnittstelle von Kunst und Architektur. Ein jüngeres Schlüsselprojekt des Teams ist WTC 911, „ein sich selbst generierendes und programmierendes Hi-Res-Gebäude, das sich in Form, Inhalt und Art im Ablauf eines Jahres seines Lebenzyklus neu konfiguriert". Andere Arbeiten sind neun Kataloghäuser, Typ „Variomatic" (Deventer, 2000), das TT-Monument (Assen, 2000) sowie eine Lärmschutzwand (Leidsche Rijn, Utrecht, 2002), alle in den Niederlanden. Oosterhuis hat außerdem an technisch aufwendigen Projekten gearbeitet, bei denen mithilfe von Computerspielsoftware neuartige Raumtypen entwickelt wurden. ONLs „Protospace"-Projekt an der TU Delft beschäftigt sich mit der Entstehung virtueller, interaktiver Architektur. Die Lärmschutzwand, der Showroom für Ekris sowie das Hessing Cockpit (Leidsche Rijn, Utrecht, 2000–05) bilden eine Kombination aus Autohaus und Lärmschutz. Derzeit arbeitet das Büro am Space Xperience Center am Flughafen Hato (Curaçao, Niederländische Antillen, 2011–12, hier vorgestellt).

ONL se décrit comme une « agence d'architecture multidisciplinaire où des architectes, des plasticiens, des concepteurs de sites web et des programmeurs travaillent ensemble et unissent leurs forces ». Kas Oosterhuis est né à Amersfoort (Pays-Bas) en 1951. Il étudie l'architecture à l'Université de technologie de Delft (1970–79), et a enseigné à l'Architectural Association (AA) de Londres (1987–89). Il est professeur à l'Université de technologie de Delft depuis 2000. Il est membre du conseil d'administration du musée Witte de With de Rotterdam. Il a réalisé le pavillon Salt Water (Neeltje Jans, Zélande, 1994–97), le pavillon multimédia de la Floriade (Hollande-Septentrionale, 2000–01) et le siège True Colors (Utrecht, 2000–01). Ilona Lénárd est l'autre directrice d'ONL [Oosterhuis_Lénárd]. Plasticienne née en Hongrie, elle a résidé et travaillé dans l'ancien atelier de Theo van Doesburg à Meudon, en France (1988–89). Elle travaille avec Kas Oosterhuis sur divers projets mêlant art et architecture. Un de leurs récents projets notables est le projet WTC 911 proposant un « bâtiment haute-résolution auto-programmable et auto-exécutable qui reconfigure sa forme, son contenu et sa personnalité au cours d'une année de son cycle de vie ». D'autres réalisations incluent neuf maisons Variomatic sur catalogue (Deventer, 2000), le monument TT (Assen, 2000) et une « barrière acoustique » (Leidsche Rijn, Utrecht, 2002), toutes situées aux Pays-Bas. Oosterhuis a également travaillé sur des projets utilisant des logiciels de jeux vidéos ou d'ingénierie pour développer de nouveaux types d'espace. Le projet « Protospace » d'ONL à l'Université de technologie de Delft fait appel à la création d'architecture virtuelle interactive. Leurs projets Acoustic Barrier, Ekris Showroom et Hessing Cockpit (Leidsche Rijn Utrecht, 2000–05) développent le thème d'une infrastructure combinant un magasin d'exposition automobile et une barrière acoustique. Ils participent actuellement au projet Space Xperience Center, de l'aéroport de Hato (Curaçao, Antilles néerlandaises, 2011–12, publié ici).

SPACE XPERIENCE CENTER

Hato Airport, Curaçao, Netherlands Antilles, 2011–12

Area: 10 000m². Client: Space Xperience Center. Cost: €50 million
Initiative: Ben Droste and Harry van Hulten

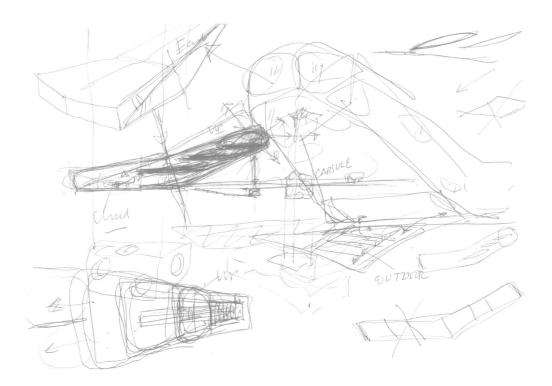

The ambition of the initiators Harry van Hulten and Ben Droste of **SPACE XPERIENCE CURACAO**© BV supported by the Curaçao authorities and entrepreneurs "is to create a major tourist attractor for the Caribbean, hosting the future operator for Galactic Travels, and offering a venue for international scientific space research." Several operators, including Richard Branson's Virgin Galactic, are potential users of the Spaceport. As has been the case of many of their recently designed projects, ONL here seems to have just the right futuristic style. Parametric modeling is used for all aspects of the design, including integrated furnishings. The profile of the building is meant to be visible and iconic. The project includes an open-air theater "cut out from the rocky coastal land and shaded by the lifted part of the structure. The actual body of the building is inspired by the form of the maple tree seed. Hangars are located in the base of the building. A guest lounge is situated in the higher part of the building, offering views of the Hato Airport runway. Though space travel for tourists is in its early phases, this project expresses a first, more "concrete" vision of what the point of departure might look like.

Das ehrgeizige Ziel der Initiatoren von **SPACE XPERIENCE CURAÇAO**© BV, Harry van Hulten und Ben Droste, die von Behörden und Unternehmern auf Curaçao unterstützt werden, ist „die Schaffung einer Plattform für zukünftige Reisen ins Weltall sowie eines Standorts für wissenschaftliche Weltraumforschung und damit einer neuen Haupttouristenattraktion für die Karibik". Verschiedene Anbieter, einschließlich Richard Bransons Firma Virgin Galactic, sind die potenziellen Nutzer des Weltraumbahnhofs. Wie bei zahlreichen ihrer neuen Entwürfe, so scheint ONL auch hier das richtige Maß an Futurismus zu zeigen. Für sämtliche Bestandteile des Entwurfs, einschließlich der integrierten Möbel, wurde mit parametrischen Entwurfswerkzeugen gearbeitet. Das Profil des Bauwerks zielt darauf ab, weithin sichtbar und unverwechselbar zu sein. Es umfasst ein Amphitheater, das „aus der felsigen Küstenlandschaft herausgeschlagen" und vom schwebenden Überhang des Bauwerks beschattet wird. Die Form des Baukörpers wurde von Ahornsamen inspiriert. Im unteren Teil des Gebäudes sind Hangars untergebracht, im oberen Bereich liegt eine Besucherlounge, die Blick auf die Start- und Landebahnen des Flughafens Hato bietet. Obwohl touristische Reisen in den Weltraum noch weitgehend Zukunftsmusik sind, vermittelt dieses Projekt eine erste Ahnung, wie ein solcher Abflughafen aussehen könnte.

L'ambition des initiateurs du projet, Harry van Hulten et Ben Droste de **SPACE XPERIENCE CURACAO**© BV, soutenu par les autorités de Curaçao et des entreprises privées, « est de créer une attraction touristique majeure pour les Caraïbes, et un lieu d'accueil pour le futur opérateur de Galactic Travels et la recherche spatiale internationale ». Plusieurs opérateurs, dont Virgin Galactic, la compagnie de Richard Branson, sont des utilisateurs potentiels du futur spatioport. Comme pour nombre de ses projets récents, ONL semble avoir ici le style futuriste qui convient. La modélisation paramétrique a été utilisée pour tous les aspects du projet, y compris le mobilier intégré. La silhouette du bâtiment se veut évidente et symbolique. Le projet comprend une salle à ciel ouvert « taillée dans le terrain côtier rocailleux, et ombragée par la partie surélevée du bâtiment. La forme du corps du bâtiment s'inspire du fruit de l'érable. Les hangars sont situés à la base du bâtiment. Un salon se trouve dans la partie haute du bâtiment, offrant une vue sur la piste de l'aéroport de Hato. Bien que le tourisme spatial soit encore dans sa phase naissante, ce projet exprime une première vison, plus « concrète », de ce à quoi pourra ressembler le point d'embarquement.

As befits the concept of a spaceport, the architecture is clearly futuristic. A sketch on the left page shows that the architect sometimes resorts to the pencil as opposed to the computer.

Dem Konzept eines Raumfahrtbahnhofs angemessen, wirkt die Architektur klar futuristisch. Die Skizze auf der linken Seite belegt, dass die Architekten mitunter zum Stift greifen, statt am Computer zu arbeiten.

Comme il convient au concept de spatioport, l'architecture est nettement futuriste. Une esquisse, page de gauche, montre que l'architecte recourt parfois au crayon plutôt qu'à l'ordinateur.

PERKINS EASTMAN

Perkins Eastman
115 Fifth Avenue
New York, NY 10003
USA

Tel: +1 212 353 7200
Fax: +1 212 353 7676
E-mail: info@perkinseastman.com
Web: www.perkinseastman.com

PERKINS EASTMAN was founded in 1981 by Bradford Perkins, who was the Principal in Charge of the TKTS Booth project published here (New York, New York, USA, 2006–08), and Mary-Jean Eastman. Nicholas Leahy was born in 1963 in Billericay, England. He received his graduate diploma in Architecture from Oxford Brookes University (Headington, Oxford). He is a Principal of Perkins Eastman and was the Lead Architect for the TKTS project. The firm's work includes Brooklyn Supreme and Family Courthouse (Brooklyn, New York, 2004); American Museum of Natural History Hall of Human Origins (New York, New York, 2006); Sun City Ginza East (Tokyo, Japan, 2006); Victorinox/Swiss Army Brands Headquarters (Monroe, Connecticut, 2007); Hopkins-Nanjing University: Center for Chinese and American Studies (Nanjing, China, 2007); Centria at 18 West 48th Street (New York, New York, 2007); Concordia International School (Shanghai, China, 2007); Chongqing Library (Chongqing, China, 2007); the Evelyn H. Lauder Breast Center of Memorial Sloan-Kettering Cancer Center (MSKCC) and MSKCC Imaging Center (New York, New York, 2009); and Greater Hanoi Development Master Plan (Hanoi, Vietnam, 2010), all in the USA unless stated otherwise.

PERKINS EASTMAN wurde 1981 von Mary-Jean Eastman und Bradford Perkins gegründet, der als geschäftsführender Partner das hier vorgestellte TKTS-Projekt leitete (New York, 2006–08). Nicholas Leahy wurde 1963 in Billericay, England, geboren. Er machte sein Diplom in Architektur an der Oxford Brookes University (Headington, Oxford). Leahy ist ebenfalls geschäftsführender Partner bei Perkins Eastman und war als Chefarchitekt für das TKTS-Projekt verantwortlich. Arbeiten des Büros sind u. a. der Oberste Gerichtshof und das Familiengericht Brooklyn (Brooklyn, New York, 2004), der Saal zur Entstehung der Menschheit im American Museum of Natural History (New York, 2006), Sun City Ginza East (Tokio, Japan, 2006), die amerikanische Hauptniederlassung von Victorinox (Monroe, Connecticut, 2007), das Zentrum für China- und Amerikastudien der Hopkins-Nanjing University (Nanjing, China, 2007), das Apartmentgebäude Centria, 18 West 48th Street (New York, 2007), die Concordia International School (Shanghai, China, 2007), die Bibliothek Chongqing (Chongqing, China, 2007), das Evelyn H. Lauder Brustzentrum am Memorial Sloan-Kettering Cancer Center (MSKCC) sowie das Röntgenzentrum am MSKCC (New York, 2009) und schließlich der Masterplan für den Großraum Hanoi (Vietnam, 2010).

PERKINS EASTMAN a été fondé en 1981 par Bradford Perkins, directeur du projet TKTS Booth publié ici (New York, 2006–08) et Mary-Jean Eastman. Nicholas Leahy est né en 1963 à Billericay, en Angleterre. Il est diplômé en architecture de l'université Brookes d'Oxford (Headington, Oxford). Il est un des directeurs de Perkins Eastman et architecte principal du projet TKTS. Les réalisations de l'agence incluent l'immeuble de la Supreme and Family Courthouse à Brooklyn (New York, 2004) ; la rénovation de la salle des origines de l'humanité du Muséum d'histoire naturelle américain (New York, 2006) ; le Centre Sun City de Ginza East (Tokyo, Japon, 2006) ; le siège de Victorinox/Swiss Army Brands (Monroe, Connecticut, 2007) ; le Centre d'études sino-américaines des universités Hopkins et de Nanjing (Nanjing, Chine, 2007) ; la tour Centria, à l'intersection de la 18e Avenue ouest et de la 48e Rue (New York, 2007) ; l'École internationale Concordia (Shanghai, Chine, 2007) ; la bibliothèque de Chongqing (Chongqing, Chine, 2007), le Evelyn H. Lauder Breast Center pour le Memorial Sloan-Kettering Cancer Center (MSKCC) et le Centre d'imagerie MSKCC (New York, 2009) ; et le plan directeur pour le développement du Grand Hanoï (Hanoï, Vietnam, 2010), toutes situées aux États-Unis sauf mention contraire.

TKTS BOOTH AND THE REVITALIZATION OF FATHER DUFFY SQUARE

New York, New York, USA, 2006–08

*Address: 1560 Broadway, New York, NY 10036–1518, USA, www.timessquarenyc.org
Area: 79 m². Clients: Times Square Alliance, Theatre Development Fund, Coalition for Father Duffy, and City of New York
Cost: not disclosed*

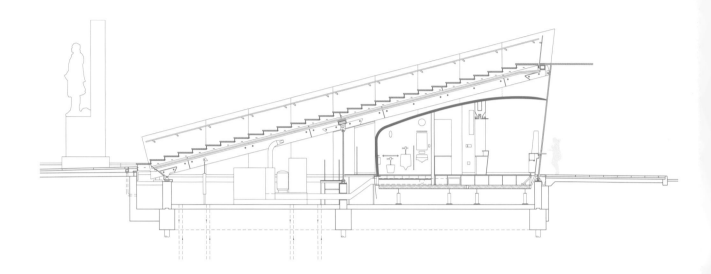

Operated by the Theatre Development Fund, this very visible project is a discount outlet for tickets to Broadway and off-Broadway shows. A red glass roof with 27 steps encloses a fiberglass shell. The steps can support up to 500 people. The entire building is built with glass, including 8.5-meter-long glass beams, making it the largest load-bearing glass building in the world. LEDs illuminate the staircase from below the steps, while a geothermal system with radiant panels that provide heating and cooling assure a low-energy profile. The booth was fabricated by the shipbuilders Merrifield Roberts. The TKTS Booth was designed by Perkins Eastman, inspired by the Van Alen Institute Design Competition-winning entry by the Australian-based firm Choi Ropiha, who had envisaged using red resin. William Fellows Architects, now part of PSKB Architects, designed the plaza of Father Duffy Square.

Das vom Theatre Development Fund betriebene, höchst prominent platzierte Projekt ist eine Theaterkasse für günstige Tickets für Broadway- and Off-Broadway-Shows. Ein rotes Glasdach mit 27 Stufen umschließt das Glasfasergehäuse. Die Stufen bieten bis zu 500 Personen Platz. Die gesamte Konstruktion besteht aus Glas, einschließlich der 8,5 m langen Träger, was sie zum größten tragenden Glasbauwerk der Welt macht. LED-Dioden unter den Stufen beleuchten die Treppe, während ein Erdwärmesystem mit Flächenheizung bei geringem Energieverbrauch für Wärme bzw. Kühlung sorgt. Gefertigt wurde das Gebäude vom Schiffsbauer Merrifield Roberts. Das Design der Theaterkasse von Perkins Eastman wurde von einem Entwurf des australischen Büros Choi Ropiha inspiriert, der ursprünglich in rotem Kunstharz hätte ausgeführt werden sollen und den ersten Preis beim Entwurfswettbewerb des Van Alen Institute gewonnen hatte. William Fellows Architects, inzwischen in PSKB Architects aufgegangen, gestaltete die Plaza des Father Duffy Square.

Ce projet très visible, est un kiosque de billets à tarifs réduits, exploité par le Theatre Development Fund, pour les spectacles programmés à Broadway ou « off-Brodway ». Un escalier vitré rouge de vingt-sept marches surplombe une coque en fibre de verre. Les marches peuvent accueillir 500 personnes. L'édifice entièrement en verre, y compris des poutres de 8,5 mètres, est le bâtiment en verre supportant la plus grosse charge au monde. Des LEDs illuminent l'escalier par-dessous les marches et un système géothermique associé à des panneaux assurant un chauffage et un refroidissement par rayonnement garantit un bas profil énergétique. Le kiosque a été fabriqué par le constructeur naval Merrifield Roberts. Le kiosque TKTS a été conçu par Perkins Eastman, qui s'est inspiré du projet de la société australienne Choi Ropiha, lauréate du concours lancé par l'Institut Van Alen, qui avait prévu d'utiliser une résine rouge. Et c'est l'agence William Fellows Architects, maintenant intégrée à PSKB Architects, qui a conçu la place de Father Duffy Square.

The relatively simple, double-function platform has an obviously central location in Times Square, one of the busiest areas in Manhattan.

Das vergleichsweise schlichte, doppelfunktionale Podium liegt mitten auf dem Times Square, einem der belebtesten Gegenden Manhattans.

La plateforme relativement simple, dotée d'une double fonction, occupe une place nettement centrale sur Times Square, un des quartiers les plus animés de Manhattan.

DOMINIQUE PERRAULT

Dominique Perrault Architecture / 6 rue Bouvier / 75011 Paris / France
Tel: +33 1 44 06 00 00 / Fax: +33 1 44 06 00 01
E-mail: dpa@d-p-a.fr / Web: www.perraultarchitecte.com

DOMINIQUE PERRAULT was born in 1953 in Clermont-Ferrand, France. He studied in Paris and received his diploma as an architect from the École des Beaux-Arts in 1978. He received a further degree in Urbanism at the École nationale des Ponts et Chaussées in 1979, as well as a Master's in History at the EHESS (École des hautes études en sciences sociales) in 1980. He created his own firm in 1981 in Paris. His first well publicized works were the Engineering School (ESIEE) in Marne-la-Vallée (1984–87); the Hôtel industriel Berlier (Paris, 1986–90); the Applix factory in Cellier-sur-Loire (1991–99), all in France; and the Town Hall / Hybrid Hotel (Innsbruck, Austria, 2000–02). His most significant projects include the French National Library in Paris (1989–95); and the Olympic Velodrome, Swimming and Diving Pool (Berlin, Germany, 1992–99). Recent buildings include the Media Library in Vénissieux (France, 1997–2001); the design of several supermarkets for the M-Preis chain in Austria (1999–2003); the master plan for Donau City in Vienna (Austria, 2002–03); and the refurbishment of Piazza Gramsci (Cinisello Balsamo, Milan, Italy, 1999–2004). More recent projects include the Habitat Sky Tower in Barcelona (Spain, 2002–07); the Olympic Tennis Center in Madrid (Spain, 2002–07); the Ewha Women's University in Seoul (South Korea, 2004–07); a redesign of the urban waterfront "Las Teresitas" (2000–06), and the construction of a five-star hotel (2000–08), both in Tenerife (Canary Islands); the Sky Tower in Vienna (Austria, 2004–08); an extension of the Court of Justice of the European Union (Luxembourg, 2004–08, published here); the redevelopment of the banks of the Manzanares in Madrid (Spain, 2005–08); Priory Park Pavilion (Reigate, UK, 2007–08, also published here); and the new Mariinsky Theatre (Saint Petersburg, Russia, 2003–09).

DOMINIQUE PERRAULT wurde 1953 in Clermont-Ferrand geboren. Er studierte in Paris und machte sein Architekturdiplom 1978 an der École des Beaux-Arts. 1979 folgte eine weiterer Abschluss in Städtebau an der École Nationale des Ponts et Chaussées sowie 1980 ein Master in Geschichte an der EHESS (École des Hautes Études en Sciences Sociales). 1981 gründete er sein Büro in Paris. Seine ersten weithin publizierten Arbeiten waren die Hochschule für Bauingenieurwesen (ESIEE) in Marne-la-Vallée (1984–87), das Hôtel industriel Berlier (Paris, 1986–90), das Applix-Werk in Cellier-sur-Loire (1991–99) sowie der Rathauskomplex in Innsbruck (2000–02). Seine bedeutendsten Projekte sind u. a. die Französische Nationalbibliothek in Paris (1989–95) sowie das Velodrom und die Schwimm- und Sprunghalle in Berlin (1992–99). Zu seinen neueren Bauten gehören u. a. die Mediathek in Vénissieux (Frankreich, 1997–2001), mehrere Filialen der Supermarktkette MPreis in Österreich (1999–2003), der Masterplan für die Donau City in Wien (2002–03) und die Sanierung der Piazza Gramsci (Cinisello Balsamo, Mailand, 1999–2004). Aktuelle Projekte sind der Habitat Sky Tower in Barcelona (2002–07), das Olympische Tenniscenter in Madrid (2002–07), die Frauenuniversität Ewha in Seoul (Südkorea, 2004–07), auf Teneriffa die Neugestaltung der Promenade „Las Teresitas" (2000–06) und ein Fünfsternehotel (2000–08), der Sky Tower in Wien (2004–08), die Erweiterung des Europäischen Gerichtshofs (Luxemburg, 2004–08, hier vorgestellt), die Neuerschließung der Ufer des Manzanares in Madrid (2005–08), der Priory-Park-Pavillon (Reigate, Großbritannien, 2007–08, ebenfalls hier vorgestellt) sowie das neue Marijinski-Theater (St. Petersburg, Russland, 2003–09).

DOMINIQUE PERRAULT est né en 1953 à Clermont-Ferrand. Il étudie à Paris et obtient son diplôme de l'École des beaux-arts en 1978. Il obtient aussi un diplôme en urbanisme à l'École nationale des ponts et chaussées en 1979, ainsi qu'une maîtrise d'histoire à l'École des hautes études en sciences sociales en 1980. Il fonde sa propre agence en 1981 à Paris. Ses premières réalisations remarquées sont l'École supérieure d'ingénieurs en électrotechnique et électronique (ESIEE) de Marne-la-Vallée (1984–87), l'hôtel industriel Jean-Baptiste Berlier (Paris, 1986–90), l'usine Applix à Cellier-sur-Loire (1991–99), toutes situées en France, et l'hôtel de ville/hôtel Hybrid d'Innsbruck (Innsbruck, Autriche, 2000–02). Ses réalisations les plus marquantes incluent la Bibliothèque nationale de France (1989–95) ; et le vélodrome et la piscine olympique de Berlin (1992–99). Ses récentes réalisations incluent la médiathèque de Vénissieux (France, 1997–2001) ; plusieurs supermarchés M-Preis, en Autriche (1999–2003) ; le plan directeur pour Donau, à Vienne (2002–03) ; et le réaménagement de la Piazza Gramsci (Cinisello Balsamo, Milan, Italie, 1999–2004). Ses projets plus récents incluent la tour Habitat Sky à Barcelone (Espagne, 2002–07) ; le Centre olympique de tennis de Madrid (2002–07) ; l'université féminine d'Ewha, à Seoul (Corée du Sud, 2004–07) ; la restructuration du front de mer « Las Teresitas » (2000–06) et la construction d'un hôtel 5 étoiles (2000–08), tous deux à Ténérife (îles Canaries) ; la tour Sky, à Vienne (2004–08) ; une extension de la Cour de justice des Communautés européennes (Luxembourg, 2004–08, publié ici) ; la restructuration des rives du Manzanares, à Madrid (2005–08) ; le pavillon du Priory Park (Reigate, Royaume-Uni, 2007–08, également publié ici) ; et le Théâtre Mariinsky II (Saint-Pétersbourg, Russie, 2003–09).

PRIORY PARK PAVILION

Reigate, UK, 2007–08

Address: Bell Street, Reigate, Surrey RH2 7RL, UK
Area: 350 m². Clients: Reigate and Banstead Borough Council. Cost: €1.172 million
Local Architects: CRGP Architects

Dominique Perrault won the international competition organized for this project in 2005. As he says, it "questions in a playful way the uncertain limit between architecture and landscape." Indeed, this work has at least a superficial resemblance with works of art by Dan Graham, who plays on reflection, opacity, and transparency. Floor-to-ceiling glazing arranged in a "zigzag pattern," together with vertical elements clad in mirror-polished stainless steel, make the point of transition between exterior and interior all the more ambiguous. The pavilion is meant for entertainment events, or even "tranquility and contemplation," as the architect says. This relatively small project shows the range of Perrault's creative capacity, often focused more on large buildings or complexes.

Dominique Perrault gewann den internationalen Wettbewerb für dieses Projekt 2005. Ihm zufolge „hinterfragt er auf spielerische Weise die fließende Grenze zwischen Architektur und Landschaft". Tatsächlich erinnert das Bauwerk zumindest auf den ersten Blick an Kunstwerke von Dan Graham, der mit Spiegelungen, Opazität und Transparenz spielt. Die zu einem „Zickzackmuster" angeordnete, deckenhohe Verglasung, in Kombination mit Längselementen aus hochglanzpoliertem Edelstahl, lässt den Übergang zwischen Innen- und Außenraum höchst mehrdeutig werden. Geplant wurde der Pavillon für Veranstaltungen, laut Aussage des Architekten jedoch auch für „stille Momente und Kontemplation". Das vergleichsweise kleine Projekt stellt die Bandbreite der Kreativität Perraults unter Beweis, die oftmals eher in Großbauten ihren Ausdruck findet.

Dominique Perrault a gagné le concours international organisé pour ce projet en 2005. Comme il le dit : « il questionne d'une manière ludique la limite incertaine entre architecture et paysage ». En effet, ce projet ressemble, au moins superficiellement, aux œuvres de Dan Graham, qui jouent sur la réflexion, l'opacité et la transparence. Un vitrage du sol au plafond, disposé selon un « motif en zigzag », et des éléments verticaux revêtus d'acier inoxydable poli, font un point de transition d'autant plus ambigu entre l'extérieur et l'intérieur. Le pavillon est destiné à des spectacles ou même, selon l'architecte, à « la tranquillité et la contemplation ». Ce projet relativement petit montre l'étendue des capacités créatives de Perrault, plus souvent concentrées sur de grands bâtiments ou de grands ensembles.

A section shows the simplicity of the structure, rendered somewhat less minimalist by the layered placement of the full-height glazing (right).

Ein Querschnitt belegt die Schlichtheit der Konstruktion, die durch die Überschneidungen der deckenhohen Glassegmente jedoch wieder weniger minimalistisch wirkt (rechte Seite).

Une coupe montre la simplicité de la structure, dont le minimalisme est un peu atténué par la disposition en zigzag des vitres de pleine hauteur qui se chevauchent (page de droite).

The somewhat enigmatic appearance of the Pavilion contrasts to some extent with the exuberant colors and unexpected vortex-like column seen in the image below.

Die fast rätselhafte Erscheinung des Pavillons kontrastiert in gewisser Weise mit den leuchtenden Farben und der überraschenden, an einen Strudel erinnernden Stütze im Bild unten.

L'aspect quelque peu énigmatique du pavillon contraste avec les couleurs exubérantes et la surprenante colonne en forme de vortex, visible sur la photo ci-dessous.

The round shape of the building is echoed in the floor pattern and the desk seen above (right). The floor plan shows the irregular disposition of the interior spaces.

Die Kreisform des Pavillons wird im Muster des Bodenbelags oder dem Empfangstresen oben (rechts) wieder aufgegriffen. Der Grundriss zeigt die unregelmäßige Aufteilung des Innenraums.

Ci-dessus, la forme arrondie du bâtiment est reprise dans le motif du sol ainsi que dans le comptoir, à droite. Le plan montre la disposition irrégulière des espaces intérieurs.

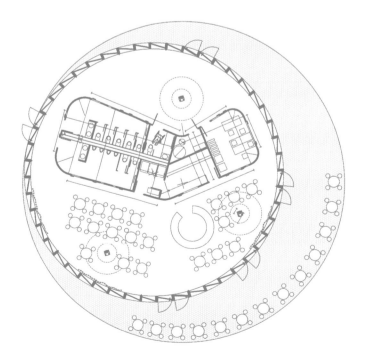

COURT OF JUSTICE OF THE EUROPEAN UNION EXTENSION

Luxembourg, Luxembourg, 2004–08

Address: Rue du Fort Niedergrünewald, 2925 Luxembourg, Luxembourg
Area: 100 000 m². Client: European Court of Justice. Cost: € 350 million
Associated Architects: Bureau CJ4 (Dominique Perrault Architecte, Paczowski & Fritsch, m3 architectes)

The architects won this project, located on the Kirchberg Plateau, in a 1996 international competition. The scheme involved tripling the Court's capacity, and the rehabilitation, including asbestos removal, for the original 20 000-square-meter building. First inaugurated in 1973, when the European Community included only six member states, the **COURT OF JUSTICE** had already been extended in 1988, 1993, and 1994. An extra 100 000 square meters to house 2000 judges, clerks, and translators were required. The original building, made of Cor-ten steel, was hollowed out to accommodate courtrooms, and is encircled by an orthogonal ring containing offices, chambers for the judges and advocate generals, and the Great Hall of Justice. Dominique Perrault used anodized, gold-tinted, aluminum mesh for sun-shades on the two towers, a screen for the judges' chambers, and on the ceiling of the main courtroom, giving material unity to the entire, originally disparate complex. The 24-story towers are both 107 meters high and house the 600-strong translation services, with a further 5000-square-meter structure at their base for administrative offices, services, and archives. The 24 131-square-meter Gallery structure is described as the "vertebral column" that creates the functional unity between the existing buildings and the newer construction. It contains restaurants, a library, professional training rooms, and public services such as kiosks and banks, and provides direct access to the towers, the ring, and the Courthouse. A 700-car parking facility is reserved for Court members.

Mit diesem Projekt auf dem Kirchberg-Plateau konnten sich die Architekten 1996 in einem internationalen Wettbewerb durchsetzen. Ziel war es, die räumliche Kapazität des Gerichtshofs zu verdreifachen und zugleich den 20 000 m² großen Altbau zu sanieren (einschließlich Asbestsanierung). Seit seiner Einweihung 1973, als die Europäische Gemeinschaft neun Mitgliedsstaaten hatte, war der **GERICHTSHOF** bereits dreimal erweitert worden: 1988, 1993 und 1994. Nun waren weitere 100 000 m² Fläche gefordert, um 2000 Richter, Verwaltungsbeamte und Übersetzer unterbringen zu können. Der aus Cor-Ten-Stahl errichtete Altbau wurde entkernt, um Platz für Gerichtssäle zu schaffen. Ergänzt wurde der Komplex um einen Ringbau mit Büroräumen, Kammern für die Richter und Generalanwälte sowie den zentralen Gerichtssaal. Als Sonnenschutz für beide Hochhaustürme sowie bei den Wandschirmen vor den Kammern und bei der Decke im zentralen Gerichtssaal verwendete Dominique Perrault goldfarbenes, eloxiertes Aluminiumgewebe. Durch dieses gemeinsame Material gewann der ursprünglich disparate Komplex an Homogenität. Die beiden 24-stöckigen Türme sind je 107 m hoch und bieten Platz für die Übersetzerteams mit ihren 600 Mitarbeitern. Auf 5000 m² zusätzlicher Grundfläche unterhalb der Türme sind die Büros der Verwaltung, Dienstleistungen und Archive untergebracht. Die 24 131 m² große sogenannte Galerie gilt als „Rückgrat" des Komplexes und sorgt für die funktionale Einheit der Alt- und Neubauten. Hier befinden sich Restaurants, eine Bibliothek, Ausbildungsräume und öffentliche Dienstleistungen wie Kiosks oder Banken. Darüber hinaus bietet die Galerie Zugang zu den Türmen, zum Ringbau und zum Gerichtsgebäude. Der Parkplatz für 700 Fahrzeuge ist den Mitarbeitern des Gerichtshofs vorbehalten.

Les architectes ont gagné ce projet situé sur le plateau du Kirchberg en 1996, à l'issue d'un concours international. Le programme prévoyait de tripler la capacité de la Cour, et de réhabiliter (désamiantageinclus) les 20 000 mètres carrés du bâtiment d'origine. Inaugurée en 1973, alors que la Communauté européenne ne réunissait que six États membres, la **COUR DE JUSTICE** avait déjà été agrandi en 1988, 1993 et 1994. Cent mille mètres carrés supplémentaires étaient nécessaires pour héberger les 2000 juges, greffiers et traducteurs. Le bâtiment d'origine, en acier Corten, qui a été évidé pour accueillir des salles d'audience, est encerclé d'un anneau orthogonal contenant des bureaux, des cabinets pour les juges et avocats généraux et la grande salle des délibérés. Le grillage d'aluminium anodisé doré, utilisé par Dominique Perrault dans les brise-soleil des deux tours, un écran pour les cabinets des juges et au plafond de la grande salle d'audience, apporte une unité matérielle à un ensemble disparate à l'origine. Les deux tours de vingt-quatre étages et de 107 mètres de haut chacune hébergent les services des 600 traducteurs. À leur pied, un autre bâtiment de 5000 mètres carrés héberge des bureaux, les services administratifs et les archives. Une galerie de 24 131 mètres carrés, décrite comme « l'épine dorsale » du projet, crée une unité fonctionnelle entre les bâtiments existants et les nouvelles constructions. Elle contient des restaurants, une bibliothèque, des salles de formation, des kiosques à journaux et des agences bancaires et autres services, et donne directement accès aux tours, à l'anneau et au palais. Un parc de stationnement de 700 places est réservé aux membres de la Cour.

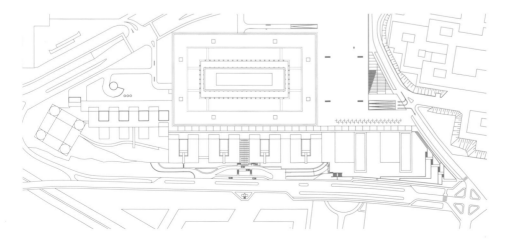

An overall plan of the complex shows the orthogonal disposition of the elements. To the right, Perrault renders the buildings more complex and unexpected by using gold-tinted aluminum mesh.

Der Grundriss zeigt die rechtwinklige Anordnung der einzelnen baulichen Elemente. Durch Einsatz goldfarbener Aluminiumgitter verleiht Perrault den Gebäuden eine komplexere und ungewöhnliche Erscheinung.

Un plan d'ensemble du complexe montre la disposition orthogonale des éléments. Par l'utilisation d'un grillage d'aluminium doré (page de droite), Perrault donne un aspect plus complexe et plus inattendu aux bâtiments.

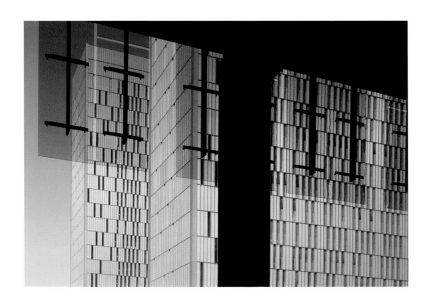

Perrault's towers are strictly rectangular blocks and yet their cladding gives them an irregular appearance that changes according to the angle of view.

Perraults Türme sind strenge, rechteckige Blöcke, die jedoch dank ihrer Verblendung – je nach Standpunkt – unregelmäßig wirken.

Les tours de Perrault sont strictement parallélépipédiques et pourtant leur revêtement leur donne une apparence variant selon le point de vue.

Elevations and a general view (below) show the rapport between the long, low-lying volume of the Court and its high towers.

Aufriss und Gesamtansicht (unten) verdeutlichen den Bezug zwischen dem langgestreckten, niedrigen Gerichtsgebäude und den hoch aufragenden Türmen.

Les élévations et une vue d'ensemble (ci-dessous) montrent la relation entre le long volume bas du palais et ses hautes tours.

Perrault mixes his very personal
brand of strong and present architecture with a sense for the efficient
operation of the buildings. Below,
section drawings show the low-lying
preexisting renovated structures vis-
à-vis the towers.

Perrault verbindet seine sehr persön-
liche, eindringliche Architektur, die
von starker Präsenz ist, mit einem
Gespür für die funktionale
Nutzbarkeit der Bauten. Querschnitte
(unten) zeigen die sanierten niedrigen
Altbauten vis à vis der Türme.

Perrault allie un style très personnel
d'architecture, puissante et actuelle,
avec un sens de l'efficacité fonctionnelle des bâtiments. Ci-dessous, des
sections montrent les bâtiments bas
d'origine rénovés, face aux tours.

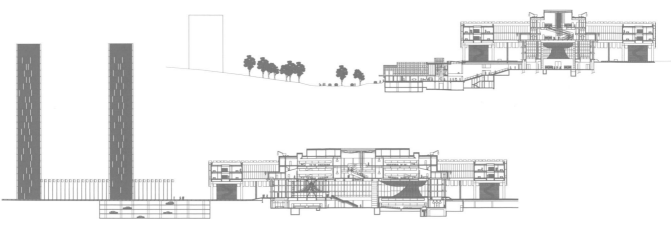

Drawings from the office of Dominique Perrault show the shimmering gold color intended for the buildings. Below, a contrast between white in the lower areas and black window frames or roof details.

Zeichnungen aus Dominique Perraults Studio zeigen die für die Bauten vorgesehene schimmernde Goldtönung. Unten ein Schwarz-Weiß-Kontrast zwischen der unteren Zone und den schwarzen Fensterrahmen sowie der Dachkonstruktion.

Les dessins provenant de l'agence de Dominique Perrault montrent la couleur dorée scintillante prévue pour les bâtiments. Ci-dessous, le contraste entre le blanc des parties basses et le noir des fenêtres ou des détails de la toiture.

Above, left, the great chandelier of the main Palace entrance. Above, right, main courtroom view from the Palace entrance stairs. Below, the main courtroom.

Oben links der große Kronleuchter in der Hauptlobby des Gerichtshofs. Rechts ein Blick in den zentralen Gerichtssaal von der Treppe des Hauptgebäudes. Unten der Hauptgerichtssaal.

Ci-dessus à gauche, le grand lustre de l'entrée du palais. Ci-dessus à droite, la grande salle d'audience vue de l'escalier d'entrée du palais. Ci-dessous, la grande salle d'audience.

Above, link stairs between the
entrance and the main courtroom.
Right, the main conference room.

Oben Verbindungstreppen zwischen
Eingang und Hauptgerichtssaal.
Rechts der Hauptkonferenzsaal.

Ci-dessus, l'escalier d'honneur
reliant la salle des pas perdus à la
grande salle d'audience. À droite, la
salle de conférences.

PLAN:B + JPR/CR

Plan:b Arquitectos / Carrera 33 #5G - 13 Ap. 401
Edificio El Atajo / Medellín-Antioquia / Colombia
Tel: +57 4 312 6947 / E-mail: juanfelipemateo@gmail.com
Web: www.planbarquitectura.com

JPR/CR / J. Paul Restrepo Santa Maria / Camilo Restrepo Ochoa
Calle 5g # 32 – 103 int 9903 / Medellín / Colombia
Tel: +57 310 829 7838 / Fax: +57 310 389 4783
Web: www.jpaulrestrepo.net / www.camilorestrepo.net

JUAN FELIPE MESA RICO was born in 1975 in Medellín, Colombia. He studied Architecture at the Universidad Pontificia Bolivariana (Medellín, 1993–98) and received his M.Arch degree from the Universidad Politécnica de Cataluña (UPC Barcelona, 1999–2000). He founded Plan:b Arquitectos in 2000, and took Alejandro Bernal Camargo as an Associate in 2005. **ALEJANDRO BERNAL CAMARGO** was born in Medellín in 1973. He also studied at the Universidad Pontificia Bolivariana (1991–95). Their work includes a new building for the Colegio Hontanares (Medellín, Antioquia, 2006); Gráficas Diamante (Envigado, Antioquia, 2006); the Orchideorama of the Botanical Garden of Medellín (Medellín, Antioquia, 2006–07, published here); and the Time Out Bar (Medellín, Antioquia, 2008), all in Colombia. **CAMILO RESTREPO OCHOA** was born in Medellín in 1974 and graduated from the Universidad Pontificia Bolivariana in 1998. Like Juan Felipe Mesa, he received a Master's degree from the UPC in Barcelona (2005). Recent projects of JPR/CR include a hotel in Medellín. **J. PAUL RESTREPO** was born in Medellín in 1944, graduating from the Universidad Pontificia Bolivariana in 1970. He worked with Camilo Restrepo from 2002 to 2007 at JPR/CR Arquitectos.

JUAN FELIPE MESA RICO wurde 1975 in Medellín, Kolumbien, geboren. Er studierte Architektur an der Universidad Pontificia Bolivariana (Medellín, 1993–98) und machte seinen M. Arch. an der Universidad Politécnica de Cataluña (UPC Barcelona, 1999–2000). 2000 gründete er sein Büro Plan:b Arquitectos, 2005 wurde Alejandro Bernal Camargo sein Partner. **ALEJANDRO BERNAL CAMARGO** wurde 1973 ebenfalls in Medellín geboren und studierte 1991 bis 1995 an der dortigen Universidad Pontificia Bolivariana. Zu den Arbeiten des Büros zählen ein neues Gebäude für das Colegio Hontanares (Medellín, Antioquia, 2006) und für Gráficas Diamante (Envigado, Antioquia, 2006), das Orchideorama im Botanischen Garten Medellín (Medellín, Antioquia, 2006–07, hier vorgestellt) sowie die Time Out Bar (Medellín, Antioquia, 2008). **CAMILO RESTREPO OCHOA** wurde 1974 in Medellín geboren und erhielt seinen Abschluss 1998 an der Universidad Pontificia Bolivariana. Wie Juan Felipe Mesa schloss auch er einen Master an der UPC in Barcelona (2005) an. **J. PAUL RESTREPO** (geboren 1944 in Medellín) beendete sein Studium 1970 an der Universidad Pontificia Bolivariana. Von 2002 bis 2007 arbeitete er mit Camilo Restrepo bei JPR/CR arquitectos. Zu den jüngeren Projekten von JPR/CR gehört u. a. ein Hotel in Medellín.

JUAN FELIPE MESA RICO est né en 1975 à Medellín, en Colombie. Il étudie l'architecture à l'université Pontificia Bolivariana (Medellín, 1993–98) et obtient son diplôme à l'Université polytechnique de Catalogne (UPC Barcelone, 1999–2000). Il fonde Plan B Arquitectos en 2000, et prend Alejandro Bernal Camargo comme associé en 2005. **ALEJANDRO BERNAL CAMARGO** est né à Medellín en 1973. Il étudie également à l'université Pontificia Bolivariana (1991–95). Leurs réalisations incluent un nouveau bâtiment pour le Colegio Hontanares de Medellín (Antioquia, 2006), un autre pour Gráficas Diamante (Envigado Antioquia, 2006), l'Orchidéorama du jardin botanique de Medellín (Antioquia, 2006–07, publié ici), et le bar Time Out à Medellín (Antioquia, 2008), toutes situées en Colombie. **CAMILO RESTREPO OCHOA**, né à Medellín en 1974, obtient son diplôme de l'université Pontificia Bolivariana en 1998. Comme Juan Felipe Mesa, il obtient un master de l'UPC de Barcelone (2005). Les réalisations récentes de JPR/CR incluent un hôtel à Medellín. **J. PAUL RESTREPO** est né à Medellín en 1944. Il est diplômé de l'université Pontificia Bolivariana en 1970 et a travaillé avec Camilo Restrepo de 2002 à 2007 chez JPR/CR arquitectos.

ORCHIDEORAMA OF THE BOTANICAL GARDEN OF MEDELLÍN

Medellín, Antioquia, Colombia, 2006–07

Address: Carrera 52, Sevilla, Medellín, Antioquia, Colombia
Area: 4200 m². Client: Medellín Botanical Garden. Cost: $2.2 million. Collaboration: Plan B Architecture—Felipe Mesa,
Alejandro Bernal; JPR/CR Architects—Camilo Restrepo, J. Paul Restrepo

The orchid exhibition facilities of the Botanical Garden of Medellín are located at 1540 meters above sea level with an average temperature between 18°C and 28°C. The architects sought "not to make any distinction between natural and artificial" in their project. Their honeycomb or flower design with the size and properties of a tree permits the creations of shade or a forest garden. Water facilities are located in the hollow trunks of the supports. The **ORCHIDEORAMA** is composed of ten "flower-tree" structures, which can be built individually, allowing the system to grow or respond to uncertainties, such as budgetary constraints, construction problems, or political decisions. Different areas are intended for small temporary gardens, orchids, exotic and tropical flowers, and bird or butterfly areas.

Die Orchideenhäuser im Botanischen Garten von Medellín liegen 1540 m über N.N. und sind durchschnittlich mit 18°C bis 28°C temperiert. Den Architekten ging es darum, bei ihrem Projekt „nicht zwischen ‚natürlich' und ‚künstlich' zu unterscheiden". Die bienenwaben- bzw. blütenförmigen Konstruktionen sind in Größe und Eigenschaften mit Bäumen zu vergleichen, spenden Schatten und bilden so etwas wie einen Wald. Die Wasserversorgung ist in den hohlen Stämmen untergebracht. Das **ORCHIDEORAMA** besteht aus zehn „Blüten-Baum"-Strukturen, die auch einzeln errichtet werden können, sodass das Gesamtsystem flexibel auf Unwägbarkeiten wie Budgetbeschränkungen, technische Probleme oder politische Entscheidungen reagieren kann. Geplant sind verschiedene Bereiche für kleine temporäre Gärten, Orchideen, exotische und tropische Gewächse sowie Vögel und Schmetterlinge.

Les installations d'exposition des orchidées du jardin botanique de Medellín sont situées à 1540 mètres d'altitude et sont soumises à une température moyenne comprise entre 18°C et 28°C. Les architectes ont cherché à « ne faire aucune distinction entre naturel et artificiel » dans leur projet. Leur projet d'éléments arborescents, en forme de nid d'abeille ou de fleurs, permet de créer un jardin d'ombre ou un jardin forestier. Les équipements d'arrosage sont logés dans les troncs creux des supports. **L'ORCHIDÉORAMA** est composé de dix « arbres-fleurs » pouvant être construits individuellement, ce qui permet au système de croître ou de s'adapter aux incertitudes des contraintes budgétaires, des problèmes de construction ou des décisions politiques. Des zones différentes sont affectées à des petits jardins temporaires d'orchidées, de fleurs exotiques ou tropicales, ou à des espaces pour les oiseaux et les papillons.

Left, a site plan shows the Orchideorama right of center. Right, an aerial
photo of the site, and above, a
ground-level view of the structures.

Der Lageplan links zeigt das Orchideorama auf der rechten Seite.
Rechts eine Luftaufnahme des Areals,
oben ein Blick auf die Bauten aus der
Froschperspektive.

À gauche, un plan de situation
montre l'Orchidéorama juste au
centre. À droite, une photo aérienne
du site, et ci-dessus, une vue des
structures prise du niveau du sol.

Clearly inspired by the vegetal
forms that surround them, the Orchideorama structures fit well into the
environment and shelter plants
and visitors.

Eindeutig formal inspiriert von der
Vegetation, fügen sich die Bauten des
Orchideorama ideal in ihre Umgebung
und bieten Pflanzen und Besuchern
Schutz.

Nettement inspirées des formes
végétales qui l'entourent, les structures de l'Orchidéorama s'intègrent
bien dans l'environnement et
abritent plantes et visiteurs.

ROJKIND ARQUITECTOS

Rojkind Arquitectos
Campos Eliseos # 432, Col. Polanco
México D.F. 11560
Mexico

Tel: +52 55 280 8396 / 5280 8521
Fax: +52 55 280 6000
E-mail: info@rojkindarquitectos.com
Web: www.rojkindarquitectos.com

MICHEL ROJKIND was born in 1969 in Mexico City, where he studied Architecture and Urban Planning at the Universidad Iberoamericana. After working on his own for several years, he teamed up with Isaac Broid and Miquel Adria to establish Adria+Broid+Rojkind (1998–2002). In 2002, he established his own firm in Mexico City. With Arturo Ortiz, Derek Dellekamp, and Tatiana Bilbao, Michel Rojkind cofounded the non-profit MXDF Urban Research Center (2004). The main goal of MXDF is to intervene in specific areas, modifying the production of urban space in Mexico through the systematic study of social, political, environmental, global, and cultural conditions. In order to achieve this, MXDF has been collaborating with several universities in Mexico, Studio Basel, ETH Zurich, and MIT in Boston. His built work includes the F2 House (Mexico City, 2001); Tlaxcala 190 apartment building (Colonia Condesa, Mexico City, 2002); Mexico City National Videotheque (Mexico City, 2002); Falcon Headquarters (San Angel, Mexico City, 2004); Boska Bar (Mexico City, 2004); the Nestlé Auditorium (Toluca, 2007); the Nestlé Chocolate Museum (Phase I, Toluca, 2007); and the Nestlé "Application Group" (Querétaro, 2009, published here), all in Mexico. Work in progress includes the renovation of the Hotel Del Angel (Mexico City, 2007–); and of the San Francisco Hotel (Mexico City, 2007–).

MICHEL ROJKIND wurde 1969 in Mexiko-Stadt geboren, wo er Architektur und Städtebau an der Universidad Iberoamericana studierte. Nach einigen Jahren selbstständiger Arbeit schloss er sich mit Isaac Broid und Miquel Adria zu Adria+Broid+Rojkind zusammen (1998–2002). 2002 gründete er in Mexiko-Stadt sein eigenes Büro. Gemeinsam mit Arturo Ortiz, Derek Dellekamp und Tatiana Bilbao schuf er 2004 das gemeinnützige Zentrum für Stadtforschung MXDF. Hauptanliegen von MXDF ist es, in spezifische Bereiche einzugreifen und die Entstehung von Stadtraum in Mexiko-Stadt durch die systematische Erforschung sozialer, politischer, umwelttechnischer, globaler und kultureller Bedingungen zu beeinflussen. Zu diesem Zweck kooperierte MXDF bereits mit zahlreichen Universitäten in Mexiko, mit dem Studio Basel, der ETH Zürich sowie dem MIT in Boston. Zu den gebauten Projekten des Büros zählen das Haus F2 (Mexiko-Stadt, 2001), das Apartmenthaus Tlaxcala 190 (Colonia Condesa, Mexiko-Stadt, 2002), die Nationale Videothek von Mexiko-Stadt (2002), die Geschäftszentrale von Falcon (San Angel, Mexiko-Stadt, 2004), die Boska Bar (Mexiko-Stadt, 2004), das Nestlé-Auditorium (Toluca, 2007), das Nestlé-Schokoladenmuseum (1. Bauabschnitt, Toluca, 2007) sowie die Nestlé „Application Group" (Querétaro, 2009, hier vorgestellt), alle in Mexiko. In Arbeit sind derzeit die Sanierung des Hotels del Angel sowie des Hotels San Francisco (beide Mexiko-Stadt, seit 2007).

MICHEL ROJKIND est né en 1969 à Mexico, où il étudie l'architecture et l'urbanisme à l'Université ibéro-américaine. Après avoir travaillé seul plusieurs années, il s'associe avec Isaac Broid et Miquel Adria pour fonder Adria+Broid+Rojkind (1998–2002). En 2002, il crée sa propre agence à Mexico. Avec Arturo Ortiz, Derek Dellekamp et Tatiana Bilbao, Michel Rojkind fonde le centre de recherche en urbanisme MXDF, une organisation à but non lucratif (2004). L'objet principal de MXDF est de modifier l'évolution de l'espace urbain du Mexique, en intervenant sur des zones spécifiques par l'étude systématique des conditions sociales, politiques, environnementales, globales et culturelles. MXDF a ainsi collaboré avec différentes universités mexicaines, l'Institut Studio Basel, l'ETH de Zurich, et le MIT de Boston. Ses réalisations incluent la maison F2 (Mexico, 2001) ; un immeuble de 190 appartements à Tlaxcala (Colonia Condesa, Mexico, 2002) ; la vidéothèque de Mexico (Mexico, 2002) ; le siège de Falcon à San Angel (Mexico, 2004) ; le bar Boska (Mexico, 2004) ; l'auditorium Nestlé (Toluca, 2007) ; le musée Nestlé du chocolat (Phase I, Toluca, 2007) et le laboratoire Nestlé « Application Group » (Querétaro, 2009, publié ici), tous situés au Mexique. Leurs projets en cours incluent la rénovation de l'hôtel Del Angel (Mexico, 2007–) et de l'hôtel San Francisco (Mexico, 2007–).

NESTLÉ "APPLICATION GROUP"

Querétaro, Mexico, 2009

Address: Avenida 5 de Febrero No. 1412, Zona Industrial Benito Juárez, 76130 Querétaro, Mexico
Area: 776 m². Client: Nestlé. Cost: not disclosed
Team: Agustin Pereyra, Paulina Goycoolea, Juan Carlos Vidals
Furniture: Esrawe Diseño, Arne Quinze, PM Steele

Located in Querétaro, in south-central Mexico, this is a laboratory for development of new products, a packaging center, and a satellite office for the firm's product technology center that works on the development of new beverages. The classification of the historic center of Querétaro's Old Town as a UNESCO World Heritage site in 1996 imposed the creation of a traditionally inspired arched porch for this building, despite the fact that it is in the industrial area. Michel Rojkind's reaction to this constraint was to seek the basic geometric form of the arch, which is to say a section of a sphere. He inscribed spherical shapes in the interconnected, unaligned, four or five-sided, satin mirror-clad boxes that provide the functional spaces. The inner faces of the sphere are colored in bright yellow, affirming the surprising modernity of the composition. Although this project concerns research, the building can be visited, hence its classification as a "public" building.

Der im zentralmexikanischen Querétaro gelegene Komplex umfasst ein Entwicklungslabor für neue Produkte, ein Verpackungszentrum sowie ein Außenbüro des Unternehmens für Produkttechnologie, das an der Entwicklung neuer Getränkeprodukte arbeitet. Die Ernennung der Altstadt von Querétaro zum Weltkulturerbe 1996 führte zur Auflage, das Gebäude mit traditionell inspirierten Torbögen auszustatten, obwohl der Komplex in einem Industriegebiet liegt. Michel Rojkind reagierte auf diese Auflage, indem er auf die geometrische Grundform des Bogens zurückgriff, ein Kreissegment. Er schrieb sphärische Formen in die ineinandergreifenden, vier- bzw. fünfseitigen Bauten ein, die mit satiniertem Spiegelglas verblendet wurden und in denen die Funktionsräume liegen. Die Innenseiten der kreisförmigen Ausschnitte sind leuchtend gelb gehalten und unterstreichen mit ihrer Farbgebung die überraschende Modernität des Ensembles. Obwohl sich hier Forschungslabors befinden, ist der Komplex offen für Besucher und somit ein öffentliches Bauwerk.

Situé à Querétaro, au centre du Mexique, ce projet est un laboratoire pour le développement de nouveaux produits, un centre d'emballage et une succursale du centre de recherche de la compagnie travaillant à l'élaboration de nouvelles boissons. Le classement du quartier de la vieille ville du centre historique de Querétaro au patrimoine mondial de l'Unesco en 1996 imposait pour ce bâtiment la création d'une porte en arche d'inspiration traditionnelle, bien qu'il soit implanté dans une zone industrielle. Michel Rojkind a réagi à cette contrainte en utilisant la géométrie élémentaire de l'arche, c'est-à-dire une section de sphère. Il a inscrit cette forme sphérique dans les quatre boîtes interconnectées, non alignées, de quatre et cinq côtés, avec un revêtement de miroir satiné, qui abritent les espaces fonctionnels. Les faces internes des sphères colorées d'un jaune vif affirment la modernité surprenante de la composition. Bien que ce projet concerne le domaine de la recherche, le bâtiment peut se visiter, d'où sa classification dans la catégorie des édifices « publics ».

Rojkind's use of hollowed-out and colored volumes gives an unusual, dynamic appearance to the structures.

Rojkinds Einsatz von räumlichen Aushöhlungen und Farbe lässt die Bauten ungewöhnlich und dynamisch wirken.

Les volumes évidés et colorés de Rojkind donnent un aspect inhabituel et dynamique aux bâtiments.

As the plan on the right shows, the overall design is made up of three unequal elements carved from an original, rectangular solid.

Wie der Grundriss rechts zeigt, besteht der Gesamtentwurf aus drei ungleichen Segmenten, die aus einem ursprünglich massivem, rechteckigen Körper herausgeschnitten wurden.

Comme le montre le plan à droite, le projet d'ensemble est constitué de trois éléments inégaux taillés dans un parallélépipède.

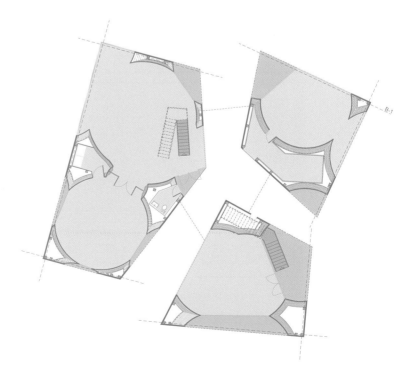

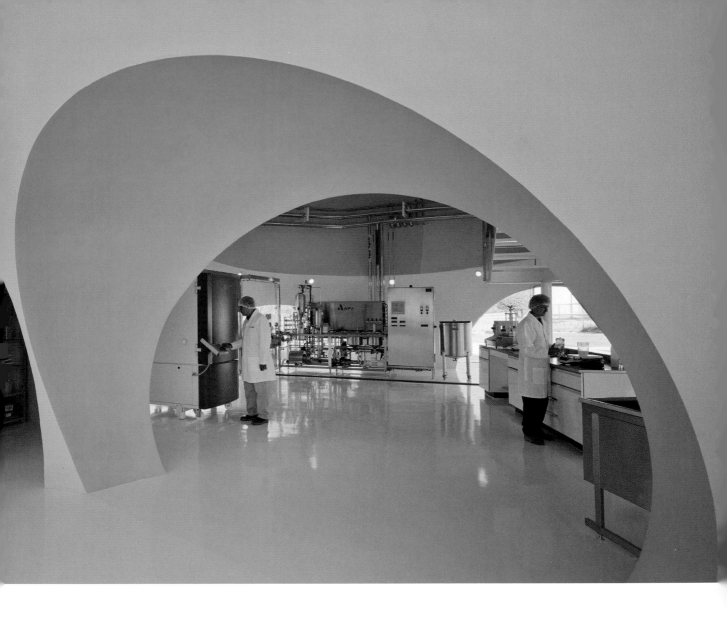

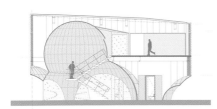
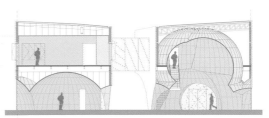

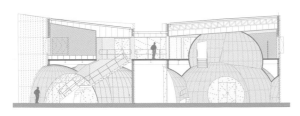
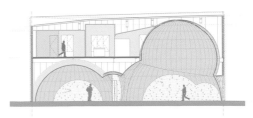

Section drawings (left page, bottom)
show how the architect has made use
of the cut-out, bulging forms visible
from the outside in the interior
design. A plan (right) outlines the
main uses of the space..

Querschnitte (linke Seite unten)
machen deutlich, wie der Architekt
die gewölbten Aushölungen, die auch
außen sichtbar sind, nutzt. Ein Grundriss (rechts) gibt Aufschluss über die
funktionale Aufteilung des Raums.

Les coupes (page de gauche, en bas)
montrent comment l'architecte a utilisé les formes bombées découpées,
visibles à l'extérieur, dans l'aménagement intérieur. Un plan (à droite)
souligne les fonctions principales de
l'espace.

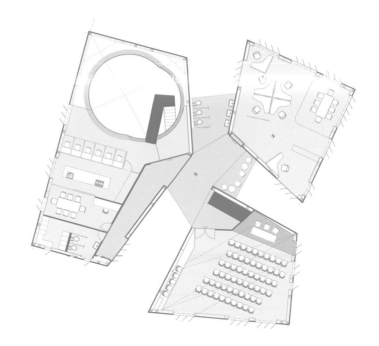

ÁLVARO SIZA VIEIRA

Álvaro Siza Arquitecto, Lda
Rua do Aleixo 53 2
4150–043 Porto
Portugal

Tel: +351 22 616 72 70
Fax: +351 22 616 72 79
E-mail: siza@mail.telepac.pt

Born in Matosinhos, Portugal, in 1933, **ÁLVARO SIZA** studied at the University of Porto School of Architecture (1949–55). He created his own practice in 1954, and worked with Fernando Tavora from 1955 to 1958. He has been a Professor of Construction at the University of Porto since 1976. He received the European Community's Mies van der Rohe Prize in 1988 and the Pritzker Prize in 1992. He has built a large number of small-scale projects in Portugal, and has worked on the restructuring of the Chiado (Lisbon, Portugal, 1989–); the Meteorology Center (Barcelona, Spain, 1989–92); the Vitra Furniture Factory (Weil am Rhein, Germany, 1991–94); the Porto School of Architecture (Porto University, Portugal, 1986–95); and the University of Aveiro Library (Aveiro, Portugal, 1988–95). More recent projects include the Portuguese Pavilion for the 1998 Lisbon World's Fair; the Serralves Foundation (Porto, 1998); the Adega Mayor Winery, Argamassas Estate—Campo Maior (2005–06); Viana do Castelo Public Library (Viana do Castelo, 2001–07, published here); and the Multipurpose Pavilion (Gondomar, 2005–07, also published here), all in Portugal. He designed the 2005 Serpentine Pavilion (Kensington Gardens, London) with Eduardo Souto de Moura. His Museum for the Iberê Camargo Foundation in Porto Alegre (Brazil) opened in 2008, as did his extension of the Hombroich Museum (Neuss-Hombroich, Germany, in collaboration with Rudolf Finsterwalder).

ÁLVARO SIZA, 1933 in Matosinhos, Portugal, geboren, studierte Architektur an der Universität Porto (1949–55). Sein eigenes Büro gründete er 1954, von 1955 bis 1958 arbeitete er mit Fernando Tavora. Ab 1976 war er Professor für Konstruktionslehre an der Universität Porto. 1988 erhielt er den Mies-van-der-Rohe-Preis der Europäischen Union, 1992 den Pritzker-Preis. Neben zahlreichen kleineren Bauprojekten, die Siza in Portugal realisierte, wirkte er auch bei der Sanierung des Stadtbezirks Chiado mit (Lissabon, Portugal, seit 1989), baute ein Meteorologisches Zentrum (Barcelona, 1989–92), eine Produktionshalle für den Möbelhersteller Vitra (Weil am Rhein, Deutschland, 1991–94), die Architekturfakultät der Universität Porto (1986–95) sowie die Universitätsbibliothek von Aveiro (Portugal, 1988–95). Aktuellere Projekte sind u. a. der portugiesische Pavillon für die Expo 1998 in Lissabon, die Stiftung Serralves (Porto, 1998), das Weingut Adega Mayor in Herdade das Argamassas, Campo Maior (2005–06), die Stadtbibliothek in Viana do Castelo (2001–07, hier vorgestellt) sowie ein Mehrzweckpavillon (Gondomar, 2005–07, ebenfalls hier vorgestellt), alle in Portugal. Gemeinsam mit Eduardo Souto de Moura entwarf er 2005 den Serpentine Pavilion (Kensington Gardens, London). Sein Museum für die Stiftung Iberê Camargo in Porto Alegre (Brasilien) wurde 2008 eröffnet, ebenso wie sein Erweiterungsbau für das Museum Insel Hombroich (Neuss-Hombroich, in Zusammenarbeit mit Rudolf Finsterwalder).

Né à Matosinhos, au Portugal, en 1933, **ÁLVARO SIZA** a étudié à l'École d'architecture de l'université de Porto (1949–55). Il crée sa propre agence en 1954 et travaille avec Fernando Tavora de 1955 à 1958. Il est professeur de construction à l'université de Porto depuis 1976. Il a reçu le prix de la Communauté européenne Mies van der Rohe en 1988 et le prix Pritzker en 1992. Il a construit un grand nombre de petits projets au Portugal et a travaillé sur la restructuration du quartier du Chiado (Lisbonne, Portugal, 1989–). Il a construit le Centre de météorologie de Barcelone (Espagne, 1989–92) ; l'usine de meubles Vitra (Weil-am-Rhein, Allemagne, 1991–94) ; le bâtiment de l'École d'architecture de Porto (université de Porto, Portugal, 1986–95) ; et la bibliothèque de l'université d'Aveiro (Aveiro, Portugal, 1988–95). Ses réalisations plus récentes incluent le Pavillon portugais de l'Exposition universelle 1998 de Lisbonne ; la Fondation Serralves (Porto, 1998) ; l'établissement vinicole et chais Adega Mayor d'Argamassas – Campo Maior (2005–06) ; la bibliothèque publique de Viana do Castelo (2001–07, publié ici) ; et le pavillon polyvalent à Gondomar (2005–07, également publié ici), toutes situées au Portugal. Il a conçu le pavillon de la Serpentine Gallery de 2005 (Kensington Gardens, Londres) avec Eduardo Souto de Moura. Son Musée pour la fondation Iberê Camargo à Porto Alegre (Brésil) a été inauguré en 2008, ainsi que son extension du musée Insel Hombroich (Neuss-Hombroich, Allemagne, en collaboration avec Rudolf Finsterwalder).

VIANA DO CASTELO PUBLIC LIBRARY

Viana do Castelo, Portugal, 2001–07

Address: Alameda 5 de Outubro, 4900–049 Viana do Castelo, Portugal, +351 2588 400 10, www.biblioteca.cm-viana-castelo.pt
Area: 1605 m². Client: Câmara Municipal de Viana do Castelo. Cost: not disclosed
Team: Tatania Berger, José Manuel Pelegrin

This Library, situated between the broad Lima River and the Avenida Marginal, is part of the urban plan for Marginal Viana conceived by Fernando Távora. The library is formed by a 45 x 45-meter volume that includes a 20 x 20 meter central void, continuing under part of the upper level to create the kind of dramatic overhang that Siza often uses. Recommendations defined by the Portuguese Institute of Books and Libraries (IPLB) for the national network of public libraries have been used to lay out the Library facilities. Two staircases and elevators link the two levels. The building is characterized by large horizontal openings, and is orthogonal in plan and elevation. Sunscreens are used where appropriate and the external finishing is in white-painted concrete and stone for the base. Working with other architects involved in the area plan, such as Eduardo Souto de Moura, Álvaro Siza praised the "rewarding and open dialogue between architects, developers, and managers" that allowed this project to come to fruition.

Die zwischen dem breiten Fluss Lima und der Avenida Marginal gelegene Bibliothek entstand im Einklang mit den städtebaulichen Planungen Fernando Távoras für das Stadtviertel Marginal Viana. Die Bibliothek besteht aus einem 45 x 45 m großen Baukörper mit einer 20 x 20 m großen zentralen Aussparung. Der Bau setzt sich nur teilweise unter dem Obergeschoss fort, wodurch jene dramatischen Auskragungen entstehen, mit denen Siza so häufig arbeitet. Empfehlungen des Portugiesischen Buch- und Bibliotheksinstituts (IPLB) für das landesweite Netz von Stadtbibliotheken wurden bei der Planung berücksichtigt. Zwei Treppenhäuser und Aufzüge verbinden die beiden Gebäudeebenen. Der Bau zeichnet sich durch großzügige horizontale Fensterbänder aus und ist in Grund- wie Aufriss orthogonal angelegt. Wo nötig, wurden Sonnenschutzblenden installiert; außen präsentiert sich der Bau mit weiß gestrichenem Beton und einem Boden aus Stein. Álvaro Siza, der mit Architekten wie Eduardo Souto de Moura kooperierte, die ebenfalls in die städtebauliche Planung eingebunden waren, lobte den „lohnenden und offenen Dialog zwischen Architekten, Bauunternehmern und Projektmanagern", der dazu beitrug, das Projekt zu realisieren.

Cette bibliothèque, située entre le large fleuve Lima et l'avenue Marginal, fait partie du plan d'urbanisme conçu par Fernando Távora pour Marginal Viana. Elle est formée d'un volume de 45 x 45 mètres qui inclut un vide central de 20 x 20 mètres se prolongeant sous une partie du niveau supérieur pour créer un surplomb spectaculaire, un dispositif souvent utilisé par Siza. L'aménagement de la bibliothèque suit les recommandations de l'Institut portugais du livre et des bibliothèques (IPLB) pour le réseau national de bibliothèques publiques. Deux escaliers et des ascenseurs relient les deux niveaux. Le bâtiment se caractérise par de larges ouvertures horizontales et par l'orthogonalité de son plan et de son élévation. Des brise-soleil sont utilisés où ils apparaissent nécessaires, et la finition extérieure est en béton peint en blanc avec une base en pierre. Ayant travaillé avec d'autres architectes intervenant sur le programme de cette zone, comme Eduardo Souto de Moura, Álvaro Siza loue « le dialogue ouvert entre les architectes, les constructeurs, et les gestionnaires » qui ont permis à ce projet de se réaliser.

Lifted off the ground and marked by a broad, horizontal band window, the Library is typical of Siza's unusual use of modern forms—the architecture is simple, and yet unexpected.

Die Bibliothek schwebt über dem Boden und ist mit ihrem markanten, horizontalen Fensterband typisch für Sizas ungewöhnliche Interpretation moderner Formen – eine Architektur, die schlicht und dennoch überraschend ist.

Soulevée du sol et soulignée par une large bande horizontale vitrée, la bibliothèque est caractéristique de l'usage original fait par Siza des formes modernes – l'architecture est simple et pourtant surprenante.

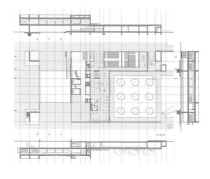

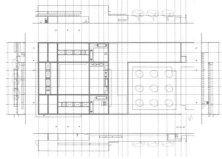

The overall plan is orthogonal, but full of surprises, like the overhead natural lighting seen in the Library view below. Furnishings are simple, in the spirit of Siza's architecture itself.

Der Grundriss ist im Großen und Ganzen rechtwinklig, birgt jedoch zahlreiche Überraschungen, etwa das Oberlicht in den Bibliotheksräumen unten. Ganz dem Geist der Architektur Sizas entsprechend ist auch das Mobiliar schlicht gehalten.

Le plan d'ensemble est orthogonal, mais plein de surprises, comme l'éclairage zénithal de la bibliothèque, visible ci-dessous. Le mobilier est simple, dans l'esprit de l'architecture de Siza.

The building sits on the water, contrasting with its environment, but not in contradiction with the town. Above, the band windows frame views of the town.

Das Gebäude liegt am Wasser und bildet einen deutlichen Kontrast zu seinem Umfeld, steht jedoch nicht im Widerspruch zur Stadt. Oben das Fensterband, das Ansichten der Stadt rahmt.

Le bâtiment, comme posé sur l'eau, contraste avec son environnement sans s'opposer à la ville. Ci-dessus, la bande de fenêtres cadre des vues sur la ville.

MULTIPURPOSE PAVILION

Gondomar, Portugal, 2005–07

Address: Rua de Pevidal, São Cosme, 4420 Gondomar, Portugal
Area: 10 309 m². Client: Câmara Municipal de Viana do Castelo. Cost: not disclosed
Team: António Mota, José Manuel Pelegrin

The site of this rather large project measures 29 208 square meters. A main room measuring 54 x 32 meters is conceived to allow for international-level sports such as handball, roller hokey, basketball, or volleyball. The flexibility of the elliptical space allows for numerous different uses, including meetings or shows seating up to 6400 people. The "support services" structure, laid out in the prolongation of the major axis of the ellipse, is 33.6 meters wide and 9.5 meters high. The first floor contains two patios and six groups of spas, massage rooms, locker rooms for coaches and referees, health services, and a gym. The second floor is intended for the VIP rooms, press-conference area, meeting rooms, and administrative offices. Álvaro Siza points out that with its large, symmetrical hall, and rooms of variable size, the facility allows for a very broad variety of uses. Air-conditioned and thermally isolated, the structure can also be divided to reduce the cost of routine maintenance.

Das vergleichsweise große Projekt liegt auf einem 29 208 m² großen Grundstück. Der 54 x 32 m große Hauptraum lässt sich für internationale Sportwettkämpfe in Handball, Rollhockey, Basketball oder Volleyball nutzen. Dank der Flexibilität des elliptischen Raums sind ebenso andere Nutzungen möglich, etwa Kongresse oder Bühnenaufführungen mit bis zu 6400 Sitzplätzen. Ein zweiter Bau mit Nebenräumen schließt sich in Verlängerung der Hauptachse der Ellipse an, ist 33,6 m lang und 9,5 m hoch. Im ersten Stock befinden sich zwei Höfe und sechs Zonen mit Wellnessbereich und Massageräumen, Umkleideräumen für Trainer und Schiedsrichter, sportärztlichen Einrichtungen und einem Fitnessraum. Das Obergeschoss ist den VIP-Lounges vorbehalten, dem Pressekonferenzbereich, Tagungsräumen sowie den Büros der Verwaltung. Álvaro Siza weist darauf hin, dass der Komplex dank der großen symmetrischen Halle und der übrigen Räumlichkeiten verschiedener Größe vielseitig nutzbar ist. Der klimatisierte und wärmegedämmte Bau lässt sich zudem unterteilen, um die Kosten für die Wartung zu minimieren.

Ce projet assez important est implanté sur un site de 29 208 mètres carrés. Il dispose d'une salle principale de 54 x 32 mètres, conçue pour permettre une pratique de niveau international de sports comme le handball, le roller hockey, le basket-ball, ou le volley-ball. La souplesse de l'espace elliptique permet de nombreux autres usages, et offre jusqu'à 6400 places assises pour des rencontres ou des spectacles. Le bâtiment auxiliaire, disposé dans le prolongement du grand axe de l'ellipse, mesure 33,6 mètres de large et 9,5 mètres de haut. Le rez-de-chaussée comprend deux patios et six groupes de spas, des salles de massage, des vestiaires pour les entraîneurs et les arbitres, des services de soins et une salle de gymnastique. L'étage est réservé aux espaces VIP, à la salle de presse, aux salles de réunions et à l'administration. Álvaro Siza indique qu'avec son vaste hall symétrique et ses locaux de tailles diverses, l'installation permet une grande variété d'usages. Le bâtiment équipé d'une isolation thermique et climatisé peut également être divisé pour réduire les coûts d'entretien courant.

The largely blank brick surfaces of the building are marked by the light, arching entrance canopy.

Die überwiegend schmucklosen Backsteinflächen des Baus werden vom leichten, geschwungenen Vordach am Eingangsbereich belebt.

Les surfaces du bâtiment, principalement en briques nues, sont soulignées par l'arche légère de l'auvent de l'entrée.

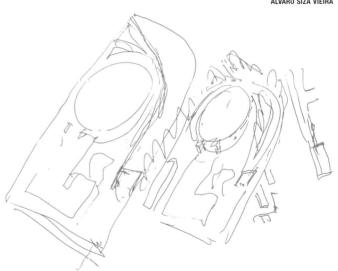

A sketch by the architect (right) and a closer view of the thin shell entrance canopy.

Eine Skizze des Architekten (rechts) und eine Ansicht der leichten Vordachschale aus größerer Nähe.

Une esquisse de l'architecte (à droite) et une vue rapprochée de la fine coque en béton de l'auvent de l'entrée.

Several pictures and a sketch (below) highlight the soaring lightness of the concrete canopy, which might recall Siza's larger canopy for the Portuguese Pavilion in Lisbon.

Verschiedene Aufnahmen und eine Skizze (unten) streichen die außergewöhnliche Leichtigkeit des Betondachs hervor, die manche auch an Sizas größeres Dach für den Portugiesischen Pavillon in Lissabon erinnern dürfte.

Plusieurs photos et une esquisse (ci-dessous) soulignent la légèreté aérienne du voile de béton de l'auvent, qui rappelle le voile plus grand de Siza pour le Pavillon portugais à Lisbonne.

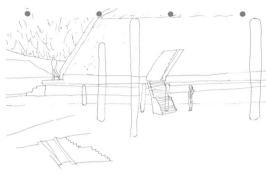

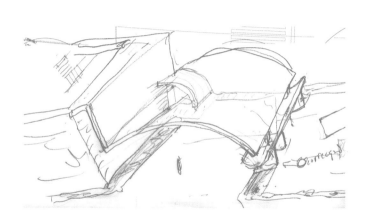

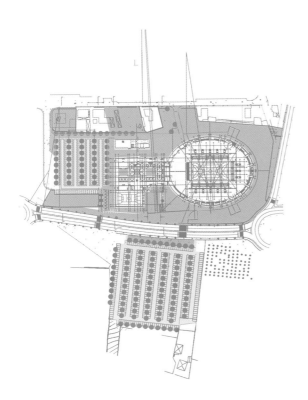

The main sports hall is seen above, and in the overall site plan to the left.

Oben im Bild die große Sporthalle, links ein Lageplan.

La grande salle de sport, ci-dessus, et dans le plan de situation, à gauche.

A section drawing of the main sports hall and, below, images showing the spectator stands and approach area for the hall.

Oben ein Querschnitt durch die große Sporthalle. Unten Aufnahmen der Zuschauertribünen und des Eingangsbereichs der Halle.

Une coupe de la grande salle et, ci-dessous, des photos montrant les tribunes des spectateurs et l'accès à la salle.

SUBSTANCE

Substance SIA
Skunu 6–8
1050 Riga
Latvia

Tel/Fax: +371 67 22 16 02
E-mail: substance@substance.lv
Web: www.substance.lv

Arnis Dimins was born in 1968 in Latvia. He received his degree in Architecture from Riga Technical University in 1992. He worked with the Latvian firm Arhis from 1993 to 2000, establishing his own firm **SUBSTANCE** SIA in 2000. The architect received the Acknowledgement for Innovation at the Best Design Awards in Latvian Architecture in 2007 for the Majori Primary School Sports Ground (Jurmala, 2007–08, published here). Brigita Barbale was born in Latvia in 1979. She received her degree in Architecture from Riga Technical University in 2002. She joined Substance SIA in 2000, and in 2006 began work with Balta istaba SIA, and in 2008 with VI. Neilands arhitekts IK. Recent work by Substance includes Stadium Stands (Jurmala, 2007); an Apartment House (Riga, 2007); Dzintari Forest Park (Jurmala, 2009); the Fizkult Fitness Club (Riga, 2009); and a Sports Complex (Jurmala, 2009), all in Latvia.

Arnis Dimins wurde 1968 in Lettland geboren. Sein Architekturstudium schloss er 1992 an der Technischen Universität Riga ab. Von 1993 bis 2000 arbeitete er für das lettische Büro Arhis, 2000 gründete er sein eigenes Büro **SUBSTANCE** SIA. Für die Sportanlagen der Majori-Grundschule (Jurmala, 2007–08, hier vorgestellt) erhielt er 2007 den Innovationspreis für lettische Architektur. Brigita Barbale wurde 1979 in Lettland geboren. Sie schloss ihr Architekturstudium 2002 an der Technischen Universität Riga ab. Sie kam 2000 zu Substance SIA, arbeitet seit 2006 auch für Balta istaba SIA sowie seit 2008 für VI. Neilands arhitekts IK. Jüngere Projekte von Substance sind u. a. die Stadiontribünen in Jurmala (2007), ein Wohngebäude in Riga (2007), der Waldpark Dzintari (Jurmala, 2009), der Fitnessklub Fizkult (Riga, 2009) sowie ein Sportkomplex in Jurmala (2009), alle in Lettland.

Arnis Dimins, né en 1968 en Lettonie, obtient son diplôme d'architecte à l'Université de technologie de Riga en 1992. Il travaille avec l'agence lettone Arhis de 1993 à 2000 et fonde sa propre agence, **SUBSTANCE** SIA, en 2000. L'architecte a reçu le prix de l'innovation aux Best Design Awards de l'architecture lettone en 2007 pour la salle de sport de l'école primaire de Majori (Jurmala, 2007–08, publié ici). Brigita Barbale, née en Lettonie en 1979, obtient son diplôme d'architecte à l'Université de technologie de Riga en 2002. Elle rejoint Substance SIA en 2000, commence à travailler avec Balta istaba SIA en 2006 et depuis 2008 avec VI. Neilands arhitekts IK. Les récentes réalisations de Substance incluent les tribunes d'un stade à Sloka (Jurmala, 2007); un immeuble d'appartements (Riga, 2007); le parc forestier de Dzintari (Jurmala, 2009); le club de fitness Fizkult (Riga, 2009); et un complexe sportif (Jurmala, 2009), toutes situés en Lettonie.

MAJORI PRIMARY SCHOOL SPORTS GROUND

Jurmala, Latvia, 2007–08

Address: 1 Rigas Street, Jurmala, Latvia
Area: 3425 m². Client: Jurmala City Council. Cost: €1.714 million
Collaboration: Brigita Barbale

Jurmala is a Baltic Sea resort, where the architects were asked to create an all-weather sports area. Closed on the side of a neighboring railway line, the facility opens to a riverfront. In warm weather, the synthetic surface is used for track and field, basketball, volleyball, and handball, while it is turned into an artificial hockey and ice-skating rink in winter. Located on a former marketplace, the facility makes use of an existing market building for the changing rooms, administrative office, and equipment storage. The second floor of the building accommodates spectator stands. The facility is visible from the rail, street, and river entrances to Jurmala. Its form is inspired by the amber or crystallized resin of pine that sometimes washes up on the seacoast. The ceiling structure is made with polycarbonate and the architects decided to leave its supports on the exterior in order to make the interior as simple as possible.

Jurmala ist ein Badeort an der Ostsee, wo die Architekten eine Allwettersportanlage realisieren sollten. Der Komplex zeigt sich zur angrenzenden Bahntrasse hin geschlossen, öffnet sich jedoch zum Flussufer. Bei warmer Witterung wird der synthetische Hallenboden für Leichtathletik, Basketball, Volleyball und Handball genutzt. Im Winter dient die Halle als Eishockey- und Eislauffeld. Die am ehemaligen Marktplatz gelegene Anlage nutzt ein altes Marktgebäude für Umkleideräume, Büros und als Geräteraum. Der zweite Stock des Gebäudes dient als Tribüne. Die Halle wird sichtbar, sobald man Jurmala per Zug, auf der Straße oder über den Fluss erreicht. Formal wurde das Gebäude vom Bernstein inspiriert, der mitunter an den Stränden angespült wird. Die Dachkonstruktion besteht aus Polycarbonat, wobei die Architekten das Tragwerk nach außen verlegten, um den Innenraum so schlicht wie möglich zu halten.

Jurmala est une station balnéaire de la mer Baltique, où les architectes devaient concevoir une aire de sport tous temps. Situé en bordure d'une voie ferrée, le bâtiment est ouvert sur un front de fleuve. À la belle saison, le sol synthétique est utilisé pour de l'athlétisme, du basket, du volley et du handball. En hiver, il se transforme en patinoire artificielle de hockey et de patinage sur glace. Un des bâtiments de l'ancien marché sur le site duquel est implantée l'installation a été conservé pour les vestiaires, les bureaux administratifs et le rangement des équipements. L'étage du bâtiment accueille des tribunes de spectateurs. Sa forme s'inspire des morceaux d'ambre ou de résine de pin cristallisés que rejette parfois la mer sur le rivage. La toiture est faite de polycarbonate et les architectes ont décidé de laisser ses supports à l'extérieur pour rendre l'intérieur aussi simple que possible.

The ribbed polycarbonate shell of the Sports Ground is its most surprising feature, allowing for broad openings and ample natural light—as well as a glowing presence in the night.

Die gerippte Polycarbonathülle der Sportanlage ist das wohl überraschendste Element des Gebäudes. Sie erlaubt großzügige Öffnungen und reichlich einfallendes Tageslicht – und lässt den Komplex nachts eindrücklich leuchten.

L'élément le plus surprenant de la salle de sport est sa coque nervurée en polycarbonate offrant de larges ouvertures et un généreux éclairage naturel – ainsi qu'une présence lumineuse dans la nuit.

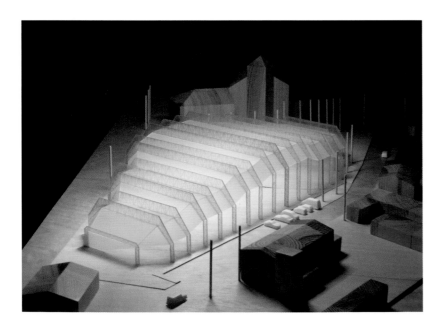

A model (left) shows the overall form
of the building, while a broad view of
the hockey rink (above) reveals the
ample interior space.

Ein Modell (links) veranschaulicht die
formale Gestaltung des Baus in seiner Gesamtheit. Die Weitwinkelauf-
nahme des Eishockeyfelds (oben)
zeigt den großzügigen Innenraum.

Une maquette (à gauche) montre la
forme d'ensemble du bâtiment, tandis
qu'une vue large de la piste de hockey (ci-dessus) révèle le vaste espace intérieur.

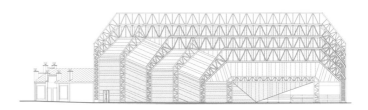

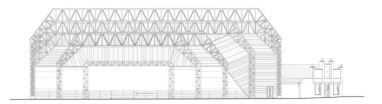

Elevations of the entire building with its openings and unusual articulated roof. Below, a view of the faceted polycarbonate roof.

Aufrisse des gesamten Bauwerks mit Fensterflächen und dem ungewöhnlich gestalteten Dach. Unten eine Ansicht des facettierten Polycarbonatdachs.

Des élévations du bâtiment entier, avec ses ouvertures et son toit articulé original. Ci-dessous, une vue du toit à facettes de polycarbonate.

TIDY ARQUITECTOS

Tidy Arquitectos
Marchant Pereira 407, Providencia
Santiago de Chile
Chile

Tel: +56 2 223 8489
E-mail: info@tidy.cl
Web: www.tidy.cl

ALBERT TIDY was born in 1967 in Santiago, and graduated from the University of Chile in 1992. In 1998, he graduated from Yale School of Architecture as a Fulbright Scholar obtaining his M.Arch degree and the Samuel J. Fogelson Memorial Award for Excellence in Design. He has been an Associate Professor at Universidad de Chile School of Architecture since 1999. Between 2005 and 2007 he served as Director at the school, and in 2007 he was named Director of the San Sebastian School of Architecture in Santiago, Chile. He founded Tidy Architects with his brother and partner, Ian Tidy, in 2000. IAN TIDY was born in 1974 and graduated from the Pontificia Universidad Católica de Chile (UC) School of Architecture in 2000. He currently teaches Interior Design and Object Design as an Associate Professor at the Universidad del Desarrollo (Santiago, 2007–08). His furniture design work has received recognition in numerous exhibitions and publications in Chile. They have completed the Organiko Restaurant (Providencia, Santiago, 2002); the Stryker Offices (Las Condes, Santiago, 2002); a number of private houses, such as the Casa Muñoz (Algarrobo, 2002–03); and the Amorio Restaurant (Santiago, 2005–06). Other recent work includes private residences, such as the Casa Martinez (Acuelo Lake, 2006); Schckolnick House (El Arrayán, Santiago, 2007); and the Alvarez House (Chicuero, 2007); as well as the University of Chile School of Arts Renovation (Santiago, 2007); and the San Sebastian Elementary School (Melipilla, 2007–08, published here), all in Chile.

ALBERT TIDY wurde 1967 in Santiago geboren und schloss sein Studium 1992 an der Universidad de Chile ab. 1998 machte er den M. Arch. an der Architekturfakultät von Yale, wo er ein Fulbright-Stipendium hatte und mit dem Samuel J. Fogelson Memorial Award für herausragendes Design ausgezeichnet wurde. Ab 1999 war er Lehrbeauftragter und 2005 bis 2007 Dekan der Architekturfakultät der Universidad de Chile. Seit 2007 steht er der Architekturfakultät der Universidad San Sebastian in Santiago, Chile, vor. Gemeinsam mit seinem Bruder Ian Tidy gründete er 2000 das Büro Tidy Architects. IAN TIDY wurde 1974 geboren und schloss sein Architekturstudium 2000 an der Pontificia Universidad Católica de Chile (UC) ab. Derzeit unterrichtet er als Lehrbeauftragter Innenarchitektur und Objektdesign an der Universidad del Desarrollo (Santiago, 2007–08). Seine Möbelentwürfe wurden in Chile bereits in zahlreichen Ausstellungen und Publikationen gewürdigt. Gemeinsam realisierte Projekte sind u. a. das Restaurant Organiko (Providencia, Santiago, 2002), ein Bürogebäude für Stryker (Las Condes, Santiago, 2002), verschiedene private Wohnbauten, darunter die Casa Muñoz (Algarrobo, 2002–03) sowie das Restaurant Amorio (Santiago, 2005–06). Weitere aktuelle Arbeiten sind mehrere Privathäuser wie die Casa Martinez (Lago Acuelo, 2006), Casa Schckolnick (El Arrayán, Santiago, 2007) und die Casa Alvarez (Chicuero, 2007) sowie die Sanierung der Kunstfakultät der Universidad de Chile (Santiago, 2007) und schließlich die Grundschule San Sebastian (Melipilla, 2007–08, hier vorgestellt), alle in Chile.

ALBERT TIDY, né en 1967 à Santiago, a obtenu son diplôme à l'université du Chili en 1992. En 1998, il poursuit ses études à l'École d'architecture de l'université Yale grâce à une bourse Fulbright et obtient son master (M. Arch.) et le Samuel J. Fogelson Memorial Award for Excellence in Design. Il est professeur associé à l'École d'architecture de l'université du Chili depuis 1999. Il a été directeur de l'école de 2005 à 2007, année où il est nommé directeur de l'École d'architecture San Sebastian, à Santiago, au Chili. Il fonde Tidy Architects avec son frère et associé Ian Tidy en 2000. IAN TIDY, né en 1974, a obtenu son diplôme à l'École d'architecture de la Pontificia Universidad Católica de Chile (UC) en 2000. Il enseigne actuellement l'architecture intérieure et le design d'objets comme professeur associé de l'Universidad del Desarrollo (Santiago, 2007–08). Ses réalisations de mobilier ont été vues dans de nombreuses expositions et publications au Chili. Ils ont réalisé le restaurant Organiko (Providencia, Santiago, 2002); les bureaux Stryker (Las Condes, Santiago, 2002); plusieurs habitations privées, comme la maison Muñoz (Algarrobo, 2002–03); et le restaurant Amorio (Santiago, 2005–06). D'autres projets récents incluent des habitations privées, comme la maison Martinez (Acuelo Lake, 2006); la maison Schckolnick (El Arrayán, Santiago, 2007); et la maison Alvarez (Chicuero, 2007), ainsi que la rénovation de l'École des beaux-arts de l'université du Chili (Santiago, 2007); et l'école élémentaire San Sebastian (Melipilla, 2007–08, publié ici), tous situés au Chili.

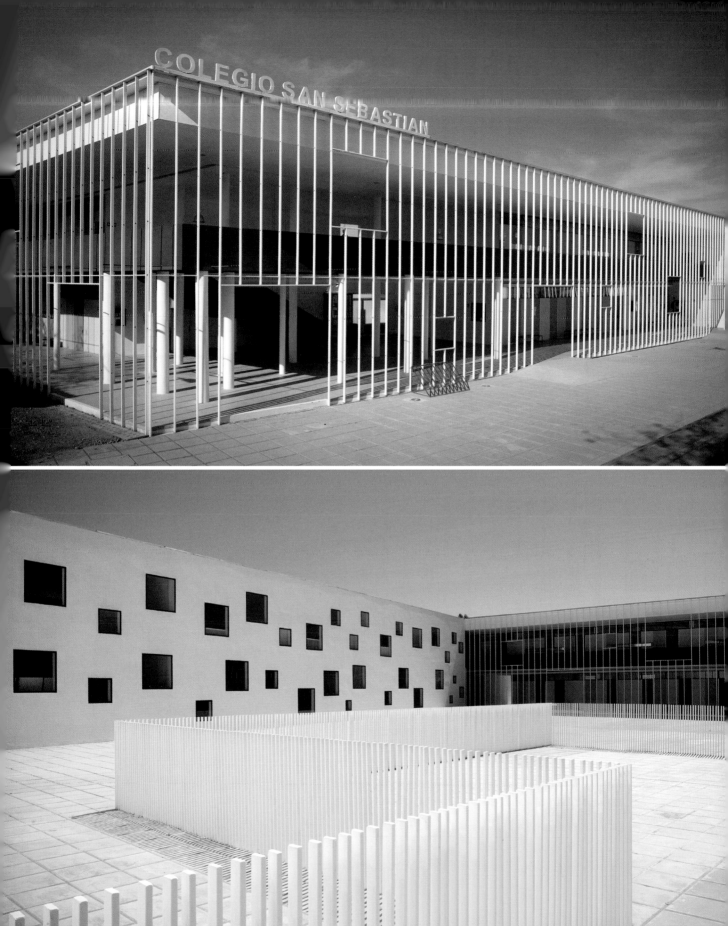

SAN SEBASTIAN ELEMENTARY SCHOOL

Melipilla, Chile, 2007–08

Address: Mozart 131, Melipilla, Chile, +56 2 831 8750, www.sansebastianmelipilla.cl
Area: 3743 m². Client: Sociedad Educacional San Sebastian. Cost: $2.2 million
Collaboration: Cecila Aldunate Montes

The regular lines of these courtyard façades are enlivened by the use of lighting and a yellow-to-green color scheme.

Der Innenhof mit seinen regelmäßigen Linien gewinnt durch den Einsatz von Licht und einer Farbpalette in Gelb- und Grüntönen an Lebendigkeit.

Les lignes régulières de ces façades de cour intérieure sont animées par l'éclairage et l'emploi d'une gamme colorée jaune et verte.

Built on a 7881-square-meter site in Melipilla, a town located 80 kilometers from Santiago, this new structure was built for a private educational institution founded in 1997 that is aided by public funds. The site has a privileged view of the Chilean central valley and Andes Mountains. The architects explain: "Our client had a clear idea of the functioning scheme for his needs based on an 'S' shaped configuration that was the base for the architectural proposal." Openings and windows face the view, with classrooms facing east and south to avoid solar gain. One public patio with a prefabricated concrete floor faces the valley, while a more private courtyard space surfaced in grass echoes the patios of historic central valley houses. Cost was limited to $600 per square meter, a fact that complicated the design of the essentially concrete and stucco building.

Der Neubau auf einem 7881 m² großen Grundstück in Melipilla, 80 km von Santiago entfernt, wurde für eine 1997 gegründete, staatlich geförderte Privatschule errichtet. Der Standort bietet einen besonders beeindruckenden Ausblick auf das Valle Central und die Anden. Die Architekten führen aus: „Unser Auftraggeber hatte klare Vorstellungen vom Funktionsschema, das auf seine Bedürfnisse zugeschnitten war und auf einer S-förmigen Grundform basierte. Sie war Grundlage des architektonischen Entwurfs." Wandöffnungen und Fenster öffnen sich zum Panorama, während die Klassenräume nach Osten und Süden ausgerichtet sind, um eine allzu starke Aufheizung durch die Sonne zu vermeiden. Ein öffentlicher, mit Betonplatten ausgelegter Hof orientiert sich zum Tal, während ein weniger öffentlicher Innenhof mit Rasenbelag an die Patios der traditionellen Häuser im Valle Central erinnert. Das Budget war auf 600 US Dollar pro m² begrenzt, was sich als Herausforderung für den Entwurf des Gebäudes erwies, das überwiegend in Beton und Gipsputz realisiert wurde.

Implanté sur un site de 7881 mètres carrés, à Melipilla, une ville située à 80 kilomètres de Santiago, ce nouveau bâtiment a été construit pour une école privée subventionnée, créée en 1997. Le site bénéficie d'une vue sur la vallée centrale du Chili et les Andes. Comme l'expliquent les architectes, leur client « avait une idée claire du plan de fonctionnement adapté à leur besoin, une configuration en "S" qui a servi de base à la proposition architecturale ». Les ouvertures et les fenêtres donnent sur le paysage, et les salles de classe sont orientées à l'est et au sud pour éviter l'apport solaire. Un patio public, avec un sol préfabriqué en béton, donne sur la vallée, tandis qu'une cour plus privative, gazonnée, évoque les patios des maisons traditionnelles de la région. Le budget était limité à 600 dollars par mètre carré, ce qui compliquait la conception du bâtiment construit essentiellement en béton et en stuc.

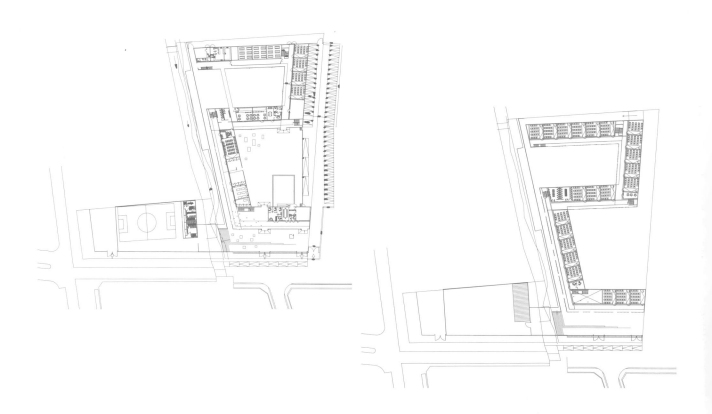

Plans show the overall form of the school, somewhat akin to the number "2", while the photos on the right reveal the differences in façade treatments imagined by the architects.

Die Grundrisse veranschaulichen die Gesamtkomposition des Schulkomplexes, die vage an eine „2" erinnert. Die Fotos rechts zeigen die verschiedenen Fassadenkonzepte der Architekten.

Les plans montrent la forme en « 2 » de l'ensemble de l'école, et les photos à droite montrent les différences de traitement des façades imaginées par les architectes.

UNSTUDIO

UN Studio Van Berkel & Bos / Stadhouderskade 113
1073 AX Amsterdam / The Netherlands
Tel: +31 20 57 02 04 0 / Fax: +31 20 57 02 04 1
E-mail: info@unstudio.com / Web: www.unstudio.com

BEN VAN BERKEL was born in Utrecht in 1957 and studied at the Rietveld Academy in Amsterdam and at the Architectural Association (AA) in London, receiving the AA Diploma with honors in 1987. After working briefly in the office of Santiago Calatrava in 1988, he set up his practice in Amsterdam with **CAROLINE BOS**. He has been a Visiting Professor at Columbia and a visiting critic at Harvard (1994). He was a Diploma Unit Master at the AA (1994–95). As well as the Erasmus Bridge in Rotterdam (inaugurated in 1996), Van Berkel & Bos Architectural Bureau has built the Karbouw and ACOM office buildings (1989–93), and the REMU Electricity Station (1989–93), all in Amersfoort; and housing projects and the Aedes East Gallery for Kristin Feireiss in Berlin. Projects include an extension for the Rijksmuseum Twente (Enschede, 1992–96); the Möbius House (Naarden, 1993–98); Het Valkhof Museum (Nijmegen, 1998); and NMR Laboratory (Utrecht, 2000), all in the Netherlands; a Switching Station (Innsbruck, Austria, 1998–2001); an Electricity Station (Innsbruck, Austria, 2002); VilLA NM (Upstate New York, USA, 2000–06); the Mercedes-Benz Museum (Stuttgart, Germany, 2003–06); the Arnhem Station (The Netherlands, 1986–2007); and a Music Facility (Graz, Austria, 1998–2007). UNStudio was also a participant in the competition for the new World Trade Center in New York, in collaboration with Foreign Office Architects, Greg Lynn FORM, Imaginary Forces, Kevin Kennon and Reiser + Umemoto, RUR under the name of United Architects. Recent work includes a Tea House (Groot Kantwijk, Vreeland, 2005–07); a Research Laboratory at Groningen University (Groningen, 2003–08); MUMUTH Music Theater (Graz, Austria, 2006–08, published here); and Burnham Pavilion (Chicago, Illinois, USA, 2009, also published here).

BEN VAN BERKEL wurde 1957 in Utrecht geboren und studierte an der Rietveld-Akademie in Amsterdam sowie der Architectural Association (AA) in London, wo er 1987 das Diplom mit Auszeichnung erhielt. Nach einer kurzen Tätigkeit 1988 bei Santiago Calatrava gründete er mit **CAROLINE BOS** sein eigenes Büro in Amsterdam. Er war Gastprofessor an der Columbia University und Gastkritiker in Harvard (1994). 1994 bis 1995 war er Diploma Unit Master an der AA. Neben der 1996 eingeweihten Erasmusbrücke in Rotterdam bauten Van Berkel & Bos in Amersfoort die Büros für Karbouw und ACOM (1989–93) sowie das Kraftwerk REMU (1989–93) und errichteten in Berlin Wohnbauprojekte sowie die Galerie Aedes East für Kristin Feireiss. Zu ihren Projekten zählen ein Erweiterungsbau für das Rijksmuseum Twente (Enschede, 1992–96), das Haus Möbius (Naarden, 1993–98) und das Museum Het Valkhof (Nijmegen, 1998), alle in den Niederlanden, eine Umschaltstation (Innsbruck, 1998–2001), ein Elektrizitätswerk (Innsbruck, 2002), die VilLA NM (bei New York, 2000–06), das Mercedes-Benz-Museum (Stuttgart, 2003–06), der Bahnhof von Arnhem (1986–2007) und ein Musikzentrum in Graz (1998–2007). UNStudio beteiligte sich am Wettbewerb für das neue World Trade Center in New York in Zusammenarbeit mit Foreign Office Architects, Greg Lynn FORM, Imaginary Forces, Kevin Kennon und Reiser + Umemoto, RUR, unter dem Namen United Architects. Jüngere Arbeiten sind u. a. ein Teehaus (Groot Kantwijk, Vreeland, 2005–07), ein Forschungslabor an der Universität Groningen (2003–08), das MUMUTH Musiktheater (Graz, 2006–08, hier vorgestellt) sowie der Burnham-Pavillon (Chicago, 2009, ebenfalls hier vorgestellt).

BEN VAN BERKEL est né à Utrecht, en 1957, et a étudié à l'Académie Rietveld, à Amsterdam, et à l'Architectural Association (AA) à Londres, où il a obtenu son diplôme avec mention, en 1987. Après avoir brièvement travaillé dans l'agence de Santiago Calatrava en 1988, il fonde son agence à Amsterdam avec **CAROLINE BOS**. Il a été professeur invité à l'université Columbia et critique associé à Harvard (1994). Il a enseigné à l'AA (1994–95). Outre le pont Erasmus, à Rotterdam (inauguré en 1996), le cabinet d'architecture Van Berkel & Bos a construit les immeubles de bureaux Karbouw et ACOM (1989–93) et la sous-station électrique REMU (1989–93), tous situés à Amersfoort, ainsi que des projets de logements et la galerie Aedes East, pour Kristin Feireiss, à Berlin. Ses projets incluent une extension du Rijksmuseum Twente (Enschede, 1992–96) ; la maison Möbius (Naarden, 1993–98) ; le musée Het Valkhof (Nijmegen, 1998) ; et le laboratoire NMR (Utrecht, 2000), tous situés aux Pays-Bas ; une sous-station électrique (Innsbruck, Autriche, 1998–2001) ; une station électrique (Innsbruck, Autriche, 2002) ; la VilLA NM (au nord de New York, 2000–06) ; le musée Mercedes-Benz (Stuttgart, Allemagne, 2003–06) ; la gare d'Arnhem (Pays-Bas, 1986–2007) et un complexe musical (Graz, Autriche, 1998–2007). UNStudio a également participé au concours pour le nouveau World Trade Center de New York, en collaboration avec Foreign Office Architects, Greg Lynn FORM, Imaginary Forces, Kevin Kennon et Reiser + Umemoto, RUR, sous le nom United Architects. Leurs réalisations récentes incluent un salon de thé (Groot Kantwijk, Vreeland, 2005–07) ; un laboratoire de recherche à l'université de Groningue (2003–08) ; l'auditorium du MUMUTH Theater (Graz, Autriche, 2006–08, publié ici) ; et le pavillon Burnham (Chicago, Illinois, 2009, également publié ici).

MUMUTH MUSIC THEATER

Graz, Austria, 2006–08

*Address: Leonhardstr. 15, 8010 Graz, Austria, +43 316 3890, www.mumuth.at
Area: 4407 m². Client: BIG Bundesimmobiliengesellschaft m.b.H. Cost: €19.2 million
Team: Hannes Pfau, Miklos Deri, Kirsten Hollmann*

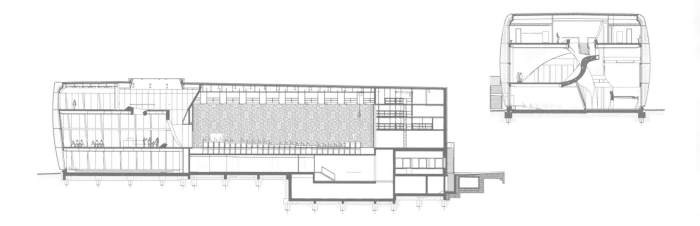

The **MUMUTH THEATER** is part of the University of Music and Performing Arts Graz and is therefore a place where young musicians receive their instruction in the performing and musical arts. The architects felt that it was "appropriate to let the architecture communicate that this is a building in which music lives." A spiral "spring" is seen as the main organizing element of the building. In the course of the design process, this spiral divided "itself into a number of interconnected smaller spirals that take on a vertical and diagonal direction becoming an important design model for us that we called the blob-to-box model," according to Ben van Berkel and Caroline Bos. The result is a dynamic and freely flowing structure. Separate entrances are provided for students and staff and for outside public. The student entrance becomes the wardrobe on performance nights, while a removable ticketing desk is installed under the staircase. The multipurpose auditorium seats 450, and can be used for solo instruments, opera, or a full orchestra. The "spiraling" constructive element connects the entrance to the auditorium and to the music rooms above. A massive concrete "twist" is another central design element. A repetitive pattern designed by the architects is used in varying degrees of density on the exterior, covered by glittering mesh.

Das **MUMUTH – HAUS FÜR MUSIK UND MUSIKTHEATER –** ist Teil der Kunstuniversität Graz, ein Ort, an dem junge Musiker ihre Ausbildung in Schauspiel und Musik erhalten. Die Architekten wollten, „dass die Architektur vermittelt, dass dies ein Bauwerk ist, in dem die Musik zu Hause ist". Eine „Spirale" dient als zentrales Organisationselement des Gebäudes. Ben van Berkel und Caroline Bos zufolge teilte sich diese Spirale während des Entwurfsprozesses „in mehrere kleinere, ineinander verschlungene Spiralen mit vertikaler oder diagonaler Laufrichtung, was sich zu einem zentralen Entwurfsmodell entwickelte, das wir ‚Blob-to-Box-Modell' nannten". Das Ergebnis ist ein dynamischer, fließender Bau. Für Studenten und Mitarbeiter sowie für Besucher sind separate Eingänge vorhanden. An Aufführungsabenden dient der Studenteneingang als Garderobe, unter der Treppe wird eine mobile Theaterkasse aufgestellt. Der Mehrzwecksaal hat 450 Plätze und kann für Soloabende, Opern oder volles Orchester genutzt werden. Die tragende Spirale verbindet die Lobby mit dem darüber liegenden Saal und bietet Zugang zu den Musikräumen in den Obergeschossen. Ein weiteres gestalterisches Element ist die monumentale „Verzwirbelung" aus Beton. Ein von den Architekten entworfenes, sich wiederholendes Muster in unterschiedlicher Dichte bedeckt das Äußere des Gebäudes, das, der vollständig mit glänzendem Gewebe überzogen ist.

L'auditorium du **MUMUTH THEATER**, qui fait partie de l'Université de musique et d'arts dramatiques de Graz, est donc un endroit où de jeunes musiciens reçoivent leurs formations théâtrale et musicale. Les architectes ont pensé qu'il était « approprié de laisser l'architecture exprimer qu'il s'agit d'un bâtiment où vit la musique ». Un « ressort » en spirale constitue l'élément structurant principal du bâtiment. Ben van Berkel et Caroline Bos expliquent qu'au cours de l'élaboration du projet, cette spirale s'est « divisée en plusieurs spirales plus petites, interconnectées, adoptant une direction verticale et diagonale, et est devenue pour nous un modèle essentiel que nous avons appelé « blob-to-box ». Le résultat est une structure dynamique et fluide. Des entrées séparées sont prévues, l'une pour les étudiants et les enseignants et l'autre pour le public extérieur. L'entrée des étudiants se transforme en vestiaire les soirs de représentation et un guichet amovible est installé sous l'escalier. L'auditorium polyvalent a une jauge de 450 spectateurs et peut être utilisé pour des solos, de l'opéra, ou pour des orchestres. Les éléments constructifs « spiralants » relient l'entrée de l'auditorium et des salles de musique situées en haut. Une « torsade » massive en béton constitue un autre élément central du projet. Un motif répétitif dessiné par les architectes est utilisé en densité variable sur l'extérieur du bâtiment qui est recouvert d'un grillage scintillant.

Section drawings reveal the inner workings of the building and show the placement of the stunning spiral staircase seen on the right page.

Querschnitte geben Einblick in das Innere des Gebäudes und verraten die Positionierung der rechts abgebildeten, beeindruckenden Wendeltreppe.

Les coupes révèlent les rouages internes du bâtiment et montrent le positionnement du surprenant escalier en spirale visible sur la page de droite.

The bulging form of the theater entrance is seen with a red lighting pattern above. The overall plan is essentially rectangular.

Der sich vorwölbende Eingangsbereich des Theaters mit roter Beleuchtung (oben). Der Grundriss ist mehr oder weniger rechteckig gehalten.

Ci-dessus, la forme bombée de l'entrée du théâtre avec ses motifs lumineux rouge. Le plan d'ensemble est essentiellement rectangulaire.

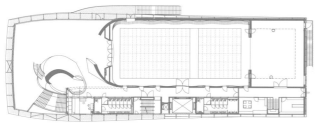

Computer-assisted renderings are naturally important in designs such as that of the massive concrete "twist" seen in these drawings and the photo below.

Bei Entwürfen wie der massiven „Betonschraube" (siehe Zeichnungen und Foto unten) sind CAD-Programme zweifellos von besonderer Bedeutung.

La conception assistée par ordinateur est bien sûr importante pour des créations comme cette « torsade » massive en béton, visible sur ces dessins et la photo ci-dessous.

BURNHAM PAVILION

Chicago, Illinois, USA, 2009

Address: 201 East Randolph Street, Chicago, IL 60602, USA, www.burnhamplan100.uchicago.edu
Area: 300 m². Client: (TBC) The City of Chicago, Burnham Plan Centennial Committee. Cost: not disclosed
Team: Christian Veddeler, Wouter de Jonge

The two planes of the pavilion appear to hover in space in this night image where a red lighting scheme makes the structure stand out against the Chicago skyline.

Auf dieser nächtlichen Ansicht scheinen die zwei Ebenen des Pavillons frei im Raum zu schweben. Das rötliche Lichtkonzept hebt den Bau von der Chicagoer Skyline ab.

Les deux plans du pavillon semblent flotter dans l'espace, dans cette vue de nuit où une mise en lumière de couleur rouge fait ressortir la structure sur la ligne d'horizon de Chicago.

Located in Millennium Park near the Chicago Art Institute, the **BURNHAM PAVILION** is one of two temporary structures (the other is by Zaha Hadid) commissioned to celebrate the 100th anniversary of Daniel Burnham's Plan of Chicago. The architects call their structure an "urban activator." The structure is made of steel columns and beams, a secondary wooden rib element covered with plywood paneling and finished with *bondo* (elastic plaster) and paint. The architects sought to add a "floating and multidirectional space" to the rigid geometry of the city. It is open on all sides, allowing continuous views of the city, thus paying homage to the original Burnham plan but at the same time questioning or augmenting it. A system of computer-variable 49 LED lights built into the podium interacts with the rhythm of activity, providing another variable element to the architecture.

Der **BURNHAM-PAVILLON** liegt im Millennium Park unweit des Chicago Art Institute und ist einer von zwei temporären Bauten (der zweite stammt von Zaha Hadid), die anlässlich der 100-Jahrfeiern des von Daniel Burnham entworfenen Chicagoer Stadtgrundrisses in Auftrag gegeben wurden. Die Architekten nennen ihren Bau einen „urbanen Aktivator". Er besteht aus Stahlstützen und -trägern sowie einer sekundären Holzrippenkonstruktion, die mit Sperrholz verblendet, mit einer elastischen Masse versiegelt und schließlich lackiert wurde. Den Architekten ging es darum, einen „fließenden, multidirektionalen Raum" in die strenge Geometrie der Stadt einzufügen. Der Pavillon ist allseitig offen und erlaubt einen Rundumblick auf die Stadt. So ist er einerseits eine Hommage an den ursprünglichen Entwurf von Burnham, hinterfragt und erweitert ihn jedoch zugleich. Ein System aus 49 computergesteuerten LED-Dioden ist in das Podium integriert und reagiert interaktiv auf den Rhythmus der Besucheraktivität, wodurch die Architektur ein weiteres variables Element hinzugewinnt.

Implanté dans le parc Millennium, près du Chicago Art Institute, le **PAVILLON BURNHAM** est l'un des deux bâtiments temporaires (l'autre est de Zaha Hadid) commandés pour célébrer le centième anniversaire du « Plan de Chicago » de Daniel Burnham. Les architectes ont qualifié leur structure d'« activateur urbain ». Celle-ci est constituée de colonnes et de poutres en acier, d'un élément secondaire fait de nervures de bois, recouvert de panneaux de contreplaqué et d'une finition au bondo (un enduit élastique) et à la peinture. Les architectes cherchaient à ajouter un espace « flottant et multidirectionnel » à la géométrie rigide de la ville. Le bâtiment, ouvert sur tous ses côtés, permet de voir toute la ville et rend ainsi un hommage original au plan de Burnham, tout en le questionnant et en l'intensifiant. Un système de 49 LEDs, géré par ordinateur, modulable en intensité et intégré au podium, interagit avec le rythme de l'activité, ajoutant un élément variable à l'architecture.

Although it does constitute something of a shelter, the Pavilion in these views might well be taken for an abstract modern sculpture as well.

Obwohl der Pavillon in gewisser Weise schützender Unterstand ist, könnte man ihn auf diesen Aufnahmen ebenso gut für eine abstrakte moderne Skulptur halten.

Bien qu'il s'agisse vraiment d'un abri, le pavillon peut être vu, sur ces photos, comme une sculpture moderne abstraite.

VICENS + RAMOS ARCHITECTS

Vicens + Ramos
C/ Barquillo, No. 29. 2º IZQ.
28004 Madrid
Spain

Tel: +34 91 52 10 00
Fax: +34 91 521 65 50
E-mail: info@vicens-ramos.com
Web: www.vicens-ramos.com

IGNACIO VICENS Y HUALDE received his degree in Architecture from the ETSA in Madrid (ETSAM) in 1976 and a Ph.D. in Architecture from the same institution in 1985. He was a full Professor of Design at the ETSAM from 1989 to 1996, and Chair of Design there beginning in 1997. **JOSÉ ANTONIO RAMOS ABENGOZAR** received his degree in Architecture from ETSAM in 1982 and has been a full Professor of Design there since 2007. Their work includes Ephemeral Architecture for the visit of Pope John Paul II (Madrid, 2003); the Stone House (Madrid, 2002–04); Glass House (Ibiza, 2002–04); Concrete House IV (Madrid, 2005–06); Concrete House V (Madrid, 2005–07); Santa Lucia Headquarters (Madrid, 2002–07); Santa Monica Parish Church (Rivas Vaciamadrid, Madrid, 2004–09, published here); Madrid New Opera House (Madrid, 2002–); Buen Pastor Parish Church (Ponferrada, León, 2007–); and the National War Museum (Toledo, 2007–), all in Spain.

IGNACIO VICENS Y HUALDE schloss sein Architekturstudium 1976 an der ETSA in Madrid (ETSAM) ab und promovierte 1985 an derselben Hochschule in Architektur. Von 1989 bis 1996 war er Professor für Entwerfen an der ETSAM, seit 1997 leitet er das dortige Institut für Entwerfen. **JOSÉ ANTONIO RAMOS ABENGOZAR** machte seinen Architekturabschluss 1982 an der ETSAM und ist dort seit 2007 Professor für Entwerfen. Zu den Arbeiten des Teams zählen temporäre Bauten für den Besuch Papst Johannes Paul II. (Madrid, 2003), ein Haus aus Stein (Madrid, 2002–04), ein Haus aus Glas (Ibiza, 2002–04), das Haus aus Beton IV (Madrid, 2005–06), das Haus aus Beton V (Madrid, 2005–07), das Hauptbüro Santa Lucia (Madrid, 2002–07), die Pfarrkirche Santa Monica (Rivas Vaciamadrid, Madrid, 2004–09, hier vorgestellt), die Neue Oper in Madrid (seit 2002), die Pfarrkirche Buen Pastor (Ponferrada, León, seit 2007) sowie das Nationale Kriegsmuseum (Toledo, seit 2007), alle in Spanien.

IGNACIO VICENS Y HUALDE a obtenu son diplôme de l'ETSA de Madrid (ETSAM) en 1976 et un doctorat en architecture de la même institution en 1985. Il a été professeur titulaire de design à l'ETSAM de 1989 à 1996 et est professeur titulaire de la chaire de design depuis 1997. **JOSÉ ANTONIO RAMOS ABENGOZAR** a reçu son diplôme de l'ETSAM en 1982 et y est professeur titulaire de design depuis 2007. Leurs réalisations incluent une architecture temporaire pour la visite du pape Jean-Paul II (Madrid, 2003) ; la maison Stone (Madrid, 2002–04) ; la maison Glass (Ibiza, 2002–04) ; la maison Concrete IV (Madrid, 2005–06) ; la maison Concrete V (Madrid, 2005–07) ; le siège de Santa Lucia (Madrid, 2002–07) ; l'église de la paroisse de Santa Monica (Rivas Vaciamadrid, Madrid, 2004–09, publié ici) ; le nouvel Opéra de Madrid (Madrid, 2002–) ; l'église de la paroisse de Buen Pastor (Ponferrada, León, 2007–) ; et le Musée national de la guerre (Toledo, 2007–), toutes situées en Espagne.

SANTA MONICA PARISH CHURCH

Rivas Vaciamadrid, Madrid, Spain, 2004–09

Address: Avenida de la Integración/Calle de Los Nibelungos, 28523 Vaciamadrid, Spain
Area: 1404 m². Client: Bishop of Alcalá. Cost: not disclosed

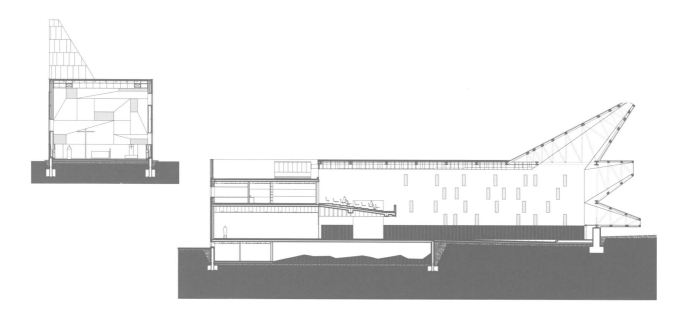

Given the nature of the site, both long and narrow, the architects decided to "develop a continuum that unifies the building housing the priests and the parish center to the church." A number of artists were involved in the project, including José Manuel Ciria, Javier Viver, José Luis Sánchez, Fernando Pagola, and José Antonio Ramos. Working with a small budget, the architects "started from a firm conviction: that the church must stand out clearly within the residential fabric. A church is a community building and as such should have the presence and prominence of a monument.... This is not sculpture, but representative architecture," conclude the architects. Their use of Cor-ten steel for the exterior cladding does indeed bring to mind the idea of sculpture, however. The interior spaces are contrasted with the exterior, evoking a contemplative character that is highlighted by the use of natural light filtered through skylights.

Aufgrund des langen und schmalen Grundstücks entschieden sich die Architekten, „ein räumliches Kontinuum zu entwerfen, welches das Gebäude für die Priesterwohnungen und das Gemeindezentrum mit der Kirche verbindet". Mehrere Künstler waren am Projekt beteiligt, darunter José Manuel Ciria, Javier Viver, José Luis Sánchez, Fernando Pagola und José Antonio Ramos. Trotz eines geringen Budgets waren die Architekten „der festen Überzeugung, dass die Kirche im Kontext des Wohngebiets deutlich auffallen sollte. Eine Kirche ist ein Bauwerk, das die Nachbarschaft angeht und sollte deswegen eine ebenso starke Präsenz haben und ebenso auffallen, wie ein Monument ... Hierbei handelt es sich nicht etwa um eine Skulptur, sondern um repräsentative Architektur", fassen die Architekten zusammen. Allerdings lässt die Außenverkleidung mit Cor-Ten-Stahl tatsächlich an Skulpturen denken. Die Innenräume kontrastieren mit dem Äußeren und wirken kontemplativ, was durch das natürliche Licht, das durch die Oberlichter gefiltert wird, unterstrichen wird.

Étant donnée la nature du site, long et étroit, les architectes ont décidé de « développer un continuum qui unifie le presbytère et le centre paroissial avec l'église ». Plusieurs artistes ont participé au projet, dont José Manuel Ciria, Javier Viver, José Luis Sánchez, Fernando Pagola et José Antonio Ramos. Travaillant avec un petit budget, les architectes ont « démarré avec une ferme conviction : l'église devait trancher clairement avec le tissu résidentiel. Une église est un bâtiment communautaire, et, comme tel, devrait avoir la présence et la prééminence d'un monument... », tout en concluant que : « Ce n'est pas de la sculpture, mais de l'architecture représentative. » Leur utilisation de l'acier Corten pour le revêtement extérieur évoque cependant bien l'idée de la sculpture. Les espaces intérieurs contrastent avec l'extérieur et évoquent un caractère contemplatif souligné par l'utilisation de la lumière naturelle filtrée par des lucarnes.

Section drawings of the church (above) are seen opposite two pictures of the unusual, sculptural, Cor-ten-steel-clad building.

Querschnitte durch die Kirche (oben) und zwei Ansichten des ungewöhnlichen skulpturalen, mit Cor-Ten-Stahl verkleideten Gebäudes (gegenüber).

Des coupes de l'église (ci-dessus) et, page de droite, deux photos du bâtiment sculptural et insolite, revêtu d'acier Corten.

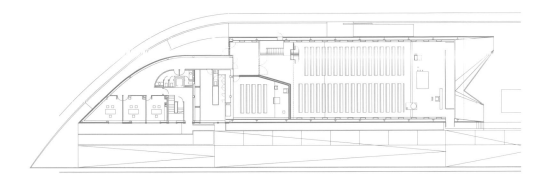

The rectangular church space is animated by irregularly placed vertical windows and the geometric composition behind the altar.

Der auf einem Rechteck basierende Kirchenraum wird von unregelmäßig platzierten vertikalen Fenstern und der geometrischen Komposition hinter dem Altar belebt.

Le volume intérieur parallélépipédique de l'église est animé par les fenêtres verticales distribuées irrégulièrement et la composition géométrique derrière l'autel.

MAKOTO SEI WATANABE

MAKOTO SEI WATANABE / ARCHITECT'S OFFICE
#2806 Azumabashi 1–23–30
Sumida-ku, Tokyo 130
Japan

Tel: +81 3 3829 3221
Fax: +81 3 3829 3837
E-mail: are@makoto-architect.com
Web: www.makoto-architect.com

Born in 1952 in Yokohama, **MAKOTO SEI WATANABE** attended Yokohama National University from which he graduated with an M.Arch in 1976. He worked from 1979 to 1984 in the office of Arata Isozaki, before creating his own firm. His first built work, the Aoyama Technical College (Shibuya, Tokyo, 1989), created considerable controversy because of its unusual bionic, but also mechanical, forms. Since that time, Watanabe has worked more and more with computer-generated designs. His work includes Chronospace (Minato-ku, Tokyo, 1991); Mura-no-Terrace gallery, information office and café, Sakauchi Village (Ibi-gun, Gifu, 1995); *Fiber Wave*, environmental art (Gifu and Tokyo, 1995–96); Atlas, housing (Suginami-ku, Tokyo, 1996); K-Museum (Koto-ku, Tokyo, 1996); and *Fiber Wave*, environmental art (The Chicago Athenaeum, Chicago, Illinois, USA, 1998). The Iidabashi Subway Station, Tokyo (2000), the Shin-Minamata Shinkansen Station and two stations on the Tsukuba Express Line, which opened in 2005, show his considerable interest in rail facilities. Recent and current work includes the Tokyo House (Tokyo, 2006); RIBBONs Open-Air Theater (Taichung City, Taiwan, 2008–09, published here); and Web Frame II (Tokyo, 2010).

MAKOTO SEI WATANABE wurde 1952 in Yokohama geboren und besuchte dort die Universität, wo er sein Studium 1976 mit einem M. Arch. abschloss. Von 1979 bis 1984 arbeitete er für Arata Isozaki und gründete anschließend sein eigenes Büro. Sein erster realisierter Bau, das Aoyama Technical College (Shibuya, Tokio, 1989), sorgte mit seinen ungewöhnlichen bionischen und doch maschinenartig wirkenden Formen für erhebliche Kontroversen. Seither arbeitet Watanabe mehr und mehr mit computergenerierten Entwürfen. Zu seinen Arbeiten zählen Chronospace (Minato-ku, Tokio, 1991), Galerie, Informationsbüro und Café Mura-no-Terrace, Sakauchi Village (Ibi-gun, Gifu, 1995), das Environmental-Art-Projekt „Fiber Wave" (Gifu und Tokio, 1995–96), das Wohnbauprojekt Atlas (Suginami-ku, Tokio, 1996), das K-Museum (Koto-ku, Tokio, 1996) sowie ein weiteres Environmental-Art-Projekt „Fiber Wave" (Chicago Athenaeum, Chicago, 1998). Die U-Bahnstation Iidabashi in Tokio (2000), der Shinkansen-Bahnhof Shin-Minamata sowie zwei Stationen auf der Tsukuba-Expresslinie, die 2005 eröffnet wurde, belegen sein großes Interesse an Bahnhofsarchitektur. Aktuellere Projekte sind u. a. das Tokyo House (Tokio, 2006), das Freilichttheater RIBBON (Taichung, Taiwan, 2008–09, hier vorgestellt) und schließlich Web Frame II (Tokio, 2010).

Né en 1952 à Yokohama, **MAKOTO SEI WATANABE** a étudié à l'Université nationale de Yokohama, dont il a obtenu un master en architecture (M. Arch.) en 1976. Il travaille de 1979 à 1984 dans l'agence d'Arata Isozaki, avant de fonder sa propre agence. Son premier projet construit, le Collège technique Aoyama (Shibuya, Tokyo, 1989), a créé une considérable controverse en raison de ses formes inhabituelles, bioniques, mais également mécaniques. Depuis, Watanabe a travaillé de plus en plus à des projets générés par ordinateur. Ses réalisations incluent Chronospace (Minato-ku, Tokyo, 1991); la galerie Mura-no-Terrace; un bureau d'information et café, Sakauchi Village (Ibi-gun, Gifu, 1995); Fiber Wave, un projet d'art environnemental (Gifu et Tokyo, 1995–96); l'ensemble d'habitations Atlas (Suginami-ku, Tokyo, 1996); le K-Museum (Koto-ku, Tokyo, 1996); et Fiber Wave, un autre projet d'art environnemental (The Chicago Athenaeum, Chicago, États-Unis, 1998). La station de métro Iidabashi, Tokyo (2000); la gare Shinkansen de Shin-Minamata; et deux gares de la ligne Tsukuba Express, ouvertes en 2005, démontrent son intérêt considérable pour les infrastructures ferroviaires. Ses projets récents ou en cours incluent la maison Tokyo (Tokyo, 2006); le théâtre de plein air RIBBONs (Taichung, Taiwan, 2008–09, publié ici); et Web Frame II (Tokyo, 2010).

RIBBONS OPEN-AIR THEATER

Taichung City, Taiwan, 2008–09

*Address: Taichung Wen-Hsin Forest Park, Taichung City, Taiwan
Area: 3000 m² (covered area, not including existing facility). Client: City of Taichung.
Cost: not disclosed. Collaboration: J. C. Yang Architect and Associates (Co-Architect),
Envision Engineering Consultants (Structural Design)*

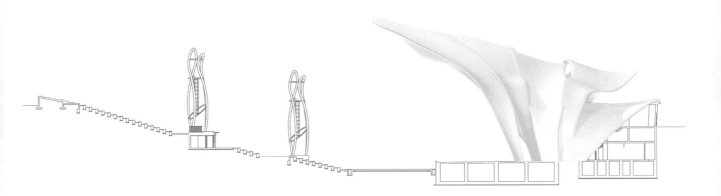

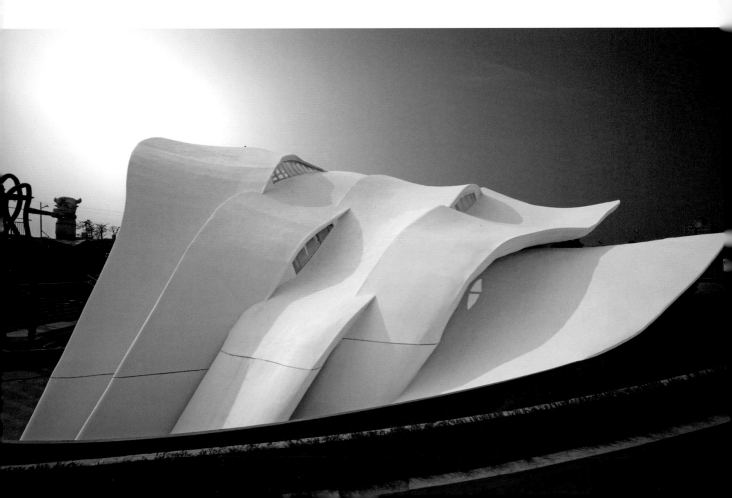

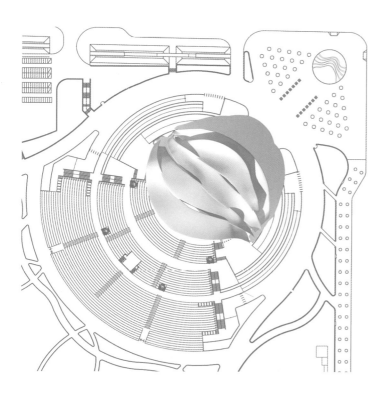

The successive ribbons that
constitute this theater shell are
visible in the photos and drawings
reproduced here. Below, a site plan
showing the fan-shaped seating
radiating out from the shell.

Die einander überlappenden Bänder
des Bühnendachs sind auf den
Fotografien und Zeichnungen deutlich
zu erkennen. Unten ein Lageplan, der
die fächerartig von der Bühne aus-
strahlenden Zuschauerplätze zeigt.

Les rubans successifs constituant la
coque du théâtre sont visibles sur les
photos et les dessins présentés ici.
Ci-dessous, un plan de situation
montre la disposition des sièges en
éventail, comme rayonnant de la
coque.

The architect was asked to design a canopy, backstage rooms, and other new facilities for an existing outdoor theater in a city park. Makoto Sei Watanabe had already created a work called RIBBON for a Japanese art presentation in Graz (2005) and his work there led to this new design. As Watanabe says, he decided after two earlier proposals to make use of five wavelike ribbons in a parallel configuration. Though no special computer program was developed for this project, it is an example, according to the architect, of "algorithmic design." Thus, a relatively simple repetition of wave forms results in a complex pattern. Makoto Sei Watanabe concludes: "This project will be a success if performances in the theater escape the limitations of the physical stage and extend out into the city. If it can achieve this, **RIBBONS** will transcend its role as canopy and play a role in expanding the functions of the theater."

Der Auftrag des Architekten lautete, eine Bühnenüberdachung, Hinterbühnenräume und weitere Einrichtungen für ein bereits bestehendes Freilichttheater in einem Stadtpark zu entwerfen. Zu diesem Zeitpunkt hatte Makoto Sei Watanabe bereits eine Arbeit namens „RIBBON" für ein japanisches Kunstprojekt in Graz realisiert (2005), auf der dieser neue Entwurf basiert. Wie Watanabe ausführt, beschloss er nach zwei früheren Entwürfen, fünf wellenförmige Bänder (engl. ribbons) parallel anzuordnen. Obwohl für dieses Projekt kein spezielles Computerprogramm entwickelt wurde, ist es laut Watanabe ein Beispiel für „algorithmisches Entwerfen". Dank dieser Methode entsteht aus einer einfachen Wiederholung wellenartiger Formen ein komplexes Muster. Watanabe fasst zusammen: „Dieses Projekt kann als Erfolg gelten, wenn es gelingt, die Aufführungen auf der Bühne über die physischen Grenzen des Theaters hinaus- und in die Stadt selbst vordringen zu lassen. Glückt dies, wird **RIBBONS** über seine Funktion als reine Bühnenüberdachung hinauswachsen und die Wirkung des Theaters erweitern."

L'architecte avait à concevoir un auvent, des installations d'arrière-scène et d'autres nouveaux équipements pour un théâtre de plein air existant, situé dans un parc urbain. Makoto Sei Watanabe avait déjà réalisé un projet intitulé RIBBON pour une exposition d'art japonais à Graz (2005) qui l'a conduit à cette nouvelle création. Après deux premières propositions, Watanabe déclare qu'il a décidé d'utiliser cinq rubans en forme de vagues dans une configuration parallèle. Bien qu'aucun programme d'ordinateur n'ait été spécialement développé pour ce projet, il s'agit selon l'architecte d'un exemple de « dessin algorithmique ». Ainsi, la répétition relativement simple de formes de vagues produit un motif complexe. Makoto Sei Watanabe conclut : « Ce projet sera un succès si les représentations dans le théâtre échappent aux limitations de l'espace physique de la scène et se propagent à l'extérieur dans la ville. S'il y réussit, **RIBBONS** transcendera son rôle d'auvent en élargissant les fonctions du théâtre. »

The ribbons are lit for evening performances, as seen in the image below.

Bei Abendveranstaltungen werden die Bänder angestrahlt, wie unten im Bild zu sehen.

Les rubans sont illuminés les soirs de spectacle, comme sur la photo ci-dessous.

The actual ribbons that make up the design are seen in the computer drawing above, and in their finished form to the left.

Auf der Computerzeichnung oben die Bänder, auf denen der Entwurf beruht; unten die Bänder in ihrer tatsächlich realisierten Form.

Les rubans qui composent le projet sont visibles sur le dessin ci-dessus, généré par ordinateur, et sous leur forme concrète, à gauche.

RENÉ VAN ZUUK

René van Zuuk Architekten b.v.
De Fantasie 9
1324 HZ Almere
The Netherlands

Tel: +31 36 537 91 39
Fax: +31 36 537 92 59
E-mail: info@renevanzuuk.nl
Web: www.renevanzuuk.nl

RENÉ VAN ZUUK received an M.Sc. degree from the Technical University of Eindhoven (1988), and created his own firm in 1993. He has a design staff of five people. Prior to 1993, he worked for Skidmore, Owings & Merrill in London and Chicago (1988–89), at Facilitair Bureau voor Bouwkunde Rotterdam, and at Hoogstad van Tilburg Architecten (1989–92). His notable completed projects include Eight Bridges (Nieuwsloten, 1993); Lock House "Oostersluis" (Groningen, 1995); Villa van Diepen (Almere, 1995); Four Canal Houses (Java Island, Amsterdam, 1997); Educational Farm "Griftsteede" (Utrecht, 1999); Center for Plastic Arts "CBK" (Alphen aan de Rijn, 2000); Art Pavilion "De Verbeelding" (Zeewolde, 2001); and ARCAM Architectural Center (Amsterdam, 2003). Recent work includes Blok 16 housing and fitness complex (Almere, 2003); bridge for bicycles and pedestrians (Almere, 2003); Bridge Keeper's House (Middelburg, unbuilt); and "Zilverparkkade" Office Building (Lelystad, 2004). More recently, he has worked on a group of 20 houses (Bosrijk, Eindhoven, 2005); a ten-story apartment building (Dudok, Hilversum, 2006); a multifunctional first-aid post (Dordrecht, 2007); Project X (Almere, 2004–08); a villa in Wageningen (2008); and Roosendaal Pavilion (Roosendaal, 2006–09, published here), all in the Netherlands.

RENÉ VAN ZUUK erwarb 1988 seinen Master of Science an der Technischen Universität Eindhoven und gründete 1993 sein Büro. Er hat fünf Mitarbeiter. Vor 1993 war er für Skidmore, Owings & Merrill in London und Chicago (1988–89), am Facilitair Bureau voor Bouwkunde Rotterdam, Hoogstad, und für van Tilburg Architecten (1989–92) tätig. Zu seinen wichtigsten Projekten zählen acht Brücken (Nieuwsloten, 1993), das Schleusenhaus „Oostersluis" (Groningen, 1995), die Villa van Diepen (Almere, 1995), vier Kanalhäuser (Java Island, Amsterdam, 1997), der Kinderbauernhof „Griftsteede" (Utrecht, 1999), das Zentrum für bildende Künste „CBK" (Alphen aan de Rijn, 2000), der Kunstpavillon „De Verbeelding" (Zeewolde, 2001) sowie das Architekturzentrum ARCAM (Amsterdam, 2003). Jüngere Projekte sind u. a. Blok 16, ein Wohnkomplex mit Fitnesseinrichtungen (Almere, 2003), eine Radfahrer- und Fußgängerbrücke (Almere, 2003), ein Brückenwärterhaus (Middelburg, nicht gebaut) sowie das Bürohaus „Zilverparkkade" (Lelystad, 2004). In jüngster Zeit arbeitete van Zuuk an einer Gruppe von 20 Häusern (Bosrijk, Eindhoven, 2005), einem zehnstöckigen Apartmenthaus (Dudok, Hilversum, 2006), einer multifunktionalen Erste-Hilfe-Ambulanz (Dordrecht, 2007), am Projekt X (Almere, 2004–08), einer Villa in Wageningen (2008) und dem Roosendaal Pavillon (Roosendaal, 2006–09, hier vorgestellt), alle in den Niederlanden.

RENÉ VAN ZUUK obtient un master en sciences de l'Université de technologie d'Eindhoven (1988), et crée sa propre agence en 1993. Il emploie une équipe de création de cinq personnes. Avant 1993, il a travaillé pour Skidmore, Owings & Merrill à Londres et à Chicago (1988–89), au Facilitair Bureau voor Bouwkunde de Rotterdam, et chez Hoogstad van Tilburg Architecten (1989–92). Ses réalisations notables incluent huit ponts (Nieuwsloten, 1993) ; une maison éclusière « Oostersluis » (Groningue, 1995) ; la villa van Diepen (Almere, 1995) ; quatre maisons sur le canal (Java Eiland, Amsterdam, 1997) ; la ferme pour enfants « Griftsteede » (Utrecht, 1999) ; le Centre d'arts plastiques CBK (Alphen aan de Rijn, 2000) ; le pavillon d'art « De Verbeelding » (Zeewolde, 2001) ; et le pavillon d'architecture ARCAM (Amsterdam, 2003). Ses projets récents incluent l'ensemble d'habitations Blok 16 et un centre de fitness (Almere, 2003) ; une passerelle cyclable et piétonnière (Almere, 2003) ; la maison du Gardien de pont (Middelburg, non construit) ; et l'immeuble de bureaux « Zilverparkkade » (Lelystad, 2004). Plus récemment, il a travaillé sur un lotissement de vingt maisons (Bosrijk, Eindhoven, 2005) ; un immeuble d'appartements de dix étages (Dudok, Hilversum, 2006) ; un poste d'urgence multifonctions (Dordrecht, 2007) ; la maison Project X (Almere, 2004–08) ; une villa à Wageningen (2008) ; et le pavillon de Roosendaal (Roosendaal, 2006–09, publié ici), tous situés aux Pays-Bas.

ROOSENDAAL PAVILION

Roosendaal, The Netherlands, 2006–09

Address: Nieuwe Markt 23, 4701 Roosendaal, The Netherlands
Area: 620 m². Client: City of Roosendaal. Cost: not disclosed
Design Team: Jorrit Spel, Chimo Villa Belda

This project was the result of a staged process in which the municipality of Roosendaal in the southwest of the Netherlands decided in 2001 to remove automobile traffic from the New Market square in the city center and then to build a large, two-story, underground parking lot. An urban design firm called Quadrat was called on to imagine the new square. Their scheme called for the extensive use of brick, the planting of 15 trees, and the creation of a restaurant and coffee pavilion. René van Zuuk was brought into the process in 2005 and asked to design a pavilion in the square in a period of five weeks. This short design period led the architect to adopt the original positioning and form of the buildings proposed by Quadrat, but René van Zuuk decided to create a cantilevered, sloped structure clad in wood (sucupira amarela). The slope allows pedestrians to walk onto the roof, or to use it as a stage for live performances. Its form makes it part of the square rather than allowing it to become a dividing element. The building cantilevers above the entrance to the parking garage on the south side, allowing light to penetrate the lower levels. Convivial and practical, the structure, containing shops, a lunchroom, and the parking lot, entrance improves on the postwar architecture of the square and encourages meeting and activities.

Das Projekt entstand in einem mehrstufigen Planungsprozess: Ziel der Stadt Roosendaal in den südwestlichen Niederlanden war die Realisierung der 2001 beschlossenen autofreien Zone am Neumarkt im Stadtzentrum sowie der Bau eines großen zweigeschossigen unterirdischen Parkhauses. Das Stadtplanungsbüro Quadrat wurde mit der Neugestaltung des Marktplatzes beauftragt. Sein Konzept setzte insbesondere auf den Einsatz von Backstein, die Anpflanzung von 15 Bäumen sowie die Ansiedlung eines Restaurants und eines Cafépavillons. 2005 wurde René van Zuuk hinzugezogen und erhielt den Auftrag, in nur fünf Wochen einen Pavillon für den Marktplatz zu gestalten. Wegen der kurzen Entwurfsphase übernahm der Architekt die von Quadrat vorgesehene Platzierung und Form der Bauten, entwarf jedoch ein auskragendes, abgeschrägtes, mit Holz (Sucupira amarela) verkleidetes Gebäude. Dank der Abschrägung des Pavillons können Passanten das Dach des Baus besteigen oder als Bühne für Liveveranstaltungen nutzen. Durch seine Form wird der Bau zu einem Bestandteil des Platzes, statt ihn zu teilen. Über dem Parkhauseingang auf der Südseite kragt der Bau stark aus und lässt so Licht in die Untergeschosse einfallen. Der freundliche und praktische Pavillon beherbergt neben dem Parkhauseingang auch Läden und ein Café. Er trägt nachhaltig zur Belebung der Nachkriegsarchitektur am Platz bei und lädt zu Begegnungen und gemeinsamen Aktivitäten ein.

Ce projet est le résultat d'un processus par étapes, à l'initiative de la municipalité de Roosendaal, dans le sud-ouest des Pays-Bas, qui avait décidé en 2001 de supprimer le trafic automobile sur la place du Nouveau Marché située dans le centre-ville et de construire un vaste parking souterrain de deux étages. Le programme élaboré par le cabinet d'urbanisme Quadrat, auquel avait été confiée la conception de la nouvelle place, prévoyait un usage extensif de la brique, la plantation de quinze arbres, et la création d'un restaurant et d'un café. René van Zuuk est entré dans le projet en 2005, avec la mission de concevoir en cinq semaines un pavillon pour la place. Ce temps de conception très court a conduit l'architecte à adopter l'implantation et la forme des bâtiments initialement proposées par Quadrat, mais il a décidé de créer une structure en porte-à-faux inclinée, revêtue de bois (sucupira amarela). Grâce à sa pente, le toit est accessible aux piétons ou peut se transformer en scène de spectacle. Sa forme est plus perçue comme une portion de la place que comme un élément de partition. Le bâtiment en surplomb au-dessus de l'entrée du parking permet à la lumière de pénétrer dans les niveaux inférieurs. Convivial et pratique, le bâtiment, qui abrite des commerces, une cafétéria et l'entrée du parking, embellit l'architecture d'après-guerre de la place et favorise les rencontres et l'animation.

The cantilevered, sloping, wood-clad
building imagined by Rene van Zuuk
is an unusual, but unprovocative
presence in the town of Roosendaal.
Pedestrians are seen on the roof of
the building at nightfall (right).

Das auskragende, holzverschalte
Gebäude mit seinem geneigten Dach,
ein Entwurf von René van Zuuk,
präsentiert sich als ungewöhnlicher,
wenn auch kaum provokanter
Zuwachs für die Stadt Rosendaal.
Rechts Fußgänger auf dem Dach
bei Anbruch der Nacht.

Le bâtiment, revêtu de bois et en
porte-à-faux incliné, imaginé par
René van Zuuk, marque Rosendaal
de sa présence originale, sans être
provocante. À droite, des piétons
sur le toit du bâtiment, la nuit.

Walkways allow the public to climb to the top of the roof of the building and to see the town from a new vantage point.

Rampen erlauben es Besuchern, das Dach bis zum höchsten Punkt hinaufzulaufen und die Stadt aus einer neuen Perspektive zu sehen.

Des allées permettent au public de grimper jusqu'au sommet du toit et de découvrir la ville depuis un nouveau point de vue.

INDEX OF ARCHITECTS, BUILDINGS, AND PLACES

CREDITS